NO TIME FOR THE TRUTH

NO TIME FOR THE TRUTH

THE HADITHA INCIDENT AND THE SEARCH FOR JUSTICE

NATHANIEL R. HELMS and HAYTHAM FARAJ

Arcade Publishing • New York

First Edition

Arcade Publishing books may be purchased in bulk at special discounts for sales promotion, corporate gifts, fund-raising, or educational purposes. Special editions can also be created to specifications. For details, contact the Special Sales Department, Arcade Publishing, 307 West 36th Street, 11th Floor, New York, NY 10018 or arcade@skyhorsepublishing.com.

Arcade Publishing® is a registered trademark of Skyhorse Publishing, Inc.®, a Delaware corporation.

Visit our website at www.arcadepub.com.

10 9 8 7 6 5 4 3 2 1

Library of Congress Cataloging-in-Publication Data

Names: Helms, Nathaniel R., author. | Faraj, Haytham, author.
Title: No time for the truth: the Haditha incident and the search for
    justice / by Nathaniel R. Helms & Haytham Faraj, Esq.
Description: First edition. | New York: Arcade Publishing, 2016. | Includes
    bibliographical references.
Identifiers: LCCN 2016016444 (print) | LCCN 2016020260 (ebook) | ISBN
    9781628726855 (hardcover: alk. paper) | ISBN 9781628726862 (eBook) | ISBN
    9781628726862 (ebook)
Subjects: LCSH: Wuterich, Frank, 1980—Trials, litigation, etc. |
    Courts-martial and courts of inquiry—United States. | War crime
    trials—United States. | Marines—Legal status, laws, etc.—United States.
    | Iraq War, 2003-2011—Atrocities—Iraq—?Had?ithah.
Classification: LCC KF7654.5.W88 H45 2016 (print) | LCC KF7654.5.W88 (ebook)
    | DDC 345.73/02523--dc23
LC record available at https://lccn.loc.gov/2016016444

Cover design by Laura Klynstra

Printed in the United States of America

CONTENTS

PREFACE

When the case of eight Marines accused of murder and cover-up at the so-called Haditha Massacre in Iraq was finally adjudicated on January 24, 2012, nobody knew for sure the general courts-martial of these eight was never intended to discover the truth. That astounding fact was revealed two years later.

The inquiry began on November 20, 2005, the day after eight children were slaughtered in Haditha, Iraq, by five US Marine infantrymen reacting to an ambush that had killed one of their own. The Marine's gruesome death was the opening gambit of an operation financed and led by al-Qaeda to paint in the world press a picture of the US Marine Corps as merciless killers. The plan, as brilliant as it was insidious, began with a tremendous bang.

The Iraqi children who would die were asleep in their beds on November 19, 2005, when a bomb commonly called an IED exploded under a nearby road. The huge blast shattered a US Marine Corps Humvee and three men riding in it. The detonation flung a dense, black cloud of greasy smoke hundreds of feet over the ancient Mesopotamian city, the only public announcement that the complex citywide attack was under way.

The children were probably awake by the time a twenty-year-old Marine lance corporal named Miguel "T. J." Terrazas flopped wetly back on the road in two parts in the deluge of debris that fell from the rising cloud. Two more Marines riding with him were wounded, one grievously. The simultaneously erupting crackle of gunfire no doubt frightened the children. The terror created by rapid gunfire and exploding grenades cannot be explained, only experienced. Along with their mothers and aunts, they ran into the back bedrooms of their stout stone homes to hide in the sanctuary the Iraqi government prescribed to keep them safe. In one house an unarmed father and a crippled old man and his wife stood their ground. There may have been an insurgent shooter there as well, although no evidence of his existence was ever produced. In another house across the way, the only man at home also declined to hide. The children in both places dived under the broad beds occupied by huddled grownups while exploding American 40 mm rifle grenades shook the thick stone walls of their momentary sanctuaries.

A few minutes after the initial blast, the petrified family probably heard shouting in bad Arabic, accompanied by several sharp bursts of automatic weapons fire coming from somewhere nearby. The sharp, distinctive cracking sound of automatic gunfire was insurgent Kalashnikov AK-47 assault rifles dueling with the battered Marines. Moments later that sound was replaced by the staccato rap of M16s, the noise of five unarmed Iraqi men being killed by American rifles. A few moments after that sudden burst of rifle fire ended, they probably heard five distinct, well-spaced shots. That was the sound of dead checks. A Marine was shooting each prostrate man in the head to make sure he was dead. Then the Marine urinated into the evacuated skull of one of his victims. After that timeless interlude an eerie silence descended over the neighborhood. Still, the innocents waited. There was nowhere else to run.

About an hour later, five American Marines forced their way inside the first house where children were huddled. It was one of three occupied dwellings they had assaulted that morning, shouting, shooting, and throwing grenades. What happened inside those homes after the initial explosion and gunfire shattered the dawn is mostly conjecture. The facts remain hidden behind an official wall of secrecy the Marine

Corps built brick by brick, slathering each block with impermeable mortar stiffened by distortions, deceit, omissions, and intentional lies.

The ambushed Marines belonged to First Squad, Third Platoon, K (for Kilo) Company, Third Battalion, First Marines, a light infantry battalion on its third deployment to Iraq in three years. The tumultuous year before, hardcore Kilo earned entry into the Corps's pantheon of heroes for its exemplary performance at bloody Fallujah. The battalion lost thirty-three men killed and more than five hundred wounded while killing or capturing at least 1,500 insurgents in the fiercest battle of the second Iraq war.

The Kilo Marine commanding the charge into the occupied houses was then-Sergeant Frank A. Wuterich, a handsome man of twenty-four experiencing his first and only day of combat. He was leading his twelve infantrymen on a routine resupply convoy when they were attacked. In an instant, a quarter of his tiny command was rendered ineffective. About sixty minutes later, Wuterich led four of his Marines to "clear south," the command he was given by his platoon commander to rid the area of unseen shooters. His actions during his only day in the sun sparked the criminal investigation that lasted seven years.

ONE MAN THE Department of the Navy sent to investigate what happened at Haditha that Saturday in 2005 was retired NCIS special agent and forensic specialist Michael S. Maloney. He was among a team of five forensic and crime scene experts tasked in March 2006 with discovering the so-called ground truth of the incident. Time was of the essence. The longer it took to explain what happened, the more embarrassing questions somebody would have to answer.

"We were told it was the My Lai [investigation] of the Iraq War," Maloney would recall in Independence, Missouri, almost ten years later.

Their mission in March 2006 was to use accepted scientific methods of crime scene reconstruction, coupled with physical evidence, witness statements, and hundreds of photographs taken by Marines in and around the bloodied ground to discover why and how the five Marines undoubtedly killed eight innocent children, as well as seven helpless adults. Maloney identified nine other decedents killed the same day as suspected insurgents—military-age males, or MAMs—so their deaths didn't matter, he recalled. "The MAMs . . . didn't follow instructions. That made them legitimate targets. Once they were identified as MAMs and possible insurgents, there was no more interest in how they died."

Maloney had been doing crime scene investigations for about thirteen years when NCIS summoned him to Haditha from faraway Okinawa. He is a disciplined former Marine still passionate about his craft. He planned to conduct his business by the numbers. To his chagrin, Maloney swiftly discovered it was not to be. He was told by his superiors that the real mission of the team was to ensure that the forensic evidence uncovered was presented the way the government wanted it revealed. Never mind what the physical evidence really showed. There was no time for the truth.

"It [the Haditha investigation] put me in conflict with senior management and limited my effect in NCIS. Our investigation and findings displeased a number of middle and senior management people," he recalled. "I received an email communication from lower headquarters—a mid-level manager—how did he put this—I needed to 'recognize what version of events the prosecution was supporting and that I was to make certain it (our findings) didn't go any further.' Essentially I was told to 'get with the program.'

"The director [Special Agent Thomas A. Betro] was being briefed every week or two weeks. I was told he expected the evidence we developed to reveal circumstances that weren't there. Clearly, the senior management was not happy with the facts we were uncovering. Our findings did not follow the preconceived notion of events. The evidence was showing findings that the prosecution was not welcoming."

It soon became clear to Maloney that Wuterich was selected early on to take the fall for the enlisted men. It was all laid out in 2007 by the "theory of prosecution" his superiors at NCIS headquarters in Washington, DC, told him to prove. The theory was at a minimum the work product of the Marine Corps's handpicked prosecution team, led by Chicago reservist Lieutenant Colonel Sean Sullivan. His orders came "straight from the top," Maloney was told. The NCIS agent's evidence was never revealed in open court and remains locked away to this day.

Seven years later, Staff Sergeant Frank Wuterich found himself in a Camp Pendleton, California, courtroom, standing before a general court-martial draped in the trappings of blind justice. The weeks ahead promised high drama. Who knew the splendid California morning was the beginning of a carefully choreographed play only pretending to decide the rest of his life?

In fact, Wuterich's fate had already been decided long before by a cabal of powerful men organized by Secretary of Defense Donald Rumsfeld, who was getting his advice from the best legal minds in the Marine Corps. Although Wuterich didn't yet know it, the evidence that would exonerate him and implicate several member of his squad for alleged war crimes had already been set aside. All that was left was the storied play.

Wuterich was the last Marine standing before the bar of justice in the matter of the United States of America versus the so-called Haditha Eight, a common reference to the indicted defendants. Along with three of his men and four superior officers, Frank Wuterich had been charged with a long laundry list of crimes topped by eighteen counts of intentional multiple murder and closed out with allegations of intentional lies and official malfeasance by his officers to cover up the truth. The incident that fueled the fire was dubbed the Haditha Massacre, a fallacious name that inflamed the uninformed and flummoxed the senior Marines and politicians charged with giving an understandable reason for the bestial deaths of innocent children the United States had sworn to protect. By January 3, 2012, the other seven original defendants had been immunized to tell the truth, deemed not responsible, or found not guilty of anything following the longest and most expensive criminal investigation in Marine Corps history. When Wuterich came to trial, few people cared about what everybody else had already forgotten.

Wounded survivor Eman Walid Abdul Hamid had not forgotten. She was nine when she hid under the bed with her younger brother, seven-year-old Abdul Rahman Hamid. Eman said she watched her Aunt Hiba run out of the bedroom with her baby, Asia, in her arms after men poked their rifles through the door shouting in strongly accented Arabic about bombs and hidden insurgents, threw in a grenade, and then tried to shoot everybody inside the room. She remembered that as quickly as they appeared, they were gone, leaving behind a room full of dead. Seconds later, her Aunt Hiba grabbed up her infant daughter and fled.

The Marines agree somebody yelled "runner" soon after clearing Eman's room, so they took off in pursuit of the fleeing figure. Later, they argued about who called out the alarm and whether anybody actually saw a running person. In any event, Aunt Hiba's unexpected departure caused the Marines to abandon House #1 to pursue her. Somehow she had disappeared. Later, she reappeared at her father-in-law's house with unharmed Asia. It was the only happy moment in the seven-year affair.

Five months later, the little girl told journalists in Baghdad a man with a "pistol" and another Marine came into her refuge after the first group left to finish off anyone still alive. Her interpreter cared little about what she said and his translation was poor. Her recollections passed unnoticed. Her story, however, was consistent with statements offered by two indicted Marines under grueling NCIS interrogation. They told NCIS investigators at Haditha Dam in early March they later returned to House #1 to clear their rear, a routine security precaution to ensure no threats are left behind. Their return visit lacked precision, they explained. One man threw a fragmentation grenade in House #1 that didn't explode so they cleared the rooms with 40 mm grenade blasts before entering. Afterward, the men went inside the smoke-filled building, where one Marine said he emptied his borrowed fifteen-shot 9 mm Beretta automatic into a room after throwing in a grenade, spreading his bullets across the dim space. He claimed another Marine had told him to frag the room. There were bodies there—he was sure of that, he said—but he could not tell the size, age, or gender. Then they visited another house where seven more women and children had died and cleared it again. He didn't know until much later one little girl survived. His partner told a similar tale, although he omitted any reference to ordering up a grenade or someone shooting a pistol.

The evidence Maloney examined showed that at least two and probably three Marines had shot into the group of women and children there at very close range, the same bullets passing through two or more bodies on their way to oblivion. Only *when* it happened was impossible to determine. Picture evidence, however, is inconclusive, and most of the forensic evidence had been cleaned up before NCIS was summoned. Despite Maloney's recommendation for further testing, there would be no forensic corroboration.

The Marines' damning statements were dismissed two years later by military judge Lieutenant Colonel Paul Ware for being inconsistent with the evidence the prosecution presented. He decided their revelations were the result of confusion and reaction to psychological trauma.

The forensic evidence never introduced was equally traumatic. The NCIS reconstruction showed that after attempting to kill everyone in House #1, the entire fire team had pursued the chimerical figure thought to be Aunt Hiba to another substantial dwelling, subsequently labeled House #2. Wuterich said he told his men to treat it as "hostile." The Marines said they either knocked on the door of the second house or rang the doorbell, nobody could remember which. Either would be an astounding way to assault a house already declared hostile. They do remember a squad member named Humberto Mendoza shooting the man who answered their summons with his rifle. The man died where he fell. The NCIS forensic reconstruction showed that Mendoza fired his rifle from twenty-one feet away. At first, Mendoza claimed Wuterich told him to do it. Later, he said he shot the unarmed man because the house had been declared hostile and shooting the occupants of hostile houses is what Marines are trained to do.

Moving through the dimly lit house, the three Marines who later admitted being inside swept it by the numbers. Corporal Hector Salinas reportedly stayed outside the front door providing security. A lance corporal named Justin Sharratt remained outside as well at the rear of the house with his M240 Golf medium machine gun, he said. Nobody ever explained how a spent 9 mm pistol casing was discovered and photographed there by a Marine Corps staff sergeant later the same day. Sharratt was the only Marine armed with a 9 mm. Years later, he told Major Haytham Faraj it must have arrived stuck to his boot. If so, who shot it?

Meanwhile, the two surviving children in House #1 stayed under the protective shield of their dead relatives until discovered hours later by two different Marines. Blood was dripping on Abdul "like a faucet," he said. Eman's little brother was too traumatized to remember how or why his mother and father had been killed. He was fixated on the "flash bang" of an explosion and the "meat" that flew from his grandfather's body after the Marines arrived. Neither story ever penetrated the veil of secrecy that kept them well hidden. The judge at Wuterich's court-martial denied a defense motion to have the children brought to Camp Pendleton to testify. After seven years, there was still no time for the truth.

Whether or not any serious crime was ever committed at Haditha is still the bone of contention. Nobody was ever convicted of one. How Marines are supposed to treat hostile buildings and the people who inhabit them had been relentlessly drummed into their heads during MOUT training in California, Kuwait, and Iraq. Their mission was to eliminate resistance.

MOUT is the acronym for military operations in urban terrain, or how to clear a house of perceived human threats by lethal means. The Marines had rehearsed the scenario hundreds of times. Stack on a wall; pack tightly together back to front covering all directions; slowly slide down the wall until discovering a door or opening; carefully look around the corner; gradually turkey peek into the targeted room, "pie-ing" it by cutting it into slices, examining each piece to discover where the threats are before throwing in a fragmentation grenade. It happens very quickly. After the blast, rush inside with guns blazing with waist-high bursts to riddle anyone still standing. Then shoot them again to be sure they are down. Nobody is supposed to survive. It is automatic, second nature. Some of the shooters had experienced it for real, over and over in the hell hole called Fallujah the year before. They knew how to kill by the numbers. They taught the new guys what to do. They were among the best light infantrymen in the world.

The ad hoc fire team from House #1 moved like wraiths through House #2, stacking and clearing in a choreographed ballet of utter destruction. Frank Wuterich was still in charge; Hector Salinas, a corporal pretending to be squad leader for a day, later testified he was nominally leading Humberto Mendoza, Justin Sharratt, and Stephen Tatum, a rookie private and two salty lance corporals, who had survived the Hell House at Fallujah, who composed the rest of the team.

Wuterich ordered them to frag the house after Mendoza shot the man who answered the door. Tatum said that upon entry he threw a borrowed grenade into a room that housed the plumbing. The explosion caused the pipes to leak. Water spread across the floor. He thought he borrowed the grenade from Salinas, but nobody was ever sure.

A few seconds later, Mendoza opened a door and threw in a second grenade. It failed to explode because he forgot to remove the safety tape that held the arming handle secure until it was time to throw it—a rookie mistake. Explosive ordnance disposal experts recovered it the next day. Inside the room, later determined to be a back bedroom, Mendoza saw eight women and children. He initially claimed Tatum ordered him to go inside and kill them after Mendoza told Tatum there were only women and children inside. Tatum followed close behind to provide backup. Mendoza changed his story several times over the years. So did everybody else who was there. After several years of procrastinating, the prosecution decided it was Tatum and Wuterich who did most of the killing. In another version, an older woman opened the door after Mendoza threw in his grenade and screamed, so he shot her first. In another version, Wuterich followed Tatum inside the room when he encountered the victims and began firing. Doing so, according to the rules of engagement (ROE) and the Uniform Code of Military Justice (UCMJ), is not a crime. It is a mandate. The lone Iraqi survivor was certain it was a short man, shorter than she, who threw in the grenade and then came back in shooting. Mendoza was the only Marine to fit that description. He was never charged.

Tatum denies Mendoza's stories ever happened. Sharratt says he wasn't even there. Their word held particular credence because they survived the Hell House at Fallujah, where two Marines earned the Navy Cross. Despite his story and service, Tatum was indicted along with Wuterich for shooting the seven victims. Tatum was charged with two counts of unpremeditated murder, four counts of negligent homicide, and assault. The dead women and children in House #2 were included among the eighteen murdered Iraqis Wuterich was initially charged with killing.

In response to numerous defense motions, the convening authority (Lieutenant General James N. Mattis) subsequently reduced the charges against Tatum to two counts of involuntary manslaughter, reckless endangerment, and aggravated assault. Meanwhile, Sharratt was charged with similar crimes in still another shooting. He, too, was later immunized from prosecution, lauded for his bravery by Mattis, and honorably discharged a certified hero. Tatum's grant of testimonial immunity and honorable discharge soon followed. Wuterich suddenly faced the rest of his life in prison alone.

The only event already certain when Sharratt and Tatum were shielded was that by the time the firing ceased, seven of the eight innocents hiding in House #2 were dead, literally shredded by Marine gunfire received from only a few feet away. No weapons, contraband, or evidence of insurgent presence was ever discovered. The room they died in was not smoke filled, nor was it too dim to otherwise see. Tatum admitted—and later recanted—that he knew some of the victims were children. It was possible. The sun was up and shining through the windows. The victims were not obscured by blankets or covers. There was no reason not to realize women and children were cowering there. Among the 5.56 mm shell casings found on the floor was an expended 9 mm pistol round. Somebody with a handgun had been there. Marines carried 9 mm handguns. Only Sharratt had one, but he said he was never inside the house. Were insurgents using the houses to hide? Did one insurgent have a pistol? Why were expended AK-47 rounds reportedly lying on the floor of House #2? Despite the questions such circumstances raised, they were never answered.

Later in the day, Second Lieutenant William T. Kallop, the Third Platoon commander and the Marine who ordered "clear south," and

Salinas returned to the alleged crime scene to count the dead. To their reported surprise they discovered the two little survivors in House #1. Their visit might have been the second time Marines entered the blasted houses, or perhaps it was the third or fourth. That important number remains an official mystery despite the immolated man later discovered melted into the kitchen floor. Neither man was ever charged with a crime.

Salinas said he was taken aback to discover that the first man to die in House #1 had mysteriously dissolved into the scorched lino-leum kitchen floor, turned into a grotesque silhouette of gray and black ash. Salinas recalled that the last time he saw him, the dead man had merely been shot to death. It was later revealed that Kallop was car-rying a white phosphorus grenade when he arrived on the battlefield that morning. The enlisted Marines denied they had been carrying any pyrotechnic devices. Kallop was the only Marine in the platoon to pos-sess one, although he was never asked what he did with it. Unlike most of the other sensational NCIS reports, his suspected involvement in the atrocity was never leaked to the press.

His possession of the device apparently caused NCIS obvious con-sternation when the investigators learned he was carrying a white phos-phorus grenade. The dead man had been consumed by one. During Kallop's questioning by two NCIS special agents on March 6, 2006, at nearby Haditha Dam, he said he never noticed any smoke or fire com-ing from House #1. Salinas, who accompanied him, had already told investigators he noticed smoke coming out of an air conditioner vent, but nothing else. The smoke was caused by a fire so hot it scorched the dead old lady in the hallway fifteen or more feet away.

The subject apparently left Kallop in a nervous state, which NCIS special agents noted in their March report. "Kallop's hands began to shake and he was sweating profusely," the agents detailed in their writ-ten narrative. Subsequently, Kallop said he wanted to speak to a lawyer before making a statement. He soon after obtained a civilian lawyer and dummied up. Kallop's wealthy father also hired a crackerjack pub-lic relations firm to speak for him. Ultimately, investigators revealed nothing that tied the two incidents together. To this day nobody has figured out how a dead man managed to cremate himself.

"It was a challenge [to understand] why Kallop was never investigated or charged," Maloney says. "He told his Marines to treat the house as hostile. Somebody was covering up what he did with his pyrotechnic device. Iraq was different war, a war of sergeants and corporals. They didn't plug in a lieutenant until the whole platoon is involved. The only reason Kallop got involved was that the FAST (Fleet Antiterrorism Security Team) team was called to the coordinated ambush. It was an anomaly for him to be in the field."

Another decedent was the old man in House #1. He lost a leg when a grenade exploded beneath him. Even so, it was not necessarily a crime. As gruesome and heartless as it seems, a human dismembered by a grenade is not necessarily evidence of murder. The ROE and the Rules of Land Warfare the United States Armed Forces ostensibly defer to provide rationalizations for random killings during close combat. Maloney was well aware of the limitations of laws written to limit killing civilians while fighting wars:

> I wouldn't call them [defendants] murderers. I would call them unreluctant killers. There wasn't a high threshhold for killing; there was no moral restraint. The lives of the people they took simply didn't mean anything. House #2 was the end of the feeding frenzy. After it was over the reinforced fire team thought, "Oh my God, what has happened?" They just couldn't get to their off switch quick enough.

The Marines detailed to clean up the mess found the old man's leg lying where he died when they entered House #1. Marines from the same company later used the leg for an impromptu soccer ball in a pickup game they played outside the charnel house. NCIS special agents confiscated a grisly digital image of the game from a Marine's personal camera. It remains an official secret. "We found prohibited images on Marines' personal cameras, the HET (human intelligence exploitation team) camera, even on the server in battalion headquarters," one agent revealed years later.

Inside House #1, other Kilo Marines were using red markers to ink numbers on the dead people's foreheads—if they had one. Six noncombatants died there: the old man, an old woman, two military aged males, a young woman, and a little boy. Only the two children, infant Asia, and her mother survived. The dead MAMs were all deemed insurgents. The remainder of the departed were defined as unavoidable collateral damage.

The same afternoon, Marines detailed to count and remove the corpses began their gruesome task, throwing the wrapped or bagged cadavers into three Humvees for a ride to the local morgue. Their leader was First Lieutenant Max Frank. Frank later reported he was told by his superiors to provide an explanation to local hospital officials when he delivered the bodies to the facility's morgue the night of November 19, 2005.

"We were to explain to the Iraqis that the Marines were sorry about this, but this is what happens when you allow terrorists to use homes to attack Marines," Frank testified two years later.

After tagging and bagging the dead in House #1, the body detail, accompanied by an HET staff sergeant documenting the deaths, moved to House #2. Behind the front door they found the man Mendoza shot. In a back bedroom they found two young women, two adolescent boys, and three little girls literally torn apart by close-range rifle and pistol fire. Somebody had leaned over them while firing to ensure their deaths, the survivor said. The forensic evidence was inconclusive when it was scrutinized five months later, but there is nothing inconclusive about the pictures NCIS found. Investigators did determine from them that one little girl had simultaneously been shot in the head by two different weapons. A picture of her body shows her head split in half, the parts opened like an obscene flower. The image is among the pictures a military judge has prohibited by court order from ever being publicly revealed. They remain hidden on one of the digital discs holding the investigative record.

A section of the body recovery detail was sent to another building labeled House #4, a compound of sorts with several separate domiciles inside a thick-walled courtyard. Inside that dwelling, they removed the remains of four men who died in a back bedroom, one of them while inside a large wooden wardrobe. Two of the men were allegedly armed with AK-47s. The man in the closet had been shot through the door behind which he was hiding. A fifth man purportedly escaped for a time. The victims had undisputedly been killed by Sharratt and Wuterich.

At least three of the decedents had been shot in the head at close range by the borrowed pistol Sharratt produced when his light machine gun jammed. It was a remarkable display of combat shooting in a kinetic environment where both sides were trying to kill one another. Although Wuterich entered the room in time to shoot the last Iraqi to die, Sharratt always maintained he had already killed them all. One of them was alleged to be an Iraqi traffic cop, and another supposedly had a Marine-issue pass identifying him as a good guy, but they were deemed terrorists anyway. The two Marines who killed them testified they seized and turned in two captured assault rifles to the battalion armorer and gave the HET a recovered suitcase containing numerous Jordanian passports, some cell phones, and money. The armorer later testified the weapons had disappeared. The passports and telephones never showed up in evidence. NCIS thought the situation very suspicious.

The fog of war that descended like a wet woolen blanket over Haditha after the clearing operation ended had affected the memories of the surviving Iraqis as badly as it did the Marines. Najla Abid-al-Razak Hamad, the wife and mother of two men killed in the back bedroom of House #4, offered an account to investigators five months later that was deemed "irreconcilable" with the recounting of events at House #4 by the Marines and the NCIS forensic reconstruction of the alleged crime scene, Maloney revealed.

Najla told NCIS Special Agent Nadya Mannle that Marines showed up outside her house several hours after the IED exploded, yelling "*erhab*" (terrorists), "*mujahedin*" (insurgents), and "*qunbehlah*" (bombs). Najla claimed that the Marines were angry and repeatedly referred to the bomb while pointing in the direction of the explosion. The Marines lined them up near a patio, allegedly dividing them into two lines. The elderly father of the four decedents and four women were placed in one row, and the four doomed men and a young boy were ordered to the second row. A different witness told Mannle that one of the Marines then set his rifle with a tripod or bipod down on top of the car and racked it. Sharratt was by now carrying his so-called SAW, a squad automatic weapon equipped with a bipod. In Sharratt's account that never happened.

Still another witness told Mannle the Marine guarding the women was taller than the other Marines. Another said all the Marines had pistols. Neither was true. Sharratt, the only Marine with a sidearm, is much taller than both Salinas and Wuterich. In murder investigations it is the little details that are important.

Najla alleged that she soon heard muffled gunfire and four distinct gunshots, leading her to believe her husband, son, and their two brothers were executed. Maloney says her allegation is completely undermined by the NCIS forensic reconstruction of the combat engagement. It shows that Sharratt and Wuterich performed as they claimed. Sharratt even passed a polygraph test.

THIRTEEN MONTHS LATER, four of the five Marines who cleared the houses were indicted for murder, manslaughter, aggravated assault, suborning witnesses, and a bevy of lesser charges. Four of their officers, including their battalion commander and company commander, were indicted as well. The charges against the officers were procedural offenses, failing to write adequate reports, failing to investigate the Iraqi claims, and failing to fill out important forms. Their real crime was failing to give the big brass in Baghdad a heads up that a shit storm was brewing. Events would show that the Marines had a contingency plan for all manner of storms, except this one. The defendants all pled not guilty.

About the same time in March that 3/1's Marines were packing for home, the unintended consequences of the ambush at Haditha began to emerge. The deaths had triggered inquiries by the press, in particular *TIME* magazine. In news parlance, the incident was growing legs—never a good thing for anyone accused of a crime. Initially, the brass in Baghdad sent an Army colonel to investigate the Marines in response to the magazine reporter's allegations of murder and massacre. The colonel reported they had done their duty in trying circumstances. To hedge his bets he suggested a more formal investigation be conducted anyway.

At the same time, the reporter, a dogged scribe named Tim McGirk, was conducting his own investigation, one more attuned to the perspective of the victimized Iraqis. He got his information from a bogus Marine press release assigning blame to the insurgents, the surviving women and children, Iraqi lawyers and doctors, and two Sunni male insurgent sympathizers claiming to be human rights workers. One worked for Reuters News Service, and the other was a middle-aged "budding journalist" when not protecting humanity, according to *TIME*. McGirk asked for nothing from the Marines.

McGirk's report was published in *TIME*'s online edition on March 19, 2006, about the same time the Army brass was digesting its hand-picked investigator's diametrically opposed findings. No matter that McGirk was never at Haditha. He said his editor told him it was too dangerous to venture there. The victims found him in Baghdad instead, accompanied by the self-proclaimed champions of civil liberties, now armed with a gruesome videotape and several witnesses who claimed the Marines had hunted the deceased like rabbits.

The Marine Corps could have discredited them all immediately. Marine signals intercept specialists had known about the alleged human rights workers long before they had emerged from the fog hovering over the events at Haditha. One of them had just been released from six months of Marine-mandated confinement at notorious Abu Ghraib prison for anti-government activities. The budding journalist was an ardent insurgent supporter, according to the Marines. The signals team eavesdropped while the men talked on their cell phones, discussing ways to both incite and videotape Marines killing Iraqis. They were known associates of the insurgents who planned and executed the ambush. When the same two men showed up in Haditha within hours of the skirmish, it was not a surprise. Even so, the Marines kept their knowledge of the individuals secret for more than a year.

Unlike McGirk, the Iraqis were eager and willing to defy the local insurgency's edict against journalists operating in their domain. After interviewing the keening survivors, taking pictures of the dead women and children, and commiserating with the local dignitaries, they began shopping their grisly story around Baghdad. How they encountered McGirk has never been revealed. He refused several requests to testify or be interviewed. McGirk brought them into *TIME*'s fold before the Marine Corps had any idea it had happened. His reporting became the basis for the spurious allegations of a so-called massacre.

Two disparate events rose from the carnage of the ambush. One was a purely legal struggle that occurred in the United States, at Camp Pendleton, and in the boardrooms of Headquarters, Marine Corps, and the offices lining the E-Ring of the Pentagon. That struggle was about who should be prosecuted, what kind of damage could be wrought from not doing so, and what had to be concealed to shield Iraqi sensibilities while protecting US geopolitical interests. All of it together determined who was going to take the fall. The scapegoats' prosecution—labeled a persecution by its opponents—was designed from the get-go to ensure that their convictions for war crimes were accomplished without ever revealing what specifically those war crimes might be. The sensationalized reporting, overt lying, and obfuscation began the day after events in Haditha exploded and continued until Frank Wuterich was brought to general court-martial on criminal charges not even the prosecutor believed.

Before the senior Marines and their Army commanders in Baghdad realized the profound effect the events in Haditha had on world opinion, it was too late to take a proactive stance. The intentionally dishonest press release that ignited the scandal could not be called back, nor could it be adequately explained. The genie was out of the bottle. Although it would take several years for the Marines to concoct a plan that would appear to be a search for justice while concurrently ameliorating the harm already done to the morale of combat-ready Marines, the time for truth had passed.

The Haditha Marines' disproportionate effect on the international stage is what *No Time for the Truth* is about.

ACKNOWLEDGMENTS

This book is the product of many people who both wittingly and unknowingly provided the ardor and passion for its creation. The gruesome deaths of at least fifteen innocent civilians at Haditha, Iraq, on November 19, 2005, at the hands of a reinforced fire team of ambushed Marine infantrymen caused a furor as divisive as any that has touched the United States Marine Corps during its long and colorful history.

Understanding the reason for prosecuting the Marine infantrymen and four of their officers for alleged massacre in the middle of a vicious three-sided hit-and-run civil war and why it was simultaneously both their just deserts and a travesty of American jurisprudence stretches the illogical concept of blind military justice to the breaking point. Dozens of Marines from every side of the issue, as well as high-ranking Pentagon officials, obdurate generals, self-serving politicians, rabid journalists, biased and well-meaning civilians, apprehensive friends, grieving parents, and skeptical attorneys also searching for answers never managed to produce any reasonable explanation how such a perversion of justice could be perpetrated. Of particular influence while writing this book was my coauthor, Haytham Faraj, a fiery retired Marine Corps enlisted mortar man, mustang infantry officer, lawyer, and finally a Marine Corps staff judge advocate with clear and uncompromising principles. Faraj was first appointed and later retained as a civilian defense attorney to represent defendant Staff Sergeant Frank Wuterich from the time of his indictment for eighteen murders and related offenses in December 2006 until the final disposition of his case on January 24, 2012. Faraj once said he was reminded every day of the cruel ironies and uninformed biases endemic among the lawyers, warriors, scribes, and laymen trying to cope with the frequently incomprehensible situation the United States Marine Corps found itself in while in Iraq. His insights and understanding of the Arabic language and Iraq's culture and customs were instrumental in understanding how the incident at Haditha could have ever come to pass. Without Faraj this book was impossible.

As important was David Allender, publisher and contributing editor of the immensely popular blog *Defend Our Marines*, both the voice and archivist of the events that followed the ambush at Route Chestnut on a cool Saturday's dawn. His efforts were so inclusive that a State Department spokesman called it "the only" comprehensive record of what happened while the Haditha incident dragged on. The State Department sought out and used his archive for pertinent facts while negotiating its failed Status of Forces Agreement with the "new" Iraqi government before the United States' complete—albeit temporary—withdrawal from Iraq on January 1, 2012. The last defendant's general court-martial began three days after that agreement was rejected.

Allender gave his voice and money for seven years while demanding justice and fair play for eight Marines, four officers and four enlisted men, ultimately charged with massacre and cover-up after one of their own died in an ambush. Early on, Allender was often aided by long-time conservative journalist Phillip V. Brennan, a *Newsmax* columnist and aging former Marine who was once Admiral Chester Nimitz's houseboy during World

War II. Before the so-called Haditha Massacre ever became a worldwide issue, Brennan was already unlimbering his war chest of invectives to decry what he saw as grave injustice. His counsel is missed.

Contributing greatly to putting it all together was Thomas J. Cutler, a retired Naval officer and fine author and researcher in his own right. He originally accepted the manuscript for publication at the Naval Institute Press, a decision that sorely tried him. There are many other people to recognize. My agents, Murray Weiss at Catalyst Literary Management in New York and Joel Gotler at Intellectual Property Group in Los Angeles, took the time and made the effort to get the project restarted after the Naval Institute Press unexpectedly rejected the book on the eve of publication. Also essential in the production of this work is Maxim Brown, the editor at Skyhorse Publishing in New York City, who took a shine to the manuscript, and Cal Barksdale, the executive editor of Arcade Publishing, the imprint of Skyhorse that the book is published under; Colonel Walt Ford, publisher of *Leatherneck* magazine, who encouraged me to write it; former 3/1 commanding officer Bob Weimann, a retired Marine light colonel and frequent contributor to *Defend Our Marines*; Mark Walker, who ably covered the story from its inception for Oceanside, California's now defunct *North County Times*; and Tony Perry, the *Los Angeles Times*'s skeptical reporter and devil's advocate who kept us thinking. There are many more reporters, investigators, Marine Corps PAOs, and ordinary citizens who contributed mightily, but unfortunately I have only limited space, so let me thank everyone mentioned and overlooked, especially those who undoubtedly know they deserve a name on this page. Last but not least, I wish to recognize my departed friend, consummate Illinois politician and advisor Bruce Pitchford, the only enlisted man who hung with our star-studded corps commander in Japan. He was wise about many things, especially people. Last and never least, my lifelong wife and partner, Marsha, and our children, Cecily and Nathaniel, a prosecuting attorney and former Coast Guardsman, respectively, who offered great legal advice and ribald observations of military life with good humor while putting up with undeserved orneriness. God bless America.

Nathaniel R. Helms
St. Charles, Missouri
December 24, 2015

When Nathaniel Helms approached me in January of 2012 in the midst of the Haditha trial to discuss the idea of coauthoring a book about the case, I was initially suspicious. He was one of the many people who made regular appearances in the courtroom. They seemed to be a collection of devoted, unquestioning supporters of the accused Marines, regardless of the facts. To many of the supporters in the courtroom gallery, dead Iraqi children were mere collateral victims of a war for "freedom" brought by the benevolent Americans. But the children who died in Haditha on November 19, 2005, were not collateral victims of a house-clearing operation gone terribly wrong. They had been murdered. The photos of well-aimed head shots—or no heads at all—from high velocity American rifles proved it. That was my state of mind when I listened to and quickly, but politely, dismissed Nat's idea of a book.

Over the next few days, I researched his background and discovered that he was not some myopic supporter but an accomplished journalist, author, former police officer, and warrior. I contacted him and let him know that I was interested, but that the project could not be biased and would have to be intellectually and factually honest. He, of course, agreed. Little did we know then that telling the story would be met with such resistance. The Naval Institute Press, the publisher that originally agreed to publish the book, came back to us time and again for months, perhaps years, with concerns about the book and made its publication conditional on making changes they wanted. We resisted, as did they. The differences appeared irreconcilable and caused me to abandon the project. Without a publisher, the book was dead.

Nat Helms, however, was undeterred. His obstinate insistence that the story be told led him to Skyhorse Publishing, who agreed to publish the manuscript as originally drafted. To them we owe a debt of gratitude.

This book is a story of a quest to defend an innocent Marine and to discover the truths about who was responsible for the murder of children and babies as they huddled in terror on their mother's bed, dressed in their pajamas, awaiting the completion of a house-clearing operation. Along the often tumultuous journey of telling this story I crossed paths with, and was accompanied by, a number of people who must be acknowledged. They are the talented filmmaker Michael Epstein, whose command of the facts made him a trusted sounding board (we became and remain good friends); my friend Colby Vokey, who set the example for courageous and zealous advocacy in the defense shop that came to be known as the pirate ship; my good friend and confidant Joseph H. Low IV, whose home in LA became my sanctuary during the years of litigation and trial; the inspirational Gerry Spence, his Trial Lawyers College, and its extraordinary faculty and staff who selflessly devoted their time in helping me prepare to defend Frank Wuterich; Nathanial Helms, who took on the herculean task of bringing this book to life and prevailed; and last, to my family, my wife, and my son Hasan. This is for you.

Haytham Faraj
June 15, 2016

ABBREVIATIONS

3/1 –Third Battalion, First Marines
COIN—counterinsurgency
COC—Combat Operations Center
COP—combat outpost
CPA—Coalition Provisional Authority
DIIR—Draft Information Intelligence Reports
DOD—Department of Defense
EOD—explosive ordnance disposal
EOF—escalation of force
FAST—Fleet Antiterrorism Security Team
FB Sparta—Firm Base Sparta
HET—Human Intelligence (HUMINT) Exploitation Team
IED—improvised explosive device
LOAC—laws of armed conflict
MAM—military-aged male
MNC–I—Multi-National Corps–Iraq
MNF—Multi-National Force

MNF–I—Multi-National Force–Iraq
MNF–W—Multi-National Force–West
MOUT—military operations in urban terrain
NCIS—Naval Criminal Investigative Service
NCO—noncommissioned officer
OP—overwatch position
PAO—public affairs officer
PID—positive identification
QRF—quick reaction force
RCT—Regimental Combat Team
RIAT—reportable incident assessment team
ROE—rules of engagement
SAF—small-arms fire
SASO—security and stabilization operations
SAW—squad automatic weapon
sitrep—situation report
TTP—tactics, techniques, and procedures
UAV—unmanned aerial vehicle
UCMJ—Uniform Code of Military Justice
VBIED—vehicle-borne improvised explosive device

NO TIME
FOR THE TRUTH

CHAPTER 1

THE HADITHA MASSACRE—
SETTING THE STAGE

Camp Pendleton, California. The longest criminal inquiry in Marine Corps history ended on Tuesday, January 24, 2012, with a solitary smack of the military judge's gavel. The so-called Haditha Massacre inquiry had not settled a thing except to ensure that the six-year-long prosecution of US Marine Corps staff sergeant Frank D. Wuterich was finally over. The thirty-one-year-old career infantryman was the last Marine among eight charged with massacre and cover-up to walk away a free man.

His ordeal had begun six years earlier—at 0730, Saturday, November 19, 2005—in the city of Haditha, Iraq, when the twelve-man rifle squad Wuterich led lost a Marine to ambush before killing eight suspected insurgents and fifteen civilians. The skirmish was provoked by enemy soldiers on a road the Marines called Route Chestnut, a modern, paved boulevard into the ancient city. The Marines belonged to "K" for Kilo Company, Third Battalion, First Marines, a First Marine

Division light infantry battalion of about 650 men on its third deployment to the Iraq War.

Included among the dead were ten women and four children. They died pathetically, huddled together in the bedrooms of two separate houses. Marines under Wuterich's command killed them with grenades and pistol and rifle fire. By Sunday the civilian deaths were known to most of the top Marine commanders in Iraq. The gruesome deaths elicited absolutely no interest among the harried brass. The Second Marine Division commanding general in charge of 3/1 while the First Marine Division asset worked through its third deployment was briefed two days later.

"I sat there and took the brief and no bells and whistles went off," Major General Richard A. Huck later ruminated.[1]

All the senior officers required to care about such things categorized the civilians as collateral damage and moved on. Their only response was a bland press release. The Army generals in faraway Baghdad said they never got a heads-up about the grisly nature of the innocents' deaths until a magazine reporter told them.

It was feasible—even likely—the civilian deaths could have slipped by unnoticed. The events at Haditha were relatively insignificant among the dozens of horrible incidents reported every week during the second year of the three-way Iraq war. The week before, November 12, the Associated Press reported that a car bomb placed by Sunni insurgents exploded outside a public market in the predominantly Shiite neighborhood of New Baghdad, killing eight people and wounding twenty-one more. Iraqi police lieutenant colonel Hassan Chaloub said among them was a woman and her eight-year-old daughter.

The same morning Wuterich's squad was ambushed, five American soldiers from the 101st Airborne Division died in two car bombing attacks near Mosul. The next morning, a British patrol was attacked by a roadside bomber in the southern city of Basra. One soldier was killed and four others were wounded, a British Defense Ministry official said.

The next day, Dr. Ahmed Fouad of the Baqouba city morgue claimed that five people, including three children, were killed and two others wounded by American soldiers manning a checkpoint. The following Monday, a US spokesman said, "US forces mistakenly fired on a civilian vehicle outside of an American military base north of Baghdad, killing at least three people, including one child."

Two days later, insurgents set off a car bomb outside a hospital in Mahmoudiya, killing thirty and wounding thirty-five, a doctor there said. Among the dead were three women and two children. American forces played no part in the incident. The Pentagon reported that eighty-eight Americans died in Iraq during November. No one was sure about the number of Iraqis killed.[2]

In the United States, nobody noticed. President George W. Bush was in Mongolia thanking folks there for supporting the war.[3] He needed friends anywhere he could find them. His poll numbers were slipping after his contentious reelection; unemployment and gas prices were rising, the economy was tanking. Without weapons of mass destruction, the voracious press circling the Pentagon demanded reasons why the United States invaded Iraq. Meanwhile, the rabid war fever that raged in the country after 9/11 was waning. The Pentagon responded with more parades, more heroes, and more hoopla at football games.

In Iraq, Lieutenant General John R. Vines, the Army general to whom top Marines in Iraq reported, apparently never received—or never shared—the information about Haditha with his superiors in Baghdad. At the time, Vines was the commanding general of the coalition forces in Iraq, then officially designated Multi-National Corps–Iraq (MNC–I). Nobody involved in the Haditha investigation is certain about what he knew and when because high-level protocol prevented Vines from ever officially being questioned.[4] Ultimately, the buck stopped with the Marines. Haditha was their baby and the Army generals and Washington politicians running the war came down hard on the Marine Corps three months later, when a story about the obscure town hit the big time, the cover of *TIME* magazine.

Thirteen months after that, Wuterich was indicted for murdering eighteen civilians. Seven other Marines from his battalion were also indicted for murder, assault, cover-up, and lying about the same incident. The defendants were accused of slaughtering twenty-four innocent civilians during an out-of-control rampage and then conspiring to cover it up. Somebody dubbed it the "Haditha Massacre" and the name stuck.

Inside the Corps, everybody's eyes were on the first Marine Corps general ever appointed chairman of the Joint Chiefs of Staff. General Peter Pace had been in command only six weeks when the events at Haditha erupted. Everyone was looking to him to take the lead. Pace is a moral man who tried to lead with the principles he learned at the US Naval Academy and practiced as a platoon leader in Vietnam. He said nothing publicly for six months.

Pace broke his silence in Singapore on June 4, 2006, when telling Marines stationed there that "the ongoing investigations of events in Haditha, Iraq, presented an opportunity for all service members to revisit ourselves and see where we are on our moral compass."[5]

Asked his thoughts about news coverage of the alleged Haditha incident, Pace told the group he supported the new ethics training requirement for deployed troops and believed it supported "what 99 percent of Marines are doing right." Pace acknowledged that as the investigations unfolded, there would likely be "a bumpy road" ahead.

He probably didn't realize just how bumpy the road would be. The scandal that evolved overshadowed his tenure as the country's highest-ranking military officer almost as soon as it was revealed. He would last two years. On June 8, 2007, Secretary of Defense Robert Gates announced that he would advise President George W. Bush not to nominate Pace for a second term. The only Marine ever so honored stepped down as chairman on October 1, 2007, replaced by Chief of Naval Operations Admiral Michael Mullen. Pace was the first Marine to fall.

At a Pentagon briefing the next day, Marine Corps Commandant General Michael W. Hagee reiterated his boss's concern without adding anything relevant to the budding imbroglio. Instead of offering excuses, he said he couldn't comment on specifics regarding ongoing investigations of alleged Marine misconduct at Haditha on November 19, 2005, or another alleged murder that followed on April 26 in Hamdaniya, a village west of Baghdad.

"As commandant, I am gravely concerned about the serious allegations concerning actions of some Marines at Haditha and Hamdaniya," Hagee told reporters. "I can assure you that the Marine Corps takes them seriously. We want to ensure the investigations are complete with respect to what actually happened on the ground and actions taken or not taken by the chain of command."[6]

THE CIVILIAN DEATHS at Haditha were not secret. The day after the November 19 skirmish, a routine Marine Corps press release from Camp Blue Diamond in Ramadi reported that one Marine and fifteen Iraqi civilians were killed there when a convoy was hit by an IED blast. The Marine Corps's colorless account noted that "gunmen attacked the convoy with small-arms fire." When the shooting ended, the announcement said, eight insurgents were dead and a wounded insurgent was captured. It sounded like a tiny victory. Good news in the perverse order of things.

The report was written by Second Marine Division public affairs officer Captain Jeffrey Pool, a career Marine responsible for briefing the vociferous press in Al Anbar Province. In November 2005, Al Anbar was the hot ticket in Iraq for determined reporters, the place where they could make a name for themselves, dancing briefly with the terrible danger the Marines faced every day. Pool was there to accommodate them.

Regrettably, Pool's account was erroneous. He knew it at the time. Pool later claimed he released the inaccurate report because he believed the civilian deaths were attributable to the roadside bombing because "it led the Marines to counter-attack the hidden insurgents" who had set it off.[7]

The communiqué was not Pool's personal opinion; a colonel named Richard A. Sokoloski told him what to say. Colonel Sokoloski was chief of staff of the Second Marine Division, a lawyer, and Pool's boss.

The Marine who died was twenty-year-old Lance Corporal Miguel "T. J." Terrazas, the son of a retired Army staff sergeant from El Paso, Texas. At the time, the senior officers knew only that a faceless Marine was dead and eleven others had been wounded in a sharp contest that lasted an entire day. The attack that started on Route Chestnut ended when Marine jets and attack helicopters destroyed a suspected enemy safe house down the road after a handful of insurgents sought refuge there. A scene from video of the event recorded by a ScanEagle unmanned aerial vehicle shows an enemy soldier diving over a wall while a five-hundred-pound bomb is descending on his position. A few days later, some Marines found half a stinking corpse not far away wearing the same kind of chest rig the jumper did.

Three months after the IED killed Terrazas, *TIME* detonated its own bomb from the internationally known magazine's Baghdad bureau. *TIME* claimed the twenty-four Iraqi citizens who died at Haditha were massacred, the victims of Marine vengeance.[8] The reporter telling the tale was Tim McGirk, a particularly resourceful journalist who claimed the Iraqis were gunned down by merciless Marines gone berserk. Regrettably, like Pool, McGirk also got it wrong, remarkably wrong, but for different reasons. He was never there. His editors decided it was too dangerous for him to find out for himself.[9] Before the Marine Corps could make McGirk's specious account right, it was too late. To steal a time-worn phrase, the Marines had landed, but the situation was entirely out of hand. It is also where this story begins.

Wuterich's court-martial ended abruptly on a gorgeous January Monday morning after a secret plea deal was reached the preceding weekend. He had been well investigated. He was investigated by an Army major general and his staff, an Army colonel and his smaller staff, sixty-five NCIS special agents, and a committee of top-notch Pentagon lawyers reporting to then secretary of defense Donald Rumsfeld. After that, he faced a five-year prosecution effort by dozens of Marine Corps lawyers reinforced by reservists called to active duty to put him and seven other disgraced defaulters away. In the end, Wuterich pled guilty to speaking ineptly during his personally led counterattack. Nobody else was convicted of anything.

His admission of guilt was a small victory for the Marine Corps—almost infinitesimal, in fact. But it was a victory nonetheless. In return for a guilty plea to one count of negligent dereliction of duty, the government dismissed thirteen far more virulent charges, including nine counts of voluntary manslaughter, two counts of aggravated assault, and three charges of willful dereliction of duty. Wuterich was charged initially on December 21, 2006, with eighteen murders, aggravated assault, and lying to cover up his offenses at Haditha. He faced a possible death sentence. The charge he admitted to was on the same level as failing to put on his cover, or cap, when he went outside. It was the only conviction the Marine Corps managed to obtain during the most extensive criminal investigation in its history.

"Not bad," civilian defense lawyer James Culp drily observed shortly afterward. The former Army paratrooper from Round Rock, Texas, represented one of the enlisted shooters indicted alongside Wuterich.

On December 12, 2006, the US Marine Corps Forces Central Command "detailing authority" Lieutenant Colonel Phillip Simmons assigned Lieutenant Colonel Colby C. Vokey to represent Wuterich. Until his appointment, Vokey had been the regional defense counsel for West Coast Marines. Without him there weren't enough defense attorneys to go around.

Two weeks after Wuterich was indicted, Simmons assigned Major Haytham Faraj to represent him as well. Before this assignment, Faraj had worked for Vokey. He was already up to his neck in the court-martial of another grunt charged with murder at Hamdaniya, Iraq, five months after Wuterich had led his squad into Haditha.

"We already knew it was going to be big," Faraj said. "It was going to be as big as My Lai. But I put it on the back burner. Puckett and Mark Zaid (civilian cocounsel at the time) were putting it in the media. I avoided getting involved. You don't put criminal cases in the media. I told them I would be happy staying in the background writing motions."

At first, it seemed the government was holding all the cards. Then the case against Wuterich began falling apart. Disintegration started slowly when the government announced that one of the defendants had decided to testify against his former squad leader. On April 17, 2007, the Marine Corps dropped all charges against accused murderer Corporal Sanick P. Dela Cruz in exchange for his testimony. Soon after he was promoted to sergeant, Dela Cruz led the subsequent parade of eyewitnesses and participants who would walk away from prosecution in return for their testimony. His claim to fame was urinating into the skull of one of the dead men.

On August 9, 2007, Lieutenant General James N. Mattis, the convening authority and final arbiter in the Haditha affair, dropped all charges against Lance Corporal Justin Sharratt and Captain Randy Stone. Sharratt was a trigger puller, and Stone was the battalion lawyer. He was charged with failing to thoroughly investigate what Wuterich's squad allegedly did.

On September 18, 2007, LtGen Mattis dropped all charges against Captain Lucas McConnell in exchange for immunity and his cooperation with the investigation. The Annapolis graduate was the commanding officer of K Company when the events on Route Chestnut exploded onto the world stage. He had been relieved for cause the preceding April along with his boss, Lieutenant Colonel Jeffrey Chessani, and India Company commander Captain James Kimber, who had nothing to do with the events at Haditha. McConnell's career was later rehabilitated and he was promoted to major.

On March 28, 2008, all charges against Lance Corporal Stephen Tatum were dropped. He was with Wuterich during the entire event and had admitted shooting at least five civilians. He was the last shooter to be exonerated. Charges of involuntary manslaughter against Tatum were dismissed "in order to continue to pursue the truth-seeking process into the Haditha incident," the Marines said in a written statement.[10]

On June 5, 2008, First Lieutenant Andrew Grayson was acquitted by a general court-martial of all charges stemming from his participation in the Haditha incident. He was the only officer to stand court-martial. Grayson was an intelligence officer attached to Wuterich's battalion. He was charged with deleting photos of the deceased Iraqis in order to obstruct the investigation. He was later charged with failing to notify the Marine Corps administrative chain of command of his murky legal status when his term of service expired before he was "accidentally" discharged from the Marine Corps. It was a circus.

On June 17, 2008, all charges against Chessani were dismissed by a military judge citing unlawful command influence. He was accused of failing to follow orders by not following up on the civilian deaths with an investigation and failing to adequately detail timely battlefield reports. The Marine Corps appealed that ruling a month later. On March 17, 2009, a military appeals court upheld the dismissal of the charges against Chessani. An administrative board of inquiry was then convened for one final shot at the highest-ranking officer charged with crimes in the incident. The board found no evidence of misconduct and recommended that Chessani be allowed to retire without loss of rank or benefits. He did so a few days later.

Wuterich was the last Marine standing.

IED ON ROUTE CHESTNUT

Seven years after "T. J." Terrazas's death, it wasn't easy to remember that the events in the Camp Pendleton courtroom on January 24, 2012, were precipitated by the remotely detonated roadside bomb that killed him. (The bombs are universally referred to as IEDs—improvised explosive devices—one of the more well-known acronyms in the alphabet soup this story floats in.) Two other Marines were wounded in the attack.

The bomb was buried in the hard-surfaced road and then concealed with fresh paving material in plain view of the people who lived nearby. The decimated squad was then fired upon by unseen gunmen they believed were hiding in and around the two houses south of their position and more to the north. The survivors did what Marines always do—they counterattacked. They say they did it by the numbers, well-trained automatons moving through squat concrete houses like remorseless wraiths. Wuterich was leading the fire team that reportedly massacred the Iraqi men, women, and children, the act that ignited the furor.

NEGOTIATIONS TO DISMISS the charges against Wuterich had been going on since the previous Wednesday afternoon, when unpredictable civilian defense attorney Neal Puckett and veteran prosecutor LtCol Sean Sullivan struck up a secret conversation to consider a deal. Faraj was not included. He says he found Puckett's behavior extraordinary. Puckett was supposed to be Faraj's partner and confidant.

Faraj thought Puckett's timing was terrible as well. The government case was in tatters. Puckett told Sullivan he never had more than a negligence case to begin with. Sullivan replied that the case could have been settled the year before. Within moments they were standing in front of military judge LtCol David Jones asking for a recess. Faraj was not invited to participate.

Faraj is a former Marine enlisted man, a "mustang" officer who went to law school after a career as a grunt. He tore the government case to shreds. Puckett's unilateral decision to cut a deal caused an irreparable breach between the two lawyers.

The only two eyewitnesses Sullivan and lead government prosecutor Major Nicholas Gannon produced to impeach Wuterich had already been branded habitual liars and subpar Marines in previous hearings. Faraj destroyed their remaining credibility on the witness stand in the days preceding the proffered deal. After Wuterich's court-martial, they were kicked out of the Marine Corps by Secretary of the Navy Ray Mabus.[11]

Faraj didn't know a deal was in the works until later in the day when Gannon told him Sullivan and Puckett were working on one. The information was a shock. The potential deal had not even been referred to the convening authority for approval. Until LtGen Thomas D. Waldhauser agreed, all the negotiating in the world was meaningless.

Faraj told Puckett the deal "was premature and ill advised." The government's case had no depth, and the defense had yet to speak.

Nine government witnesses had already sided with the defense. The Iraqi witnesses either were prohibited from testifying or refused to, and the forensic evidence was almost nonexistent. Faraj was certain the case was won. Puckett told him his job was now to help convince Wuterich the deal was a good one.

On Friday the court-martial resumed without Jones offering an explanation. He was so sure the court-martial would move forward, he warned counsel to anticipate ten-hour days and Saturday sessions to make up for the lost time.

The final Friday of the trial began the way it had ended the previous Wednesday, with prosecution witness Sergeant Humberto Mendoza on the witness stand. He had risen from private first class to sergeant while Wuterich's case ground on. Mendoza was one of four Marines who swept through two houses killing almost everyone inside. The pint-sized infantryman was going to reveal that Wuterich told him the houses were hostile. It was why Mendoza said he killed two men up close and personal with his M16. He killed the second man when the unarmed victim answered a polite summons to his front door. The prosecution was trying to prove Wuterich made Mendoza do it by speaking irresponsibly.

Faraj was hard on the Venezuelan for a time before offering a carrot instead of his usual stick. He said Mendoza was a brave Marine who was so devastated by his own actions he was sure he must be guilty of something. Faraj gently convinced the battle-rattled former infantryman to admit he had second-guessed himself into believing he had done something wrong. Faraj coaxed and cajoled, reaching into the depths of Mendoza's soul for the spark of truth he was trying to tuck away.

"If I train a dog to attack and then he does, who is the blame, responsible [sic]—the dog or the person who taught him to behave that way? Mendoza was responding to his training," Faraj declared.

In the end Mendoza admitted he didn't hear any orders from Wuterich and didn't have a clue what happened in the charnel houses now innocuously labeled House #1 and House #2.

After watching Faraj finish reducing Mendoza's shaky testimony to irrelevancy, the jury "panel" of eight combat-hardened officers and senior NCOs dutifully settled back to watch more than three hours of five-year-old "outtakes" from the CBS television news show *60 Minutes* in which Wuterich gives a candid interview to CBS TV personality Scott Pelley. The video snippets were the government's last best chance to seal Wuterich's fate. Outtakes are video clips that end up on the cutting room floor instead of on TV. It was great theater.

The interview aired first in March 2007. During Wuterich's interview, he told Pelley he ordered his squad to "shoot first and ask questions later" or "something like that." The first time Wuterich said it was to an Army colonel on a fact-finding trip to Haditha in February 2006. It wasn't a smart thing to say before he had an opportunity to speak with legal counsel and absolutely devastating to his defense when he repeated himself on national television.[12]

Faraj was in the choir of defense attorneys who called Puckett's decision to put Wuterich on national television one of the most irresponsible decisions they had even seen a defense attorney make.

"The first time I met Puckett I asked him why he did it," Faraj recalled five years later. "I was still starry eyed. I thought it was a bad decision, but I needed to understand at this point. I did not attack."

Navy and Marine Corps lawyers spent three subsequent years in appeals courts fighting to obtain the unused portions from CBS while Wuterich helplessly waited in the wings.[13]

The smoking gun the government sought wasn't there. It never had been. The panel heard Wuterich calmly repeat over and over that he had done nothing wrong while Pelley groped for proper tone in lieu of any substance. Wuterich's calmness was unnerving.

Watching Wuterich watch himself five years later was somehow sad. Time had not been kind to him. The hollow-eyed man watching from the defense table and the young staff sergeant full of earnest conviction on TV in 2007 scarcely looked the same. Three years of bickering between lawyers who cared little about what happened to Wuterich had wounded him.

Trial resumed on schedule at 8:30 a.m. Monday with two forensic pathologists drily explaining the subtle differences of stippling and identifying evacuated skulls. It was important evidence because most of the victims suffered head wounds. Some of them appeared to have arrived from very close by. Air Force Lieutenant Colonel Elizabeth A. Rouse, MD, a pathologist and regional medical examiner from San Antonio, Texas, was the government's expert on the victims' manner of death. She offered her usual explicit, definitive view that the Marines had been very efficient while dispatching the victims residing now only in white loose-leaf notebooks of grisly photographs each juror possessed. They contained the images recorded by several Marines after the shooting ended. Rouse had used them to help determine her findings. One of the images was of the man set on fire.[14] Nobody officially ever figured out why. Officially, no one tried. Rouse had already testified several times and knew the litany by heart. Many of them had been alive when the headshots evacuated their skulls. Then everybody went to lunch.

When trial resumed at 1:30 p.m., it was immediately suspended "until further notice." In the witness room, a group of NCIS special agents were waiting to testify. They were serious guys in suits, the G-Men of the Naval Service. Among them was Special Agent Michael S. Maloney, a forensic reconstructionist assigned to the Forensic Consultant Unit, Violent Crimes Division of NCIS.

The Marines despised them. The defense made them the arch villains of their play. Some of them performed brilliantly. Some of them were Keystone Cops. No doubt the agents anticipated a cold reception knowing the panel had already heard at great length about their alleged borderline treatment of Wuterich and the other defendants during their defamed investigation in Iraq in February and March 2006. Instead, they were sent home.

On Tuesday morning, Wuterich told Jones he wanted to confess to a single count of negligent dereliction of duty, part of a plea deal Sullivan and Puckett negotiated. This time the deal was approved by LtGen Waldhauser, the final arbiter of the matter. He was the fourth general to oversee the Haditha investigation.

Puckett told Jones the secret negotiations that led to the guilty plea had in fact continued through the weekend before the deal was struck. He offered that observation after Jones told the court that the first round of bargaining announced the week before "fell through" before trial resumed the preceding Friday morning.

"Nothing ever fell through," Puckett corrected Jones before the settlement was announced. "I'd like to get that on the record."

Eighteen months earlier, prosecutor Sean Sullivan had offered Wuterich eighteen months' confinement in return for pleading guilty to something. Faraj talked Wuterich out of it. He convinced Wuterich he had the case won:

> This time he was broken. The Marine Corps had broken him down. LCpl [Stephen] Tatum broke down after twelve hours of interrogation by NCIS at Haditha Dam. Wuterich had been getting battered for five and a half years. He didn't have it in him anymore to fight.

Wuterich's admission had little to do with killing people. Negligent dereliction of duty is a relatively minor charge. It is a lesser included offense detailed in Article 92 of a Uniform Code of Military Justice violation, titled "Failure to Obey Order or Regulation.[15] There is nothing quite like it in civilian law, but it is still an admission of guilt.

The government's acceptance of the deal was a wildly waved white flag. Considering an unlikely but still possible life sentence as the alternative, it was a remarkable defense victory, a big bass drum. And like a drum it was empty. It allowed Puckett to lay claim to an elusive legal victory without doing a lot of heavy lifting in court.

Dereliction comes in many forms. It exists to ensure the good order and discipline of the armed forces is maintained no matter how ambiguous the offense threatening it may be. Willful dereliction is a much more severe offense than negligent dereliction, which comes with a six-month jail term. Even so, Wuterich could have wound up in jail for three months.

Compared to murder his conviction was meaningless, more a vengeful act than the ministrations of justice. According to Article 92, a person is derelict in the performance of duties "when that person *willfully* or *negligently* [emphasis added] fails to perform that person's duties or when that person performs them in a culpably inefficient manner." *Willfully* means intentionally. *Negligently* means the accused failed to use due care "which a reasonably prudent person would have exercised."

Wuterich was convicted of failing to act like a reasonably prudent person should when he led his squad into a counterattack he knew had already wiped out 25 percent of his command. Negligent dereliction calls for a maximum forfeiture of two-thirds pay per month for three months and confinement for three months. Instead, Wuterich was demoted to private, although the punishment applied was not part of the sentence mandated by the crime. That probably hurt the most.

The lawyers already knew the only sentence Jones could impose on Wuterich was reduction in rank to private (E-1) and a general discharge. LtGen Waldhauser saw to that. His decision says a lot about what the Marine Corps thought of the court-martial. The only other sanction that could be applied was the type of general discharge Wuterich received—either under "honorable" conditions or "other than honorable" conditions. If given an "other than honorable" discharge, the onus of misconduct would forever haunt him. That, too, was decided by the convening authority. No other punishments were authorized by the deal set up between Wuterich and the general who made the rules. The UCMJ is very flexible in matters of retribution.

Before Wuterich was sentenced, he told the court he was a single parent. His former wife, Marisol, had left him years before. He testified that his income was $3,486 a month for being a staff sergeant with more than fourteen years of service. With that he took care of three young daughters on his own. There was a touching home movie featuring his little girls at his sentencing hearing the next morning. They skipped and danced and played while Frank strummed his guitar.

It was as touching as it was incongruent, being shown on the same screen that had showed dead Iraqi babies the week before. The video was produced by New York videographer Michael Epstein, who had been recording the events for Puckett since he was retained.

Before sentence was handed down Tuesday morning, the judge asked Wuterich if the defendant understood the implications of his decision before he admitted being guilty of speaking badly. Wuterich still had the option of continuing the good fight he had waged for more than six years. A conviction for any of the felonious charges could cost him the balance of his lost youth in federal prison. Sitting behind him were two Marine officers deeply wounded by his decision. Major Jeffrey Dinsmore and Major Lucas McConnell were there to remind him who he was letting down.

It was impossible to tell what was going through Wuterich's mind. His face was as blank as it had been for six years. After telling Jones he understood the ramifications of his decision, it was time for coming clean. The last scene in the play required Wuterich to fall on his sword. It was grand theater. In the moment, it was easy to forget that the lives of twenty-five human beings were now forfeited without explanation.

Wuterich admitted he failed to maintain "adequate tactical control" of four Marines he was leading by uttering a "negligent verbal order." Wuterich told the court that comments he made to troops "may" have led to the "tragic" deaths of the women and children.

"I took a team of Marines to clear houses to the south of the site [where the civilians died] and did use the words 'shoot first, ask questions later,' or something to that effect prior to clearing or entering there," Wuterich testified.[16]

The veracity of his only admission had repeatedly been debunked. Evidence already admitted showed that his fire team didn't remember him saying anything like that. Two team members testified Wuterich didn't say anything at all before they cleared the houses; one team member said he wasn't there to hear what his squad leader said; and another claimed the first time Wuterich gave anybody an order was when he told the team to "shoot whoever answered" their polite summons to the front door. "Just wait until he opens the door and shoot," Lance Corporal Mendoza testified Wuterich ordered them.

The incongruity of this was incredible. Ringing doorbells and knocking on doors was simply not done by Marines storming hostile houses. Now it was too late to ask why.

WHEN TIM MCGIRK'S story of massacre and mayhem at Haditha hit the ether on March 19, 2006, almost nobody except the people who lived there and the uninvited foreigners who were killing them and each other in large numbers had ever heard of the place.

McGirk had never gone to Haditha for his facts. He relied on two known insurgent sympathizers masquerading as human rights workers and two small children for his answers. McGirk's helpful human rights advocates—one just released from Abu Ghraib prison for anti-government agitation and the other a person of lasting interest among Marine signal-intercept specialists—were heard talking on cell phones before the attack. They were discussing how to record just such an event for propaganda purposes, maybe even get a Western reporter to look at it.

"How did you follow up with it, did you send Iraqi stringers out to investigate?" former *Columbia Journalism Review* writer Paul McLeary asked McGirk in a story that ran on June 16, 2006.[17]

"[Even] our stringers who had really good contacts with the insurgents, who wanted to go, were told by the insurgents, 'Don't even try it, because the guys out there are all crazy foreign fighters, and they'll kill you as a CIA spy,'" McGirk replied. So nobody went.

Twenty-four Iraqis were killed that day, the Marine Corps initially claimed, many by the horrific bomb blast that demolished the Marine Humvee. Nine were immediately identified as insurgents. McGirk wasn't sure of the number of innocent victims when he made his allegations. He just knew there were many.[18] He watched a color video showing them piled in a morgue. He listened to the mourners mourning without understanding what they said. He talked to the wounded survivors. He talked to their lawyer. He talked to the man who made the movie. He talked to the doctor at the morgue. But he didn't talk to the Marines he accused of doing it.

The women and children who died in two houses belonged to two families in the same Sunni tribe. Some of the dead MAMs were their husbands, brothers, and friends. By 2005 the acronym was a pejorative for Iraqi men old enough to carry weapons—like Gook, Kraut, and Chink in other conflicts. Some were foreigners. They all died in a neighborhood the Marines said had a well-deserved reputation for harboring insurgents and sympathizers. It had the best routes in and out of town.

Five Iraqi men died first by Hay al-Sinnai Road, the same road the Marines called Route Chestnut. It was the only hardpan thoroughfare into the southern part of the city. They were unfortunate to be on the road when the blast occurred. Wuterich testified he took a knee and shot all five MAMs when they tried to flee on foot after inexplicably showing up in a white car seconds before the bomb exploded. Wuterich said he believed them to be insurgents. Events would show he had good reason to think that.

Ten of the other dead Iraqis were women and kids—six women and four children—who died huddled in bedrooms. Another victim was an old man reportedly confined to a wheelchair, an allegation Faraj vehemently disputes, though later-revealed NCIS photos suggest it was true. Squad member Hector Salinas, a sergeant when he left the Corps, later testified he saw a one-legged dead man by a wheelchair after he later returned to the home. He thought his leg was amputated during his killing. Salinas shot an old woman there as well, he said.

The questionable wheelchair homily was revealed by *Washington Post* reporter Ellen Knickermeyer on May 27, 2006, in an account by a Haditha resident identified only as a man named Fahmi.[19] Knickermeyer, who managed to get to Haditha despite the danger, quoted Fahmi as saying he watched the Marine counterattack the suspected ambush site from his roof. He saw the Marine direct other Marines into the house closest to the blast, about fifty yards away.

It was the home of seventy-six-year-old Abdul Hamid Hassan Ali, Fahmi claimed. He lost a leg to diabetes and was confined to a wheelchair. Even so, Ali was always one of the first on his block to go out every morning, scattering scraps for his chickens and hosing dust from his driveway. NCIS, however, determined the victim's leg was blown off by a grenade that exploded under him.

WUTERICH SAID HE didn't know the old man, women, and children were there. The rest of the dead were MAMs. Some of them were not armed when they died. Two with guns died inside their house when the Marines stormed in. One unarmed man was killed answering a polite summons to come to his front door. One died running for his life. Four brothers with two loaded assault rifles died in a back bedroom of a tiny apartment with pistol bullets in their foreheads. It was remarkable shooting, testimony to the training of Marines.

Conventional wisdom suggests six of the victims died in the first house after three Marines led by Wuterich stormed it. The other eight civilians died in the second house when the same four-man stack cleared it with grenades and rifle fire. It all supposedly happened in the time it took a lance corporal running with a machine gun to cross roughly two hundred meters of uneven ground to reinforce them. That story was offered early and often while the incident was under examination.

The lance corporal was Justin Sharratt. He tells a different story, one nobody ever heard outside of interrogation rooms and bars. In February 2006 he told an Army colonel the team returned to the scene of carnage that became House #1 and House #2 and cleared the buildings a second time before finishing up. He told a similar story to NCIS investigators at Haditha Dam on March 19, 2006.

His civilian lawyers took great pains to paint Sharratt as a grand spinner of "sea stories." Telling the court your client is a habitual liar is not a common strategy, particularly a murder defendant seeking immunization from prosecution for telling the truth. Sharratt's account could easily have been dismissed as hyperbole if he hadn't left behind signature Beretta 9 mm shell casings he said he used to shoot his victims. They were reportedly found in all three death houses.

Sharratt told Faraj they must have arrived stuck in somebody's boot. Faraj didn't buy it. Sharratt was the only Marine among the shooters armed with a pistol. Sharratt had borrowed it from Navy corpsman Hospitalman Third Class Brian "Doc" Whitt so he could fire warning shots at Iraqis that drove too close. At the end of the day he gave it back, Whitt told investigators:

> Immediately after the meeting was over, LCpl Sharratt gave me possession of my nine-millimeter back. He gave it to me with one magazine empty (fifteen rounds expended) and the other was half full (approximately eight rounds gone). I asked him "where did all my rounds go," he had said, "sorry I had to pop your nine-mil's cherry [use it to kill someone]." I asked what exactly did he mean. . . . That is when he told me very nonchalantly "the number was nine and most of them were headshots."[20]

The second time the team cleared the houses, Sharratt said, it was a ragged, slow-moving affair. Nobody stacked. After throwing a grenade into the south end of House #1 that failed to explode, they cleared the structure using an M203 grenade launcher before moving inside. There, the Marines chose sectors and meandered from room to room throwing in grenades and shooting rapid fire without looking around any corners, he said. He didn't mention House #2.

Sharratt was supposed to testify that Salinas told him the initial clearing operation was interrupted when a runner disappeared out of House #1 and presumably disappeared into House #2, the house where eight Iraqis died. The houses needed securing. Tatum and Sharratt volunteered to go back and finish the job, he said.

It could have happened that way. At Wuterich's court-martial Salinas testified he was in command. He claimed Wuterich never gave an order all morning. At the Wuterich court-martial, nobody asked him about a second visit to the death houses and he never mentioned it.

Sharratt did mention it, however, several times, just not in court. He twice drew diagrams that showed the path they took, once for the Army and again for NCIS. Whether the victims died in the first fusillade or a second was never revealed. Four wounded children were orphaned as well. Sharratt said he just pointed his pistol at the figures sprawled in the rooms and emptied his magazine.

The little girl who survived in House #1 said somebody came back and shot at them with a pistol. So did her brother. Sharratt said Faraj wanted to know how spent American-made 9 mm cartridges found their way into two homes that the government conceded Sharratt had never entered. He never got to ask. Faraj stated:

> I believe Sharratt shot in the back bedroom of H2 [House #2] because there was 9 mm ammo on the floor. From there I believe he went back to H1 [House #1] to finish the clearing operation that was interrupted when they saw a runner.

Sharratt had been in an Oceanside, California, bar drinking beer when he told his story to this reporter. The court-martial was over and he was going home the next day. He said he first told his version of events in February 2006 to an Army colonel named Gregory A. Watt. A month after that, he told NCIS investigators a slightly different version in a urine-soaked dungeon at the bottom of Haditha Dam while being interrogated. Sharratt called his interrogation the "ol' good guy–bad guy routine" that lasted for sixteen hours. Both accounts are written down in signed statements he made to Watt and NCIS. He told them the second clearing operation started outside House #2 when someone, probably LCpl Tatum, threw a grenade into the structure after being told to sweep through the house again. It was a dud. He never told them they were afraid it might explode so they continued clearing the rooms from the outside using an M203 grenade launcher to shoot through windows. Two Marines—Salinas and Mendoza—had M203s. Sharratt couldn't remember who used theirs. Afterward, they went inside.

"Someone threw a frag in the room, 'he' was hearing shit and told me to clear by fire," Sharratt recalled in his written statement to Watt.

"The frag went off and I stuck my 9 mm around the corner and fired inside until it was empty without entering. We then entered the room and there were a few dead insurgents lying on the ground. I could not make out gender or type. The others were clearing other rooms. I believe it was Tatum who threw the frag and said clear by fire. I stayed in the house about ten seconds afterwards."

At the bar, Sharratt estimated at least four hand grenades were thrown into the rooms during the slow-motion operation. Two failed to explode. Two dud grenades were later recovered. He did not remember how many M203 rounds were fired.

Faraj maintains Mendoza's inexperience was the reason they had to clear the buildings a second time. The first time Mendoza threw a grenade in House #2 he did so without removing the safety tape he placed around the arming handle to prevent accidentally arming the grenade while carrying it. If insurgents were still inside, they now had a fine US-made grenade. The squad had to make sure nobody still inside was capable of using it. It wasn't pretty, but it was doctrine. Faraj was certain they lied to protect Mendoza because the squad thought he had done pretty well in his first fight.

Sharratt told the NCIS investigators that the second time they went through the houses, Tatum and he were certain the house was clear—those inside were dead. Sharratt said he was later surprised to discover that two wounded children were found in House #1 by Lieutenant Kallop, the officer commanding Third Platoon. Tatum testified he was "shocked" to discover anyone had lived.

Kallop told investigators he remembered giving Sharratt one of his 9 mm magazines to replace the rounds the machine gunner had fired in Houses 1 and 2. Doc Whitt gave him two magazines when he lent him the pistol. Each holds fifteen rounds. If that is so, Sharratt fired at least thirty-seven times. Kallop said he didn't ask Sharratt what he used his pistol for. Afterward, Sharratt was issued a pistol of his own, according to his platoon sergeant.

Both Tatum and Sharratt told NCIS investigators they returned to both houses for a second clearing operation while being questioned by the same agents at Haditha Dam. For reasons never explained, the NCIS agents refused to believe them. After Tatum retained legal counsel, he never mentioned it again. Faraj opines the NCIS theory of the crime didn't leave room for an alternative set of circumstances.

Special Agent Matthew Marshall testified twice that Tatum was confused about what time he entered the rooms to clear them. He said the same thing about Sharratt. Sharratt's expended 9 mm cartridges offered ample proof there was reason to investigate further because all the Marines who were there testified Sharratt stayed outside when they cleared the houses the first time, the only time the government acknowledges the houses were cleared.

The implications were huge if Marshall talked two defendants out of their own noose. If Faraj is right, the luckiest break either Marine received was Marshall's determination that Sharratt and Tatum were screwing up the government's theory by insisting they returned to Houses #1 and #2 a second time. When the two Marines returned and fired on the occupants again, positive identification would have been required and murder would have been committed.

NCIS Special Agent Michael Maloney said he wanted to pursue the leads provided by the two grunts' recollections but was prohibited from doing so by his superiors in Washington, DC. They told him to drop any further investigation into that line of reasoning because it did not fit into the carefully crafted narrative Marine Corps prosecutors intended to present.

In the end, the story revealed by Sharratt and Tatum in early February and again in March 2006 was not supported by the evidence prosecutors decided to present rather than the Marine Corps's inability to bring the four enlisted Marines' accounts into serious question.

LtCol Paul Ware, the officer in charge of Wuterich's Article 32 preliminary hearing, agreed in a report to then LtGen Mattis about Tatum's case:

Special Agent [Mathew W.] Marshall testified that LCpl Tatum was confused of what time he entered the room to clear it. If a grenade was thrown and then the Marines left returning after the events of House #2 and then fired at the occupants, positive identification would surely be required. However, this theory is entirely unsupported by the evidence. The government provided no evidence to demonstrate that these Marines proceeded to House #1 for illegitimate reason.[21]

Three months after the attack, the two children who survived in House #1 told Tim McGirk an entirely different account of what happened. They said the Marines purposely shot everybody they could see. They were little and scared and hurt and had just lost their parents. Their pathetic stories suffered from profound inconsistencies. The Iraqi interpreter McGirk used and the manner in which their story was told suggested they had been carefully coached. Faraj, who speaks fluent Arabic, said the interpreter simply told him a story without too much consideration for what the children were saying. Faraj would have been able to prove it had the trial continued.

One of the circumstances the interpreter ignored was the arrival in House #1 of a Marine armed with a pistol. Nine-year-old survivor Eman Waleed Abd Al Hameed said she remembered seeing a Marine with a "pistol" enter the room after her family was killed.

"That was the Arabic word she used for a handgun," Faraj explained.

The interpreter never told McGirk what she said, Faraj says. Her little brother Abd Al-Ralunan Waleed Al Hameed remembered the Marine with the "pistol" as well. The Marines dismissed their claims as fabrication. Even so, their surviving family received thousands of dollars in so-called *solatia* payments to make amends.

One thing is certain: Eman's parents were dead, killed by Marines who stormed their home and left a spent handful of US-issue 9 mm pistol shells behind to tell about it. All Sharratt said at the bar was they went back and everyone was dead.

When the hearing concluded about 9:00 a.m. on January 23, Wuterich shook hands with his attorneys before hugging his parents, David and Rosemarie Wuterich, who had been in the courtroom every day since testimony began. They had a tough time of it. The next day, Wuterich accepted responsibility for the events at Haditha and the matter was officially closed.

CHAPTER 2

MAJOR HAYTHAM FARAJ, USMC (RET.)

Major Haytham Faraj met Frank Wuterich for the first time after Wuterich was indicted. Faraj was a rookie judge advocate assigned as senior defense counsel at Camp Pendleton when he was detailed to be Wuterich's attorney. Faraj got into law after sixteen years as a grunt. He is as passionate about the profession as he was about the infantry. With his shaved head and fierce scowl he seems imposing before he opens his mouth. Faraj proved to be a force multiplier. He intended to win.

Faraj figures a lifetime of being a grunt trumped the knowledge and understanding of practitioners who fought their battles in stilted briefs sent silently over email. He worked for LtCol Colby C. Vokey, Wuterich's other Marine lawyer. Their unshakable resolve didn't go down well with a lot of brass hat Marines. Nor was Vokey making any friends among the prosecutors at Camp Pendleton in his role of regional defense counsel for West Coast Marines. The Corps's legal apparatus was overwhelmed. Even so, Vokey demanded respect for his defense team, and that included sharing some of the slender resources the Marine Corps budgets for handling courts-martial.

Vokey refused to compromise merely for the sake of good order and discipline. During September 2007 he was briefly fired before outraged current and former Marine lawyers raised so much hell he was reinstated.[1] He was fired by Colonel Rose M. Favors, the command defense counsel of the entire Marine Corps, who reported to the staff judge advocate, Brigadier General Kevin Sandkuhler—the Corps's top lawyer. Favors fired Vokey for allowing the defendants to have more than one Marine Corps lawyer assigned to represent them. Vokey said Favors told him that assigning more defense lawyers was unnecessary for them to receive adequate representation. At the same time, the prosecution was reinforcing with called-up reservists. Vokey said he protested the decision, so she fired him.

Among the critics who spoke openly about the firing was retired Marine Corps brigadier general David M. Brahms. He was already enmeshed in the Haditha murder investigation when he exploded into anger over Vokey's firing. Brahms is a Harvard Law School graduate who climbed through Marine Corps ranks after completing the Platoon Leaders Course to become the director of the Judge Advocate Division for three years prior to his retirement in 1988.

"I am pissed," Brahms told the blog *Defend Our Marines*. "The danger here is not malevolence; it is the appearance of evil and the effect upon those in the defense bar."[2]

Faraj thought Vokey's firing was totally inappropriate:

It wasn't just about ethics. I think the Corps has outstanding ethics. Lawyers, on the other hand, played a lawyerly game of straddling the ethical line to win. That type of conduct was despicable because I grew up in a Corps where right and wrong were not gray areas.

When Faraj retired from the Corps after twenty-two years of service he joined forces with civilian Neal Puckett, himself a retired

Marine lieutenant colonel and former military judge who represented Wuterich. Puckett has a fearsome reputation inside the Beltway as an effective defense advocate for ailing Marines. It was supposed to be an equal partnership, Faraj says.

Puckett is a different breed of cat than Faraj. He never swings when he can duck. Puckett was getting paid tens of thousands of dollars donated by outraged Americans, many of them current and former Marines, to defend America's son. Faraj thought they would be an effective team.

For Faraj, teaming up was the easiest way to continue representing Wuterich. Puckett was very good in the courtroom. Faraj brought a dogged legal style and intimate knowledge of the facts to win his case. Faraj had a practitioner's understanding of the tactics and techniques used by the accused Marines. He had cleared hundreds of structures in his sixteen years in the infantry; he attended the MOUT training courses as an enlisted Marine and officer. He had thrown live grenades and dummy grenades, cleared rooms, and understood that in the universe of military operations, room-clearing operations always ended up pitting one man against another.

"It is nothing less than an old-fashioned shootout where the man quickest to the trigger and surest aim survives to try his luck once more and the other is dead. MOUT erases technological advantages in weapons and equipment. It evens the odds," he says.

Faraj and Puckett's relationship was destined to be contentious and temporary. Faraj is direct, like an M1 tank; what you see is what you get. Puckett is a charming chameleon, a sleight-of-hand genius who works best in the spotlight of center stage. Faraj is most comfortable away from the limelight. He found their relationship a strange dichotomy.

"Puckett had a well-known reputation in the military criminal defense community. He was known as a deal maker. Through his charm, charisma, and an affable personality he usually won over younger prosecutors into supporting guilty pleas. Prosecutors in the military, like their defense counterparts, looked up to more senior lawyers, especially those in private practice. Senior lawyers, like Neal Puckett, provided a model to emulate, perhaps at least learn from. Eventually, every military lawyer would become a civilian. The path to civilian employment promised many challenges that people like Neal Puckett had already figured out.

"He knew that younger lawyers looked up to him and tried to learn the secret to his apparent success. He used their admiration to talk them into reasonable deals and in return rarely betrayed them by fighting for his clients at trials and beating them. Prosecutors, especially Marine Corps prosecutors, hate to lose, and when they do, they become a lot less agreeable to deals. Neal [Puckett] fared well in this world. He made a decent living and rarely had to worry about wasting time reading voluminous discovery or interviewing witnesses. He would get the story from the client, build the case into a herculean task that can only be handled by Neal Puckett, then go back to the client with a deal that the client accepts with overwhelming gratitude," Faraj explains.

That style of lawyering served Puckett well until Haditha, Faraj says: "Haditha was different, but Puckett did not grasp it. Puckett would use Haditha to earn hundreds of thousands of dollars for himself while intending all along to plead Wuterich guilty. Puckett had one problem. Vokey and I were seasoned ground combat veterans who were not going to be led into a guilty plea."

Vokey and Faraj intended to work the case by taking the government to task. When they joined the Wuterich defense team, they had little idea of Puckett's intentions or style, and Puckett, likewise, knew nothing about the two detailed Marine lawyers who grew in the Corps leading troops. Faraj found himself at odds with Puckett immediately, he said.

"When the defense teams for other codefendants began to vigorously fight the charges, Puckett found himself in a difficult position. He lacked the inclination or desire to read the discovery. He instead spent his time making friends with Wuterich's parents. The intent behind developing that relationship sought to win their support for the inevitable deal."

Meanwhile, Vokey and Faraj interviewed witnesses and buried their noses in the discovery. Faraj was appalled to learn Puckett wanted to waive Wuterich's Article 32 evidentiary hearing. He thought it was a grave blunder. So did Vokey. Doing so held far bigger consequences at Camp Pendleton than in civilian court where the defendants routinely waive a preliminary hearing before a judge. Civilians usually know why they were arrested and booked and whether or not they did what they were accused of. Waiving the obvious saves both sides' time and money.

Wuterich's Article 32 hearing was different. It was a way for both sides to get everything out on the table for LtGen Mattis, the "convening authority" that brought the charges and the general they believed would eventually decide Wuterich's fate. The procedure has no equivalent in the civilian world. Faraj knew appearance was everything when defending Marine Corps honor before LtGen Mattis, unarguably the most respected senior Marine officer on active duty at the time. In some Marine circles, Mattis was known as the "Warrior Monk."

Faraj was astounded to discover Puckett hoped that by waiving the Article 32 hearing he would win some favor with the prosecutors. Faraj and Vokey vehemently disagreed. In the end, Wuterich agreed to an abbreviated Article 32. Faraj and Vokey did most of the work. Puckett enjoyed the media spotlight, even privately bragged about it, presuming he was ingratiating himself with the media, Wuterich, and his parents. Faraj says he was never comfortable joining that kind of parade.

Extreme self-assurance sometimes proves lethally self-serving. However, Haytham Faraj was an extraordinary Marine officer in an institution endowed with remarkable men and extraordinary characters. The Haditha investigation was full of them. Even so, Faraj stood out. He was first an enlisted infantry man, the soul of the Corps. He was commissioned after nine years in the ranks, a proud mustang. He joined the Corps in July 1986, a seventeen-year-old high school kid who wanted to be a Marine so badly he signed up under the delayed-entry program when he was still sixteen. He made staff sergeant in six and a half years, an accomplishment by itself.

Faraj's rapid rise up the career ladder was a big jump for a kid who immigrated from Beirut, Lebanon, when he was twelve years old, an Arabic-speaking child who learned English at the same time he was trying to learn how to be a typical American kid. Now forty-seven, he is one of two sons in a family of four children who left Beirut with their mother and father, Hassan and Nawal. It was a long journey that ended in a Greek-Jewish neighborhood on the north side of Chicago. Both sons would eventually join the Marines. Faraj's brother didn't like it as much. He left after his first enlistment ended.

Growing up in Chicago was tough at first. His parents were not wealthy refugees who fled the war-torn little country under a golden parachute. There was no Lebanese community in Chicago to settle among. Faraj grew up in a lower-middle-class neighborhood where diversity was practiced long before it was labeled: "My parents were not wealthy in Lebanon. Lebanon was war torn. No one was wealthy except the warlords and the large land-holding dynastic families who use sectarian differences to divide the country and strengthen themselves.

"I was just a kid who wanted to play football and wrestle. It was exciting, scary, and different. Chicago was dark and depressing in January 1980. Black snow piled in mounds on street corners and biting cold made for a stark contrast with the bright sunny streets of Lebanon— even a war-torn Lebanon. No one spoke to anyone. People wrapped up from the cold seemed to mind no one else. Lebanon was different. People stopped to chat and greet each other. There is a familiarity in a country so small. Stick around long enough and faces become familiar. Chicago was different. It was big. It was cold. And it was a lonely place. Once I got into the Chicago schools, it was all right."

Things really began to change once he got into Mather High School.

"The unfamiliar became less alien. As for most American teenagers, high school became the place where a social network developed that would provide friends, bonds, and a place to belong.

"I did well in school, had good friends, and was for the most part happy. We didn't have much but then I never really thought about it.

I know that my family could not afford to send me to college. Desire for adventure, a rambunctious best friend who kept talking about the Marines, and a recruiter who promised very little except being 'one of the few' and some money for college led me to make a decision that would affect my entire life."

It was a remarkable transition for a kid who'd already tasted war. Lebanon had been under siege when he left. Nobody in his family could speak a word of English when he had arrived in Chicago. Two years later all four siblings were fluent. His mother and father had a tougher time. His father had a strong accent until he died. Faraj, however, sounds like a guy from Chicago, the garrulous John Belushi edge on his words evident on occasion.

Faraj tackled school and making friends and getting accepted among his persnickety peers with the same aplomb he later showed on the athletic fields and in the Marines. He had one advantage going into junior high school: he came from a country where soccer ruled supreme. He was good at it and that gave him segue into the rest of an adolescent's complex social life. By the time Faraj entered Mather High School he was big and strong. He wrestled at 167 pounds and managed to win all the way to the Illinois regionals in arguably the toughest physical challenge in high school athletics. When he wasn't getting slammed onto mats, he was playing football—linebacker on defense and pulling guard on offense—getting slammed into the frozen Chicagoland turf.

His pursuit of athletics was not without purpose. Even then, he intended to be a warrior. Faraj liked to run, to pump iron, and stay strong. He loved to compete, to try and be the best. He is still doing Ironman triathlons in his forties. His passion for a challenge led him to the Marines. When football ended in junior year he was already on a contract with the Marine Corps, training with a pool of like-minded recruits. While he waited to go, he prepared himself physically and mentally for the biggest challenges of his life.

"I had always been interested in the military. I read *Soldier of Fortune*, talked to the Marine recruiters, talked with guys who had been in or were joining. I decided the Marines were the roughest and toughest. At seventeen I was physically fit; my football team had gone all the way to the city championships. Soon after I graduated I left for the Marines."

On July 28, 1986, Faraj began boot camp at the Marine Corps Recruit Depot at San Diego, California. After that and three months of training to be a mortarman at the Infantry Training School at Camp Pendleton, he joined the fleet. Instead of water, he got sand, training troops with 1/4 at miserable 29 Palms in the Mojave Desert. He managed lots of training doing field support, playing the aggressors and defenders against other infantry battalions cycling through the regimens in the hottest spot Marines train in the United States. After a year with 1/4, Faraj was promoted to corporal and selected to attend Marine Security Guard School in Quantico, Virginia, followed by an assignment to embassy duty. Faraj distinguished himself at Marine Security Guard School. He picked Djibouti, in the Horn of Africa, as his first assignment. He was assigned to the American embassy in Djibouti, next to the notorious Camp Lemonnier, home of the Thirteenth Demi-Brigade of the French Foreign Legion.

A French officer this reporter knew in Bosnia during the civil war there said he had commanded French Foreign Legion troops at Djibouti in the late 1980s. He fondly recalled his days in the emptiness "chasing the natives across the desert."

The Frenchman was at Camp Lemonnier long before it was a United States Naval Expeditionary Base. He said the Legion occupied Camp Lemonnier because it was so miserable it couldn't have been anything else. The Marines stationed there unanimously agreed. They claimed it was sometimes 140 degrees during the day inside the canvas tents they lived in. A man could drink six quarts of water a day in Djibouti without ever taking a piss, Faraj recalled.

Faraj's choice of duty stations was more a statement about his personality than about some well-thought-out decision. He selected Djibouti because the barren desert outpost promised something different, exotic, and unknown. That it was, he discovered. In 1988, the poverty-wracked land was an austere newly liberated former French colony. There was nothing to do except "drink, work out, and stand post defending the embassy."

Faraj spent his free time voraciously devouring books, running long distances in above one-hundred-degree temperatures, and riding an old Peugeot bicycle that he bought for $200 from the outgoing US AID officer.

Life in Djibouti wasn't all hot weather and austere hardships. The Marines regularly held parties at the Marine House for Embassy staff and other diplomats. The Marine House served as the social hub for those assigned to diplomatic duty. Marines received invitations to embassy parties and diplomatic social functions. Marines in Djibouti also received two R&R trips during their tour. Faraj went to Kenya and Ethiopia.

"This was embassy duty. It was hard, but not like being in the fleet. No sympathy for me here. I had a maid and driver. We could use the Embassy boat to water-ski and deep-sea fish."

After fifteen months in Djibouti, Faraj was pardoned. He requested to go—and was miraculously sent—to Stockholm, Sweden, about the best gig an enlisted Marine could ever hope to have. Fourteen months later the high life ended. Faraj's days of dalliance were interrupted by a war. In 1990, Iraq's strongman Saddam Hussein sent his troops next door to occupy almost defenseless Kuwait. The United States said he was making a bid to take over the world's oil supply and told him to leave. Most of the world agreed. Saddam refused and at twenty-one Faraj found himself in his second hot war in a decade. At least this time he could defend himself.

Faraj received orders to Second Battalion, Fifth Marines (2/5) at Camp Pendleton. He arrived there in August 1990, destined for Fox Company—affectionately called the Black Hearts. He took over the 60 mm mortar section. Sixty millimeter mortars—usually referred to as "sixty mike-mike"—are an infantryman's artillery. A good mortar team can change the initiative in a battle. Either offensively or defensively it can be a playmaker. Unfortunately, Faraj discovered, this mortar section was a disciplinary time bomb.

"They were proficient at what they did but were headed for a disciplinary disaster."

The section reminded him of the recon platoon from the movie *Heartbreak Ridge*. They challenged him at every turn. They wanted to test him. He had been an 81 mm mortarman. They were 60 mm mortarmen. That's a big difference. Sixty mike-mike gunners are up front; 81 mm mortars, with their greater range and hitting power, are stationed in the rear with the gear, at least from a frontline grunt's perspective. Being at the front is relative.

Faraj took up the challenge by making sure he was there to wake them up at 0530 every day. From August to December 1990, they ran daily and trained in the "backyard" doing gun drills and firing pneumatic mortars. They were going to war. They all knew that, but none of them knew the place where they were headed better than Faraj. He had spent six years in Kuwait between the ages of three and ten.

On January 10, 1990, now Sergeant Faraj arrived off the coast of Kuwait as a mortar section leader. Fox CO, 2/5. The company was part of the Fifth Marine Expeditionary Brigade. After two months playing decoy, the Fifth finally came ashore, moving across the blazing desert where Saddam Hussein's madmen had set all the oil wells on fire to secure Kuwait City. It was a quick war, one hundred hours of mean in Dante's Inferno.

On its way home, the Fifth joined Operation Sea Angel, the international humanitarian effort to assist Bangladesh in dealing with the devastation of Cyclone Marian. From fire to water; the only thing that didn't change was suffering people.

Next was Okinawa, where Faraj ended up being a weapons platoon commander, a billet usually filled by a senior first lieutenant. There is a lot of responsibility there. Weapons Platoon shoots the mortars and the rockets that don't care who they blow up. Get it wrong and good men will die.

The Marine Corps must have already been grooming Faraj for more responsibility. In April 1992, not long after being promoted to staff sergeant, Faraj was accepted into the Marine Enlisted Commissioning

Education Program (MECEP). The extraordinary program provides a way for deserving Marines to finish their college educations so they can be commissioned officers. They earn while they learn and then come back to the Corps with their newfound knowledge. Unlike the other services, the Corps likes to make its own officers, picking and choosing from among the aspirants. "Ring knockers" from the service academies aren't always graciously welcomed.

Faraj chose the historic Citadel, founded in 1842 as the the "Military College of South Carolina." He said good-bye to Okinawa and hello to Charleston, a beautiful place full of beaches and belles. During the 180 years since its founding, the Citadel has produced dozens of generals who endured a tough academic regimen replete with ritualized hazing and quaint Old South military traditions. Its most illustrious graduate is Army General Mark Clark of World War II and Korean War fame. Most of the hazing bounced off the career warrior who wore his hard-earned stripes during class. He was already a Marine.

The physical hazing didn't bother Faraj either. He graduated magna cum laude in less than three years, earning a bachelor of arts in political science, focusing on international relations and military affairs. After graduation it was back in the Corps, on to the various staff and command billets infantry officers fill during their careers. His training made him an infantry expert.

One of the more interesting assignments Faraj drew was revitalizing the Air Naval Gunfire Liaison Company (ANGLICO) concept that had fallen on hard times after Vietnam. On the battlefield line, grunts depend on especially trained observers and communicators to get naval artillery and air assets on the target and not on the Marines. On the fluid, fast-moving battlefield knowing where the bad guys are—and, more important, knowing where the good guys are—is essential. ANGLICO teams are attached to maneuvering units to assure timely on-call intervention by naval gunfire and fast movers off aircraft carriers just over the horizon. It takes a lot of concentration and iron nerves to control artillery and air assets on the battlefield. The "best billet" he filled was being an 81 mm mortar platoon commander with Third Battalion, First Marines, a plum assignment for junior officers on their way up the chain of command. After that, it was on to be the executive officer and company commander of Field Company, Weapons and Field Training Battalion. This company is made of fifty to fifty-five drill instructors who train all the recruits on the West Coast in fundamental field combat skills.

In 2002, Faraj was selected for the law education program. He left the Corps for three years to take on the law, attending school at American University in Washington, DC, before returning to the Corps as a judge advocate with a promotion to major. Less than a year later, Faraj met Frank Wuterich. He didn't know it yet, but the young Marine squad leader from Connecticut would occupy most of his time for the next six years.

THE END

How the court-martial ended was entirely Wuterich's choice, Faraj told the press. His job was to do what was best for his client. Faraj's face, however, belied the story. He wasn't happy. Neither was Faraj in the habit of carping to the press. He didn't need to. The roiled black cloud thundering over him when he walked into the Media Center said it all.

Faraj says he wrote much of the admission of guilt Wuterich uttered verbatim in the closing hour of the court-martial. Wuterich's statement to the court made no mention of the last-minute appeals from former 3/1 Marines for Frank to hang tough; or of a confrontation in a courtroom restroom between an enraged Marine officer and Neal Puckett; and nothing about the appeals for Frank to take it to the finish that drove his mother to tears and his father to distraction. In the end, Wuterich's children and parents and Puckett had the leverage. Wuterich told the court he was ready to take responsibility and the consequences for his actions.

Frank Wuterich's parents weren't fools; they knew it was very tough on their son to appear to cave in when victory was almost at hand. Nor did they understand why the United States Marine Corps their son professed to love was trying to ruin his life for defending himself. None of it made any sense. It hadn't made sense from the beginning, his dad said. Down the road that same day, Marine Corps pilots using Hellfire missiles and five-hundred-pound bombs had shredded a "hostile building" full of surrounded enemy soldiers. It took the Marines a week to find all the enemy parts. Nobody was accused of a crime for blowing them to bits. Nobody had known who was inside the house when the rockets and bombs destroyed it.

Besides, they had more immediate things to worry about than obtuse arguments. Duty and honor don't pay for anything. Who was going to take care of Frank's three daughters with him in prison? It could still happen. Frank's court-martial was proof positive that crazy things happened. They implored Frank to take the opportunity Puckett arranged and run with it. Frank's parents believed the sun rose and set on Neal Puckett. They said so.

Major Jeffrey Dinsmore—one of their favorite Marines—was beside himself with disgust. His opinion of Puckett wasn't nearly as flattering as Wuterich's parents'. Nor was his opinion of their son. It is problematic that Mr. and Mrs. Wuterich knew that at the time. Dinsmore cornered Puckett in the courthouse men's room the preceding Wednesday when negotiations for a deal began. Dinsmore claimed he accused Puckett of selling out his client. He raged at Puckett, accusing him of selling out the Corps, the worst crime of all. Haditha was a stain on the honor of the institution that wouldn't ever go away without Wuterich being exonerated completely. He said Faraj believed as he did.

Dinsmore took his case to Wuterich in the defense counsel's office down the hall from the courtroom where he was soon expected to testify. He was risking his career for tampering with a witness if his appeal backfired. Prosecutor LtCol Sean Sullivan would drop a hammer on the outspoken infantryman if he found out a subpoenaed witness was urging the defendant to resist the prosecution's best chance of salvaging even the tiniest of victories. He would have probably already been stepped on if he weren't such a damn fine Marine. Dinsmore passionately urged Wuterich to reconsider anyway. For two days he said Wuterich tried to meet his expectations. Then he agreed to the deal.

After the verdict was in, Dinsmore said he wasn't surprised, only disappointed. He thought Wuterich had more of what makes Marines different. He was troubled with the hypocrisy the deal underscored: America sent its sons to war and then turned on them. It didn't matter if the reason for the war in Iraq was a pretext. It didn't matter whether world opinion held the war in Iraq just or unjust. Marines are sent where the action is the toughest because they are expected to win. The phrase "send in the Marines" was pregnant with examples of what Marines are capable of doing.

When the same advocates got to see for themselves what sending in the Marines really means, many of the same shock-and-awe crowd found they didn't have either the heart or guts for it. Dinsmore raged that their change of heart cost Marine lives. They did what they did at Haditha, and Fallujah the year before, because that is how Marines are trained to fight. Fighting any other way is fratricide. Marines fight to win, not to die. If the policymakers wanted a different outcome, they should have sent in the Army. In Dinsmore's mind the successful prosecution of Wuterich was grounded on an incomprehensible moral dichotomy Puckett refused to consider and Faraj was forced to defend. Wuterich was caught in the middle. It was an impossible situation.

To make sure he was understood, Dinsmore took the unusual step of publishing his opinion on the *Defend Our Marines* website the night Wuterich was sentenced. After it was posted on January 24, he said it was the only thing he could do to refute the guilty plea Wuterich had accepted for "convenience." He didn't necessarily blame Wuterich; Dinsmore simply couldn't forgive him:

> For six years, the officers and men of 3rd Battalion, 1st Marines firmly believed that no unlawful action took place on November 19th. We believed this based on the available intelligence before, during, and after November 19th, based on the enemy's stated objective of a propaganda victory that would erode our combat effectiveness, and based on our detailed knowledge of the context of November 19th's day-long, high-intensity combat. We accepted challenges to our

integrity, accusations of a unit cover-up, and institutional condemnation by our Corps. Men like LtCol Chessani and 1stLt Grayson
refused numerous plea offers from the government, including letters
of reprimand with no punishment whatsoever. With SSgt Wuterich's
admission of guilt, however, we must accept that a cover-up took
place, even if unwittingly. With his admission of guilt, we must
accept that some unlawful action was committed by a member of
SSgt Wuterich's squad.

Today the judge handed down the maximum possible sentence.
While a portion of that sentence was restricted by the terms of the
plea agreement, it is right and just that Frank Wuterich no longer
be a Staff Non-commissioned Officer in the Marine Corps. I wish
Frank the best in his future endeavors, and empathize with his difficult personal decision to accept responsibility for the unlawful
actions committed by one or more members of his squad. But any
Marine who is guilty of negligence and dereliction with results on
the scale of November 19th, 2005, cannot lead Marines. Ever again.[3]

Dinsmore's statement said a lot about how fighting Marines think and
even more about how they are made.

When Wuterich and the other seven defendants were indicted in
December 2006, Faraj was already underwater defending a Marine
named Corporal Trent D. Thomas, accused of murder and cover-up
in the town of Hamdaniya, near Abu Ghraib, where seven enlisted
Marines and one sailor were charged with murdering an Iraqi man on
April 26, 2006.

The government charged that the Marines abducted an Iraqi man
there, killed him a half hour later, placed an AK-47 and a shovel next
to his body along the road, then falsified the formal report of the incident, asserting he was shot while digging a hole for a roadside bomb.
The Marines thought he was responsible for setting up IEDs while
killing and maiming Kilo, 3/5 Marines. Unfortunately, the defendants
knew far more about killing than committing murder. They grabbed
the wrong guy.

Congressman John P. Murtha (D-PA) told ABC television "some Marines pulled somebody out of a house, put them next to an IED, fired some AK-47 rounds so they'd have cartridges there. And then tried to cover that up."[4]

The country would hear plenty more from him.

Meanwhile, the investigation of the Hamdaniya incident by NCIS resulted in charges of murder, kidnapping, housebreaking, larceny, obstruction of justice, and conspiracy for the alleged cover-up of the incident. Faraj was detailed to defend Thomas. The two cases were collectively overwhelming. Faraj was still in training. Most trial attorneys don't start their careers representing alleged high-profile war criminals.

Until August 2007 Faraj only met with Wuterich two or three times. His biggest impression was "how nice a guy he was. In Iraq he went outside the wire to play soccer with the kids. It was dangerous. He didn't hate anybody."

Being detailed to a Marine represented by civilian counsel meant Faraj was going to be second string. At the time Wuterich didn't seem at immediate risk. Puckett had a reputation for being a kick-ass defense attorney with lots of steam. After all, he had been a Marine Corps military judge and a lieutenant colonel. He had already been on television.

Wuterich's Article 32 hearing, the precursor to the court-martial, was filled with drama. Although Puckett was still getting most of the face time in the news, Faraj and Vokey were emerging stars in the usually drab and colorless proceedings. In two separate hearings, they set themselves upon the government's witnesses and shredded them. Marines are remarkably disciplined, and that discipline has a way of stifling emotion. Not that summer. Their hard-charging tactics grated on Sullivan, the prosecutor. That led to some sharp exchanges that livened up the attorneys' otherwise carefully modulated monotone. That made Faraj and Vokey stand out even if nothing else did. Both detailed Marine defense attorneys started getting some face time of their own.

At Camp Pendleton, the Marines were working full time readying the arena where the games would be played. The facility was grandly called the Justice Center. By civilian standards it was a small, austere, no-nonsense courtroom across an asphalt grinder from the barren Media Center equipped with enough desks to accommodate the laptops of a platoon of reporters.

Inside, public affairs officers (PAOs) and enlisted media guides, called "minders," were making sure the carefully screened scribes adhered to the laundry list of don'ts they dared not do on pain of being barred. In 2007 most of the chairs in both buildings were filled with reporters from around the world. The video displays worked, the sound system was crisp and loud, and the PAO running things kept a tight rein on reporter access to the players. By the time Wuterich's court-martial actually happened five years later, all that had changed. With a few exceptions everything was different except the buildings. The world had moved on. The wars in Iraq and Afghanistan had produced so many tragedies, so many scandals; it was hard to remember which one was about Frank Wuterich. The Iraq War officially ended before Wuterich's court-martial even began. It was old news. The passion was gone. Although all the trappings were in place, the court-martial never seemed to really get going. It was an old donkey that needed flogging to move along.

The defendant was the same, and prosecutor Sullivan hadn't changed too much. He was thinner, and he'd received a couple of new gold stars in lieu of second awards for his Legion of Merit and Navy and Marine Corps Commendation medals. Gannon, Sullivan's younger partner, was lead prosecutor, an unenviable position when cocounsel is senior and aggressive. Gannon looked like a youthful major. He rarely made his presence felt. When he did, it was jousting against Puckett. In the end it boiled down to a contest between Sullivan and Faraj.

During the court-martial Wuterich usually sat next to Faraj. He looked much older now, although the same dark rings were under his eyes. Through it all he remained stoic and unemotional.

His parents were behind him—aging, spare people with harried looks. They both smoked and would speed out of the court room to the smoking area during each recess. Mrs. Rosemarie Wuterich was never comfortable with the attention she generated when she went outside the Legal Center to light up. Her emotional state was fragile. It was painful to watch her worry. Mrs. Wuterich's husband, David, is a quiet fellow who taught industrial cooking in happy obscurity for twenty-two years in Connecticut while raising his son. He was always pleasant. They are good people who shared their son with the Marine Corps and got him back broken. Their faces plainly asked who was going to make him whole again.

Both of them deferred to Puckett, a dapper peacock among the crisp, dour Marines and the usually scowling Haytham Faraj. Puckett took care of the procedural things, clearly enjoying himself bantering with the judge. Faraj always looked like he was getting ready for combat. He even had a war face. He was a brilliant interrogator of infantrymen and intuitively knew what made grunts tick, but he sometimes wasn't good with soothing hyperbole.

Puckett was as silky as Faraj was rough. Puckett interrogated the gentlemen and ladies of the trial. Faraj was there for the proles. Faraj was relentless in cross-examination, sparing nothing to get at the truth. His style was the most interesting thing about Wuterich's abbreviated court-martial save the outcome. Faraj seemed real. Who else really understood what it meant to have life and death under a finger without without having ever pulled a trigger?

The two-story building where everything happened used to be squad bays for enlisted men and still has the rectangular plainness of a barracks. The motif is red, white, and yellow. Golden oak paneling and functional carpet were the only amenities in the second-floor courtroom. The judge sat at one end and the lawyers and Wuterich at the other. Against one wall was the panel box where the eight members— jurors to civilians—sat in swivel chairs. Several armed Marine military policemen guarded the door to ensure everybody gave up their cell phones.

The panel was professional Marines, a study of tough, hard men with blazes of color over their hearts. The lowest ranking among them was a gunnery sergeant, a demigod to an enlisted defendant. The highest ranking juror was a lieutenant colonel, an archangel who rarely appears in enlisted Marines, daily lives. A full-bird colonel had been dismissed from the jury pool before it was empanelled. The panel was the Corps's version of the defendant's peers. In the caste system of the Marines, Wuterich was just over the line into the exclusive club of Marine leadership. Although Puckett and Faraj were now civilians, they had both done a lifetime in the Corps. At least they had the respect of the panel. The panel's venom seemed to be reserved for Sullivan, a Chicago reservist who earned his pension prosecuting fellow Marines.

During the selection process, lawyers ask the panel questions to discover if they have any biases that might influence their decisions. The process is called a *voir dire*, from the French phrase literally meaning to speak the truth. In the military system, judges ask that the questions be submitted beforehand for approval.

Faraj took up the defense voir dire. He was certain he could prove then that Wuterich did not kill any women and children. He could also show that any shots fired by Wuterich outside the houses were consistent with the ROE. The central issue, "the danger point," as Faraj called it, was whether these jurors would hold Wuterich responsible for the action of his squad. It was a seemingly simple question lost in the cacophony of moral outrage stirred by pundits and commentators masquerading as America's conscience.

At the beginning of the court-martial the eight-member jury panel asked numerous questions, as is their right under military law. Faraj usually answered them for the defense. They were often hard, penetrating questions about actions and reactions of Marines under fire. Puckett didn't know anything about that. Neither did Sullivan.

The rest of the time they sat impassively, occasionally snorting derisively at the government's enlisted witnesses when they testified. They stared at Dela Cruz like he was a curious bug. Mendoza got short shrift as well. The only one they really seemed to pay attention to was retired 3/1 sergeant major Edward Sax. The entire panel was leaning forward while he testified. The old NCOs frequently exchanged knowledgeable glances when Sax talked about close-quarters combat. After listening to him they looked like they had already made up their minds. Especially after they heard him laconically explain how the NCIS special agents abused the suspected junior Marines in a urine-soaked cell during their marathon investigation in Iraq.

Faraj was angered but not surprised the enlisted Marines were interrogated in a Russian-built dungeon at the bottom of Haditha Dam. It was good psychology. Several of the defendants told Faraj they had been questioned up to sixteen hours straight without even being allowed to urinate except in a bottle or on the floor. Faraj made sure the jury heard all the details.

"NCIS was interrogating your Marines, in one case one Marine had to hold his pee until he signed his statement?" Faraj demanded from Sax.

Sax said that when he heard what was happening to his Marines, he went to the NCIS special agents and told them, "If one of my Marines had to urinate they were to take their penis out and pee on the table."[5]

It was a wasted effort. Still unbeknownst to Faraj, the deal was in the works. Sullivan and Puckett had already started to talk.

"They actually started to talk in the middle of my cross-examination of Mendoza. I went for a run in the hills behind the courtroom during the lunch break. I came back to a grinning and jovial Puckett standing in the parking lot waiting for me. 'They want a deal' he says to me, 'dereliction of duty.'

"'What does Frank want?' I say.

"'They want a deal' he [Puckett] says. 'Dereliction of duty.'

"'What does Frank want?' I said."

Faraj barely heard the answer. The revelation shocked him. Not only because a deal was being offered, but because Puckett's tone gave the news the air of certainty. Puckett responded that Frank was interested and thinking about it. Faraj walked away dejected. Instead of a clear-cut victory, Faraj now faced the very real possibility that he would have to stand next to Wuterich while he pled guilty. Faraj felt defeated. Unfortunately, the events before him reflected the uncertainty of trial work, when pride, reputation, and the desire to prevail are always trumped by reality.

"I lived this case for six years because of . . . delays," Faraj recounted after the trial. "All to end up in a deal where his client admits to making a benign statement that no one heard and one he hardly remembers making which magically results in his squad members forgetting the ROE and killing over a dozen civilians. It was absurd. It was false. It did not make sense. Yet it happens in courtrooms every day all over the United States where snake oil salesmen posing as lawyers stand next to innocent clients as they plead guilty to crimes they did not commit because the grave risk of punishment after a loss at trial is so much greater than the plea bargain."

Faraj had resolved never to force or persuade a client to plead guilty, and now he was doing it. It was a rocky road to walk on for a product of the Gerry Spence Trial Lawyers College in Dubois, Wyoming.

Gerry Spence himself, along with a number of notable trial attorneys from around the United States, flew to Camp Pendleton in the late summer of 2007 to help Faraj and Vokey prepare the defense of Wuterich. It didn't include a lesson in giving up. To Faraj a plea was surrender, a betrayal of all the people who had committed to stand by Wuterich while he battled to prove his innocence:

> His plea was a farce. His general court-martial was never about words. Suggesting words alone caused a massacre or its aftermath of course was total nonsense. Even prosecutor Sullivan didn't buy that one. Wuterich's Marines were so pumped up on excitement and fear and rage and adrenaline—especially adrenaline—they would have mowed down everybody they saw had Wuterich uttered 'eat your veggies,' or nothing at all. Their platoon leader had already told them 'clear south.' That was all they needed to hear. Everyone in the courtroom except some of the civilians knew that.

During opening arguments the first day, Gannon set the tone when he told Jones, "I can't think of a single witness desiring of being helpful to the government." His was a startling admission arriving before the court-martial even began.

Faraj didn't expect to hear that. He had to assume the case could still go against Wuterich despite the distaste for the prosecution evident in the expressions of the panel's members.

The drama passed almost unnoticed in the American news media. There was more interest in Wuterich's court-martial in Iraq than Middle America. The atmosphere was nothing like the electrically charged environment in 2007 when the heavy hitters from the *New York Times* and *Washington Post* were pontificating from Camp Pendleton. Among the missing was former *TIME* reporter Tim McGirk.

The reporter who started it all was nowhere in evidence until the whole thing was over. He briefly came out of the San Francisco fog to appear on a San Diego PBS podcast. He even wrote a note to the popular blog *Defend Our Marines,* warning it to tread carefully where he was concerned. McGirk seems sensitive about his failure to actually visit the location of the story he broke. He said his boss prohibited him from going.

The junior Marine minders who watched the reporters were friendly guys with short-timer attitudes. All of them had deployed at least once. Their boss was PAO Lieutenant Colonel Joe Kloppel, his hands full just keeping the clapped-out audiovisual equipment working.

The minders were tasked with escorting the reporters back and forth across the grinder separating the media center from the court room so they wouldn't talk to anyone. They weren't supposed to get chatty. Few of them had any idea what the court-martial was about. Some of them asked. They were in high school when Haditha happened.

Kloppel was the go-to guy. Everyone went to him to find out how much the investigation and trials cost. He never found out himself. The government refuses to reveal what it spent trying eight Marines caught up in the transition from "shock and awe" to "shock and uh-oh" when the United States changed its mission from regime destroying to so-called nation building after two bloody years of intense combat.

In 2006, there seemed to be a reason for the court-mar-tials. Americans don't accept massacre as an operational necessity. Meanwhile, the ignoble lie that produced the noble gesture of ridding

Iraq of a despot rapidly morphed into a perverse kind of reconstruction. "Winning the hearts and minds," a jaded concept dragged off the
junk pile of Vietnam, was the new mantra.

In pursuit of those elusive hearts and minds was the 3/1, the aptly
nicknamed "Thundering Third." Without their loyalty and dedication,
the great minds running the war wouldn't have been nearly as capable of turning Iraq into a smoking hole and America into a pariah in
record time. With the insurgents gone along with most of Iraq, the
same postulates of political correctness started arresting the young men
and women they trained to a razor's edge for being too aggressive. Faraj
thought their prosecution was a grave injustice, and his sentiments
were implicit in much of what he said in court.

In the early days the Marine Corps's top lawyers huddled with
Secretary of Defense Donald Rumsfeld to map out an acceptable outcome. They told the top dogs the foul deeds would all come out in the
"32s."

Vokey said the lawyers overstated the case to the secretary of
defense's crisis committee.

"The prosecution actually believed—and still believes—it can win
a conviction. It oversold that to General Sandkuhler and he believed
it," Vokey said in an interview with *Defend Our Marines* in 2008.[6]

"The Rumsfeld team was briefed by high-ranking Marine Corps
lawyers sent by Brigadier General Kevin Sandkuhler, staff judge advocate to the commandant of the Marine Corps," Vokey said. Also in
the mix was Peter M. Murphy, former general counsel to the Marine
Corps—a civilian who had counseled commandants and their lawyers
for twenty years. Murphy and Sandkuhler have since retired. Vokey
said he was informed of the study group during briefings he received
from Sandkuhler in June 2006.

"Sandkuhler believed they were all guilty and the case was going to
quickly be over. I tried to tell him I didn't think so. I said, 'General, I
don't believe that is correct,' but he thought that the prosecutors were
going to win, that everybody was going to roll over on each other. It
didn't happen that way.

"I was briefed by my boss [Colonel Rose Favors], who was briefed by Sandkuhler on Hagee's presentation to Murtha, Senator Carl Levin, and the other congressional leaders who control the money. There was nothing in his [Hagee's] remarks about cold-blooded murder or massacre or anything like that."

No matter. Sandkuhler's appreciation of the situation was the basis of Rumsfeld's apparent acquiescence to the Pentagon's decision to publicly crucify the Marines. The only thing left was piling on Wuterich before pounding him into submission the Marine Corps way. When Wuterich's court-martial finally got underway, it seemed a certainty the government would win. Even Faraj thought so.

In one respect, the seemingly endless investigation did produce positive results, although not the kind criminal trials are usually held for, California defense attorney Kevin McDermott opined the day the court-martial ended. "Certainly, justice was never served," he observed.

McDermott represented Lucas McConnell, the Annapolis graduate who was relieved of command of Kilo Company, 3/1, while a captain and then rehabilitated. He appeared at trial the last day without his Combat Action Ribbon on his chest. Now Major McConnell testified he doesn't wear it because Wuterich never received his. His testimony was a bright moment of nobility in this otherwise sordid tale. The next day he would feel betrayed.

CHAPTER 3

SHARRATT'S WAR

The same night Wuterich decided to offer his plea, Justin Sharratt was talking about what it was like to be in Iraq. Sharratt had been waiting two weeks to testify in an all-expenses-paid squatter hotel in Oceanside on the Marine Corps's dime when the trial unexpectedly ended. It was his last night in town. He was sitting with his observer in a Marine hangout where he used to drink before the war. He had been summoned from his new job mining coal deep under Pennsylvania to tell his story and never got to.

Sharratt said he was called as a defense witness. The twenty-seven-year-old did two hellacious tours in Iraq with Third Platoon. He wasn't shy about what he did. He was proud to be known as a shit-hot Marine. He was crushed that Wuterich had folded so close to the end of the trial. Sharratt complained that a lot of Marines suffered through their own agonies, making sure they protected their brother when it was his turn to face the judge. He still couldn't get his head around Wuterich giving up.

In 2005, Sharratt was a machine gunner in the Marine Corps, a twenty-first-century baby-faced killing machine. Wuterich was his squad leader. The big man could run full speed for two hundred meters in a 110-degree desert carrying a 25.5-pound machine gun and 250 rounds while clad in almost forty pounds of helmet and body armor. He could field strip a SAW in forty-nine seconds, a battalion record. He could knock down a running man with it from one hundred meters away. He was just as good with his pistol. Sharratt could even piss in a plastic water bottle he just drank from going thirty miles an hour down a rough road standing in a bouncing Humvee. In a terrible place called Fallujah, the year before Haditha, he spent an entire afternoon shooting it out with grenade-throwing Chechens inside a little house filled with death. He said he fired a thousand rounds. In Marine vernacular, Sharratt was very salty.

Most days in Iraq were a routine grind that got on everybody's nerves. Bad food, heat, disagreeable Iraqis—he called them "rag-heads" and "MAMs"—and constant fear of being attacked did bad things to good people. One hot day, he almost got into a fist fight with Dela Cruz while they were searching the house of a suspected high-value insurgent. The bad guy was a known shooter still at large in the neighborhood. The platoon leader had to break it up. It was the heat and grime that did it. The filth was everywhere all the time, a combination Sharratt described as dust, dirt, sweat, and stink that coated everything in gritty tan rouge. Filth seemed to bother him the most. There was no escaping it. He said combat was a kind of weird release.

Former sergeant Francis W. Wolf, Sharratt's squad leader at Fallujah in 2004 and still in the same platoon in 2005, said Sharratt was one of the best Marines in the company. On November 19, Wolf helped kill an insurgent he suspected of sniping at his squad while they were en route on foot to Chestnut after the ambush. Wolf was being questioned by government prosecutors on June 12, 2007, via telephone from his home in Kentucky when he made his remarks to listening lawyers.[1]

Question: You were Lance Corporal Sharratt's squad leader in Fallujah?

Answer: Squad leader, no, sir. I was his team leader.

Q: How well, then, do you think you now know Lance Corporal Sharratt?

A: I know Sharratt pretty good, sir.

Q: Certainly, as his superior in the military, you have a lot of experience?

A: Yes, sir.

Q: What is your opinion of Lance Corporal Sharratt as a Marine?

A: As a Marine, sir, I think he is one of the better ones out there, no doubt about it.

Q: Why do you say that?

A: He is willing to learn. He never bitches, he never moans, he doesn't need help, and as far as knowing his weapons system, as far as employing his weapons system, as far as helping others out, and as far as not being scared and doing what he needs to do, he is, by far, up there.

Sharratt's skills were still desperately needed when he went back in 2005. Nothing had improved. It wasn't as bad as Fallujah, but the town was tense. It was a week before Thanksgiving, and they were a long way from turkey and all the trimmings. Sharratt said it was a filthy dump where he expected trouble all the time. "The whole fuckin' place is a garbage pile," Sharratt remembered. "Imagine everywhere you look is garbage piled higher than your fence and that is Iraq."

His squad was chugging along a modern highway in the Euphrates River Valley of northwestern Iraq about a mile from the dirty brown river. The correct name is the Hay al-Sinnai Road. The ancient Persian armies probably walked it. The Marines called it Route Chestnut. Sharratt's Humvee had just passed Route Viper on the right and was ready to cross Route Zebra on the left. He was paying close attention; intersections were danger zones. They were driving back from resupplying the combat outpost (COP) at Banir

Dahir where a squad of Third Platoon Marines was stationed. They had overwatch on an Iraqi Army traffic control checkpoint. They had just delivered chow, a corporal with the day's crypto ciphers, and five Iraqi Army replacements to relieve the ones manning the checkpoint.

The squad was riding in four "up armored" sand-colored Humvees moving along at thirty-five miles per hour in a two-hundred-meter-long column. Sharratt was riding in the makeshift armored cupola sticking out the roof of the lead vehicle. He was manning an M240 Golf 7.62 mm medium machine gun. Each Humvee was separated from the next by about fifteen meters of open road to keep more than one vehicle from being destroyed by a single roadside bomb.

Sharratt's primary job was watching out for possible IEDs and other infernal devices strewn by enemy "insurgents," the English name chosen for the Iraqi guerrilla fighters. They called themselves *mujahideen*—the "people doing jihad," fighting a holy war. The Thundering Third was trained to destroy them with overwhelming firepower.

There was good reason for the Thundering Third's precautions. Four months earlier, on the morning of August 4, 2005, an amtrack carrying Marines from the Ohio reserve battalion that 3/1 replaced hit a huge roadside bomb. The vehicle was destroyed, and fifteen of the sixteen passengers inside were killed.[2] The bombs were still everywhere. Ever since the Thundering Third had arrived at the edge of Haditha in early September, the EOD specialists and combat engineers from Regimental Combat Team 2 (RCT-2) had been detecting and destroying them in place every day. Often they were common IEDs, homemade land mines triggered by pressure or trip wires. More and more often they were sophisticated remotely detonated devices, the handiwork of al-Qaeda technicians and former Iraqi Army loyalists practicing their unique brand of jihad.

Since they arrived on October 5, the battalion had discovered dozens of IEDs secreted on the roads in and around the city. During November alone, twenty-two of the hidden bombs had been removed from Route Chestnut before they could kill anybody. Sharratt was supposed to detect them before he got blown up.

In the instant Sharratt was not looking for the omnipresent IEDs. He sensed danger ahead from a very ordinary-looking white Opel sedan. He had just been briefed to watch out for very ordinary-looking white cars driving around filled with explosives. When it drew closer, he saw it was filled with people. The white car was driving in the convoy's direction on the bisected hard pan road still devoid of traffic in the cool morning dawn. That was never cool, Sharratt said.

Iraqi vehicles were required by martial law to pull over when American convoys thundered across the dusty landscape. Warning signs prominently displayed on the front and rear of American military convoys in Iraq warned in English and Arabic not to approach within one hundred meters of the convoy or risk getting shot. Iraqis who failed to obey were in grave danger. The insurgency was gaining traction every day over the needless deaths of Iraqi citizens dying in pursuit of their everyday lives.

The Western press was already kicking back; the heady days of the "drive up" to Baghdad, when the journalists embedded with the warriors thought they were with Sherman marching through Georgia, were over. Dealing with the military spin doctors every day had its own morale-sapping synergy. Heady optimism was out; cynical pessimism was in among the easily jaded reporters covering the war.

When the white car got close to Sharratt he saw it was full of MAMs. They might have been innocent Iraqi males going somewhere on Saturday morning, getting an early start to avoid the tie-ups at the traffic barricades and heat. That was usually the case. Or the white car could have been a VBIED like the one that a suicide bomber had recently tried to blow up some other Marines with. The briefing he had listened to before heading out was full of BOLOs—"be on the lookouts"—warning about ordinary looking things that might prove deadly to inattentive Marines.

Wahabi fighters allied with the local Sunni fundamentalists had been active in Haditha since al-Qaeda took over Haditha after wiping out the local gendarmes in the spring of 2004. Sharratt had battled them before. They were stone killers who knew how to fight.

On August 4, 2005, adherents of Ansar al-Sunnah—followers of Sunnah—reportedly eviscerated a 3/25 sniper they captured and killed on camera for a propaganda video. Five members of the same hunter-killer team were slaughtered in a ten-minute wholesale assault by hooded jihadists. The Iraqi jihadists celebrated their deaths with a parade. The free DVD of the spectacle was reportedly very popular.

The report came from Britain's *Guardian*. The reporter on August 22 said the DVD "features a young, blond muscular man who had been disemboweled. He was said to have been a member of a six-strong US sniper team ambushed and killed on August 1. Residents said he had been paraded in town before being executed."[3]

The Marine Corps denies the report.

In response to the intensifying insurgent attacks, the Coalition launched Operation "Iraq Fist" on September 5. The newly arrived Thundering Third, along with the rest of the Second Marine Division's reinforced RCT-2, surrounded the Haditha, Barwanah, and Haqliniyah "Triad" while it prepared for another slugfest like the one at Fallujah the year before that left three thousand insurgents dead. Inside the Triad was another muj army, one made of shadows. Their most powerful weapon was propaganda.

The Coalition government cautioned the civilians trapped in the Triad that the Marines were coming. Warning leaflets were distributed, artillery was brought up, and a long column of tanks and wheeled assault vehicles spread around the cities to secure important crossroads. It was déjà vu all over again for the Fallujah vets in First Squad. Sharratt said it was hard on everybody's nerves waiting to attack. For the rest of the month, 3/1 Marines slowly and carefully placed a cordon of steel around Haditha, the largest and most volatile of the three cities. The uncertain company officers and noncommissioned officers (NCOs) of 3/1 told their Marines to stay ready for anything. The old guys were particularly keyed up.

The veterans in Third Platoon had learned some new tricks about street fighting since Kilo, 3/1 had blasted its way into Fallujah to kill an al-Qaeda army that fought to the death. After the battalion returned to Camp Pendleton in early 2005 it practiced assaulting buildings over and over until it was second nature. Form a stack, go in hot. First a grenade and then waist-high fire from corner to corner before moving on to the next room. The idea was to kill everything in the room as quickly as possible. Maximum carnage in minimum time, death as an art form called MOUT. The room-by-room attack-and-clear scenarios were built on lessons learned at Fallujah when 3/1 suffered thirty-three killed and more than five hundred wounded fighting inside enemy warrens in the ancient city.

First Lieutenant Jesse Grapes, a former Third Platoon leader who led the platoon at Fallujah, coined a phrase then that would reverberate at Haditha a year later. "Never go in a room without throwing in something that goes boom," he taught his Marines.[4] Among them were Sharratt and Stephen Tatum, who were inside the deadly Hell House when Grapes led his Marines in to take it back from foreign fighters fortified inside.

Former 3/1 commanding officer Jeffrey Chessani said he didn't know what his Marines would find when they returned to Iraq in the fall of 2005 so he had to assume the worst. They trained accordingly. A more mundane aspect of their training was learning the ROE, escalation of force (EOF), and the concept of positive identification (PID), or knowing when and who to shoot before pulling the trigger. The lawyers who taught the classes explained that Marines who violated the rules were subject to court-martial and stiff prison sentences.

One of them was a female captain, a lawyer named Kathryn Navin. She testified several times. The young Marines called her a "mattress." Few of them paid much attention to female lawyers, who would never join them in combat. The platoon leaders and NCOs reinforced the ROE training in platoon briefings. Sharratt called the repeated lectures about the rules "more of the same bullshit," among other things.

The new rules did not mean Marines could not defend themselves, his leaders told him. The ROE were intended to minimize the number of civilian casualties that were making Operation Iraqi Freedom look bad.

By the time Sharratt returned to Iraq on his second tour, the Iraq war was all about not looking bad. Civilians were getting killed by everybody at a prodigious rate. The disastrous revelation from Abu Ghraib Prison was still in the news, competing for attention with hor-rific car bombings and several new allegations of American brutality. Sharratt called the alleged American slaughters "payback."

In October 2005, the Pentagon announced that nine thousand Americans had been wounded in Iraq. Far too many young people were coming home missing limbs. Washington started looking for a way out. The generals in Baghdad ordered a kinder, gentler war in the meantime. Despite the new emphasis on the ROE, Chessani said there was nothing in it about asking questions first and shooting later when attacked. He called the notion "a perfect prescription for getting killed." His Marines were trained to be aggressive, to strike hard and fast. He had witnessed what happened when they didn't. Failure filled American body bags. He wasn't going to let that happen on his watch. "You have to let Marines have the inherent right to self-defense," he said.

The civilians of Haditha had little say in what was happening around them. Most people preferred peace to war, whatever the price. Unfortunately, the provisional Iraqi government had no influence over anything, the Americans couldn't protect them, and the insurgents had no qualms about killing them for accommodating the infidels. So they didn't have choices. Until the fall of 2005, the insurgency openly occu-pied Haditha, imparting its harsh brand of Islamic justice on the popu-lation. Three months before the events of November 19, the *Guardian* newspaper described Haditha as an "insurgent citadel" where Islamist guerillas were "the sole authority, running the town's security, adminis-tration and communications."[5]

Marines who tried to get to know the residents of the Triad said they wanted a peace that didn't include them or their Shia lackeys. The Shiites and Sunni faithful had been butchering each other since the death of the Prophet Muhammad, when Sunnis displayed the temerity to insist on choosing Islam's leaders instead of following a line of imams the Shia believe were appointed by the Prophet—or God Himself.

The Americans were caught between two competing religions they didn't understand, a culture incomprehensible to them, and dozens of tribes with shifting alliances all vying for favor with whoever they thought was going to win. There was little common ground and zero trust. By the time Sharratt lined up his 240 Golf on the white car filled with MAMs, things had been spinning out of control for almost two years.

AFTER "SECURING" IRAQ, the generals and civilians running the Coalition Provisional Authority (CPA) occupation government from Baghdad were trying to give more hometown responsibility to the "new" police and Iraqi National Guard. It wasn't going too well in Al Anbar Province. On July 16, 2003, reputedly moderate Mohammed Nayil Jurayfi, mayor of Haditha, and his youngest son, Ahmed, were assassinated by al-Qaeda gunmen for cooperating with the infidels. Their deaths came during the emergence of the Sunni rebellion against the central government in the restive region.[6]

In the late summer of 2004, the US Army occupying Anbar pulled out, leaving behind a small police force in each city to replace them. By America's election day in 2004, the insurgents had pinched it off from the occupied zones. Nobody in Washington noticed. On November 7, scarcely anyone in the United States commented on a Coalition report that armed rebels at Haditha had killed twenty-two tightly bound Iraqi soldiers and policemen—the insurgents called them traitors—who were lined up in the city soccer park and shot execution style during the day while spectators cheered them on.

On November 8, an Iraqi government spokesman said the initial report was incorrect. The deceased in Haditha were in fact fisherman. In any event, the police officers charged with capturing their killers melted away. They still hadn't come back to work eighteen months later.

Haditha was briefly in the news again when US forces nearly captured al-Qaeda poster boy Abu Musab al-Zarqawi on February 20, 2005.

In late March 2005, Iraqi Special Forces backed by US Army advisors reported killing eighty-four insurgents in a raid on a lakeside training camp at Lake Tharthar, the reservoir created by Haditha Dam. Al-Zarqawi's hand was in all of it. Besides capturing ten foreign fighters, they found dozens of passports from all over the Middle East.

On May 24, 2005, the Marines launched Operation New Market, a cordon-and-search operation in the Triad. It was the second such operation in two months, all part of the Coalition trying to capture the hearts and minds of Haditha's long-suffering residents. The battalion-sized sweep by Marine reservists from an Ohio infantry battalion designated 3/25 cleared hundreds of homes during "knock and talk" clearing operations that came up with nothing during its deployment. It was followed by another sweep impressively named Operation Iron Fist.

Jeffrey Dinsmore said the Ohio reservists had been sandbagging patrols, hanging out with the locals instead of staying sharp. Some of them were even hanging around with the mayor and his boys. It was bad business, and Marines paid for it with their lives. Dinsmore played a pivotal role in how 3/1 intended to fight. He said Iraqis were personable people and easy to like when they weren't scheming to kill you. The Ohio Marines convinced themselves they had already won enough hearts and minds. Believing their own bullshit killed them, he said. Afterward, nothing had changed.

On October 5, 2005—the start of the holy month of Ramadan—RCT-2, along with US Army and Iraqi forces, launched Operation River Gate, a follow-on operation to Iron Fist designed to catch the insurgents inside the Triad before they all disappeared. Included in the van of 2,500 Marines, soldiers, and Iraqi Army forces that invaded Haditha and its environs was 3/1. The operation's stated aim was putting down Sunni-led insurgents intensifying their campaign of violence ahead of an October 15 nationwide vote on Iraq's new constitution.

In early October, Iraqi Security Forces discovered propaganda production equipment in a house while conducting clearing operations. They found compact discs, audiotapes, three computers, printers, banner makers, multidisc copiers, and thousands of blank discs and tapes. They also discovered a bomb-making factory with prewired bombs, mortar rounds, propellants, blasting caps, and detonation cord.

The same day, three men in a white four-door sedan were stopped. A search of the car revealed a video camera. Minutes later, another white four-door sedan approached and detonated within yards of the Marines, killing the driver. While viewing the tape in the video camera, they saw the captured driver speaking to the car bomb driver. Videotaping suicide car bombings "is a known terrorist propaganda tactic" used to spread fear and to intimidate Iraqi citizens, Dinsmore said.

On October 10, two additional weapons caches were found in Haditha. The cache sites contained bomb-making material, small arms, rocket-propelled grenades, and ammunition.

Eventually, the US mission switched to providing security for the October 15 elections. Operation River Gate officially ended on October 21, 2005, although operations remained more of the same for Kilo's Marines. Instead of a bruising battle, 3/1 took the entire city of Haditha in four days without firing a shot.

It was a heartening start, but the 3/1 commanding officer said he didn't expect the insurgents to remain dormant too long. The insurgency had a way of disappearing and reappearing at times and places where it held the strongest advantage. The Marine occupiers were constantly being watched, measured, and analyzed for weaknesses. When the enemy found one, it struck hard. Their tactics were as old as time, and so were the results. That was why 3/25 was hurt so badly in August, Dinsmore learned as 3/1's intelligence officer. He was a force recon thoroughbred who took war fighting very seriously. Since this writing, he has been promoted to lieutenant colonel. In his view, the Ohio reservists had grown lax, complacent.

Sharratt says he always paid attention. It is easy to believe. Seven years after the events at Haditha he remained hyper-alert, situationally aware, always checking things out. He tried being a prison guard for awhile but didn't like it. Too confining, he said. Too bright is more likely. He liked the money coal mining brings him. He called underground coal mining "safe" and "misunderstood."

The only time Sharratt wasn't up for a fight in Iraq was inside a firm base where he could take off his gear and relax for a few hours with his buds in Third Platoon. He never felt comfortable outside the wire. He didn't trust Iraqis ever, especially the Iraqi Army soldiers they dragged along with them when they moved around. In his experience, everything about the place—its dogs, its sullen people, its Byzantine architecture, confusing roads, disloyal soldiers, language, even the children—posed sudden dangers. It is easy to believe that if the driver of the white car didn't pull over, Sharratt was going to "light them up."

Sharratt was reborn hard during Operation Al Fajr/Phantom Fury at Fallujah the year before. Thirty-three of his comrades in 3/1 died in battle there—including a Marine lance corporal named Juan Segura from Third Platoon killed minutes into the attack. Hundreds more in his battalion were wounded learning the art of survival. Nine days into the battle, his squad spent an entire afternoon inside a house the size of a small apartment exchanging grenades and machine gun fire with suspected Chechens holding the upper floor. Half the Marines who went in were carried out. Sharratt was a different man when he walked outside.

After that, all he saw was the enemy. There were no innocents, only potential threats, especially the swarthy men in "man dresses" who collected in hostile groups to glare at the Marines when they swept through Haditha searching houses.

Every squad has a Sharratt, a bigger-than-life kid who wears his emotions on his sleeve and really believes in brotherhood and loyalty. Nobody who served with him ever said he wasn't a brave, resourceful Marine. Sharratt has a penchant for overstatement, but that isn't the same as lies. The Marines breed colorful people. There is proof positive he wasn't bullshitting in Iraq. He damn sure understood payback.

At that moment, Sharratt was focused on the white car. It was still approaching the convoy from the opposite direction, heading directly toward them. His job was standing in the cupola behind his machine gun looking out for mines and IEDs and ushering Iraqi vehicles to the side of the road until their convoy passed. If the white car didn't pull over, Sharratt intended to riddle it with his 240 Golf.

Justin Sharratt was very typical of the young enlisted Marines who joined in the wave of patriotism following 9/11. He joined out of high school from Indiana. He believes absolutely it was his vocation to kill the enemy. Paraphrasing his viewpoint, 3/1 came to the palm-studded city by Haditha Dam to kick some haji ass on behalf of their brother Marines in 3/25 who were killed introducing democracy to the fucking ragheads.

Lima Company, 3/25 was so beat up it wasn't allowed outside the wire of its firm base for fear more of its hometown Marines would be killed, 3/1's Edward Sax later recalled.[7]

Suddenly, the heavy-handed combat doctrine of security and stabilization operations (SASO) was out. Establishing trust was in. It was called COIN, shorthand for counterinsurgency warfare. The underlying problem with the policy was that the Iraqis didn't want the Marines barging into their lives no matter how polite they were. Sharratt had never heard of it. His job was to kill ragheads.

If the Iraqis failed to respond to kindness, the Marines were prepared to level the city, but they were supposed to give COIN a shot first. Marines are goal oriented. It was definitely a paradox. The elections for a new central government were slated for October 15, and the CPA needed things in northwestern Iraq to settle down the way Fallujah did. The First Squad's short trip to the COP and back was part of that paradigm.

The COIN component of Operation River Gate ostensibly represented the new way to win hearts and minds. Marine officers were still measuring their effectiveness by counting the number of improvised explosive devices they found and disabled, the number of weapons caches discovered, number of enemy combatants killed, and number of humanitarian or community relations projects completed. The Marines scored big in Baghdad when they got the Haditha power generation plant back in operation. But more hearts and minds were still needed.

Marines were instructed to remember the new COIN tenet, "First, do no harm." They generally attributed the phrase to General James N. Mattis while commanding Marines in Al Anbar.[8] Then, if the Iraqis didn't cooperate, they could kill them lawfully.

BY THE TIME Sharratt was riding in his Humvee on Route Chestnut, the insurgents were driven from sight but not from the minds of the locals. Although the insurgency was suddenly absent from the streets, its influence wasn't. Brutal al-Qaeda leader Abu Musab al-Zarqawi promised that anyone who cooperated with the Americans would eventually be dealt with. Decapitation was his favorite option. There were enough DVDs of decapitated people passing around the Triad to make his point. The result was stalemate. The Marines were simply too strong for the insurgency to take on head-to-head and too weak to assert complete control.

Someone among the insurgents decided an attack severe enough to incite the Marines to slaughter was required. They knew if the Marines were attacked hard enough with a combination of buried bombs and hidden snipers, it would stir them to retaliate with all the brutality they were capable of.

The anticipated response was fundamental to US battle doctrine. It was a lesson the insurgents had learned at Fallujah. The mujahideen who survived the battles for the sacred mosques knew the Marines' ways well. Muj corpses littered the mosques in the ancient city where they tried to resist.

The attack on Hay al-Sinnai Road was planned in early November in Albu Hyatt, a nearby town where dozens of Marines and hundreds of Iraqis would be killed and wounded before the end of the war. The ambush was intended to be a local operation, something to give the home folks plenty to ponder.[9]

Local Wahabi extremists and well-paid local gunmen from Al Asa'ib al-Iraq—the Clans of the People of Iraq—led by al-Qaeda foreign fighters would carry it out. The three main elements of the complex attack were the IED-initiated ambush on Route Chestnut and two IED ambushes planned along the so-called River Road that parallels the Euphrates River about 1.5 kilometers north and east of the Chestnut location. Dinsmore said paid shooters were dangerous; they were trained fighters who knew their jobs. They were a different breed altogether than the local zealots who practiced religion and pray-and-spray with equal enthusiasm.

The local Wahabi gun fighters and well-paid local gunmen from Al Asa'ib al-Iraq followed the al-Qaeda foreign fighters for money. That required negotiation. The Marines knew something was up because there were several blabby insurgent supporters talking about the attack on their cell phones. What the Marines didn't know was when and where.[10]

Sharratt knew nothing about any of it. He later said an ambush was the farthest thing from his mind. At that precise moment, he was totally focused on the MAMs in the white car. He couldn't know the ambush on Route Chestnut was not the random event conducted in isolation the way the skirmish was later portrayed. He did know—the whole squad knew—they were going to "get in some shit" sooner or later. It still surprised him when it happened.

CHAPTER 4

THE KILL SACK

The imminent attack on Sharratt's convoy was the starting point of a daylong insurgent terrorist operation. Nothing about the ambush was random. The site chosen was a modern, paved highway on the south side of the city bisecting an important agricultural area inhabited by relatively wealthy Sunni Muslim Arabs. They despised both Americans and Shiites with an intensity only three thousand years of boiling internecine religious war can produce.

The area surrounding the kill zone was home to rabid Sunni supporters. Within a square mile of the ambush site were homes of dozens of known insurgents who had disappeared when the Americans arrived. A few days before, the platoon had encountered another IED near Route Viper. Luckily, nobody was killed.

Even 3/1's boot Marines knew Haditha was at the center of insurgent resistance in the province. Marines are briefed on why they fight. Sharratt said they were told 3/1 was always sent where the action was since it had made a name for itself kicking Fedayeen Saddam's ninja asses at the "Bridge Fight" at An Nasiriyah in 2003.[1] Kilo Company was sent to the center of the action to get things moving. At Fallujah in 2004 the battalion crashed into the city down Route Henry to the heart of the insurgent rebellion. Sharratt was there that time. It was all the reason he and his buddies needed to be ready.[2]

Sharratt motioned to the man driving the white car to pull over as soon as he made eye contact with him. He pointed his machine gun at the car, universal language in Iraq for "I'm talking to you." The driver complied immediately, pulling over in a wide spot in the road in front of a dump truck parked near large piles of sand. For a few seconds Sharratt watched them do his bidding. He doesn't remember having thought much about them being any kind of threat as he rolled by.

Then his world blew up. One second he was fixated on the white car already pulling over, and then the bomb exploded. He heard the explosion almost the same second its shock wave passed over him, momentarily blocking his vision with dirt and debris. When it cleared, the white car was empty. The five men riding in it had bailed out. They were milling around the left side of the car. MAMs were a threat. What they were up to was a complete mystery. But it didn't bode well that they were where they were when the IED exploded. Sharratt said he locked on to his prearranged defensive sector, hunkered down inside his armor, and waited. He could hear small-arms fire that sounded like the distinctive cracking of AKs. The MAMs from the white car were now the responsibility of the Marines in the Humvee behind him.

The indictments said their names were Ahmed Kutar Museleh, also known as Ahmed Fenr Muselh; Wagdi Aida Alzawi, also known as Wgedi Aida Abd; Kaled Aida Alzawi, also known as Kaled Aida Abd; Mohmed Tbal Ahmed; and Akram Hamid Flaeh, also known as Akram Hmid Fluih. They were either insurgents on a nefarious mission, four technical school students being chauffeured to class by a taxi driver, or five guys with really bad luck.

"They definitely were not insurgents," Faraj says. Had they remained inside the car, history might already know.

There were plenty of warnings to give them pause. Marking their passage along Route Chestnut—the only paved road leading into

Haditha from the southeast—was a parade of glaring yellow and red signs in Arabic, Farsi, and English, and simple pictures warning that death awaited those who disobeyed. They should have seen at least one. They were planted all over the city. If that wasn't enough warning, there were burned-out cars and trucks lying about to provide examples of what could happen if they didn't. Former 3/1 commander Lieutenant Colonel Willie Buhl opined without irony it was unfortunate so many Iraqis could neither read nor see well enough to notice the signs.

The checkpoints and menacing Americans pointing guns at them enraged the Iraqis. It was a daily reminder they were under the thumb of an invader. The influential Sunni clerics and sheiks that headed the tribes were powerless to do anything about them except to encourage the more zealous patriots among the population to actively resist. Their hostile attitudes explained to Dinsmore and Chessani why IEDs could be placed in cunning hiding spots in plain view of the local residents. Too many went unreported to explain them away as terrorist threats.

WHEN THE IED blew up, the rest of the Marines in the convoy acted instinctively. Within seconds of the blast, they had pulled over in a "herringbone" formation, the three surviving vehicles facing in opposite directions to cover their completely exposed flanks. Some of the Marines said they immediately began taking small-arms fire from the south. Others said they took some from the north as well. Sharratt said he didn't know. Down the road at the COP First Squad had just resupplied, Corporal Joe Haman said AK-47 fire was definitely cracking through the still air where the blast originated.[3] The grunts in the Humvees bailed out; they were helpless inside. Sharratt stayed on his gun.

Behind the wheel of Sharratt's Humvee when the IED exploded was Fallujah vet Corporal Rene Rodriquez, from Austin, Texas. He moved to the left front of the Humvee and took a knee. The assistant driver or "A-Driver" was twenty-two-year-old Cpl Hector Salinas. He headed toward the back of the convoy. He was from Spain, a transplanted Texan who grew up by Rodriquez in neighboring Houston.

Salinas is a blustery, tough-talking fellow, a sergeant-in-waiting slated to take over the squad. It was his first deployment to Iraq. Salinas came from 1/4 with two other Marines who wound up in Third Platoon. Along with everyone else in First Squad, Third Platoon, they were commanded by Kallop, a rich kid from New York who was friendlier with his Marines than officers usually are. His style of command would produce mixed results.

Behind them, Tatum was second in line driving a "high-back" Humvee, protected by a jury-rigged lash-up of manufactured and homemade armor. Tatum immediately tried to bail out, but the weight of the slabs protecting the doors made them sag on their hinges. He banged his shoulder against the door several times before it yielded. Getting trapped inside a Humvee was a considerable stressor.

Even so, Tatum was known as a tough, steady Marine. He sometimes wore thick glasses and took a lot of ribbing about having four eyes and that sort of thing. Seven years later, he would look and sound eerily like Buddy Holly.

Sitting beside Tatum was Corporal Sanick Dela Cruz, twenty-three, the squad's designated mean guy. He was a little Filipino man from Chicago who led the second fire team. He was reputedly vicious. Just before Wuterich's trial, the prosecution revealed that after the battalion returned from Iraq in 2006 he'd struck a Third Platoon lance corporal and threatened him with death if he ever saw him on the street.[4] Dela Cruz's usual sidekick was Private First Class Humberto Mendoza, twenty-one, the squad mutt sitting in the back of the Humvee. He was even smaller than his fire team leader. Mendoza didn't *comprende* English too well. Dela Cruz liked to pick on the Venezuelan for being stupid, blaming him for whatever went wrong. The other Marines felt sorry for Mendoza but picked on him anyway. In the back of the Humvee with him were a team of Iraqi Army soldiers on their way to the rear. Nobody is sure what happened to them later on.

Driving the third vehicle was twenty-four-year-old squad leader Sergeant Frank Wuterich, a serious Marine from Connecticut with a

friendly demeanor who played with the local kids. He was getting promoted to staff sergeant so he could take over as Third Platoon sergeant.
His men thought he was a fine squad leader, willing to listen and willing to command when he needed to. They thought he would make a
fine platoon sergeant. So did McConnell, his company commander.

Usually, Wuterich would not be driving, but he was letting Salinas
run the short resupply convoy for experience. His best fire team leader
did the planning, getting the squad ready to deploy on the convoy.
Riding shotgun next to him was LCpl Trent Graviss, another combat vet who had transferred in from 1/4 Marines. He was operating
the squad radio. He had a personality conflict with Dela Cruz, his
fire team leader and constant nemesis. They had been together in Iraq
their first tour. Graviss thought Dela Cruz was a bullshit artist with a
little-man complex. He often said so. Graviss was a straight-talking,
candid person who never really picked up the company line. The government liked him enough to make him a frequent witness. He was a
player in two unrelated Third Platoon war crimes trials. In the backseat
was "Doc" Brian Whitt, the US Navy medical corpsman temporarily
assigned to the squad for the duration of the convoy.

Bringing up the rear of the little convoy was another high-back
Humvee with three Marines in it. High backs had a neck-high armored
shield around the back of the truck, hence the name. Miguel "T. J."
Terrazas was driving it. He died instantly when two cans of compressed
propane erupted under the front of his vehicle. T. J. was the squad
jester, a popular kid who had been with Tatum and Sharratt the year
before. Several people would later claim they were his best friend.
Next to him was LCpl James Crossan, another close friend. He was
crushed under vehicle debris. Sitting in the back was LCpl Salvador R.
Guzman. He was blown onto the road. They had fought together at
Fallujah the year before.

The second-tour Marines were the heart and soul of the squad.
They set the tone for the rest of the grunts. Even Wuterich sometimes
deferred to them on tactical decisions. All of the veterans had been
in the legendary Hell House fight that produced two Navy Crosses

and a ticket for all of them into the pantheon of Marine Corps lore. After the battalion came home, these were the Marines who trained the rookies how to make war the next time they deployed. They were the hard core of Kilo, the riflemen machine gunners and assaultmen who would lead the next fight. They had been trained hard by Navy Cross recipient Sergeant Major Bradley Kasal, master tactician Staff Sergeant Christopher Pruitt, and First Sergeant A. D. Miller. In charge of them all was Sax, the battalion sergeant major. They were solid Marines who didn't believe in giving the other side any slack.

The veterans were definitely salty. They understood that esprit de corps is the glue that binds Marines together in combat. Esprit is part bravado, part macho bullshit, part tradition, a heavy dose of discipline, and very real. Outsiders can sense it, but they are never invited to partake. Esprit is what ensures that the old twenty- and twenty-one-year-old veterans tell the eighteen- and nineteen-year-old kids what they know about killing, offering ad hoc show-and-tell time using the electronic images of dead Iraqis taken at Fallujah to show the rookies what they could expect when they deployed in 2005. Possessing dead Iraqi pictures was forbidden. Everybody had them.[5]

The combat vets were responsible for instilling the cherries with the tightly knit squad's credo, one that isn't in Marine Corps training manuals. "Never give an inch, never offer a break," was in the hearts and minds of the Marines who fought down Route Henry in 2004. They'd promised themselves and they promised the rookies they would never suffer like that again. "Everybody goes home" was their motto.

Their hard-core attitudes rubbed off on the new guys. Kilo's officers and senior NCOs didn't interfere. During MOUT and SASO training before they deployed, 3/1's senior Marines fulfilled the training requirements to present the rules of engagement to their subordinates, but it would become clear they didn't believe in it themselves. Former Kilo Company commander McConnell told his company during in-country training sessions that Haditha wasn't Fallujah, but it didn't stick.[6] Nor was their attitude surprising. The leadership all the way up the line from Kallop to Major General Stephen T. Johnson, the highest-ranking Marine in Iraq, believed Marines had a legitimate right of self-defense even when the civilians got in the way. Civilian deaths were as unfortunate as sometimes they were unavoidable. Collateral damage was part of the Marine experience.

Learning from experience in combat was how the brass had learned the subtleties of warfare when they were young. Lessons Marines learned in Haiti in 1915 were still being applied in 2005. Civilians always find it unnerving when they discover that the United States trains killers in a methodical, comprehensive way. Surgically precise killing is a refined, ingenious art form that requires years to master. It is all about never giving the other guy an even break. Even so, the old veterans gave lip service to the laws of armed conflict and the ROE they personally found threatening. It was orders. But the young Marines sensed they didn't often sound like they meant it. At least that is the way most of the junior enlisted men say they remember their training.

Setting the tone for them were NCOs like Sax, a Marine's Marine, a self-professed warrior who was likely to show up in a raging firefight just to boost morale. Enlisted men respect officers and NCOs willing to chance a bullet in the face when they don't have to. He told his Marines their job was making the other assholes die. He was proud he'd inspired his charges to live by teaching them how not to die, and he said so.

Sax didn't say there wasn't a time when restraint was in order. During a half-dozen interviews and interrogations, Sax acknowledged that Marines must obey the ROE, but only when they don't interfere with a Marine's primary task of staying alive to engage and destroy the enemy. Sax did a good job selling his message to his Marines. Six years after the fight they still talked about him. The rookies wanted to be just as hard as Sax, to fight like unfeeling machines the way they were taught at the School of Infantry and practiced in 3/1 until they finally deployed in the summer of 2005.

THE AMBUSH

At 0716 on a cool, slightly overcast Saturday morning, everything that had happened before the IED exploded was suddenly background noise. Haman heard the IED go off from almost a kilometer away and knew it was ugly. Already, he could see a big cloud of black smoke rising just about where the convoy should be. A few minutes later he heard Wuterich on the radio report he had Marines down. Then he heard Wuterich tell the brass at Firm Base Sparta (FB Sparta) an insurgent had remotely detonated a buried IED under the last vehicle in the convoy. Wuterich later recalled the blast was stunning, throwing debris so high in the air it fell like steel rain. It made it easy to imagine that the insurgent who had dialed for dollars on his cell phone to set off the blast was still out there watching.

The IED demolished T. J.'s Humvee and instantly killed the twenty-year-old who had earned his moniker going out of bounds to Tijuana, Mexico. Crossan, also twenty, was severely injured, guaranteed a life of pain. Guzman, nineteen, still able to shoot, had a heel shattered. He immediately crawled toward T. J. to help. The smiling kid was in two parts, burned almost beyond recognition, his face wrecked. Under the debris that used to be the high-back, Crossan was calling for someone to help T. J. Scarcely able to breath and unable to see, the young Marine from Washington State didn't know help was not an option. Navy Corpsman Brian "Doc" Whitt and Guzman started pulling Crossan from the wreckage.

Even then, luck showed its fickle face. For reasons Wuterich still can't understand, something told him to change lanes by crossing the raised median seconds before the IED exploded. It could just have easily been his vehicle, or the third in line that was destroyed. Much speculation has been spent since that day wondering whether Wuterich's last-second decision to shift lanes momentarily threw off the insurgents' timing. A few seconds either way and the bomber would have missed the fourth Humvee as well. The blast radiated out one hundred meters. If it had gone off in the middle of the convoy, more Marines would have been hurt. That it didn't was another of the many imponderables that shrouded the truth in a wispy blanket of fog.

What happened, when, where, how, and why had to wait to be sorted out. The only thing certain at 0716 was that an IED had just killed a Marine. His death would come with a terrible price. Before an hour passed, most of the Iraqis who would die on Route Chestnut were already slaughtered, piles of bleeding human refuse created by superbly trained Marines using high-power rifles, one pistol, and grenades.

The first to die after Terrazas were the five Iraqi MAMs in the white car. Wuterich, Dela Cruz, and Salinas said they shot them. A year later, nobody was absolutely certain who knocked them down first. They all suffered "dead checks"—kill shots to the head. Wuterich said he took a knee and began firing when he heard Dela Cruz begin yelling at them to stop in bad Arabic. He admits shooting all five of them. He said they disappeared one by one as they fell out of his view behind the white car. It was damn fine marksmanship. Dela Cruz initially said he fired when they started to run. He had a straight, unobstructed view of them. After he was indicted for five murders, he changed his mind and said he waited until Wuterich shot them down before he joined in with dead checks while standing over their bodies. Much later, he demonstrated for Faraj how he leaned over the white car and shot them. Salinas also said he started shooting when the MAMs began to run. His attention was split between the fleeing Iraqis and terribly wounded Crossan. He was so engrossed trying to save Crossan he didn't have time to chase them, so he shot them instead.

Salinas described what happened in a statement he gave to an Army colonel in February 2006:

LCPL Dela Cruz saw a white four-door sedan from the overwatch position. I also saw the white four-door sedan up on the hill, at the front left of the convoy. It was located immediately to the left of our front vehicle. It may have been observing the convoy. After the blast, four or five MAMs exited the vehicle and started running south of Chestnut. We PID the MAMs so, we started shooting and they all go down. They kind of look suspicious and I didn't have time to chase him.[7]

Within seconds all five of the men were dead, strung out in a crooked line leading to the sand pile behind them. About thirty minutes later, fourteen more Iraqis would die in two nearby houses at the hands of a four-man fire team led by Wuterich. Before it happened, Kallop arrived with the quick reaction force (QRF), a squad of Marines always on standby at FB Sparta just for emergencies like the one unfolding now. After checking out the dead and wounded, and conferring briefly with Wuterich, Kallop told his squad leader to take a fire team and "clear south." The squad was still receiving small-arms fire from somewhere across the wadi, or valley, that separated a cluster of houses from the road to the south.

Meanwhile, on the north side of Route Chestnut, the rest of the squad was searching other houses. One of them showed evidence of being the IED triggerman's hidey-hole. Graviss called for Kallop to come and check it out; otherwise, Kallop would have led the way to House #1. After exploring the position, Graviss and Dela Cruz started looking around the neighborhood. Eventually, they encountered a group of women and children in a nearby house holding a large amount of American cash, a disassembled cell phone, packed suitcases, and fifteen Jordanian passports. A group of MAMs and one woman were taken into custody. Nobody died.

While that was going on, Tatum and Mendoza followed Wuterich across a wadi toward the house they believed was the source of automatic weapons fire still coming at them from about two hundred meters away. Tatum said he knew where to go because Salinas shot a grenade against the wall of the house. Salinas said he was shooting his M203 40 mm grenade launcher at a MAM two hundred meters south of his position, all the time groping for Crossan's severed fingers. He said he fired the grenade launcher as well as his M16 several times. When he saw the fire team head south, he took after them using a different route across the wadi.

Upon reaching the targeted house, the four Marines formed a loose stack before entering. Each has a different recollection of what happened next. Salinas said he was the first one in. Wuterich said he didn't remember the order of anything. Salinas downed a figure in the hallway to his right with aimed fire from his rifle. Tatum and some of the others heard an AK-47 rack in the next room. Tatum and Salinas threw in grenades. Only one of them exploded. Mendoza saw a MAM in front of him and after some hesitation blew his head off. Quickly, methodically, they went from room to room killing every living thing they saw. Six people died there. Two orphaned children lived.

While they were still clearing the house with grenades and rifle fire, somebody yelled "runner." A fleeing person reportedly streaked toward the house next door, all the Marines except for Salinas in hot pursuit. Later on, nobody could remember seeing anyone running and nobody was sure who yelled out "runner." In one statement Salinas said he did. Then he never mentioned it again and nobody asked. What is certain is that Wuterich, Tatum, and Mendoza followed the elusive ghost into the adjacent house, where a door was open. It might have been a woman named Hiba and a small child named Asia who ran out of the room when a grenade exploded. Her niece was hiding in the bedroom where almost everyone died and she watched "Aunt Hiba" run out with her baby sister.

For some reason, after cordoning the front of the second house, one of the Marines either knocked or rang a doorbell at the front door. Everybody heard it, but nobody remembers whether it was a knock or a ring of a doorbell, or who did it. A bigger question never asked was "why?" Their training didn't call for polite entry during clearing operations.

In any event, they all agree that when a man came to answer, Mendoza shot him through the glass door from about twenty-one feet away. At first he said Wuterich told him to shoot the guy when he answered the door. He later said he shot him because he had been told the house was hostile. Upon entering the foyer they treated the second house and its occupants just as roughly as those at the first house they stormed. Wuterich, however, said he never fired his weapon in the second house. Tatum says maybe he did. Salinas, standing outside, said he didn't know who was shooting. Mendoza offered several different accounts. Faraj thinks the confusion was understandable:

> Salinas never said Wuterich fired his weapon. In fact, Salinas said he never entered the house, although in an interview I conducted with him in 2007 he told me that he went through the house and cleared some rooms but never fired his weapon.

Mendoza said he did fire inside and later said he didn't. Then he changed his mind again. Tatum said he threw a grenade into a room that turned out to be a bathroom with exposed water pipes. The water pipes burst. While still hiding from the blast, Mendoza said, he heard "womans and children" in the bedroom where the women and children took shelter believing they would be safe. He claims he asked Tatum what to do. Tatum says that never happened.

Mendoza threw another grenade into a back bedroom that didn't go off. He later lied about it and said he didn't. In his second version of events, he said he opened the bedroom door, saw women and children, and closed it again without doing anything. Tatum said that was a lie. He said he followed behind Mendoza or Wuterich shooting into the room. Wuterich said he cleared the house to the left either in front of or behind Salinas. Wuterich still claims he never fired his weapon inside the house.

Tatum first said he followed a Marine but did not know who because it was dark. After his grueling interrogation by NCIS, he was sure it was Wuterich. Seven years later he wasn't sure of anything. Whatever the sequence, afterward the men congratulated Mendoza for being such a stand-up Marine in his first firefight. Wuterich told Mendoza he was proud how he had popped his cherry on his first contact.

After being held until he almost urinated on himself, Tatum relented to NCIS interrogators and adopted the story they wanted to hear. In the new version, Tatum said he witnessed Wuterich's blazing rifle. Wuterich says he stood in the hallway without joining in. Seven years later, Sharratt said Tatum had to push Mendoza out of the doorway so he could get inside the door and shoot. He never said how he knew that. Salinas said he didn't see any of it. In his final version of events, Sharratt maintained he was at the rear of the first and second house providing security.

In the official story Sharratt first offered, he selflessly dismounted his M240 Golf and tore out after the team upon realizing it was without an automatic weapon. By the time he reached the scene less than a minute later, they had already cleared the first house and disappeared inside the one next door. Inside, eight people were being shot. Sharratt said he didn't know that until later. From his vantage point he heard a grenade erupt, followed by blasts of small-arms fire. He didn't have to see inside to know the squad was clearing the house room by room. Less than a minute later, the fire team emerged.

As soon as they finished their grim deed in the second house they gathered outside before the reinforced team moved to the next home, an empty building under construction. Seeing it locked, Sharratt blasted the door open with his machine gun so they could get inside. After discovering it was empty, the winded Marines moved on to the next house, where Kallop told them to take up temporary residence on the top floor in an overwatch position. They were grateful for the break. While they were there, Sharratt borrowed a fifteen-round 9 mm magazine from Kallop. He never explained why he needed it and Kallop said he never asked. Doc Whitt said he had already given Sharratt two full magazines.

A few minutes later, Sharratt and Salinas simultaneously observed an unarmed Iraqi in a dark sweatsuit make a running break from the first house the fire team had cleared. Kallop saw him at the same time from a position north of the house. All three men opened up and the Iraqi went down hard, disappearing over a low-lying ridge he was headed for. The dead man lay there all day. He probably ran out of House #1.

About two hours later, four more Iraqi men died in a house on the north side of Chestnut. Their indiscretion was turkey peeking, looking over a wall that surrounded the house they were in and then ducking back down. They were looking at the Marines in the overwatch position (OP). It was considered by the Marines to be a hostile act. After watching them for a while, Wuterich ordered Salinas to fire several nonlethal "training" grenades at the men with his M203. Although the rounds landed close by, the Iraqis continued to pop in and out of view, a very suspicious thing to do when American Marines are on the hunt.

Tiring of the intrigue, Wuterich, Salinas, and Sharratt moved to the house in front of them. Tatum stayed behind to secure the OP and give some cover fire. Meanwhile, Mendoza had gone off on a detail ordered by Kallop. The building Sharratt, Salinas, and Wuterich approached was a multifamily structure surrounded by a wall and secured by a blue gate. In one apartment they found a large group of women and children. Among them were a man and a young boy, the women later said. One woman claimed the Marines took custody of the boy before demanding to know where the men were. She said she pleaded for the Marines not to take her young son. They eventually complied, although they took a grown man with them. The Marines said they never saw any men in the first apartment. The women said they never saw any of the Iraqi men alive again.

Wuterich said he ordered Salinas to secure the civilians while Sharratt and he went next door without any Iraqi men in custody. When Wuterich and Sharratt went to investigate they encountered four Iraqi men—two of them armed with AK-47 rifles—in a back bedroom. Before the Marines could find out why they had been spying on the squad, the Iraqis were dead, killed in a closet-sized room. Sharratt said he peeked in and saw a man pointing a locked and cocked AK-47 at him. He tried to shoot the man with his SAW, but it jammed. He jumped back behind the wall and told Wuterich he had a jam. Pulling his 9 mm pistol out he reengaged, shooting the man with the AK between the eyes. Then he shot another man with another AK in the head. Spying two more men, he continued firing until he ran out of ammunition. Most were head shots. By then Wuterich was firing as well. Sharratt said the confrontation was over in less than three minutes.

That was not the end of the fight. While First Squad was conducting its grim business, other Marines from Third Platoon were engaged as well. Gunfire was sounding all over the sun-baked city. While Wuterich was taking out the houses to the south, McConnell arrived with Third Squad, Third Platoon led by Fallujah veteran Sergeant Francis Wolf. They had walked to the ambush site, taking intermittent sniper fire along the way. They killed the two men responsible. Somewhere else on the River Road that ran adjacent to the Euphrates, an EOD team and another squad of Marines from First Platoon providing security had also been attacked. Overhead, helicopters and UAVs were orbiting the battle area. Several running MAMs were engaged by helicopters. Chessani notified RCT-2 that his battalion was in heavy contact with the enemy.

Less than a kilometer east—about 3,300 feet—a reinforced squad led by a lieutenant from Weapons Platoon, Kilo was involved in a two-hour grenade fest and firefight that culminated in a series of huge explosions caused by five-hundred-pound American bombs. The bombs were dropped from Marine attack jets on a house concealing a diehard group of cornered insurgents. Toward evening the last insurgent captured that day surrendered to pursuing mud Marines, several Iraqi Army soldiers, and an M1 tank while clutching a kidnapped baby to his chest. Blood was running from his eyes and ears, reminders of his lucky escape from the bombed safe house. The HET believed he came from House #4.

When the air finally cleared late that afternoon, at least twenty-four Iraqi men, women, and children as well as Terrazas were dead, and eleven Marines were wounded, including an officer. Five of the Iraqis died by the mysterious white car. Fourteen more of the victims—members of two families—died in the first two houses the squad cleared, two of them infants, as well as eight MAMs. Faraj says some of them were the menfolk of the slaughtered women and children who happened to be home that morning. Along with the civilians died the presumptive moral primacy of the United States in the second Iraq war.

The Iraqis who survived the skirmish told a completely different story, the one McGirk trumpeted in *TIME*. Their first interviews with NCIS investigators did not occur until March 29, 2006, 130 days after the combat engagement and ten days after *TIME's* explosive story appeared on the Internet. By then the families of some of the dead MAMs had been denied *solatia* payments because Marine intelligence discovered they lived in "bad guy houses."

On March 29, 2006, NCIS special agents Nadya Mannle and Mark A. Platt traveled to Haditha to interview the Iraqi survivors.[8] On March 29 and April 6 they met with Aiad Ahmed Hameed (father of the four suspected insurgents killed by Wuterich and Sharratt in House #4), Khadega Hassan Hameed (mother of the deceased suspects), Yosef Aiad Ahmed (the older brother who was not present on November 19, 2005), Najla Abid-al-Razak Hamad (victim Jamal's widow), and Khaled Jamal Aiad (Jamal's son). Najla did most of the talking.

According to Najla, there was an explosion that sent glass flying at around 0600 hours. The Marines arrived between 0930 and 0945. Najla, Jamal, and Khaled were in House #3. She alleged that the three Marines ordered them out of their house while yelling "*erhab*" (terrorists), "*mujahedin*" (insurgents), and "*qunbehlah*" (bombs). Najla claimed that the Marines were angry and repeatedly referred to the bomb while pointing in the direction of the explosion. She claimed that the Marines asked who lived in House #4 and Jamal explained that it was Aiad's home. The Marines then ordered Jamal, Najla, and the boy Khaled to House #4. Meanwhile, Ehab had been there with her husband Jaseb and Khatan. She claimed Nagham and Marwan were preparing to go to Baghdad—Khatan was also planning on leaving. Following the explosion, Ehab told Mannle she heard gunfire and yelling and screaming. Then it grew quiet.

At about 0945 Jaseb called out to Najla and told her that everyone had to go outside into the courtyard. Once outside, Najla claimed that the

Marines had them wait near the patio. According to Najla, the Marines ordered Aiad and the other occupants out of House #4. Once they were outside, the Marines divided them into two lines, with the father and four women sitting in the first row and the four men and Khaled in the second. Once separated, the Marines continued questioning them. Khaled claims that one of the Marines set his rifle with a tripod or bipod down on top of the car and racked it. Only Sharratt was so equipped.

Najla claims that during the questioning one Marine went into House #4. Meanwhile, Jasib insisted he was a traffic police officer while Marwan tried to show a Marine-issue "Haditha Key Persons Identification" provided to reliable Iraqis for identification. The Marines asked them if they had any weapons and Jasib told them about an AK-47 located in House #4 that was issued to him for his job. Jamal reportedly told the Marines that he, too, had an AK-47 in House #3.

According to Najla, one Marine took her and Jamal to House #3 to retrieve the AK-47, two empty magazines, and five rounds. Later, she claimed only she went with the Marine to retrieve the weapon. Nagham told Mannle that Najla went with Jasib into House #4 to obtain his locked-up weapon, but in fact, NCIS later determined, did not disclose it to Marines until days later when they returned to his house and took the weapon.

When the Marine returned with the recovered rifles, two of them allegedly went back into House #4. Najla claimed she could see them through the window talking and pointing fingers. When they came back out, they spoke with the Marine who had remained behind to guard the women. One of the Marines then directed the women and Aiad back into House #3. Najla said that she pleaded for her son Khaled's life, and the Marines let the boy go with her. Once the women were inside, Najla claimed, she tried to open the door at least twice, but was stopped by the Marine guarding them. Najla then alleged that she heard muffled gunfire and four distinct gunshots. Following the shots, the Marine guarding them left and she saw all three Marines running down the street. Her story was corroborated by the other Iraqi civilians. The indicted Marines said it was all lies.

Former 3/1 commanding officer Jeffrey Chessani tried to explain what happened in the days that followed. It was his command, it happened on his watch, so he alone was responsible. It was a clean fight, clean kills, he said. He would angrily exclaim, "My Marines are not murderers," when a reporter suggested otherwise. The dead civilians were unfortunate, just as war is unfortunate. Death, however, was inevitable when they got in the way. It was not his Marines' fault. Fate is a cruel handmaiden. The insurgents had picked the time and place to launch the attack. From the prospective of a Marine lieutenant colonel insulated by custom and tradition from ordinary civilian mores, it was plain to see what happened. Chessani thinks everyone else deserves an explanation as well.

The key to understanding the events at Haditha the way Chessani does is to go back to what happened after 2003 when the 3/1 Marines who invaded Iraq during Operation Iraqi Freedom came home from their first deployment in 2004 to train the next group of recruits. Those Marines were professional infantrymen trained to a fever pitch to destroy the enemies of the United States. They had been training relentlessly since the decade-old Gulf War. After 9/11 it got even tougher. The Thundering Third was more than ready for war when President George W. Bush ordered Operation Iraqi Freedom. They were also among the few Marines to put their training into action when on March 24 and 25, 2003, they battled fanatical Iraqis to hold open a critical road between two essential bridges at An Nasiriyah.

Therefore, it was not an accident that Chessani's men had been trained by some of the most experienced infantrymen in the Corps. That is how the Marine Corps works. Lessons learned are passed down to the next generation of war fighters so as not to reinvent the wheel every time they enter combat. The extralegal interpretations of the ROE that dominated the Iraq battlefields in 2005 were not yet a practice; they were an exception. The emphasis was on attack. The battle between the bridges at Nasiriyah taught 3/1 the enemy was a tough, brave, tenacious fighter who would kill them if given the slightest chance.

Navy Cross recipient Bradley Kasal and the other senior NCOs who led the battalion's enlisted men in 2003 took those lessons to heart. They trained the generation of leaders who led 3/1 in Iraq during 2005.

"We don't train Marines to be speed bumps," Kasal is fond of saying.

The officers and NCOs who led 3/1 into Iraq on its second deployment in 2004 were more than mere warriors; they were combat artists. Their palette was power projection, and their subject was death on call. Their reach was as far as an infantryman's weapons can shoot. Within that cone of fire, they were among the deadliest hunters in the world. They had not learned anything about the benefits of restraint, so they weren't teaching it. In this story, it is essential to remember that the Marine Corps relies on lessons learned as much as air to breathe. The lessons it learned in 2003 and 2004 were still fresh in its institutional mind.

Sometimes there is time for mercy, even tenderness, on the battlefield, but rarely, and never when fighting an enemy. Kasal always carried candy for the kiddies. Most of the Marines recall fond moments with the Iraqis. They just recall the bad times better. Regret comes after it is too late, when tired, scared Marines trying to survive are confronted by tiny bodies they just robbed of life. It was a natural part of combat in Iraq. Every war has a unique flavor, and unfortunates getting in the way spiced this one.

Typically, combat veterans view the laws and rules governing warfare as object lessons for lawyers and historians to sort out when the war is over. Once somebody shot at them, these Marine infantrymen relied on a primal rule: survival of the fittest. It was almost inconceivable to Marines who spent a decade preparing for the second Iraq War to give even the slightest advantage away in a gunfight. Their way was about winning. Sharratt later explained in detail:

By February 10, 2004, I reported to Kilo Company and met the men that I would later trust with my life in combat. Our First Sergeant in Kilo Company was then First Sergeant [Brad] Kasal, who is now a Sergeant Major. He gave his Marines a deep pride and a desire to be tactically sound. First Sergeant Kasal would coach us through patrols, help us with our land navigation skills, and show us the ropes of patrolling and ambushes.

By April 2004, all of us new-joins had settled into our squads and teams. I was placed in Second Squad, Second Team and my team leader was Sgt Wolf. We were a very tight knit team and Sgt Wolf was a great teacher. He wanted us to become the most tactically proficient Marines possible. He would often threaten to make us fire team rush everywhere if we did not get better.

Sgt Wolf made us better Marines and when we got to Fallujah we were a confident and tactically proficient team. Before I had joined the Marine Corps, I had signed up for the infantry because I wanted to be the best, I knew the Marines' training was longer and I wanted the best training. I knew that going to combat would change my life, but no one could ever really understand combat until they've been there.[9]

Occasionally before and after arriving in Iraq during July 2005, the battalion lawyer Randy Stone spoke to the Thundering Third's enlisted men about the rules of land warfare, laws of armed conflict, and the rules of engagement. They would sit in the heat sweating rivulets while the lecture droned on. Sharratt said they resented hearing about all the rules telling them what they couldn't do. Stone wasn't the man doing it; he was just talking about it.

One of the lessons came with a test. It is labeled BARGEWELL EXHIBITS 002873 THROUGH 002876. The test had one question that was eerily prescient:

You are in the lead armored Humvee escorting a four-vehicle convoy along HWY 1. There is a flash behind you followed by a loud explosion as one of the NTVs [nontactical vehicles] in the convoy disappears in a cloud of dust and smoke. You see two males 200m [meters] away from you mount a motorcycle and speed away. Three males in a roadside stand 100m up the road run into a nearby house, but you start taking small arms fire from a different house 150m west of your position. What do you do?

A. You should respond with deadly force to the hostile fire coming from the house, remain vigilant to the other possible threats in the area.

B. You should engage the fleeing men on the motorcycle first because they are beyond effective range if you wait.

C. Engage everywhere you see movement because there's no telling who detonated the IED.

Another question:

The convoy you are in suffers an IED attack on the unpopulated outskirts of Ramadi. As you focus your attention on the location of the IED, you notice two individuals in civilian clothes and no weapons jump up out of fighting hole 40 meters away from where the IED exploded and run away from you. You quickly ascertain the individuals were within command-detonation range of the IED. Command detonation is a common method of detonation. What can you do?

A. Nothing because you don't have enough information to know for certain that the fleeing men detonated the IED.

B. You can engage with deadly force ONLY after you fire a warning shot first.

C. You may engage the individuals with the necessary force, including deadly force, to prevent their escape.[10]

Stumped? The answers are:

1. A. You should respond with deadly force to the hostile fire coming from the house, remain vigilant to the other possible threats in the area.
2. C. You may engage the individuals with the necessary force, including deadly force, to prevent their escape.

The exhibits are attachments of training aids made by Stone when he was the staff judge advocate of 3/1 at the time of the Haditha incident. He used them to teach 3/1 Marines the ROE in Iraq. He is the same lawyer who managed to get himself indicted for failing to adequately investigate the battalion he was assigned to.

"But, hey," former Third Platoon squad leader and Navy Cross recipient Sergeant Robert "R. J." Mitchell once explained, "they are lawyers. Grunts don't listen to fucking lawyers. They listen to guys like Kasal."

Mitchell is an authority on close combat. He said once the fighting starts that men—even Marines—are impossible to control. Their training kicks in and they go on autopilot. Mitchell earned his Navy Cross saving Kasal when the future sergeant major of the School of Infantry at Camp Pendleton was fighting for his life in the Hell House. Both men suffered multiple wounds in a room-to-room battle with foreign fighters as well-trained and determined as they were. Mitchell killed his last victim with his KA-BAR knife after his M16 was destroyed by grenade shrapnel, using his good arm to dispatch a foreign fighter lying near death next to Kasal. It was his fourth wound in two days. The foreign fighter made gurgling sounds until he died, Mitchell said.

Kasal had seven bullet wounds in his body and forty-seven more holes made by grenade shrapnel. Bleeding out, he was still able to shoot it out with bad guys on the other side of the wall. Lying next to Kasal was Third Platoon wild man Lance Corporal Alex Nicoll. His leg had been sawed off below the knee by the same burst of weapons fire that cut Kasal's leg almost in half. Nicoll was gut shot as well. He was trying to make a joke. Afterward, they all laughed. Mitchell said the deadly situation they found themselves in was too absurd for anything else. Sharratt and Nicoll were buddies.

"War is some sick shit," former Third Platoon, Kilo squad leader Jose Nazario noted in 2008. He was being tried in federal court in Riverside, California, for allegedly murdering prisoners of war at Fallujah when he was with Third Platoon, Kilo, in 2004. He was a product of the same lessons learned as Sharratt, Tatum, and Wuterich. Mitchell was in his platoon. Nazario was the first Marine ever tried in a civilian court for following military orders. The former sergeant and two Marines under his command were accused of murdering four civilians they found in a house full of recently used weapons. The Marines said they were obviously insurgents. Nazario was accused of shooting two of the suspected insurgents with his M16 when somebody higher up the chain of command asked him why the prisoners were still alive. Nazario's trial was under way in US district court in Riverside at the same time the Haditha spectacle was being played out a hundred miles away at Camp Pendleton.[11]

One of Nazario's co-defendants was a former sergeant named Ryan Weemer. At the Hell House fight in Fallujah, then corporal Weemer emptied his fifteen-round 9 mm pistol into another insurgent's chest while taking three AK-47 rounds in the leg. Ammunition exploding in the foreign fighter's rig set the insurgent's beard on fire. The flames marked his position. Then Weemer shot him with his rifle. He stood accused of shooting an unarmed old man in the head with his 9 mm pistol after Nazario told him to. He incriminated himself during a job interview with the Secret Service to guard the White House. The ghosts were with him every night. They broke him.[12]

There were other lessons. Among them is a picture of a Marine mugging behind an Iraqi on his knees with his brains draining onto his patio. The Marine had just shot the guy in the back of the head while he was praying. A few days later, the same Marine was shot to pieces. Those stories got around as well. They were all considered lessons learned at Fallujah by the young Marines preparing to deploy to

Iraq as soon as their training cycle ended. The Marines were told they were ready for anything, thanks to lessons learned.

Unfortunately, Marines don't come with on 'and off switches. Chessani said the men who fought at Fallujah had experienced some of the worst combat in the Iraq War. "It's not like you can make the experience go away."

CHAPTER 5

DAMAGE CONTROL

The first grievous blow landed November 20 when Second Marine Division public affairs officer Captain Jeffrey Pool served up his bogus press release. Evidence later presented showed the erroneous account was authorized by Colonel Richard A. Sokoloski, chief of staff of the Second Marine Division and Pool's boss.

It may have been a badly produced product of RIAT, the acronym for a reportable incident assessment team. The Second Marine Division was supposed to have one. Before Sokoloski dove behind his Fifth Amendment right against self-incrimination, he told Bargewell's investigators he sought to capitalize on the civilian deaths by intimating that the insurgency was responsible for them. The RIAT was the appropriate vehicle for doing so.

RIAT was conceived by Colonel John R. Ewers in late 2002 while he was a lieutenant colonel and the First Marine Division staff judge advocate. He is also the Marine who questioned Sokolowski. Plenty would be heard from the colonel in the ensuing seven years. At this writing, he is the top lawyer in the Marine Corps, a major general advising the commandant.

The First Marine Division staff judge advocate is both the division's top lawyer and the division commander's personal counsel. Ewers said he created RIAT to provide First Marine Division commander then major general James N. Mattis with "ground truth" about adverse incidents ranging from friendly fire incidents to alleged war crimes by either side during the initial invasion of Iraq in March 2003.[1]

The original RIAT component included among its list of personnel Ewers, the division PAO, the civil affairs officer, the medical officer, and a handful of other specialists tasked with defusing adverse incidents and deflecting unfriendly reporters in Iraq before they could exploit harmful information. The team was successfully employed eight times during Operation Iraqi Freedom in 2003, the Marine Corps later said. The concept was eventually adopted across the whole of the Marine Corps. Ostensibly, the program was in force when the Second Marine Division relieved the First in 2005.

Major General Richard Huck, Second Marine Division commanding general at the time of the Haditha incident, said he wasn't even aware there was a problem when the twenty-four dead Iraqis showed up on his radar scope two days after they died. Nine of them were reported insurgents, and the civilian dead were collateral damage. Defusing the potential problems dead innocents presented was supposed to be the work of the RIAT. Huck said he was unaware of any problem with the situation until the Army sent an Army officer to see what was going on. That always raises the hackles of Marines.

Up the chain of command in Baghdad a lot of people were already thinking about Haditha, long before McGirk's story appeared on March 19, 2006. Among them was Army Lieutenant General Peter W. Chiarelli, commander of multinational forces in Iraq. In January, McGirk gave a copy of an extraordinarily inflammatory video and accompanying witnesses' testimony to Lieutenant Colonel Barry Johnson, a US Army military spokesman in Baghdad.[2] The video and testimony purportedly told a story of an unprovoked massacre by a handful of rogue Marines in

Haditha. According to the account handed to Johnson, the Marines had hunted down the civilians like rabbits in revenge for the death of one of their own. After reviewing the evidence, according to McGirk, Johnson passed his information up the chain of command with a request that it be given "a full and formal investigation."

McGirk's principal sources of information were two Iraqi nationals who founded the grandiloquently named Hammurabi Organization for Monitoring Human Rights and Democracy after the Haditha incident developed. He identified the founders as Taher Thabet al-Hadi Hadithi (Thabet), forty-three, and thirty-six-year-old Ali Omar Abrahem al-Mashhadani (Ali Omar), an on-and-off Reuters News Service photographer previously arrested by Marines in his hometown of Ramadi. They founded the organization a month after Ali Omar got out of Abu Ghraib after more than five months of interrogation at the infamous prison. The human rights group had been in business for about a month when Thabet went to Baghdad with his gruesome video. Three months later, Ali Omar Abrahem al-Mashhadani and Taher Thabet al-Hadi Hadithi were the darlings of *TIME* magazine.[3]

Ali Omar's American warders told the blog *Defend Our Marines* that he was released about December 15, 2005, along with about five hundred other Iraqi prisoners. He was arrested for suspicion of anti-government activities. Reuters also reported that he spent five months in US custody before being released without charges. *TIME* identified Thabet as head of the Hammurabi Organization, adding that the group was affiliated with Human Rights Watch. Almost immediately, Human Rights Watch vehemently denied it had any connection with the Hammurabi organization and *TIME* wrote a retraction.

Barry Johnson, who in 2012 was a colonel in Afghanistan, responded to an email inquiry from *Defend Our Marines* in 2007 detailing what McGirk had alluded to:

> The evidence presented to me by Tim McGirk was simply too
> detailed in events and tactics described by his Iraqi witnesses to be

ignored. It was never a matter of my passing judgment on this unit or the individuals involved. It was simply a matter of ensuring an incident was properly investigated given the extent of civilian deaths involved. There are times when Public Affairs Officers have to represent the public conscience to the command, reminding leaders how our actions can be misconstrued by others if we aren't transparent in our operations and activities to the furthest extent possible.

Yes, I said this incident had the potential to be a big PR problem. I said that as a lever, to help ensure it was taken seriously up the chain of command and fully investigated in order to know what really happened on the ground. My gut told me that bad guys likely used the first house and people living there as cover, firing from it and moving out the back to other houses. A common tactic. But I had no way of knowing that for sure when talking to Tim and the only way we could ever say this with confidence would be to open an investigation.

Had I ignored what Tim was telling me, this story would have likely been a blip, not a PR disaster. A he-said, she-said story with no conclusive evidence one way or another. It could have drug out a little while as others tried to pursue the story, but nothing would ever likely be conclusive. We'd call it enemy propaganda. I knew this at the time, but burying the story wasn't the right thing to do. At least I didn't think so, based on the circumstantial evidence I was presented, and the commanding general didn't think so when he read that evidence in my memo.

No decisions to prosecute were based on what I wrote about potential PR consequences or what Tim told us would be a story in *Time.* As you know, the memo I wrote did lead to a formal and full investigation. Decisions to prosecute were made based on that investigation. Investigating the incident was the right thing to do. I was surprised, however, from some of the findings, which in turn led to prosecutions. I did not expect this to be the case.

I did not know any of the backgrounds of anybody involved in this incident. It wouldn't have changed my recommendation to fully investigate it. [4]

On February 14, 2006, Chiarelli appointed Army Colonel Gregory A. Watt to conduct an "informal" AR15-6 investigation to find out if McGirk's allegations were true. The assignment took Watt and his three-man staff to where 3/1 was standing down at Haditha Dam. The senior Marine hierarchy told Watt al-Qaeda and its Sunni supporters had chosen to make a stand inside the city.

Haditha's seventy-five thousand residents sit squarely astride the lines of communication between Syria and Baghdad, a 220-mile artery of roads, waterways, oil pumping stations, pipelines, and people where the blood of regional commerce flows. Watt's story is heavily spiced with acronyms from the alphabet soup military officers enjoy:

By early 2005, cells from *Ansar al Sunna* (AAS) and AQIZ [Al-Qaeda in Iraq] had established the Triad (Haditha, Barwana, Haqlaniyah) as a safe haven and key line of communication (LOC) between the border and points east, such as Ramadi and Mosul. Marine Corps denial operations north of the Triad—particularly Operation River Gate—resulted in many mid-high level insurgents fleeing the three cities. . . .

While overall insurgent activity dropped precipitously, this was likely the result of overwhelming numbers of CF [Coalition Forces] on the ground within the Triad. As CF transitioned from offensive operations to a continuing security and stability mission, they expected these operatives to re-infiltrate the cities, reestablish contact with local criminal level insurgents, and conduct planning for attacks on CF firm bases and patrols. CF began to see an increase in probing attacks of the firm bases, small caliber IDF [indirect fire attacks] at close range, Small Arms Fire (SAF) attacks within the city, and VBIED/IED attacks within the city. CF also expected that local AAS operatives would establish contact with high-level foreign fighters and begin planning for spectacular attacks (SVBIED, coordinated ambush) against CF in Haqlaniyah, in an attempt to preserve access to vital LOC. AAS has begun re-infiltrating from outlying areas into Haditha, establishing contact with local criminal and insurgent operatives. They have continued intelligence gathering and passive observation of CF patterns throughout the city, while determining remaining resources that have not been discovered by CF.

Instilling democracy where tribal plutocracy and religious theocracy has reigned since biblical times was more pretense than anything else. In 1975, Saddam Hussein built the giant K3 crude oil pumping station near Haditha to service the country's new 1.4-million-barrel-per-day pipeline. In those days, Saddam wisely kept Iraqi oil cheap and plentiful. Oil money was the main ingredient in the greenback poultice he applied to the Iraqi economy to mask the tortures his supporters inflicted on the country's suffering population. To that end the Iraqi-owned North Oil Company and Western interests built the 220-mile long transnational pipeline through the northern Euphrates Valley to export oil at Syrian ports.

When the oil artery slicing through Haditha was cut by insurgents in June 2003, the CPA temporarily holding the reins of government in Baghdad estimated it would take less than a year to repair the damage to the pipeline and resume pumping operations. The endeavor was eventually abandoned when continued instability made it clear the Coalition needed to regain control of Haditha and its environs before it could fully exploit Iraq's natural gas and oil reserves. Regrettably, the struggling central government was barely managing to hang on to what it had already seized.

Military force was the only available option except for an "acceptable" peace, and al-Qaeda and its supporters had already made it very clear they weren't interested in peace of any kind that allowed a place for the United States on Arab lands. The insurgents didn't have to win the battle raging in Haditha to win the oil prize; they just had to not lose it.

Al-Qaeda soldiers, foreign fighters, and religious zealots intending to cut the arteries of commerce began flooding across the border from Syria on the highways and ancient smuggler's desert passages between Syria and Iraq almost as soon as the American-led invasion began in late March 2003.

The United States responded on March 30, 2003, when Army Delta Force "operators" tasked with investigating several suspected weapons of mass destruction sites supposedly secreted around Haditha arrived in the area. Finding nothing, they pushed east toward Haditha Dam the next day to secure the dam infrastructure and investigate Kuwaiti claims that WMDs could be hidden inside of the seventeen-story, Russian-built structure. The Delta operators were supported by a reinforced company of fabled US Army Rangers from the Third Battalion, 75th Ranger Regiment.

The destruction of the Haditha Dam by Saddam loyalists or foreign fighters was a serious concern. Its destruction would have a disastrous impact in a country that had sustained annual floods and drought before it was built. A broken dam would also upset the timetable the Coalition Army commanders had prepared for the conquest of northern Iraq. They needed to choke it off from opposition reinforcements flowing south from Syria and Ba'athist functionaries fleeing north to the party strongholds in Al Anbar Province.

About the same time, US Army Rangers received intelligence reports indicating the Iraqi military had started a disinformation campaign claiming the United States intended to bomb Haditha Dam. The reports triggered concern among Coalition commanders, who surmised that the Iraqi military was going to blow up the dam and blame it on the invaders.[5]

The Rangers, already tasked with another mission, stood down to begin planning for the hasty operation. They had less than twenty-four hours to prepare for it. The intelligence reports the Rangers received said the dam was heavily guarded with armored vehicles, including T55 tanks, and at least fifty anti-aircraft artillery pieces. The Rangers expected to encounter heavy resistance.

On the evening of March 31, 2003, the Delta operators and Company B, Third Ranger Battalion seized the dam—code-named "Objective Lynx"—that straddles the Euphrates River east of the city. At first it seemed like it was going to be an easy chore after all. After arresting two security guards manning a gate of the looming complex, they simply moved inside the compound and took up residence. Their mission to prevent its destruction and secure a line of communication across the river for follow-on forces appeared to be a walkover.

That notion of an easy victory lasted until the afternoon of April 1, when Iraqi Army forces gathering to the north of the dam counter-attacked with unusual determination. For six days and nights the Iraqi Army fiercely resisted the Delta operators and Rangers with infantry attacks and mortar and artillery barrages. When the battle ended, the Rangers reported they needed direct fire, 120 mm mortars, and close air support from attack helicopters and jets to overcome the fierce resistance. In the end the Rangers killed or captured at least 230 enemy soldiers, twenty-nine T55 tanks, three heavy cargo trucks, two motor-cycles, twenty-nine automatic anti-aircraft cannons, fourteen various heavy anti-aircraft artillery pieces, twenty-eight 155 mm artillery pieces, twenty-two 82 mm mortars, six 60 mm mortars, eight ammo caches, ten military boats, and one kayak. For a brief time, peace reigned.[6]

By April 10, US Army ground forces began fortifying the area with a reinforced heavy cavalry regiment—the equivalent of about 6,500 men. The unit initially chosen to secure the environs of Haditha was the "Tiger Squadron," Third Armored Cavalry Regiment (Third ACR)—from a unit called the "Long Rifles" that had been based in Germany for more than thirty years before returning to the United States.

Upon its arrival in theater on April 2, the Third ACR was imme-diately tasked with securing and stabilizing Al Anbar Province, a 140,000-square-mile area and the largest province in Iraq. It includes the infamous "Sunni Triangle," which Saddam Hussein, his family, and the senior leaders of the Ba'ath Party called home. The Third ACR became the nucleus of a regimental combat team named "Task Force Rifles" with the attachment of numerous support units.

The task force initiated combat operations by conducting recon-naissance missions in the Euphrates River Crescent to identify targets, removing hostile Ba'ath Party members from power and eliminating anti-coalition elements running a very effective media campaign against them. The Third ACR would call Al Anbar home for the next year.

In order to increase security in the regions, the regimental task force established the Iraqi Civil Defense Corps training facility north of the city of Hit. More than three thousand Iraqi troops were hastily trained and formed into two Iraqi Civil Defense Corps battalions that promptly deserted along with their weapons. Many of these predominantly Sunni men later used their new weapons and skills to fight against the central government.

On January 18, 2004, initial contact was made with the US Marine Corps's RCT-7 slated to replace the Army task force. The Marines began arriving in numbers by the middle of February, and beginning on March 4, joint missions were conducted by Army and Marine units. The task force continued to conduct combat operations until March 14, 2004, when control of the region passed to the Marines. During the task force's tour in Al Anbar Province, it suffered forty-nine killed and more than two hundred wounded.

In February 2004, First Marines deployed to Al Anbar Province. Upon arrival in theater, First Marines formed into RCT-1 to replace the Third Brigade of the 82nd Airborne Division. The command consisted of several major subordinate commands from First Marine Division and various smaller attachments from throughout the Marine Corps. When it was completely formed, it was the most powerful ground force in northwestern Iraq.

RCT-1's area of operation included numerous cities, specifically Al Karmah, Al Saqlawiyah, Nasser Wa Salem, and Al Fallujah, and the Haditha Triad—the centers of al-Qaeda and Sunni resistance in Iraq at the time. Its mission was to conduct SASO and train Iraqi Security Forces. That mission was put on hold when four mercenaries working for Blackwater Security were attacked, mutilated, and hung on the Brooklyn Bridge at the western edge of Fallujah. Much later Faraj would defend Navy Seal Matthew McCabe, who captured the guy responsible for the killing of the four men and hundreds of innocent civilians. McCabe was accused of assaulting the insurgent while he was tied up.

By October the Fallujah Brigade had gone over to the insurgency. In November 2004, the CPA ordered Operation Al Farj/Phantom Fury to retake the city from al-Qaeda. A month later, what was left of the city was secure. More than 60 percent of the city's 140,000 structures had been destroyed or damaged and at least three thousand insurgents were dead. The Thundering Third alone lost thirty-three men killed and more than five hundred wounded. They claimed to have killed more than one thousand insurgents and captured hundreds more. More insidious, the bloody battle of the ancient City of Mosques set the tone for how Marines were trained to fight in the year that followed.

CHAPTER 6

GETTING IN TROUBLE

B y November 19, 2005, Wuterich's First Squad had been in Haditha
for almost two months. Although 3/1 "belonged" to the First
Marine Division, it was sent to the Second Marine Division as reinforcements, thereby falling under its chain of command until relieved.
They had acquitted themselves well in September and early October,
before Operation River Gate sent RCT-2 into battle once again. The
battalion was still riding high on the honors it had earned the preceding
year while under the command and control of its parent First Marine
Division. It was the principal reason 3/1 was sent to the Triad. The
CPA needed a tough, unremitting force to bring the Haditha region
under control before the scheduled October 15 national elections to
install a new Iraqi government.

The Marines were told they were in Haditha to hunt down and kill
al-Qaeda, the faceless, formless enemy that had relentlessly bedeviled
them from the day they arrived. They were told to expect a vicious,
no-quarter contest, a repeat of Fallujah 2004. Sax testified the battalion

expected an instant replay of Fallujah despite assurances to the contrary. He said it again at Wuterich's court-martial.

Wuterich was a typical product of Marine Corps infantry training when he took over First Squad, Third Platoon before the company deployed. Still a rookie—a "cherry"—the new guy came out of a training billet at Camp Pendleton's School of Infantry full of battle-tested theories he taught well but had never applied in combat. Cherries have to prove themselves, something he managed to do even before they left the States. The men who served under him later declared Wuterich was already a good squad leader and a good Marine when they deployed. That was testament enough. Wuterich passed muster with the old hands by listening to what they had to offer from the day he arrived in the company a few months before it deployed to Iraq, maybe too much. The internal dynamics of an infantry squad are influenced as much by personality as rank, and First Squad had some real hard-asses in it.

Wuterich grew up in Meriden, Connecticut. In 2005, he was still married to a lady named Marisol. They eventually had three daughters. He had signed up for the Marines at seventeen and volunteered for the infantry. Wuterich quickly found out grunts fight on the pointy end of the spear, but they live on the shit end of the stick.

Wuterich is a smart guy. His family said he had the soul of a musician and the tattoos to match. When he joined the Corps to flee Meriden, he thought it was a temporary stop on the way to his dream of being a music producer. Then the Twin Towers collapsed under the weight of suicide bombers and he found himself at war. He reenlisted right after 9/11. He would wait four more years before he got into his first and only firefight.

By the middle of November, Wuterich and First Squad was feeling salty; they had a few minor scrapes under their belts and they had been running roads and patrols for almost three months. They had done hundreds of knock and talks; they hunted high-value targets and uncovered dozens of weapons caches and propaganda mills.

Until NCIS showed up, the Thundering Third's Marines uniformly believed the ambush on Route Chestnut was just another incident in the battalion's struggle to kill al-Qaeda. When the charges of murder surfaced among the lower ranks in late February and early March 2006, 3/1's Marines were already packing their bags to go home, celebrating a completed tour without the huge losses in life the company had endured in 2004. None of the young Marines thought anything sinister happened on Route Chestnut, certainly not anything that could be construed as a crime. On the contrary, there were meritorious promotions and decorations for valor in the works. Wuterich already knew his was a successful tour. He was up for staff sergeant—the first important rung on a career Marine's professional development. The incident at Haditha faded into the white noise of the war.

How the twenty-four Iraqis died, who they were, and who really killed them and why would probably have remained an unplumbed mystery had the issue never been thrown into the court of public opinion by *TIME* magazine.

The Marine Corps's reaction to the harsh criticism was unprecedented. The plotters who carried out the scheme at Haditha knew that the Marine Corps would have to react to the ambush with vigor. They planned the attack accordingly. Although it was a subtle, brilliant plan, they could not have possibly guessed that it would change the way Marines see themselves as well as how they want others to see them.

How the brilliant deception was planned and executed was known almost immediately to the intelligence experts in the highly compartmentalized intelligence-gathering apparatus the Corps relies on for tactical intelligence. Within a month it was clear the deadly encounter was an intentional propaganda ploy planned and paid for by al-Qaeda foreign fighters. That didn't stop the press from comparing the situation to the infamous massacre at My Lai, South Vietnam, four decades before.

A May 28 editorial in the *New York Times* described the Haditha incident as "the latest indication of what terrible things can happen when soldiers are required to occupy hostile civilian territory in the midst of an armed insurrection and looming civil war," and that it raised questions that "have awful resonance for those who remember

Vietnam, and what that prolonged and ultimately pointless war did to both the Vietnamese and the American social fabric."[1]

Three days later in an editorial titled "Duty, Honor, Investigation" the *Los Angeles Times* wrote: "If Marines 'avenged' the killing of a comrade by terrorizing and killing innocent Iraqis, they disgraced their uniform and must be punished. The same is true of anyone higher in the chain of command who helped conceal what happened on November 19, 2005, in Haditha in western Iraq." The editorial added: "If the allegations of a massacre are corroborated—and a full disclosure is overdue—the debate about the wisdom of the US mission in Iraq inevitably will become even more inflamed. But in Iraq, as in Vietnam, larger 'explanations' for atrocities cannot be regarded as excuses."[2]

The intelligence gleaned by counterintelligence operatives attached to 3/1 after the ambush shows that the battalion staff had been advised of the scheme to demonize the Marines by an informant named Muhannad Hassan Hamadi. The informant was snared by 3/1 Marines on December 11, 2005, and decided to cooperate. Defense attorney Gary Myers said he never understood why investigators who descended on Haditha in February 2006 didn't "examine the linkage" between al-Qaeda, the local insurgency, and the events at Haditha before deciding war crimes had been committed. It was information the Marines could have exploited. Unfortunately, the Corps's fumbling public affairs effort fell short once again, failing to offer mitigating circumstances that might have made even the nearly deaf ears of influential media magnates perk up enough to consider an alternative to massacre.

Muhannad was the first to reveal that the attack was carried out by cells of local Wahabi extremists and well-paid local gunmen from Al Asa'ib al-Iraq, led by al-Qaeda foreign fighters. The Iraqi turncoat's claims were bolstered by Marine signal intercepts that revealed the al-Qaeda fighters planned to videotape the attacks on Route Chestnut and elsewhere around the city on November 19 and exploit the resulting carnage for propaganda purposes.[3]

Eleven insurgents involved in the attack were identified by name and affiliation in the details of the HET summary that followed his capture. HETs worked hand in hand with infantry battalions to seize and exploit human intelligence, or HUMINT, that provided some more "ground truth" to battle commanders. All eleven insurgents were killed or captured in the days immediately following the Haditha incident.

The summary also details the Marines finding three dead bodies near the Sub Hani Mosque after the November 19 fight was over. It describes them as "military-aged males" wearing "chest rigs." Two of the decedents were "missing parts of lower torso." The authors opined the victims were foreign fighters killed in one of the Marine bombings during the daylong combat. Dinsmore said it made sense because nobody claimed their bodies; if they had been local folks somebody would have been searching for them.

At the same time, McGirk was preparing his March 19 story about murder and cover-up at Haditha. There was real reason for his suspicions. The vicious Marine response along with the bogus Pool press release and its subsequent handling by Sokoloski and later MajGen Huck set the situation up for exploitation.

When McGirk received his video evidence from Thabet and Ali Omar, the two dubious human rights advocates were still under observation by Marine Corps counterintelligence teams. They were considered useful tools by the Marines listening to them talk on their cell phones. Because McGirk never interviewed the Marines, he never heard 3/1's side of the story. It might have swayed him.

DURING A MARCH 26, 2007, deposition, Dinsmore revealed what kind of enemy the battalion had been fighting in the weeks prior to the ambush on Route Chestnut, as well as on the day in question. The videotaped evidence deposition had been ordered by the commander of US Marine Corps Forces Central Command on March 19, 2007—coincidentally the same day McGirk's story broke—in accordance with standing orders for disseminating classified intelligence, the Marine Corps said.

The enemy 3/1 could expect to encounter didn't fit into the parameters of conventional COIN operations, Dinsmore said. A unit of highly trained Force Recon Marines had already encountered insurgents in Haditha during a takedown job in October 2005. Instead of surrendering to the Marines, the insurgents killed one of them. Dinsmore was certain 3/1 would encounter the same kind of resistance.

Dinsmore's assessment had been presented to Chessani and the other senior officers in the battalion on November 17, 2005, to help them prepare for what their Marines could expect while they occupied Haditha. Pertinent pieces of the briefing were sent down to the line companies. Dead Marines always got everybody's attention. Two days later, First Squad was ambushed.

The latter portion of Dinsmore's deposition detailed what subsequently happened on Route Chestnut and why. Dinsmore reluctantly offered his observations to prosecutor Sean Sullivan.[4] Dinsmore holds Sullivan in particular contempt for judging his men without knowing anything about combat. He wasn't worried what would happen to him for making waves. He is one of those rare human beings who really are like Rambo. He later claimed he never intended to cooperate with Sullivan one more iota than he had to.

It was the slow-motion battle Dinsmore described in his narrative that made the situation of the 3/1 Marines different from that of most other service members suspected of war crimes. Most of the other alleged offenders precipitated the fatal engagements—making the Marines and soldiers charged with war crimes automatically complicit in the alleged deeds. The Haditha Marines were responding to an attack that had already killed one man and wounded two more. In mathematical terms, Wuterich lost 25 percent of his combat effectiveness instantly. Dinsmore laid it all out in a PowerPoint presentation.

From page forty-six of the deposition:

Question: (Sullivan) And could you explain what—what your assessment was?

Answer: [This] was taking it to the next step and painting a future opera—or a future intelligence picture for the Commander. The keys points that added into my intelligence assessment and to—and to paint the picture for the Commander were that we believed the— the insurgents conducted the [Route Chestnut ambush] planning in Albu Hyatt.

This was intelligence that we received on about 17 November, prior to the attack, in—in which Weapons Company conducted an operation down in Albu Hyatt, and they had intelligence reports that Syrians were planning a major operation in the City of Haditha. My—that lead to my assessment, that, and in conjunction with— with the events as they occurred, led to my assessment that it was an orchestrated attack with two main elements: IED, small-arms fire complex attack on Route Chestnut to begin the day; and then the small-arms fire ambush on EOD responders and targets of opportunity.

To me this was a—this was a typical insurgent TTP, tactic, technique, and procedure; and then—and then the fact that there were ten to fifteen insurgents involved, this was my assessment based on reporting throughout the day and the fact that this was—this was pretty robust for the insurgents to mount this type of an attack that could involve a squad size to start off the day and then—and then, you know, additional personnel throughout the city planting IEDs, conducting small-arms fire ambushes, and so forth.

Q: Now you have listed here "interaction of the populace M&I approach." What is that?

A: That's a—that—it's a couple of things, you know. The—the fact that they interacted with the locals significantly when they were driving south in the blue sedan. They were yelling out the window, talking to individuals around the area, some follow-on propaganda that we received, and—and the—the way that they interacted with the population.

Q: And I forwarded to the next exhibit page 55 of 156; and what does this depict?

A: This was my assessed enemy course of action. What I was trying to do for the Commander was to paint a picture of how the enemy executed this attack city-wide. A US Air Force Predator Unmanned Aerial Vehicle orbiting the area subsequently launched a Hellfire missile attack on fleeing insurgents running through the palm grove. Other insurgents were tracked for more than four hours as they moved from house to house trying to escape the battlefield.

The press knew nothing of Dinsmore's intelligence brief. Who needed to know is still a secret.

OFFICIALLY, BAGHDAD STAYED mum. Without some pushback from the Marine Corps to defend its own, there was no reason for the skeptical press to presume they were being fed the truth by the defendants. The war's critics quickly called the incident a "second My Lai," a putative reference to the horrific slaughter in Vietnam perpetrated by American soldiers in southern I Corps during the Vietnam War.

"The killing of Iraqi civilians at Haditha has often been referred to as a modern-day My Lai. The name is shorthand for slaughter of the defenseless, the benchmark of American wartime atrocity," thundered the BBC.[5]

Sharratt's lead defense attorney, Gary Meyers, said anyone who compares the two events is a fool. Four decades earlier, Meyers successfully defended a soldier allegedly complicit in the mass murders at My Lai while a captain in the US Army JAG Corps. The unwarranted comparisons angered Meyers, anxious to keep the Haditha incident in perspective.

"From our perspective—from a legal perspective—we knew it was a kinetic event," said Meyers. "We knew enough to present to the IO [investigating officer] that this was not an isolated event; that the entire city was in a kinetic state that day. Anyone who tries to compare this event to My Lai is an absolute fool."

The thirteen HET Draft Information Intelligence Reports (DIIRs) Bargewell footnoted without further interest were prepared by members of an HET identified as HET03. Marine HET units investigate and record local intelligence-worthy activities for interpretation and consumption by intel officers trying to understand the enemy's tactics, techniques, and procedures (TTP) as well as divine their intentions. Grayson's HET was instrumental to guiding Chessani's thinking, he said. Grayson's intelligence Marines were "critical to the success" of 3/1 locating hundreds of weapons caches around Haditha. His job was identifying what was important for Chessani, Carrasco, and Dinsmore to hear.

It was all about intuition and sound reasoning, Dinsmore said. After Grayson obtained the information, Dinsmore decided how to exploit it. Chessani said the mustang officer who considered Force Recon his second home was considered by his peers to be among the best intelligence officers they had ever worked with.

The DIIRs named five other insurgents involved in setting up the IED that killed Terrazas. One of them, Majid Salah Mahdi Farraji, was killed when Marine Corps F18s bombed the so-called "safe house" where the battle eventually migrated to after the initial IED ambush fractured Wuterich's squad. Several more insurgents were killed or captured in December and January.

HET reported the plan concocted to peddle an inflammatory video to Western reporters was prepared in Ramadi sometime in late December 2005. Thabet and Ali Omar began pitching the story to the Western media pool in Baghdad soon after. Their job was selling martyrdom, Faraj says. He surmised that in the twisted logic of the Salafi religious zealots the deaths of innocents was morally sound because their unfortunate passage brought them closer to God. Somehow, McGirk never said exactly how, he obtained a copy of the inflammatory video from Thabet.

The videotape Thabet offered revealed only one side of two wars going on at Haditha. It showed nothing of the internecine war between the Shia and Sunnis to fill the vacuum left by Saddam's departure. Both struggles were piling up civilian corpses like cordwood. The Haditha victims were very much a part of that struggle, Faraj said.

McGirk's gullibility is understandable. US-led forces were killing enough insurgents and civilians from both camps to make the reporters wonder who the United States was saving from Saddam. Faraj says Iraqi culture is revenge driven, an eye for an eye. Once the Coalition started killing Iraqis to save them from the insurgency, they unleashed a monster. Faraj wonders if McGirk ever knew.

McGirk never revealed why he always believed two Iraqis rather than going to Haditha and discovering for himself. Third Battalion, First Marines offered to provide him everything he needed to visit the battalion. Dinsmore said his allegations were serious enough that the Marines were prepared to accommodate him however he chose to arrive. He was still refusing their offers for a candid briefing and interview when the pretrial investigations began almost two years later. Then he refused to appear at Camp Pendleton after being subpoenaed.

It is doubtful he was afraid. McGirk bravely interviewed Taliban leaders in Afghanistan for *TIME* on Thanksgiving Day 2001, just seven weeks after the World Trade Center collapsed in New York City.

"There was a genuine Thanksgiving glow about the meal," McGirk said of his holiday repartee with a local Taliban chieftain. "I leave thinking that maybe this evening wasn't very different from the original Thanksgiving: people from two warring cultures sharing a meal together and realizing, briefly, that we're not so different after all."

Perhaps his sympathetic description of the men who harbored Osama bin Laden and the jackals that helped him bring down the World Trade Center made him seem particularly appealing to the insurgency. Since his massacre story began unraveling, McGirk has refused to explain. Seven years later, McGirk declined a January 22, 2012, email request for an interview with *Defend Our Marines*, but stated that he wanted to set a few points straight:

A photographer, an Iraqi translator and myself had made arrangements through the military to go to the Marine base at Haditha. Two days before we were supposed to leave on the embed, an ABC reporter was shot in the head by a sniper in Baghdad, and there was a general lock-down on press movements by media organizations in Iraq. My editor in NY, Jim Kelly, ordered me not to go to Haditha. It was as simple as that.[6]

McGirk was telling a more involved story in June 2006. That's when McGirk told *Columbia Journalism Review* reporter Paul McLeary: "I just know in my case that we deliberately got all of our facts together, and then and only then did we go to the military," he said. "We held off on reporting it until we could get their side of the story. So, I don't think we were in any great rush to accuse them of a massacre."[7]

Whatever the reason for his decision to hear only one side, McGirk's intransigence had one unintended consequence. It gave the insurgency its biggest counterintelligence coup of the Iraq War.

The Marine Corps could have revealed immediately what it knew about the two supposed human-rights workers. It already knew quite a bit. Ali Omar was the best known of the two rogues, having spent five and a half months as the Marine Corps's guest at Abu Ghraib. His thirty-six-year-old partner, according to *TIME*, was merely a "budding journalist" with a video camera. The Marines claimed he also had access to the black heart of the insurgency. What else, they frequently speculated, could explain his unmolested ability to record the victims' bloodied corpses? Apparently, the foreign fighter's penchant for killing journalists for being CIA spies did not include budding reporters.

Dinsmore believes the pair had anticipated that their agitation would help fuel some local antagonisms that would gain the insurgency a few more recruits. Recruiting new bodies during wartime is tough duty no matter what side of the fence one is leaning toward. Their success was all the more remarkable because *TIME*, an august body among the world's news journals, produced a story in which the reporter never personally went to the scene of the alleged crimes. Usually, journals of record—especially those with international reputations—insist on close scrutiny and multiple sources to verify the veracity of controversial news reports, particularly one so damning that it damages national will.

When the world press got hold of the story, critics of the conflict used the gruesome deaths of the innocents at Haditha to underscore the Americans' vicious execution of the war. By October 2005 the United States admitted at least thirty thousand civilians had died in Iraq since Operation Iraqi Freedom was launched. The reporters weren't exaggerating the US military's penchant for indiscriminately using overwhelming firepower when it suited its purpose. The muted voices from the warrior caste who tried inexpertly to separate warfare from morality asked, "Isn't that the point?" That is what the Marine Corps is trained to do and what the Pentagon spent billions of dollars making sure it could do. The American taxpayer received what it paid for.

ON JUNE 12, 2006, *TIME* declared the Gordian knot hanging over Haditha was cut. McGirk, Michael Duffy, and Bobby Ghosh wrote a follow-up piece entitled "The Ghosts of Haditha." Their condemnation was swift and uncompromising:

"The criminal investigation, which will probably produce charges against Marines for committing slayings, is expected to extend into the summer," *TIME*'s report declared.

The Marine Corps once again declined comment.

A sidebar by Jeffrey Kluger confided that *TIME*'s investigation was conducted by email with "more than a dozen witnesses," including the Haditha mayor, the morgue doctor, and a local attorney, who negotiated obtaining compensation for some of the victims. McGirk couldn't go himself because "travel between Baghdad and Haditha was extremely dangerous for Iraqis, let alone foreign journalists." There was no mention of what the Marines faced every day.

What else could it be but My Lai all over again? the pundits cried.

For more than a year after the My Lai analogies inevitably appeared, the Marine Corps resisted revealing what it knew about Ali Omar and Thabet's insidious work. Dinsmore said the Corps was reluctant to disclose its highly classified signals-intercept capabilities. Some word leaked out, but it was ignored. This writer provided direct links to indisputable sources willing to talk to reporters at the *New York Times* and *Washington Post* without obtaining any interest. In the meantime, young Marines who thought they were doing their duty were paying a fearsome price. On March 12, a week before McGirk's first story broke, and ten weeks after McGirk initiated his "investigation" in Iraq, somebody whispered to him the Marine Corps had turned the matter over to NCIS for criminal investigation. McGirk revealed the previously undisclosed inquiry in his March 19, 2006, magazine account: "Lieut. Colonel Michelle Martin-Hing, spokeswoman for the Multi-National Force–Iraq, told *TIME* the involvement of the NCIS does not mean that a crime occurred."[8]

Despite Martin-Hing's pronouncement, McGirk's reporting remained a searing indictment of the Marines' actions. The magazine's implication was that the whole situation was nothing but a giant cover-up.

Apparently unaware that Pool had intentionally misreported the facts, McGirk claimed that "after *TIME* presented military officials in Baghdad with the Iraqis' accounts of the Marines' actions, the United States opened its own investigation, interviewing twenty-eight people, including the Marines, the families of the victims, and local doctors." Only then, he said, did the Marine officers looking into the matter discover that the "the fifteen civilians killed on November 19 died at the hands of the Marines, not the insurgents."

The *TIME* account claimed the investigation of events showed that the civilians who died at Haditha were slaughtered:

"The military's own reconstruction of events . . . paint a picture of a devastatingly violent response by a group of US troops who had lost one of their own to a deadly insurgent attack and believed they were under fire."

Perhaps coincidentally, on December 21, 2006, the day criminal indictments and charges were announced against Wuterich, Colonel

Stewart Navarre (chief of staff, Marine Corps Installations West) made the following statement about what *really* happened at Haditha:

> On the morning of 19 November 2005, a four vehicle convoy of Marines from Kilo Company, 3rd Battalion, 1st Marine Regiment, 1st Marine Division was moving through Haditha when it was ambushed by insurgents employing an improvised explosive device and small arms fire.
>
> One Marine was killed and two were wounded by the explosion. Over the next several hours, 24 Iraqi men, women and children died in the vicinity of the IED explosion.
>
> On 20 November 2005, 2nd Marine Division issued a press release stating that 15 Iraqi civilians were killed in an IED explosion, and Marines and Iraqi Army soldiers killed eight insurgents in a follow-on fire-fight.
>
> We now know with certainty the press release was incorrect, and that none of the civilians were killed by the IED explosion.[9]

ENTER MURTHA

By the end of April both political and public pressure to hold a thorough investigation had grown exponentially. In Washington, the first rumblings from Democrats were rolling off the Hill, reverberating off the Pentagon before stirring pundits to notice they had a story with galloping legs. Democratic Representative John "Jack" Murtha of Pennsylvania was already getting some inside scoop on the story. His chief political advisor was married to an NCIS agent stationed at its headquarters in DC.

President Bush was vulnerable to all the allegations of war crimes and misconduct that seemed to be heating up Washington. Murtha was just the guy to fan the flames. He was a retired Marine reserve colonel with two Bronze Stars and two Purple Hearts, as well as an important seat on the House Appropriations Defense Subcommittee. His hands were never far away from the military's purse strings and the Marine Corps knew it.

Very soon the NCIS investigator's "secret" findings would ooze into the office of the eighteen-term Congressman from Pennsylvania. Using the incomplete findings by NCIS special agents still grilling Third Platoon's Marines at the bottom of Haditha Dam, Murtha went to work. His information was just the sort of evidence Democrats had been looking for to bash President Bush over the head. The war was going poorly, and the Democrats were looking for traction riding on his failed war policies. The incident at Haditha presented the perfect opportunity to get some.

In May, Murtha declared that the Marines had killed the Iraqis in cold blood. He had proof, he claimed on several television news shows. Not only did *TIME* magazine say so, no less than the USMC commandant Gen Michael W. Hagee had told Murtha so in a personal briefing. Murtha quickly hedged on his first grandiose claims when an aide to Gen Hagee declared Murtha's claim wasn't true, but the damage was already done.

On December 21, 2006, the Marine Corps announced that eight Marines, four enlisted men and four officers, were being indicted for the alleged massacre at Haditha. Secretary of the Navy Donald Winter later revealed the Marine Corps initiated its investigation as a result of the hue and cry brought on by *TIME* magazine's reporting.

The real issue was whether the tactics employed by the Marines who counterattacked were within the spirit as well as the letter of the Laws of Land Warfare and the ROE. There was no question that innocent, helpless women and children had been gunned down. In the second house, the Marines cleared by fire an entire room full of innocents who were killed.

Their ugly deaths posed a serious problem. Without weapons of mass destruction, without a clear reason for staying in Iraq once Saddam's regime was destroyed, the CPA needed moral authority to have any legitimacy at all. Where was the United States going to find the moral authority for killing women and children, toddlers, infants, and a crippled old man? Faraj thinks prosecuting eight Marines was an easy way to regain some of it. The process that started with an insurgent IED killing a single Marine had reached all the way into the White House. No doubt the insurgents were saying it didn't get any better than that.

CHAPTER 7

WHAT THE MARINES SAID WHEN NOBODY WAS LISTENING

Third Platoon considered the convoy on Route Chestnut routine despite the IED ambushes, small-arms attacks, snipers, and vehicle-borne suicide bombers who liked to blow Marines to pieces.

In Iraq, the days and nights follow the rhythms of the countryside. When the four trucks left FB Sparta, the people in the houses lining Route Chestnut were still sleeping. The crack of dawn was a good time to move. The Iraqi population stoically suffered the soldiers and Marines who came into their neighborhoods to search for arms and nebulous "high-value" targets. There was nothing to prevent the Americans from romping through their homes with guns drawn at all hours of day and night looking for enemies.

The marauding forces were not there without purpose. Dinsmore's people were hearing of large numbers of new faces around. Dinsmore tells a story about the mayor of Haditha, a man who had already lost one son to the war. Although cordial, he had no use for the Americans. Dinsmore and Chessani believed he was cooperating with the insurgents. So did the HET and the intelligence community feeding MajGen Huck the big picture. So did Colonels Davis and Sokoloski.

The mayor asked Dinsmore what was in it for him to cooperate with Marines when cooperating was dangerous to his family's health. When the Americans could protect him he might reconsider what to do. In the meantime it was in Allah's hands.

Nothing happened on the way to the COP. Joe Haman, then twenty-one, was at the COP when the convoy arrived. He said it was 0700 when his buddy Terrazas drove up. Haman was a mortarman although he was pulling security along with the rest of the Weapons Platoon. Haman was wounded twice in Iraq during tours at Fallujah and Haditha. Even today, he still looks too young and wholesome to know what he knows. In 2010, Haman was shot eight times while earning Missouri's police Medal of Valor during his brief career as a Saint Louis police officer. It earned him a feature story in *Leatherneck* magazine called "Lucky Joe Haman: Hostile Fire Magnet." When the Humvees arrived, Haman's friend Terrazas was driving the high-back bringing up the rear of the convoy. He was looking forward to getting in a few minutes of good bullshit with T. J. before the convoy had to depart. The two Marines went way back, before Fallujah, before the war, when they were just nineteen-year-old kids.

The convoy stayed thirty minutes, just long enough to share a smoke and a few jokes. T. J.'s brief visit with Haman was the last conversation they had. As soon as the convoy reassembled, it departed the combat outpost north on Chestnut toward home, the former elementary school Marines called FB Sparta. Being an infantryman is all about shitty missions and convoys and outposts and ambushes. Nobody seemed too bothered by the day, Haman said. It was just another bite out of the same shit sandwich.

It changed quickly when the four-vehicle convoy was subjected to a "complex attack," a combined-arms, multidirectional assault. It was the kind of attack Dinsmore had briefed Chessani on two days before. The ambush was initiated by "the detonation of the IED and small-arms fire in the vicinity of Route Chestnut, Haditha, Iraq," the Marine Corps determined.

All Haman knew was that something really big had just gone bang. "I knew it was bad as soon as I heard it," he said.

His suspicions were confirmed seconds after the blast when a fire-fight erupted. Haman was hearing an exchange of rifle and automatic weapons fire from a group of houses about 150 feet south of the IED blast. He remembers that the firing didn't build up gradually the way meeting engagements usually do. "It was an ambush."

So many weapons were firing Haman couldn't distinguish between them, he said. There was a brief flurry of fire immediately after the ambush and then quiet that lasted a long time. Then the firing started up again. Haman heard the loud, sustained popping of "gunfire followed by grenade explosions," the signature of an assault.

Other Marines remember other things. Salinas remembers seeing several enemy rounds smack the ground at his feet while he ran to the rear of the convoy to help the wounded. Once there, he hunkered down beside the box of armor left intact when the IED blew the fourth vehicle apart. Still under fire, he crawled to Crossan, pinned in the debris. The trapped Marine was yelling for somebody to help T. J. Knowing T. J. was beyond help, Salinas crawled to Crossan and began pulling away a heavy piece of the truck that was pinning him to the road. "Doc" Whitt was right next to him. After dragging Crossan clear, he learned his buddy had lost two fingers. He was still looking for them when enemy bullets started striking around them. He saw a "tall man" about two hundred meters away so he took him under fire with his 40 mm M203 grenade launcher.

"People look awfully small at two hundred meters," he later observed.[1]

Mendoza reported having trouble getting out of the Humvee because the weight of the add-on armor overburdened the door hinges. It took several heavy shoves to get the door open, he later claimed.

Faraj said Mendoza's recollection was a very important bit of information for the defense. "The dumb shit was in the back of the high-back with the IAs [Iraqi Army soldiers]. Wuterich was the one that couldn't get his door open because of the armor," Faraj said. "That fact is important because that slight delay means Dela Cruz fired first, which led Wuterich to key off him for HI/HT and PID. In other words, Wuterich took appropriate action shooting at the five men because one of his Marines had engaged them as a target. It was his responsibility to see it through."

Simultaneously, the radio chatter picked up inside the rented COP. It was Wuterich's convoy calling for help. Haman wondered if T. J. and the other guys were all right. Then the firing abruptly slowed down, sporadic instead of sustained, then it stopped, Haman said.

Somebody at the IED site was telling FB Sparta there were casualties. The voice put out the casualty numbers, a number assigned to each Marine that identifies them if they are killed or wounded. Three numbers went out over the ether. The convoy was "hurt bad," Haman said.

Salinas said small arms fire immediately came at the stalled convoy from the south after the IED exploded. Salinas said he returned fire while he searched for Crossan's missing body parts. It was coming from the house later labeled House #1. He said it lasted until the Marines attacked the houses.

At the center of the convoy Wuterich was facing south. To his east Dela Cruz did the same thing. Both men recalled receiving heavy small-arms fire that dinged the road and whacked against the armor plates attached to the Humvees. One hundred meters away, the Iraqis in the white car simultaneously began climbing out. Dela Cruz shouted in bad Arabic for them to stop.

Wuterich took a knee and shot at and possibly hit all five Iraqi men by the white car. He always claimed he did.

"He probably did not hit all five men," Faraj argues. "When Dela Cruz and Wuterich engaged almost simultaneously, the men would have naturally taken cover or run away as they were reported to have done. Imagine that, running away when you're getting shot at!

"Anyway, because Wuterich was positioned to the south of the vehicle when they ducked and began to run, Wuterich would not have been able to observe them as well. Dela Cruz would have had no problem.

"NCIS special agents, including Maloney and the Air Force Medical Examiner, Dr. Elizabeth A. Rouse, MD, confirmed at least three of the men were shot from a northern firing position while the two others could have been shot from either position. If Dela Cruz is to be believed they were standing around with their hands either on their heads or up in the air when he began killing them. If Wuterich is to be believed the men began running."

Several Marines testified that Dela Cruz yelled "*Qif! Qif!*"—stop-stop—when the men began to flee. Wuterich revealed immediately taking a knee and firing until the fleeing Iraqis disappeared behind the white car. By the time they hit the ground Dela Cruz was on them, giving each body a "dead check." Then he urinated on the broken skull of one of the victims. The bodies lay there in an uneven row the rest of the day.

Forensic experts later discovered the men were not dead when Dela Cruz provided dead checks. All the men had stippling on their faces. Stippling is what forensic scientists call powder burn tattooing on the skin of someone who bleeds after being shot at close range. The reddish brown tattooing means the victims were alive when shot. Dead men don't bleed. The five men dead checked by Dela Cruz all had reddish-brown stippling on their faces. Even so, dead checks aren't necessarily a crime, particularly during close, intense combat.

Haman heard on the radio that the QRF from Sparta was on the way. That got his squad leader's attention, he said. Their squad was on alert to move out in case reinforcements were called.

"As soon as it [the IED] went off Sgt Raphael, our squad leader, told us to gear up and standby. Our squad was on React because we already had another squad on patrol from the COP," Haman recalled.

React is shorthand for reaction force. Haman's job that day was to be ready to deploy immediately with the rest of his squad for backup if they were called. At about 0745 3/1 Intel hand-launched a Dragon Eye remotely piloted vehicle, a little radio-controlled spy plane, from FB Sparta, Dinsmore said. It showed that in the palm groves north and east of the ambush site, insurgents were gathering under the trees in small groups.

In the moments that followed, Marines inside the Combat Operations Center (COC) dispatched an EOD team from the firm base to find out exactly what had happened to Wuterich's convoy. About the same time, Captain McConnell, Kilo's commander, and the React Squad led by Wolf headed toward Route Chestnut on foot. It was about a mile march. Simultaneously, the EOD team was hit by small-arms fire while still a kilometer away from the ambush site. Before it could get moving, another Kilo platoon discovered yet another IED on the River Road. That slowed everybody down for a time. The EOD team dispatched to check out Wuterich's situation would eventually arrive at Route Chestnut without taking any casualties.

The EOD experts determined the device on Chestnut that killed Terrazas was made with two pressurized propane tanks full of compressed propane gas and an explosive triggered by a remotely detonated electrical fuse.

Whoever had placed the IED in a hole covered it with cleverly applied concrete to hide the device. Nobody living nearby noticed. The Marines couldn't understand how that was possible. The deadly handiwork was done in plain view of the neighborhood.

Later on, the little girl who survived the onslaught at House #1 told a CNN television reporter she knew the bomb was going to go when the Marines drove by so she covered her ears. Nobody ever asked her how she knew.[2]

Marines are trained to look for IEDs. The danger keeps them hypersensitive to their existence. Mines and booby traps have a psychological value even more powerful than the horrific explosions they make. They cause anxiety that translates into indecision, and indecision takes precious seconds away from applying the correct response. Conversely, knowing IEDs were around provided a strong incentive for Kilo's Marines to remain situationally aware. That this IED went unnoticed when two other were discovered the same morning by other Kilo Marines is testament to the bomber's skill and cunning.

The triggerman let two trucks drive over the bomb before it erupted. Wuterich had inexplicably chosen that moment to move his vehicle to the eastbound lane across a raised median. He later said it probably saved his life:

> Because our enemy goes to great lengths to exploit our patterns I chose to change our route to the traffic control point our company occupied. . . .
>
> As I made the turn on Chestnut, I decided to cross the two lane road and drive on the left side of the median. This was a decision, I'm sure, that saved the lives of the Marines in my vehicle. Vehicle four was not so lucky. An explosion louder than anything I have ever heard rocked the entire convoy. . . .
>
> The first thing I noticed outside my vehicle was a white, four-door sedan to the southwest. At this point, I realized my mission had changed. We had practiced this scenario before on white boards, in class rooms, in front of superiors, subordinates and peers. My training would take over from here. Some details of the events that occurred that day will always be vividly clear in my mind; other details will never be.

After the blast Wuterich did what Marine sergeants are supposed to do: he led the nine remaining uninjured Marines of First Squad into battle. The decisions he made would forever change his life.

THE MARINES DREW their first blood moments after the blast when Wuterich and Dela Cruz engaged and killed the five Iraqi males beside the small white Opel sedan. It proved to be a fateful incident

that cast suspicion on every subsequent action taken by the embattled Marines. From a grunt's perspective, however, their deaths
made perfect sense. Military-aged males in Iraq were a threat cate-
gory. They raised a palpable level of suspicion in Marines taught to
consider every potential threat while evaluating their surroundings.
These guys had managed to climb to the pinnacle of provocation
merely by passing by.

Marines going to Iraq in 2005 were taught that military-aged Iraqi
males inside a fluid, one-hundred-meter imaginary line that marks
the security zone around an imperiled Marines' position are always
threats. According to the yellow ROE cards always in their pockets,
the five Iraqi males beside the small white Opel sedan were subject to
lawful deadly force. Their lives were forfeited for being in the wrong
place at the wrong time. It was an ugly truth that never changed until
the Americans withdrew from Iraq in 2012. At Haditha in 2005,
Iraqi cars and trucks were routinely ordered out of the way when the
Marines drove by. Sometimes people who failed to comply were shot
at. Occasionally, they died. Marines called it "lighting them up." The
practice didn't win many hearts and minds.

The Marine Corps brass tried to diminish the number of incidents where the Iraqis died unnecessarily. Marines in the field were
subjected to occasional lectures on the subject. Conversely, the young
Marines liked to brag about lighting them up. Recruits looked forward to the opportunity. It was part of the Camp Pendleton lexicon
in 2005.

Several news reports claimed four of the men in the car were students on the way to a technical college. The fifth victim was their cab
driver. To many Americans the veracity of their purpose was murky,
clouded by news reports that it was Saturday so the technical college
they were supposedly attending was closed for the weekend. When the
NCIS tried to find out for sure the locals shot at them.

Faraj says he knows why the five men were on the road.

"Iraq is a Muslim country. The weekend is Friday. When I lived
in Kuwait the first day of the week was Saturday, not Monday. The

hype about the technical school and Saturday classes was created by the ignorant investigators Daddy Kallop (Third Platoon leader 2ndLt William Kallop's wealthy father) hired to turn attention away from his son. I always found this stuff laughable. The men in the car were students. They were not insurgents. The fact that we know their names confirms that," Faraj says.

What was known for sure on November 19 was that five MAMs were ordered to the side of the road by Sharratt when their car approached too close to the little convoy. It was standard operating procedure. That put them inside the Marines' one-hundred-meter security perimeter and within triggering range of the IED. The clash of truths about their subsequent deaths erupted months after the shooting went down, when both Marines who probably killed them faced murder charges. In the instant the ambush occured there was no hesitation. The Marines simply lit them up.

Dela Cruz initially claimed when he ordered the passengers from the car in Arabic they inexplicably began running away. After being charged with murder he changed his mind, declaring they were standing with their hands on top of their heads outside the car. He explained he told the story about them running away to stave off investigators to protect his fellow Marines.

After he was granted testimonial immunity and his murder charges were dismissed he elected to testify against his former squad leader. In a hearing at Camp Pendleton in the summer of 2007, he said the Iraqi men were milling about, apparently curious about what had transpired.

In his third version of events, Dela Cruz laid all the blame for their deaths on Wuterich. During one investigatory hearing he claimed Wuterich gunned down the five unarmed men who were standing next to the car without provocation: "They were being nosy. They had their hands up looking around; they were being nosy, being curious. . . . I did not see them as a threat, they were just standing there," Dela Cruz explained to the hearing officer.

After Wuterich mowed them down, Dela Cruz said he shot them again just to make sure they were dead. Then he urinated on one.

The emotion of the moment made him do it, he claimed. Dela Cruz added that Wuterich later told him to lie and claim that the men were running away, behavior that justified killing them under the Marines' ROE. Pissing on them was his own idea, he said.

For allegedly telling Dela Cruz to lie after he had reported the Iraqis' deaths as lawful, Wuterich was charged with violating Article 134 for providing a false statement to the HET's Staff Sergeant Laughner about the circumstances of the Iraqis' deaths. Their verbal exchange the day of the skirmish was the basis of the charge. "Apparently Gannon and Sullivan decided that by not giving a full report to a staff sergeant who had nothing to do with Wuterich, he [Wuterich] was concealing the truth—conspiring to conceal the truth," Faraj explained.

Wuterich always maintained the five Iraqi men in the white car stopped by Sharratt posed a threat to the convoy. Running away merely amplified the apparent danger: that was underscored when they attempted to run away after the IED blast.

> I remember encountering no vehicle traffic or foot traffic that morning leading up to the IED detonation. The white, four door sedan was parked on the side of the road within 100 m (meters) of the IED attack, and within the security parameters of our convoy. I heard yelling mostly from the west where Cpl Dela Cruz was shouting in broken Arabic and using expletives to the military aged males who occupied the white car. His weapon was at the ready, as it should have been. They were not complying and in fact were starting to run in the opposite direction to the south away from where Cpl Dela Cruz was approaching them. I took a knee in the road and fired. Engaging was the only choice. The threat had to be neutralized. Vehicle-borne IEDs were a serious threat and would have incapacitated our squad making us combat ineffective. I don't remember anyone else firing at the same time I was, although at a squad debrief later on I learned that Cpl Dela Cruz had engaged the men at the car at the same time as I did and Cpl Salinas reported that he had opened fire, as well.

After I watched the military aged males fall to the ground, Cpl Dela Cruz advanced on them and I saw him fire at the bodies as they lay before I turned to make my way to the casualties. That is when I started hearing small arms fire from the south.

Kallop, the first officer to arrive on the scene, later told Col Watt:

I then walked to their (Wuterich/Dela Cruz) position where there was a white four door sedan with the doors open and four dead MAMs a few meters to its south. I asked Cpl Salinas what had happened and he told me that they had been parked on the side of the road before the IED had detonated, they had stayed and observed after the IED had detonated and while the Marines had tried to cordon the area and that when Marines showed their weapons and yelled at the MAMs in the car to get out so they could detain them they opened the doors and attempted to run away . . . failed to comply with the Marine's directions so they had been shot.

When Kallop arrived, Crossan was still pinned under the wheel of the destroyed vehicle. Salinas said bullets were splattering against the armor of the high back. Crossan was going into shock. His eyes were dilated, rolling around in his head. He kept repeating over and over, "How's T. J.? Is T. J. okay?"

Tatum told him that Terrazas was fine.

Meanwhile Graviss was growing increasingly agitated because the COC couldn't understand him. They kept asking for the same information over and over. Wuterich took over the radio:

Remaining calm, I grabbed the radio from him and conveyed the information the COC requested which included a typical CASEVAC report stating the administration number of the wounded and killed, the priority of the casualties, along with the triage that was being administered by Doc Whitt.

Kallop's QRF arrived on Route Chestnut from FB Sparta at about 0745. Its primary mission was to secure the convoy site and transport Crossan and Guzman to the Battalion Aid Station for medical care.

Guzman, although injured, urged Doc Whitt to take care of Crossan. Guzman helped Tatum and the others pull off the debris covering Crossan and then lay down on the road. He pointed his weapon down range to provide security.

After the explosion on Route Chestnut, the situation at FB Sparta became frenetic. Wolf, the Second Squad leader, was lying in his rack when the explosion occurred. He went to the floor. Wolf was a savvy Marine who didn't take chances. He had already seen too many Marines die.

When the fire slackened Wolf immediately went to the COC. He arrived in time to see the first QRF, led by Corporal Sanchez, preparing to leave with Kallop. The QRF left by 0720 and probably arrived at Route Chestnut no later than 0745. It was designated Spartan 1/1.

Approximately fifteen minutes after the explosion, Wolf led Second Squad on a foot patrol to the IED site. They were accompanied by McConnell and Laughner, the counterintelligence specialist detailed to Kilo. Laughner worked for intelligence officer First Lieutenant Andrew Grayson.

Wolf said he could hear AK-47 and M16 fire coming from the area. Several times along the patrol to Route Chestnut Sgt Wolf ordered his squad to cover when 7.62 rounds from Kalashnikov assault rifles and a heavier Dragunov sniper rifle split the air. At one point, Laughner reported he saw enemy rounds striking the ground one hundred meters to their front. The fire was probably coming from his east—the area to the north of Chestnut. Heading to the sound of the guns, Wolf and some other Marines killed two armed Iraqi men in track suits who'd been shooting at them. Both of their weapons were recovered. Because of that skirmish it took Wolf's squad more than an hour to arrive at Wuterich's position. By then the reported insurgent shooters had apparently fled.

The Marine Corps later determined the complex attack consisted of two main elements. The first element was the engagement against Wuterich's First Squad on Route Chestnut. The second element consisted of a small-arms attack on the Marines and EOD personnel who were responding to another IED found about 1,500 meters away on the frequently used River Road. It was the first of two IEDs that would be discovered in the thick palm groves adjacent to the Euphrates River. Insurgent activity recorded on UAV video showed numerous insurgent cells arming up in the palm groves as well.[3]

Because of the obvious insurgent activity in the vicinity of Chestnut, another squad, Kilo's First Squad, First Platoon (Spartan 1/1), was deployed to set up a blocking position at the intersection of Routes Viper and Chestnut. While moving south on River Road, that squad was delayed by another surface-laid IED. While removing it, they also took ineffective long-range small arms that lent more credence to the Marines' assertion the incident on Chestnut was merely the opening round in the daylong battle.

Wuterich reported to his platoon leader as soon as he arrived:

> The next thing I remember was the QRF arriving on scene. Lt Kallop was the first Marine I met from the QRF and I began to present an informal situation report to him. I remember his main focus was on the WIAs (Wounded in Action). I provided him that information and showed him our KIA (Killed in Action), LCpl Terrazas.

On that particular morning, Kallop was in charge of supervising company working parties and organizing the administrative convoys such as the one Wuterich was carrying out. Kallop had the added responsibility of leading one of the QRFs always standing by to reinforce any of the company's far-flung elements needing help.

The night before Kallop had received orders to send a resupply convoy to the COP at Banir Dahir with an Iraqi relief force for the traffic control point as well as to deliver new radio codes to the platoon pulling COP duty there. Implicit in the order was a standing directive to make sure Wuterich presented a patrol plan. The Marine Corps does not rashly enter into threat situations. It proved to be the correct course of action.

Kallop had just finished his overnight shift in the COC when he heard the news that Wuterich's squad was under attack:

> I had been on duty for the night and was in the process of conducting changeover with my platoon sergeant, Staff Sergeant Fields. I was filling him in on the events of the night when we heard a large explosion outside. There was a few second delay before we heard [Wuterich make] the call for the QRF on the radio.

On February 21, 2006, Kallop told Watt what happened next:

> I heard Spartan 3/1 [Wuterich] say something along the lines of, "IED, IED, we need QRF on Chestnut." . . . 3/1 had one urgent and two routine casualties that needed to be evacuated to LZ Bull [where the battalion aid station was located].

The QRF was on the move almost immediately. While Kallop geared up and moved to the standby vehicles, Sanchez briefed his fire teams. The convoy drove south on Route Leopard toward Route Chestnut as fast as it could move. Kallop later told Watt:

> At that time I did not know that anyone had been killed and remember thinking we were lucky. Spartan 3/1's radio traffic was reporting the vehicle that had been hit was destroyed. . . . [Wuterich] told me that more had been small arms fire from the north directly after the IED but not anymore and that the rear [fourth] vehicle had been hit.

Kallop took Wuterich's situation report before moving to help Crossan. About then he heard small arms fire snapping past his head. It was coming from the south side of Route Chestnut. About the same time, Cpl Sanchez told him to take cover as the rounds were very close. Kallop moved with Wuterich to a more secure location behind the destroyed Humvee. During that conversation, Salinas reported to Kallop that a possible insurgent was turkey peeking from behind cover near House

#1. Kallop ordered the veteran grenadier to fire a 40 mm grenade from his M203. It exploded harmlessly about twenty feet short of the Iraqi man. Kallop told Watt what happened next:

> I looked out to the south and identified where the rounds were coming from with Sergeant Wuterich. They were coming from a house that was across a wadi on the south side of the road and a little to our west. I could see movement and hear the rounds cracking around me so I pointed at the house and told Staff Sergeant Wuterich to clear south to the enemy and that I would be there as soon as the casualties were away safe.

Wuterich gathered a team of Marines to "clear south," fateful, haunting words Wuterich correctly interpreted to mean assault and eliminate the threat. Wuterich later testified what happened next:

> While still receiving small arms fire, Cpl Salinas directed Lt Kallop to take cover and get down, Cpl Salinas and I then advised Lt Kallop that we were taking fire from a house to the south and we needed to assault that house. Lt Kallop agreed and gave us the order to clear south. Cpl Salinas then commenced suppressive fire on the house using his M203 grenade launcher firing high explosive rounds into the structure. I watched at least three impacts detonate on the upper portion of the house with minimal to no damage.

After radioing a situation report (sitrep) to the COC—including a notation that the Marines were taking small-arms fire from the south—Kallop asked for more reinforcements. Then he joined Wuterich's forming assault group and headed south. About halfway there he was stopped by Graviss, who told him he had found a possible trigger house on the north side of the road. Leaving Wuterich to lead the clearing operation alone, Kallop followed Graviss to the likely IED trigger house. On the way, he told Lance Corporal Rodriguez to detain every MAM around for questioning. Behind him Wuterich was assaulting the house:

I also saw Sergeant Wuterich's team breach the house. LCpl Sharratt had a M240G dismounted and was suppressing the house as the stack closed with it. I lost sight of my team after they rounded a wall and LCpl Sharratt ceased fire and moved in with the team.

"At the time, I didn't see any insurgents. I didn't see any bad guys," Kallop would later testify.

SHARRATT REFUTED KALLOP'S claim, testifying he never fired his M240G until after House #1 and House #2 were cleared the first time. Meanwhile Wuterich's squad was still taking fire. The bulk of it seemed to be coming from an area about two hundred meters southwest of the destroyed fourth vehicle, he said. They headed south toward two adjacent houses where the fire originated from south and west of their position. To reach the houses they had to cross the depression and then navigate a small hill. There was very little cover beside the natural lay of the land.

Sharratt, claiming he was still on overwatch in his vehicle's armored turret, tells a different story. He says he looked back from his security post in his Humvee in time to see Salinas and Mendoza running south up the hill. Thinking they were alone, he decided to give them a hand with his M240. When Sharratt started down the hill, he saw Wuterich and Tatum near the top of the rise, getting ready to assault the house. He insists he never fired his weapon until he shot the lock off the third house the fire team searched. Sharratt later explained:

> I decided to dismount the 240 Gulf from the turret because it was only two Marines; and I wanted to bring more firepower to the table, plus, my SAW and gear were below in the back seat of the vehicle. It was faster to grab the 240. I was also concerned that if I got separated from them while trying to catch up, I would need the extra firepower. I dismounted the 240 Gulf, I slung some rounds over my shoulder, and I jumped off the turret and started running down and back up the hill with the 240 Golf.

By the time Sharratt said he covered two hundred meters to House #1, Wuterich and his team had already cleared it and were inside the house next door—believing that they had taken additional fire from that building. Sharratt told Watt he stayed outside providing rear security and did not know there were civilians lying dead inside.

Kallop had a somewhat different recollection of events. He later told Watt:

> I left the house and started towards the road while calling another sitrep to Spartan Main when I heard more AK fire. I reported that to Spartan Main and began running to the south. About halfway I heard machine gun fire and knew that Sergeant Wuterich's team was suppressing so I called Spartan 4 at the TCP [traffic control point] and told them we were suppressing south and to hunker down as I ran south. By the time I got to the road, all firing had ceased. On the road there were about five detainees and an Iraqi Soldier was beating one with a stick. I took it away from him and yelled at him not to hit them, but to guard them and continued running across the wadi to our south, where I threw the stick, and linked up with Sergeant Wuterich. He told me that after clearing the first house there had been more enemy fire directed at him from the south so he had continued clearing in order to close with and destroy the enemy. I did not ask if they had gotten them because we were no longer receiving fire.

Wuterich had yet a different story, one in which he coined a phrase that will haunt the rest of his life:

> Small-arms fire had ceased and I and Cpl Salinas proceeded to assault that house. Simultaneously, Cpl Salinas directed the two closest squad members (LCpl Tatum and PFC Mendoza), to join us so we would have at least a fire team going into the assault. At some point previous to us departing, Lt Kallop directed me to give him my 148 [PRC-148 handheld radio] because he didn't have a radio with him at the time.

The four of us aggressively advanced on the house and on approach I advised the team something like shoot first and ask questions later or don't hesitate to shoot. I can't remember my exact words but I wanted them to understand that hesitation to shoot would only result in the four of us being killed.

Faraj thinks using such an innocuous phrase to lay the foundation for a criminal proceeding was ridiculous. "'Shoot first and ask questions later' encapsulates everything a grunt needs to know to survive in a MOUT environment. How else does one enter a hostile structure containing bad guys with guns aimed at the door of entry? Telling a trained infantryman to shoot first and ask questions later is like reminding him to breathe in before breathing out."

Gannon and Sullivan used Wuterich's statement to prove he had murder on his mind when he sent his fire team into action. Faraj says prosecutor Major Darren Erickson, who had also been an enlisted man and a grunt, found the focus on the statement laughable and lamentable. He encouraged his bosses to let the case go. The actions of the squad made tactical sense to him, although the results were tragic. Nonetheless, there was no crime here; it was war. No one listened.

In the end, the phrase turned into a get out of jail free card, but nobody could have guessed it at the time. Whatever he might have said, Wuterich was fixated on the war in front of him:

The exact details of clearing the first and second house will forever remain unclear to me. I'll never be able to pinpoint exact shooting positions, exact chronology of events, who was where and when, or even what the exact layout of the houses were. What I do know is that we cleared those houses as we were trained using forced entry, grenade employment, followed with clearing by fire.

Tatum kept a clearer head. He said he knew exactly what he had been doing when they cleared the first two houses. Tatum had lived through trial by fire at the Hell House and reacted accordingly, automatically stacking with Wuterich and Mendoza when they entered House #1. His adrenaline was pumping from the small-arms fire "he knew" was coming from the south. His attention was drawn there by the explosion of the 40 mm grenades Cpl Salinas fired, he said.

Just before they jumped off to clear the house, Wuterich told him to treat the building as hostile, he testified during Wuterich's court-martial. Tatum knew what that meant; everybody inside was going in the hurt locker. They were going in hot, grenades first, then bursts of automatic weapons fire aimed low . . . center mass . . . take out anyone still standing. MOUT!

One of his buddies told NCIS that Tatum said he thought the war should be fought like in biblical stories when everyone was put to the sword. Tatum said he moved in like it was a textbook exercise, just like he had trained for a thousand times.

After entering the first house through a kitchen, he testified he heard what he believed was an AK-47 rifle being racked from around a corner. Salinas and he each tossed a grenade into the room but only one of them exploded. The information was pulled from him by NCIS investigators during a vicious interrogation in a Haditha Dam dungeon three months later.

After lawyering up, Tatum let his $50,000-and-counting civilian lawyer do the talking. His Houston attorney, Jack Zimmermann, reconstructed his complete statement for the press. Tatum never again uttered a public word until Wuterich's court-martial. Zimmermann is a former combat Marine and a very sly guy, a fox of a Texas lawyer in the tradition of Percy Foreman and "Racehorse" Haynes. His sanitized version of events was intended to clear Tatum rather than the air:

I heard a Marine engage a target after entering the house, and I knew Mendoza engaged a target to the right inside the house. I heard an AK-47 being racked in the room to the left, and me and Cpl Salinas threw grenades in that room. After the grenade went off, I went in and followed my training, firing in my sector.

The visibility was horrible. There was dust and smoke. I really couldn't make out more than targets. Someone yelled there was a runner, so I followed my fire team to House #2.

Before we entered, Mendoza engaged someone through the door. Inside, I was told to frag a room. When I saw that room was clear, I heard another Marine engage in the next room. My duty was to help that Marine, so I went in and engaged targets.

It was dark; I couldn't make out a whole lot. Just targets! I only went in each room a few steps, and the shooting lasted only seconds in both houses. . . .

I did not know there was women and children in that house until I went back later in the afternoon with SSgt Laughner. Otherwise, I would have physically stopped everybody from shooting.

Nine-year-old survivor Eman Hamed told investigators that a grenade landed near her grandfather's bed and exploded, sending shrapnel through the room. Her mother and four-year-old brother were killed as she huddled, injured, with another brother, Abid, six.

"All rooms," Abid told NCIS investigators. "They were shooting in all rooms."

Wuterich never denied the deadly assault occurred:

I remember that after clearing the bottom floor of the first house, a door that was leading south was open. Someone shouted, "There's a runner!" and we quickly exited that house and continued the assault to the second house directly south. We ran to the second house because it was the closest structure and the only place the runner could have gone.

We treated the second house the same as the first. After PFC Mendoza fired at the man at the door, the rest of the team flowed in. Again, we used grenades and cleared the rooms by fire.

After I felt the threat was neutralized and we were no longer being fired on, I took the team back within the security perimeter on Route Chestnut. Heading along Route Zebra, the team stopped twice to search unoccupied structures. Somewhere around the intersection of Zebra and Chestnut I received my radio back. At that time I transmitted back to the COC that we had finished clearing two houses and there may be collateral damage. I was asked to provide more details as far as a number of enemy vs. neutral KIAs. This was information I did not have at the time. I estimated fifteen KIAs and that was the extent of my report.

In his reconstructed statement, Tatum makes no mention of anyone from the squad returning to House #1 or #2 to secure it after the initial assault. If he is telling the truth, what happened inside the houses at Haditha was not an unfortunate accident, nor a lapse of moral judgment. Neither was it a conscious or unconscious slip in decency and compassion. What the Marines in First Squad did on November 19 was execute a textbook perfect assault on two fortified houses believed to be occupied by the enemy. They were merciless. It was both their defense and their crime.

The Marine Corps draws heavily on "lessons learned" to create its institutional memory. The lessons learned by the Marines in 3/1 at Fallujah the preceding year had already been incorporated into Marine Corps doctrine pounded into every Marine infantryman destined for combat in Iraq. It was part of the training Wuterich and Mendoza testified they received before they deployed. It was what Tatum and Sharratt had done at Fallujah, where men died for getting it wrong.

The lessons offered and learned during the house-to-house slaughter at Fallujah carried far more weight than merely being a footnote in the military experience of Tatum and Sharratt. Fallujah was a defining battle in Marine Corps history, a battle as fierce as any small unit action Marine infantrymen have encountered in the Corps's illustrious history. It created a new legion of inductees into the Marine Corps's sacred Pantheon of Heroes and another lesson in the lexicon of Marine Corps institutional thinking. The battalion's Marines practiced them continuously at 29 Palms and March Air Base MOUT training facilities until it was a part of their soul.

That training came into play in a terrible instant at House #1. If their story is to be believed, the attack was a classic example of the lessons learned. Their counterattack was quick, sharp, brutal, and efficient: stack up, cover, throw in a grenade, follow it up with a maelstrom of automatic weapons fire, and then on to the next room and next house to repeat the process until the area is cleared. Nothing was supposed to survive—that was the object of the exercise. The clearing operation moved so swiftly Sharratt claims he was still running across a two-hundred-meter space—roughly six hundred feet—when the clearing operation in House #2 was concluding. He said he heard rather than saw eight people die.

Sharratt's story had morphed remarkably between his pleasant conversation with Watt and his vicious confrontation with NCIS in March:

> I don't know exactly what happened in Houses #1 and #2, and I didn't witness with my own eyes what happened in those houses. I shot the lock off a third house that ended up being empty. And we cleared a fourth empty house as well. I remember then moving back up to Route Zebra towards Route Chestnut.

Kallop was also heading south. He told Watt he encountered the same Iraqi soldier beating another detainee. That was not all he discovered:

> Then [I] walked back toward the detonation site where the detainees were being staged and found the same Iraqi Soldier hitting a detainee with the stick that I had confiscated earlier. I confiscated the stick again and told LCpl Rodriguez and LCpl Tatum to make sure the IA didn't beat them anymore. . . .
>
> I walked back to Cpl Dela Cruz and LCpl Graviss's position. They had found a number of Jordanian passports, approximately fifteen, two cell phones (one of which had been disassembled), and a large amount of cash which according to them the woman had tried

to hide during the search. So I called the HET team (Sgt Laughner) and gave him the situation and began taking pictures of all the MAMs in the house with the items that had been found.

I left my camera with Cpl Dela Cruz to finish taking pictures and walked back to Chestnut. On my way there was another burst of AK fire directed at the Marines in the overwatch position, and I saw a MAM in all black running from behind one of the houses that had been cleared down into the wadi on the south of the road. Believing he had been the shooter I fired my weapon at him and when he disappeared into the wadi I directed the overwatch's fire onto him.

When I got to Chestnut I linked up with Corporal Salinas and told him to take me to the houses they had cleared. The first one we went to was the original one we had taken fire from and that I had pointed Sergeant Wuterich toward. Inside, we found a number of dead people in the family room in the back of the house, to include women and some children. I looked around the room searching for weapons when one of the children moved and I noticed that he and a little girl with him was still alive. I got them up and saw that they had been hit by shrapnel so I tried to get them to come outside to a corpsman but they would not go. At that point I decided that I had to keep going and that I would come back for them. Cpl Salinas took me to the next house to the south and as we began to make entry there was more gunfire on Chestnut. We bounded [move and cover] back toward the road when Spartan 3/2 [Third Squad, Second Platoon] told us that they were coming down from the north and to cease fire. I saw Sergeant Wuterich and LCpl Sharratt firing to the west on Chestnut and told them to cease fire because 3/2 was over there.

Wuterich stood his team down and waited for orders. Sharratt was still lugging the heavy M240G machine gun. He decided to put it back in his Humvee and grab his SAW. The 5.56 mm light machine gun is a lot smaller and quicker to use during close-in fights.

THE KILLING IN the two houses south of the wadi was all over before 0800. In the sanitized narratives ultimately introduced by the prosecution, there is no mention of anyone revisiting the houses a second time or Sharratt borrowing Whitt's pistol. If the Marine Corps's intent was truly to ensure the guilty were convicted of murder, it was a strange decision to make, several defense attorneys opined at the time. Murder charges were only applicable if the alleged shooter *knew* the occupants of the houses were noncombatants and intended to kill them anyway.

For the rest of the morning of November 19, several maneuvering Marine squads from Kilo Company were attacked by insurgents. Several hours of combat led to the final fighting of the day, a battle of such intensity the Marines used four five-hundred-pound bombs and at least four Hellfire missiles to obliterate the insurgent stronghold. That fight left ten Marines wounded, including the officer leading the patrol. The half-hour exchange of grenades among rooftops and doorways was captured on video by two orbiting drones. Later on, a carload of weapons was recovered next to the ruins of the building the insurgents had fortified. It was the same blue Mercedes that was videotaped delivering weapons and instructions in the palm groves by the orbiting Scan Eagle UAV.

First Squad could see the developing action from its OP. For most of the morning Wuterich and his Marines stayed at the house north of Route Chestnut. They had been there since 0815, when Kallop instructed Wuterich to establish the OP on the roof of a house near the IED site to keep an eye on a known "muj" house directly across the street.

According to Wuterich:

> My team then occupied an over watch position at the intersection of Chestnut and Viper. Within the next several hours we located and killed insurgents in a house north of our position and we killed another suspected insurgent fleeing from the scene along a ridgeline. We watched as rotary winged aircraft deployed Hellfires and dropped bombs on houses directly to our south. We remained on over watch for the majority of the rest of the day.

Wuterich, Salinas, Sharratt, and Rodriguez moved to the roof of the house and set up temporary positions, where they remained until Kallop ordered Rodriguez to accompany him to House #1. Tatum and Mendoza stayed put on the first floor. Mendoza was eventually ordered to take a radio to Dela Cruz, searching north of Chestnut where the IED triggerman was suspected of lying in wait. Mendoza's active role in the incident was over.

THE OTHER FIGHT

Dinsmore was still in the COC at FB Sparta monitoring the cata-pult-launched Scan Eagle unmanned aircraft deployed shortly after the IED triggered the explosion. The UAV belonged to the 1st Marine Air Group. Also in the air over Haditha was a super-secret USAF RQ-1 Predator medium-altitude, high-endurance UAV. The drone's capabil-ities included downlinks that allowed any interested senior officer in faraway Baghdad a real-time view of what was happening in Haditha if they cared to look.

Between 0830 and 0900, Dinsmore observed insurgents delivering weapons from a car in the vicinity of Route Chestnut and River Road. He continued monitoring the movement of the blue Mercedes sedan until they arrived at the so-called "safe house" near Route Zebra and River Road.

Also operating in the trees was a man on a motorcycle and at least two men in a truck circling the palm grove. The Marines believed they were contacting two- and three-man insurgent cells gathering under the cover of the date palms. Eventually, the truck stopped long enough for ten to fifteen insurgents to gather around it. They took weapons and ammunition from the bed of the truck before holding a "pep rally" and disappearing into the trees, Dinsmore later recalled.

Haman was still monitoring the radios inside the rented house his squad was using for their COP. It sat on a hill overlooking Route Chestnut with a good view of the surrounding countryside. It had thick walls and a flat roof with an outer wall offering a modicum of protection. It wasn't bad by contemporary standards.

The St. Louis native had served with Sharratt, Tatum, and Terrazas at Fallujah. He says that nobody ever asked him what his squad encountered during and after the ambush.

"As soon as it [the IED] went off, Sgt (later SSgt) Raphael—our squad leader—told us to gear up and standby. Our squad was on React because we already had another squad on patrol from the COP," Haman said. They didn't have long to wait to deploy, he added.

About thirty minutes after the IED went off, Haman's squad was called into action, he said. Meanwhile, orbiting helicopters and ground commanders filled the airwaves with urgent messages. Haman could hear the rotors *whapp*ing around the area. Occasionally, he would see a helicopter darting down low and then coming back up. They were looking for something. The Marines in the COP were anxious to get into the fight. They couldn't understand what the delay was all about, Haman said. A nearby helicopter reported to headquarters that a large group of insurgents were fleeing out the back of the small cluster of houses under counterattack by Wuterich's squad. The pilot spotted the insurgents when they abandoned the houses, Haman said. The pilot reported that some of the insurgents then peeled off from the main body, fleeing into another house situated by a palm grove about one or two hundred meters south of where Wuterich was engaged.

"Air—helos—saw insurgents that split into groups. One of the groups ran into another house in a palm grove. Air picked them up going in."[4]

That put the fleeing insurgents only eight hundred meters from the COP. Haman's squad was ordered to hunt them down.

Led by Lieutenant William Zall, the platoon leader, and Sergeant Raphael, the Marines ran toward the enemy position. It was only a two-minute run to reach the houses where the insurgents had disappeared, he said.

Haman's squad consisted of twelve Marines. Among them they had two 5.56 mm SAW light machine guns, two M203 40 mm grenade launchers mounted under M16s, and eight riflemen. Haman was armed with an M203-equipped rifle, he said. It is a lot of fire-power. In most places it would be an overwhelming amount of fire-power. In Haditha on November 19, 2005, it wasn't nearly enough, Haman said.

"Then one of the helos shot two missiles into the house. It blew out the roof, put a big hole in the roof, smoke was coming out. We were told to go into a house by a blue car. The car was parked between two houses. We didn't know which house was the right one."

Haman's squad chose the first one they came to. When they got to the front door it was eerily still. Except for the orbiting helicopters and the sporadic firefight going on to the north where Wuterich was fighting, it was deathly still, Haman said.

"The point man kicked in the door. LCpl Blankenship was on point. Cpl Bautista, my fire team leader, told us to stack up and go in. I was the second man to the door. I wanted to throw a frag. I had never thrown a frag into a house before."

Haman let one fly. The orbiting Scan Eagle captured the house fill-ing with smoke. Plaster and other debris rained down inside. Haman said it was almost impossible to see inside the building.

"Our squad leader Sgt Raphael told us to wait for the smoke to clear, but our adrenaline was pumped up so we just rushed in. We couldn't see anything so we turned our flashlights on. Nobody was in the house, the house was clear," Haman continued. "We were at the wrong house.

"Somebody said it was the house to the southwest—catty cor-ner. Lt Zall said to clear the other house but don't frag it this time. Blankenship tried to kick the door down. It knocked him down, he couldn't do it. So LCpl Ghent bashed into it a couple of times. He couldn't do it either."

Despite the danger, the Marines couldn't help laughing, Haman said.

"Everybody was laughing. The third time he [Ghent] knocked it in and fell down. I jumped over him. I saw a room to the right and one way in the back corner. The door was almost closed. Then a grenade came out the door. It bounced off my foot and went off," Haman said.

"I don't remember anything after that for a while. I was hit but I didn't know it," Haman added. "Somehow I was inside the room to my right. I don't know how I got there.

"Bautista called my name. I guess I woke up. I got up and started shooting at the door. We backed out of the house. It was one of the lessons we learned at Fallujah. When there is somebody inside, just back out and call in air strikes."

Still groggy, Haman backed out the door, firing his weapon down the hallway where the grenade came from, he said. For the moment there was no return fire and everybody made it safely back outside. But it was only a momentary respite, Haman said.

"LCpl Garcia and LCpl Vetor went to the side of the house. I saw them, so I went with them. I was still real groggy. It was an American grenade and it really rang my bell," Haman added with a laugh. "I thought I was okay."

"Then Vetor looked back and yelled 'grenade.' One blew up behind me. I got hit in my right back triceps and in the back shoulder. I knew it had hit and it burned a little. It didn't hurt until hours later. Then the hole in my underarm swelled up as big as a golf ball and I was bleeding out of it. Lt Zall got hit real bad. Zall got hit in the legs. He was evacuated and 'Doc,' our [US Navy Medical] corpsman, was wounded. LCpl Garcia got hit as well."

Zall and the corpsman were out of the fight. Haman and Garcia stayed in. Iraqi grenades were dropping off the roof of the house they had just retreated from. Meanwhile, the rest of Haman's squad backfilled into the first house the fire team had just cleared. They charged up onto the roof and started throwing grenades at the insurgents attacking Haman's group. Insurgent and Marine grenades were flying back and forth. Some of the grenades seemed to be coming from the windows and some from the roof of the house occupied by the insurgents. The fight was captured by aerial eyes.

"Vetor checked Garcia and me and said we were both good. Then an AK burst came in and sprayed in front of us in an arc. We thought it came out of the window so we started lighting up this window. Then we heard an explosion go off, maybe on top of the roof."

The explosion was a Marine's grenade bursting among the Iraqi insurgents.

Garcia, with Haman, was wounded and groggy. He wanted to throw a fragmentation grenade at the window of the house they were taking fire from. The dazed Marine didn't realize it was covered with steel bars. Haman told him to put the grenade away, he said.

"Then Garcia started complaining about his arm. He couldn't lift it. Then we heard explosions going off inside," Haman added.

Haman was getting alarmed. He still didn't know where several members of the squad were and grenades and automatic weapons fire from the insurgents who fled Wuterich's position was flooding the area. It was getting very dangerous to be outside. But it wasn't any better indoors.

"We kept yelling for LCpl Ghent, Cpl Bautista, and Sgt Raphael. We couldn't get a response from them. We could see the helos flying around. We didn't want to get a rocket. We didn't know where anyone was. Vetor said to pop the white flare to let them know where we were," Haman said.

About then they heard an M240, the successor to the Vietnam-era M60 that shoots 7.62 mm rounds at about 650 rounds a minute. The welcome sound told him reinforcements were arriving, Haman said.

"Somebody started lighting up the house with the two-forty. We popped a red star cluster [pop-up flare]. Then Bautista popped a green flare," Haman recalled.

Now everybody knew where all the members of the squad were located. It was time to get out of Dodge. The Marines decided to make a run for a dirt berm pushed up by a bulldozer on the other side of the road. Vetor popped his head around the corner to see if he would get shot at. There was no more firing so he started running down the street.

"He took off running first. I went second and then Garcia came. We wanted to run across the road to where there was some cover,"

Haman said. "Then a seven-tonner [cargo truck] or two pulled up and Marines started popping out. As soon as they saw us Sgt Raphael [on the roof of the house next door to the insurgents] started yelling for cover fire."

The Marine reinforcements jumped out of the trucks at a curve on the road where a dirt mound gave them cover, Haman said.

"They were in enfilade. They had cover about fifty meters [164 feet] away on the berm from where we were at.

"We regrouped and found out where everybody was. We saw the docs putting Lt Zall and our doc into either a seven-tonner or Humvee to medevac out. Then we ran back to a house across the street from the one the insurgents were throwing grenades from.

"Marines went to the top of the roof on the house and started shooting M203 grenades at the insurgents. I stayed inside the house with LCpl Stefinitis watching over the civilians who lived there. There were eight people. We got them all in one room while everybody else went on the roof to engage. I smoked a cigarette. I still didn't know [how bad] I was hit. Stefinitis was bleeding from grenade hits to his nose and face."

Six Marines were on the roof, Haman said. They included Lance Corporal Josh Karlen, from Colorado; Lance Corporal Bury, a Texan who was usually a radio operator in the headquarters section; Corporal Bautista; Raphael, the squad leader; and two other Kilo Company Marines.

"They got into another grenade fight. Grenades were flying all over the place. I think everyone on the roof got wounded. I know we had nine guys wounded in my squad," Haman said. He had been wounded twice.

"From then everything went to shit. We called for air. I stayed downstairs. I think I smoked a whole pack of cigarettes. They were up there fifteen to twenty minutes," Haman said.

"Then we all took off, jumped about a four-foot wall, ran down to the palm grove, climbed the hill, and went back to the house we used for the COP and waited for the air to hit. We waited fifteen to twenty minutes for air to get there. I think they dropped two five-hun-dred-pounders, but it could have been thousand-pounders. They blew the house all to hell," Haman added.

After the bombing, other Marines returned to the demolished house. Overhead, the Scan Eagle was watching. Inside the demol-ished house, they found five dead insurgents and a large arms cache. Two Iraqis who survived the bombing were captured inside the house. Another insurgent was tracked to a house down the street. Marines reported to the firm base that he quickly reappeared carrying a baby. Outside, an M1 tank was waiting. He surrendered. The man was still bleeding from his ears and nose from the concussion of the aerial bomb when he was taken into custody. Both Iraqis later admitted being insur-gents, the Marine Corps said.

After the fight was over, Haman discovered he was hit multiple times by grenade shrapnel. He got a few days off to tend to his wounds, and then he went back in the fight.

"That is the way they do it in the Corps," he said.

Back at FB Sparta, video was streaming in, showing the insurgents arming in the palm groves north and east of Wuterich's position. Other insurgents were heading toward a so-called "safe house" under attack by Weapons Platoon. It was less than a quarter-mile from Wuterich's position.

Dinsmore thought the insurgents were using the house in the cor-ner of Viper and Chestnut as the gathering place for insurgent rein-forcements being fed into the battle. He kept an ear on the radio and an eye on the video, relaying the information to the maneuvering Marines closing in on the safe house.

CHAPTER 8

HOUSE #4

The grenade fight Haman's fire team found itself emeshed in was just beginning when Wuterich's small assault force stood down at their overwatch position. At about 1030, Wuterich's team observed a Marine Corps Cobra attack helicopter launch Hellfire missiles on the muj house eight hundred meters away. The Cobras had been summoned by McConnell. Dinsmore watched the attack unfold. At least two missiles misfired before two successfully went through the roof into the two-story concrete structure. Except for a large hole in the roof and a lot of smoke, the missiles didn't appear to do much structural damage.

About thirty minutes later, Haman's squad reached the housing area. Almost immediately they began trading grenades with insurgents across several rooftops in the same area where 3/1's Scan Eagle was circling the damaged muj house. The attack began with Haman throwing a grenade into the first house they approached. A huge cloud of dust exploded out the windows and door. Unfortunately, it was the wrong house. Haman's squad continued on foot to the house across the street. The lieutenant ordered no more grenades. Almost immediately, they came under grenade and automatic weapons fire. Ten Marines—including Haman and the officer—would be wounded there before the insurgents were subdued by Marine attack bombers.

Kallop, meanwhile, was still circling his platoon's position ensuring that his Marines had adequately secured the ambush site. From radio reports he knew the insurgents were infiltrating into the area in small groups from the palm grove 1,500 meters to the northeast. Dinsmore was keeping track at battalion, moving around resources to meet the growing threat, keeping Chessani and McConnell abreast of the expanding battle area.

Kallop said he returned to the house where Dela Cruz and Graviss were collecting documents and equipment they suspected had been left behind by insurgents who fled. He used his radio to relay the find to Laughner before returning to Houses #1 and #2 to take pictures of the MAMs killed and captured.

For the next few minutes the situation was relatively quiet. Later, following the Hellfire attack, Wuterich's team noticed a small group of Iraqi men watching them. The Marines took a hard look of their own. Smart MAMs were usually the first locals to disappear.

About ten minutes after the Hellfires exploded, Wuterich decided to find out what the Iraqi men across the road were doing. His intent was simply to check them out, but the squad prepared for the worst anyway. It was not time to let down their guard.

Wuterich and Sharratt spent a few minutes watching an unarmed MAM boldly walking back and forth behind the gate that enclosed Houses #3 and #4, "just asking for trouble," Sharratt recounted. Additional men would periodically come outside, check out the Marines on the overwatch position, and then go back inside the house. Sharratt didn't like it. The Marines were always suspicious of military-age Iraqi males, especially inquisitive ones that stayed around after bloody confrontations. That kind of behavior was considered suspicious on its face. Sharratt told NCIS the Iraqis' curiosity alarmed him:

Sometime around then, we noticed some Iraqi males were look-ing over the wall in front of a house on Viper. This was suspicious because they would watch us and then duck away when they saw that we were watching. They did that several times. We had been waving at them to scare them off.

After a few minutes of them watching us, Corporal Salinas fired an M203 training round at the wall in front of the house. At that point, I saw two men leave the wall in front of House #4 and run back inside House #4.

After a few minutes, they started watching us again and would peek at us and run back inside. The turkey peeking caused us to have serious concerns. We had no idea if the Iraqi males were triggermen or lookouts for other insurgents. We were trained that under certain circumstances, turkey peeking, like what we were watching, could be considered hostile intent. We had no desire to hurt these men. And for that reason, we did not fire an HE at them. Eventually, our concerns for our safety was enough that we decided to go find out why they were watching us.[1]

Wuterich decided to approach the house and conduct a so-called knock-and-search investigation. Leaving their overwatch position, Wuterich, Salinas, and Sharratt entered the compound containing Houses #3 and #4 through the common gate of the courtyard surrounding both homes. Tatum stayed behind on overwatch.

Sharratt explained what happened next:

We walked down from the OP and began walking north on Viper towards this suspicious house. At first, I actually thought both houses were one. I went through the gate from house three and walked up to the front door. During both combat tours, I searched hundreds of houses. Haditha was a very dangerous place where we were trying to develop a relationship within the community.

When we went to house three, we did not know who was at that house other than the males that were observing us. When I walked up to the house, the front door was closed but not locked. When I entered the house, there were four or five adult women in the room and a couple of children. I don't remember seeing any adult males. I began searching several rooms. I remember Sgt Wuterich and Cpl Salinas talking to the women. The SOP is usually to ask in Arabic if there are any weapons. Then the SOP is to ask if there are any males around.

Sgt Wuterich asked several women and children standing in the door of House #3 where the men were who had been watching them. The battalion SOP was to first ask if there were any weapons—"*Enta salah*" in Arabic—and then to ask where the males were—"*Entaabu.*"

Sgt Wuterich and Cpl Salinas called me over. And I think it was Salinas that told me that the women were pointing that the men were next door. I stepped outside, and Sgt Wuterich told me to go with him over to house four while Salinas waited with the women and children in house three. I was in the lead as we walked over to house four. I had my SAW and my 9 mil. We were cautioned as we entered the house because of the IED that morning. The fact that Weapons Platoon needed support from Hellfire missiles, the suspicious turkey peeking from the men, and the fact that they were hiding in a house with the women and children next door.

Salinas stayed with the women and children at House #3 while Wuterich and Sharratt investigated next door. Sharratt was in the lead as they walked to the side door of House #4 near the front of the house. He headed directly into the center meeting room common in Iraqi homes with Wuterich close behind.

Unsure of who was in the next room, Sharratt and Wuterich stacked themselves on the door that allowed access to the interior hallway and stairwell. That way, they could cover each other as they moved through the house in their curious MOUT ballet.

When Sharratt began to stack himself along the wall, he saw an Iraqi male pointing an AK-47 at him through a bedroom door. The Iraqi looked as though he was going to fire the weapon. A second later, a firefight erupted. The subsequent NCIS forensic reconstruction of Sharratt's actions would support much of what Sharratt later told NCIS:

I entered the house through the front door. It was quiet. I moved into the center meeting room, and SSgt Wuterich followed me. We cleared the room by walking along the walls. The room was mostly empty. I remember that there were some mats on the floor. Sgt Wuterich and I began to stack along the door on the wall that allowed access to the interior hallway and stairs.

As we started to stack ourselves, I glanced across the hallway and saw an Iraqi male pointing an AK-47 at me as if he was going shoot. I quickly shouldered my SAW and tried to fire, but it jammed. When the SAW jammed, I withdrew behind the wall. At the same time, I dropped my SAW letting the sling catch it near my waist. Then I jumped back. I bumped into SSgt Wuterich who was behind me. I knew that there were insurgents with weapons in that room. I had to move fast to establish fire superiority, or Sgt Wuterich and I could wind up trapped inside.

As I was pulling back in the room dropping the SAW to my side, I said, "Jam," to Staff Sergeant Wuterich, while simultaneously drew my 9 millimeter sidearm. I leaned out past the door jam [sic] waiting for the insurgent to present himself. When the insurgent popped back out from behind the door, I shot him once in the head; and he fell backwards. I began to assault through the objective and stepped forward into the bedroom doorway. I could hear an AK-47 racking its chamber.

As I stepped into the doorway, to my front was another insurgent with his AK-47 waist level as though he just completed racking it. I immediately fired at his chest and head firing several times with my pistol. After shooting him, I continued to shoot the other individuals in the room. I kept firing until my magazine was empty because I didn't know if they had body armor on or suicide vests. As I fired at the other insurgents in the room, I felt as if they were coming towards me.[2]

Sharratt hit all of them, mostly with headshots. It was remarkable shooting: four head shots in a kinetic environment against combatants armed with two automatic assault rifles. In others times and places, it would have been legendary shooting. LtGen Mattis commended Sharratt for his skill and bravery.

The close-in fighting at Fallujah had taught him to fire as long as he could. What happened next was classic Marine tactics:

After I ran out of ammo, I yelled, "I'm out." Sgt Wuterich entered the room and fired his M16 at the men too. By the time Sgt Wuterich came in the room, I felt as though I shot all the men in the room.

After clearing the room, I grabbed the two AK-47s. And Sgt Wuterich and I searched the rest of the rooms in the house. As we were leaving the house, we found a suitcase with three or four Jordanian passports in it, clothes, and hygiene gear. We left the house with the suitcase and the AK-47s.[3]

Later on, while examining the captured weapons, Sharratt said he found a live AK-47 shell with the primer indented in one of the Kalashnikovs. Luckily for him, the insurgent's weapon had also jammed.

Toting the insurgents' weapons, passports, and suitcase, Wuterich and Sharratt returned to Route Chestnut. Spent from their fierce close encounter, they placed the weapons and suitcase in the first vehicle they came across. It was the last time they ever saw the captured booty. Sometime later, the weapons disappeared. Their loss would provoke dire consequences in the months to come.

After disposing of the insurgents' equipment and documents, Sharratt hooked up with Tatum. He explained what had happened so that Tatum could report the contact to Lt Kallop. Then the two

Fallujah veterans walked over to the massive crater to pay their respect to LCpl Terrazas, collecting his destroyed rifle as well. The company armorer, Cpl Robert Stafford, would later reconstruct a rifle from the exploded pieces of T. J.'s weapon. He hung the rifle on the wall at Firm Base Sparta in loving tribute to the friendly kid with the pleasant smile.

Five years later, Sharratt's former defense attorney Jim Culp said he never entirely bought Sharratt's story about what happened in that room. Culp doesn't know what happened, and emphasized he is happy LtGen Mattis bought into his client's recollections, but he didn't believe it himself. Culp said it was too pat, too much like a bad script in an adventure movie.

CHAPTER 9

TROUBLE BREWING

From the day the Haditha incident erupted until about the middle of March 2006, no one in Kilo Company below the rank of lieutenant knew there was a scandal brewing. All the enlisted men heard were accolades for a job well done. LtCol Chessani came around to congratulate the men. So did other brass.

Kilo Company First Sergeant Albert Espinoza visited everyone as well. After the fight was over, Third and Fourth Platoons came to FB Sparta for a little R&R. Espinosa was there to congratulate the men on a job well done. The line grunts rarely saw Espinoza, who unlike his two predecessors usually stayed in the rear with the gear, Haman said.

The first sergeant visited all the platoons, doing a little glad-handing and offering words of encouragement. He told Sharratt he did a fine job. Espinoza congratulated Haman for his performance in the grenade fight and asked him if he had ever got to fire his M203 (grenade launcher) during the battle. Espinoza never suggested there was any impropriety. On the contrary, he seemed unusually friendly, Haman recalled.

Kilo Company continued to patrol in the interim, conduct cordon-and-search operations, and set up checkpoints. Eventually, Guzman and Fourth Platoon's Lt Zall returned from the hospital in Germany. LCpl Crossan never returned.

IEDs killed four more 3/1 Marines while their tour wound down. Thankfully, nothing else major happened to the squad again until the NCIS special agents showed up. With only weeks to go before 3/1 was scheduled to leave Haditha, the hammer fell. Word began spreading around Kilo that Wuterich's squad wasn't going home with the rest of the battalion. Then word got out that Wuterich and his squad were going to be held in Kuwait while criminal allegations were investigated. It was the first time Kilo's Marines heard rumors about an NCIS investigation.

"About two weeks before we left, we found out about it. We found out that the guys in [Wuterich's] squad had to stay there. We heard they were in trouble, but we didn't know why. They came home a couple of days later," Haman recalled. "Everyone knew about the dead civilians. They regretted them," Haman explained, "but it was a fight."

A couple of months after it happened, unfamiliar officers began appearing at Haditha Dam. "Usually we didn't see anyone, but I didn't know what they wanted. Nobody talked to me," Haman said. He didn't know it had anything to do with Sharratt's squad. "I talked to Sharratt a lot of times after the fight and he never said too much. He sure didn't say anything about murder. None of us thought anything had happened. We would see reporters every once in a while so we didn't think too much about it."

On February 10, 2005, McGirk officially began inquiring at the Multi-National Force–Iraq (MNF–I) headquarters regarding the November 19, 2005, engagement. It was four days later, on February 14, that Army Lieutenant General Chiarelli appointed Army Colonel Gregory Watt to head a preliminary investigation into the Haditha deaths. On February 17, Watt, two Navy lawyers, and a translator left Camp Victory in Baghdad for Al Asad Air Base in Al Anbar Province. That evening Watt's team visited Colonel Stephan Davis, the commanding officer of RCT-2 and the senior officer in tactical command in the region. Watt did not detail what the two men discussed.

The next morning, Watt's team departed Al Asad for the Haditha Dam complex. For the next eight days Watt and his team conducted an "Informal AR (Army Regulation) 15-6" investigation of the events surrounding the "3/1 Marine 19 November 2005 Haditha Complex Attack." Apparently, Watt already knew—or at least presumed—the incident at Haditha was not the mindless rampage McGirk described, but was rather a coordinated enemy attack on a Marine infantry battalion. Like McGirk, Watt said he did not intend to rush to judgment.[1]

According to Army Regulation 15-6, an "informal investigation or board may use whatever method it finds most efficient and effective for acquiring information" as long as the investigating officer confers with a staff judge advocate or similar military lawyer for guidance before proceeding. Mail, telephones, and any other method of communication that will get the job done is considered appropriate." Watt, with his two lawyers in tow, decided to simply move around the area of operation interviewing the witnesses.

Watt was seeking answers to five allegations made by McGirk to MNF officers in Baghdad. Watt labeled them "a" through "e." Each item detailed a specific complaint McGirk brought to Baghdad.

a. "Home of Addull Hameed Hasan Ali: Marines entered and killed Hameed Hasan Ali," his wife, three sons, a daughter-in-law, and a young child.
b. "Home of Younis Salim Raseef: Marines entered and killed Younis Salim," his wife, his sister-in-law, and five children.
c. "Home of Ayed Ahmad: Marines entered and killed Ayed Ahmed" and his four sons.
d. "Home of Hasan Ahmed: Marines entered and arrested family members. (No reported deaths.)"
e. "Taxi and passengers: Marines stopped the taxi and killed the occupants identified as Ahmad Fanr Mosdlih, Mohammad Tabbal,

Wajdee Eiada, and Khalid Eiada. (For the purposes of this investigation this taxi is referred to as WHITE CAR)."[2]

On March 3, 2006, Watt filed his report with Chiarelli. What Watt's team discovered didn't bode well for anyone.

At first, it appeared more like a case of smoke and mirrors than murderous fire aimed at innocent civilians.

In the section of Watt's report labeled "Facts," he told Chiarelli that the Marines were as much the victims of the complex attack as the dead Iraqis.

a. First Squad, Third Platoon, K Company, Third Battalion, First Marines four vehicle patrol was ambushed on 19 Nov 05 on RTE CHESTNT . . . (Assessment: This was a coordinated attack, initiated by an IED, and supported by anti-CF SAF from at least 3–4 mutually supporting positions).

b. Initial IED detonation resulted in 1X FKIA [Friendly Killed in Action] (LCPL Terrazas) and 2xFWIA (LCPL Guzman and LCPL Crossan).

c. First Squad, Third Platoon dismounted, secured perimeter and reacted to contact. . . . (Assessment: The 12x man Marine Squad was quickly overwhelmed between the loss of 3x Marines. They were stretched thin; the rest of Kilo Co was engaged at other locations in Haditha near simultaneously.)

d. 1/3 Kilo engaged a hostile threat in three homes (HOUSES #1, #2, and #4) and a perceived threat from one car (WHITE CAR).

e. 1/3/K entered and cleared multiple structures. During consolidation and reorganization, 26 deceased were delivered to the Haditha Hospital Morgue.

f. Between the S2 (Capt Dinsmore), the HET and the CAG it was determined that there were 15x NKIA [Neutral Killed in Action—civilians] and 8 EKIA [Enemy Killed in Action].

g. Solatia payments were made for 15x NKIA and 2x NWIA totaling $38K [$38,000].[3]

Part four of Watt's report—labeled "Findings"—determined whether any "law of armed conflict violations were committed" and to "discover whether the Marines had intentionally targeted, engaged or killed non-combatants."

Watt was equally certain that the Marines responded appropriately to the combat situation threatening their lives:

> No, there are no indications that CF (Coalition Forces) intentionally targeted, engaged, and killed non-combatants. There is no denying that civilians died during the insurgent's coordinated attack on the Marines on 19 November 05; however, there is no evidence that the Marines intentionally set out to target, engage, and kill non-combatants.[4]

Watt needed three more single-spaced typewritten pages to detail exactly what his investigation discovered. As briefly and concisely as the subject permitted, he addressed each specification of misconduct alleged by McGirk. In the end, he seemed to be satisfied that the insurgents, not Wuterich and his Marines, were responsible for the death and destruction on Route Chestnut.

On page 6, in paragraph (c) of his report, Watt offered what is perhaps his most profound finding:

> c. Were any violations of the law of armed conflict committed by insurgents? Specifically did insurgents target, engage, and kill non-combatants?
>
> Indications are that insurgents fought from homes occupied by non-combatants and used these homes for cover and concealment. Statements by numerous Marines support that they received hostile SF [small arms fire] (from HOUSE #1, HOUSE #2, and HOUSE #4 as well as a house identified as a possible trigger house). Marine statements indicate that these anti-CFs did not distinguish themselves from non-combatants.

Despite his initial finding, Watt was not completely satisfied that the Marines had acted appropriately. There was still the matter of the dead women and children.

In section 5—"Recommendations"—Chiarelli suggested that the MNF–I initiate a CID (US Army Criminal Investigation Division)/NCIS investigation into the events at Haditha. Watt qualified his recommendation by saying, "however, given time lapsed, Solatia payments, TIP/TOAs [Relief In Place/Transfer of Authority—a sequence of events for a unit being replaced by another in Iraq], renovation of HOUSE #1 and HOUSE #2, obtaining more prosecutable evidence will be extremely difficult."

Watt seemed as concerned with the potential public relations disaster looming on the horizon. Speaking specifically to McGirk's inquiry, he recommended that, "MNC–I: Prepare PAO response to *TIME*, independent and video allegations. Acknowledge event occurred; the Marines reaction to the ambush/coordinated attack was IAW published doctrine and TTP [tactics, techniques, and procedures]; Non-Combatants were killed while Marines cleared houses that they had been fired on from; and Solatia Payments were made for damages."[5]

Watt's recommendation for the Marine Corps to come clean was ignored. Either the Marine generals running the show didn't want to admit to error or, more likely, they were involved in running a shooting war—a kinetic event—that left them little time for pondering previous horrors. The US military was in a reactionary mode throughout Iraq. The insurgency had the horsepower.

On March 3—closing with the salutation "Steadfast and Loyal"—Watt presented his report to Chiarelli. On March 9, Chiarelli reviewed it and directed the situation be given a more thorough examination. The next day, Secretary of Defense Donald Rumsfeld and General Pace officially learned of the Haditha investigation. For once, they were ahead of the rumor mill. It would still be a few days before Kilo Company's embattled Marines discovered that their long-anticipated homecoming was going to be much less pleasant than the ones they envisioned in their dreams.

On March 16, a week after Chiarelli ordered an inquiry, the Marine Corps officially requested a criminal investigation of the incident at Haditha. The probe began immediately. Within twenty-four hours, three NCIS agents already in Iraq went to Haditha to investigate. The next day—the same day *TIME* revealed its Haditha story online—the existence of a criminal investigation into the deaths in Haditha was reported in the media.

At a press conference in Baghdad the next day, Chiarelli summarized the events at Haditha and Watt's preliminary investigation into the Marines' involvement in the deaths of the twenty-four civilians there and promised McGirk they would be thoroughly investigated.

Good to his word, Chiarelli announced on March 19 that he was appointing US Army major general Eldon A. Bargewell to investigate two major aspects of what happened: training and preparation of Marines prior to the engagement and the reporting of the incident at all levels of the chain of command. The next day—the timing of all these momentous events by now becoming somewhat propitious—*TIME* published "Collateral Damage or Civilian Massacre in Haditha?"

On April 7, 2006, about three weeks after 3/1 returned to Camp Pendleton from Iraq, Lieutenant Colonel Jeffrey Chessani, commander of the Third Battalion, First Marine Regiment; Captain Lucas McConnell, Kilo's commander; and Captain James Kimber, commander of the battalion's India Company, were publicly relieved of command "due to lack of confidence in their leadership abilities stemming from their performance during a recent deployment to Iraq," the Marine Corps said in a statement.[6]

On May 17, Pennsylvania Congressman John Murtha, the eighteen-term Democrat, retired Marine reserve colonel, and ranking Democrat on the House Armed Forces Appropriations Sub-Committee, said on international television that the Marines at Haditha killed twenty-four Iraqis in cold blood.

"There was no firefight," Murtha claimed. "The reports I have from the highest level: No firing at all. No interaction. No military action at all in this particular incident. It was an explosive device, which killed a Marine. From then on, it was purely shooting people.

"Our troops overreacted because of the pressure on them and they killed innocent civilians in cold blood. And that's what the [investigative] report is going to tell."[7]

Murtha claimed his source was General Michael W. Hagee, the commandant of the Marine Corps.

On May 21 Murtha was a guest on CNN's *The Situation Room with Wolf Blitzer.* By then he had changed the source of his information. The following exchange took place during the broadcast:

> **Wolf Blitzer:** How do you know [the massacre] happened?
> **Murtha:** Because *TIME* has pictures.·

On May 24, Hagee finally briefed Murtha about Haditha—seven days after Murtha claimed on international television that the briefing had already taken place. Murtha admitted to the *Philadelphia Inquirer* that General Hagee never used the phrase "in cold blood."[8]

The next day General Hagee flew to Iraq to speak with troops. His message to his Marines was that they need to better adhere to the Corps's values and standards of behavior and to avoid the use of excess force—or else.

On May 28, Murtha appeared on ABC's *This Week* and claimed that the Marines made *solatia* payments to the families of Iraqis killed in Haditha at a time when the Marines' official explanation for the deaths was a roadside bomb. Murtha also claimed that the incident in Haditha would be worse for the American war effort than Abu Ghraib.

Not to be outdone by Murtha, the same day, Virginia Republican Senator John Warner, also a former Marine, as well as chairman of the Senate Armed Services Committee, said the panel would hold hearings on the Haditha incident. On May 29, riding high on the bandwagon of his own creation, Murtha charged the Marines with a cover-up.

"There has to have been a cover-up of this thing," Murtha alleged. "No question about it."[9]

The Haditha Eight, eight Marines indicted for murder, assault, cover-up, and war crimes on December 21, 2006.

SSgt. Frank Wuterich	LCpl. Stephen Tatum	LCpl. Justin Sharratt	Cpl. Sanick DelaCruz
Squad Leader	Rifleman	Rifleman	Rifleman

LTC Jeffrey Chessani	Capt. Randy Stone	Capt. Lucas McConnell	1LT. Andrew Grayson
3/1 Battalion Commander	Intelligence Officer	Kilo 3/1 Company Commander	Lawyer 3/1 SJA

SSgt Frank Wuterich at Haditha Dam in 2007 while preparing for his general court-martial.

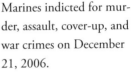

Twenty-year-old LCpl Miguel "T. J." Terrazas, who was killed that morning on Route Chestnut.

USMC

USMC

US Army

L to R: Gen Peter Pace. The Haditha investigation occurred under Pace's watch as the first Marine selected as Chairman of the Joint Chiefs of Staff; Gen James N. Mattis (ret.). Mattis was designated the convening authority in the investigation. Army MG Eldon Bargewell (ret.). Then LtGen Peter Chiarelli ordered Bargewell to conduct the formal inquiry into Haditha.

L to R: MajGen Richard A. Huck (ret.) received a Secretarial Letter of Censure for his involvement in the Haditha incident, which destroyed his career; Gen Peter W. Chiarelli (ret.) was ordered by Gen Casey to investigate Haditha; Gen George W. Casey Jr. (ret.) initiated the Haditha investigation following reports that US Marines had massacred women and children.

USMC   Courtesy of Jeffrey Chessani

to R: Attorney Neil Puckett represented SSgt Wuterich from his initial indictment in 2006 to the end
his court-martial on January 24, 2012; Coauthor Haytham Faraj was co-counsel defending Wuterich
rting in 2007; LtCol Jeffrey Chessani (L) was considered an up-and-coming officer of 3/1 until relieved
r cause.

SMC   Courtesy of Barry Johnson

to R: Col Richard Sokoloski received a Secretarial Letter of Censure for approving the erroneous press
ease detailing the Haditha incident; MajGen John Ewers was assigned by LtGen Chiarelli to investigate
aditha and provide legal counsel to LtGen Mattis; US Army Colonel Barry Johnson was the person to
nom TIME reporter Tim McGirk first brought allegations of murder and cover-up.

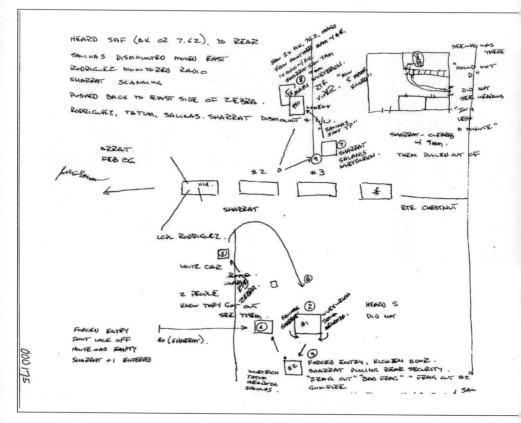

Hand-drawn map by LCpl Justin Sharratt made while he was being interrogated by NCIS at Haditha Dam. His testimony was later dismissed by investigating officer LtCol Paul Ware despite strong evidence that Sharratt, Tatum, and Salinas returned to Houses #1 and #2 to "secure their rear" by using grenades and small arms with intent to kill everyone inside both houses. Instead, Ware recommended all charges against Sharratt be dropped to give him testimonial immunity from prosecution. Diagram from the Bargewell Report.

"Went back across Route Zebra to the first house we had first went around. I asked CPL Salinas if we had already cleared it. He said no. We threw a frag in but, it did not go off so we did not go in. We cleared the house by fire with a 203. We entered and the door was opened. We each took sectors to clear. Someone through a frag in the room, said 'he' was hearing shit, and told me to clear by fire. The frag went off and I entered the room and emptied by 9 mm clip and then the next person went in with an M16 and fired in the room. There were a few dead Iraqis lying on the ground. I could not make out gender or type. The others were clearing other rooms. It happened fast, we were in and out. I believe it was LCPL Tatum who threw the frag and said clear by fire. I stayed in the house about 10 seconds afterward."

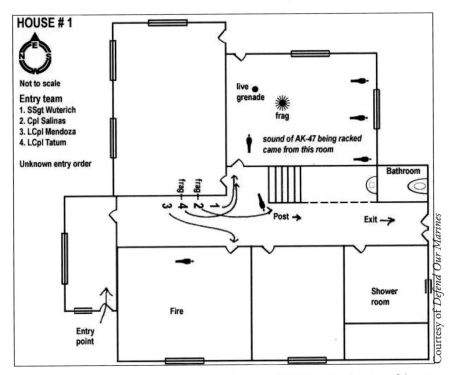

HOUSE # 1

Not to scale

Entry team
1. SSgt Wuterich
2. Cpl Salinas
3. LCpl Mendoza
4. LCpl Tatum

Unknown entry order

live grenade

frag

sound of AK-47 being racked came from this room

Bathroom

frag — 4
frag — 2
3 — 1

Post →

Exit →

Shower room

Fire

Entry point

Courtesy of Defend Our Marines

Above: NCIS diagram of shooting scene in House #1. **Below:** NCIS diagram of shooting scene in House #2. Drawings from the Bargewell Report.

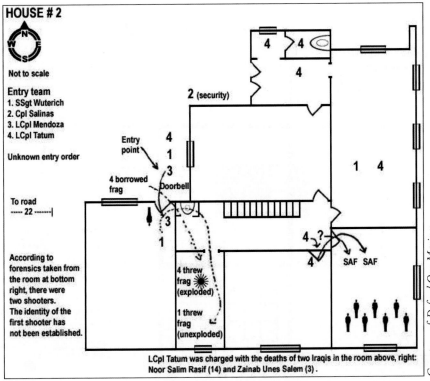

HOUSE # 2

Not to scale

Entry team
1. SSgt Wuterich
2. Cpl Salinas
3. LCpl Mendoza
4. LCpl Tatum

Unknown entry order

To road
----- 22 -------|

According to forensics taken from the room at bottom right, there were two shooters. The identity of the first shooter has not been established.

4   4

4

2 (security)

Entry point

4
1
3

4 borrowed frag

Doorbell

3
1

1   4

4 ?
4

SAF SAF

4 threw frag (exploded)

1 threw frag (unexploded)

LCpl Tatum was charged with the deaths of two Iraqis in the room above, right: Noor Salim Rasif (14) and Zainab Unes Salem (3).

Courtesy of Defend Our Marines

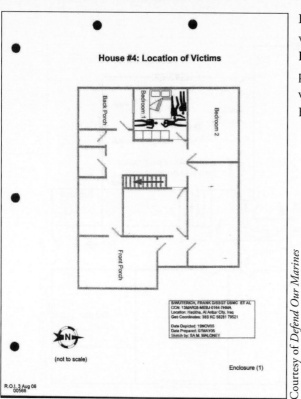

House #4: Location of Victims

Back Porch

Bedroom

Bedroom 2

Front Porch

S/WUTERICH, FRANK D/SSGT USMC ET AL
CCN: 13MAR06-MEBJ-0164-7HMA
Location: Haditha, Al Anbar City, Iraq
Geo Coordinates: 38S KC 58281 79521

Date Depicted: 19NOV05
Date Prepared: 07MAY06
Sketch by: SA M. MALONEY

N

(not to scale)

Enclosure (1)

Left: NCIS diagram of the location of the victims found in House #4.

Below: NCIS diagram of the bloodstain patterns in the bedroom where the victims were found in House #4. Drawings from the Bargewell Report.

Courtesy of Defend Our Marines

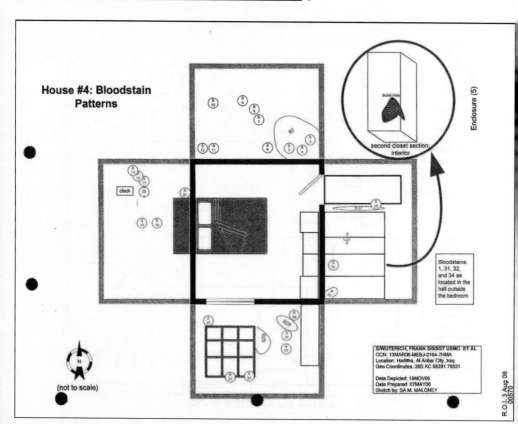

House #4: Bloodstain Patterns

clock

Bullet Hole

second closet section:
interior

Enclosure (5)

Bloodstains:
1, 31, 32,
and 34 are
located in the
hall outside
the bedroom

S/WUTERICH, FRANK D/SSGT USMC ET AL
CCN: 13MAR06-MEBJ-0164-7HMA
Location: Haditha, Al Anbar City, Iraq
Geo Coordinates: 38S KC 58281 79521

Date Depicted: 19NOV05
Date Prepared: 07MAY06
Sketch by: SA M. MALONEY

N

(not to scale)

Top: Leaked NCIS image of the bomb crater marking where one Marine died and two were wounded on Route Chestnut at the southern edge of Haditha, Iraq, on November 19, 2005. **Bottom:** Dead Iraqis lying where they were slain seconds after an IED explosion ripped through the four-vehicle convoy led by SSgt Wuterich. These images were leaked by someone with access to the NCIS investigation before the inquiry was concluded. It was later revealed that the images, originally shot in color, were confiscated from 3/1 Marines who were at the scene.

NCIS

Top: The blood-spattered bedroom in House #2 where eight women and children were killed. One child survived. NCIS used this image and many like it to conduct a forensic reconstruction of the events. They determined that at least two shooters were involved in the killings in this room.
Bottom: An unidentified dead Iraqi civilian killed by SSgt Wuterich's squad when it swept through Houses #1, #2, and #4 after being ambushed. Because of time prohibitions, NCIS was unable to determine precisely who killed whom because forensic reconstruction of the dead houses didn't begin until four months after the killings happened.

NCIS

NCIS

CFLCC ROE CARD

1. On order, enemy military and paramilitary forces are declared hostile and may be attacked subject to the following instructions:

   a. Positive Identification (PID) is required prior to engagement. PID is a reasonable certainty that the proposed target is a legitimate military target. If no PID, contact your next higher commander for decision.

   b. Do not engage anyone who has surrendered or is out of battle due to sickness or wounds.

   c. Do not target or strike any of the following except in self-defense to protect yourself, your unit, friendly forces, and designated persons or property under your control:

   - Civilians
   - Hospitals, mosques, churches, shrines, schools, museums, national monuments, and any other historical and cultural sites

   d. Do not fire into civilian populated areas or buildings unless the enemy is using them for military purposes or if necessary for your self-defense. Minimize collateral damage.

   e. Do not target enemy Infrastructure (public works, commercial communication facilities, dams), Lines of Communication (roads, highways, tunnels, bridges, railways) and Economic Objects (commercial storage facilities, pipelines) unless necessary for self-defense or if ordered by your commander. If you must fire on these objects to engage a hostile force, disable and disrupt but avoid destruction of these objects, if possible.

CFLCC ROE CARD

2. The use of force, including deadly force, is authorized to protect the following:

   - Yourself, your unit, and friendly forces
   - Enemy Prisoners of War
   - Civilians from crimes that are likely to cause death or serious bodily harm, such as murder or rape
   - Designated civilians and/or property, such as personnel of the Red Cross/Crescent, UN, and US/UN supported organizations.

3. Treat all civilians and their property with respect and dignity. Do not seize civilian property, including vehicles, unless you have the permission of a company level commander and you give a receipt to the property's owner.

4. Detain civilians if they interfere with mission accomplishment or if required for self-defense.

5. CENTCOM General Order No. 1A remains in effect. Looting and the taking of war trophies are prohibited.

REMEMBER
   - Attack enemy forces and military targets.
   - Spare civilians and civilian property, if possible.
   - Conduct yourself with dignity and honor.
   - Comply with the Law of War. If you see a violation, report it.

These ROE will remain in effect until your commander orders you to transition to post-hostilities ROE.

Above: Rules of Engagement card issued to 3/1 Marines at Haditha 2005.

Below: Rules of Engagement card issued to the author while a helicopter door gunner in Vietnam in 1968.

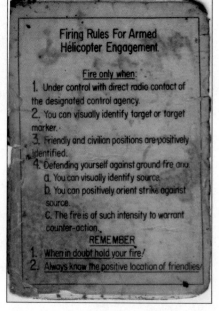

Firing Rules For Armed Helicopter Engagement

Fire only when:
1. Under control with direct radio contact of the designated control agency.
2. You can visually identify target or target marker.
3. Friendly and civilian positions are positively identified.
4. Defending yourself against ground fire and:
   a. You can visually identify source.
   b. You can positively orient strike against source.
   c. The fire is of such intensity to warrant counter-action.

REMEMBER
1. When in doubt hold your fire!
2. Always know the positive location of friendlies!

Left: Iraqi MAMs (military age males) were routinely stopped and searched for weapons and triggering devices for IEDs. **Above:** Kilo, 3/1 on guard at Haditha during Operation River Gate prior to the ambush on Route Chestnut.

Left: Every military convoy in Iraq displayed signs at front and back warning Iraqis to stay away. **Above:** Iraqi National Guard troops in Haditha were often occupied securing the population by controlling their movements in the city.

3/1 Marines on patrol in Haditha during a so-called pacification operation.

A high-back armored Humvee like the one destroyed by an IED on Route Chestnut.

igging up IEDs was a routine chore. At Haditha, 3/1 Marines found twenty-two IEDs before Wuterich's
uad was decimated by one undiscovered, homemade IED.

A Marine probes a soft spot in the road at Haditha where he suspects an IED has been buried. Some of the hidden bombs were triggered by cell phones; others were detonated by pressure or trip wires. They were often hidden in debris, dead animals, or vehicles parked on the side of the road.

Hunting IEDs at night. The second vehicle is equipped with a mine roller used to detonate conventional mines buried in the road. The sophistication of the insurgent bombmakers quickly made them almost obsolete.

above left: Marine engineers blowing up Iraqi ammunition hidden away to make IEDs.
above right: A bridge over the lake formed by Haditha Dam, a frequent target of al-Qaeda–paid and –led insurgents bedeviling 3/1 in November 2005.

120 mm mortar shells and other ammunition destined for a VBIED driven by a suicide bomber.

Above: Force recon sniper provides overwatch fire support while 3/1 Marines perform knock-and-search operations. **Right:** 3/1 Marines occupying a rooftop while other Marines search the building below.

3/1 Marines kicked down hundred of doors searching for insurgents, financed and led by al-Qaeda, engaged in producing propaganda videos and pamphlets distributed throughout Al Anbar Province.

3/1 Marines approaching a booby-trapped house in Haditha in November 2005.

S soldiers "stack up" in preparation to enter and clear a building in Fallujah, Iraq.

A hand-launched Dragon Eye unmanned aerial vehicle like this videotaped and transmitted almost the entire skirmish at Haditha to commanders in real time.

Left: Marine engineers attached to the 3/1 digging up hidden artillery shells used for making IEDs.

Right: A Kilo, 3/1 rifleman at the gates of Haditha. To his front is a Sunni minaret marking the location of
a sacred mosque. A few days before the Haditha incident, Kilo Marines located and disarmed a huge mine
hidden inside a mosque next to a well-traveled road.

Two days later—May 31—President Bush made his first public comments about the deaths in Haditha, promising that "if, in fact, laws were broken, there will be punishment."

On June 6, 2006, the Associated Press offered a detailed account of what happened in Haditha according to "activist" Thaer Thabet al-Hadithi, saying, "The case . . . is threatening to further weaken popular support for the Iraq war in the United States and has tarnished the military's image in Iraq and around the world."

The same week, the *Washington Post*, now in a headline war with *TIME* and the *New York Times*, reported that the NCIS investigators wishing to exhume the Haditha decedents, remains were stymied by the alleged victims' relatives. Not to be outdone, *Nation* magazine claimed the Marines in Haditha "perpetrated a massacre."

Four days later, Senator Warner reversed himself and announced his panel wouldn't investigate the alleged atrocities at Haditha until the Pentagon completed its own investigation. He did, however, renew his vow to hold open hearings on the incident. He never did.

On June 16, MG Bargewell's examination of the Marines' training and preparation before being sent to Haditha, as well as the veracity of the Marines' report concerning the incident, was forwarded to Chiarelli. Bargewell's 107-page report—at the time still classified "Secret"—found no evidence of a cover-up. Instead, Bargewell discovered that the senior officers failed to ask the right questions vigorously enough. In April 2007, the entire report was leaked to the *Washington Post*.

In August 2006, LtGen Mattis, the incoming commander of the I Marine Expeditionary Force at Camp Pendleton, was briefed on the Haditha investigative report by NCIS officials. Mattis announced he would convene with his lawyers to determine whether charges should be filed. One of his lawyers later recused himself to avoid the appearance of impropriety and another—Colonel John R. Ewers—became instrumental in destroying the government's case against Chessani after a military appeals court in March 2009 upheld the dismissal of war crimes charges against him by ruling Chessani was the victim of "unlawful command influence." The precipitating event was that Ewers investigated the case before counseling Mattis about what to do with Chessani and seven other Marines awaiting indictment. Ewers is currently staff judge advocate to the commandant and the Corps's senior lawyer.

A week after Mattis took on the job of Convening Authority in the Haditha affair, *TIME* superstar Ali Omar was again released from jail. The Reuters photographer and founder of the Hammurabi Human Rights organization was reportedly released after a two-week stay in military custody. It was a well-covered event. The world press blamed Omar's incarceration on American injustice. US military spokesman Lieutenant Colonel Guy Rudisill refused to say why the "thirty-six-year-old freelance cameraman and photographer" from Ramadi was in jail.

Before Omar's release, Rudisill said the ill-starred journalist was incarcerated in Baghdad's Abu Ghraib prison. "He will not be able to have visitors for the next sixty days," a Reuters story added.

Ali Omar was released eleven days later after Reuters global managing editor David Schlesinger called on the US military to explain Omar's detention and why he was held incommunicado: "We are very concerned and dismayed by this unexplained and prolonged detention of a journalist working for us and urge the US military either to release him or provide a full account of the accusations against him."

ON NOVEMBER 21, anonymous sources leaked to NPR the names of five enlisted Marines expected to face charges. Salinas, one of the Marines named as a potential defendant, was never charged. Instead, he was held past his separation date at Camp Pendleton by the prosecution as a possible witness. He remained there for eighteen more months.

Two weeks later, on December 6, 2006, Lieutenant General Richard Natonski, former commanding general of Camp Pendleton's First Marine Division, briefed members of Congress about the Haditha incident. The preceding spring, while a major general, he had relieved 3/1's commanding officer and Kilo Company's commanding officer for command failure. Meanwhile, anonymous Camp Pendleton sources told the press that charges were expected to be announced the week of December 18.

On December 21, eight Marines from the Thundering Third—four enlisted men and four officers—were charged with murder, assault, and dereliction of duty for the incident at Haditha.

CHAPTER 10

ANOTHER INCIDENT AT OWL CREEK

O n April 7, 2006, the distinguished eighteen-year Marine Corps career of LtCol Jeffrey Chessani imploded after he was relieved of command of the Thundering Third for cause—the kiss of death for a professional military officer.

Three weeks after the battalion returned to its California home, Colonel Michael Schupp, the commander of RCT-1, 3/1's parent regiment, told Chessani the Marine Corps no longer had "confidence in [Chessani's] leadership abilities." To prove it, Schupp gave Chessani a "double-signer" fitness report, one in which both the rater and endorser—then Natonski—agreed that the officer being evaluated was unworthy of command. It was a career-killing action that effectively ruined Chessani's chances of ever being promoted again. Tougher still, Chessani was Schupp's operations officer when he was CO of RCT-1 during the Battle of Fallujah. Together, they had eaten some of the same dirt.[1]

Being unpopular was not new to Schupp. In November 2004, when he was the operational commander at Fallujah, he had created a lot of bad blood with some of the infantry battalion commanders, never developing the same level of professional respect enjoyed by his predecessor Colonel John Toolen. In an interview at Marine Corps Base Quantico in November 2006, former 3/1 commanding officer Colonel Willie Buhl said Schupp ordered an armored reconnaissance by the line battalion commanders from inside M1 tanks where 3/1 and the other infantry battalions were going to cross the line of departure, thereby telegraphing their intentions. Buhl complained neither he nor the other grunts liked being inside an armored behemoth so close to the muj that they could suffer a mobility strike. The foreign fighters were reported to have French and Russian guided antitank weapons that could leave the tank and crew helpless far too close to insurgent lines for comfort. Buhl called it an unsound idea.[2]

Joining Chessani in disgrace were Annapolis graduate Captain Lucas McConnell, Kilo's handpicked young commander, and Captain James Kimber, commanding officer of India Company. McConnell's relief was at least comprehensible to Marines who understand the arcane institutions of their beloved Corps. It was, after all, Marines from his company who had killed the Iraqis. The relief of Captain Kimber, who wasn't at Haditha, seemed more of a stretch that the Marine Corps didn't seem interested in clearing up. Kimber, with remarkable candor for a serving Marine, told the press he was a "scapegoat."

SCAPEGOATS AREN'T UNKNOWN in the Marine Corps. Nearly two and a half centuries of combat against enemies foreign and domestic have produced more than a few good Marines offered up as sacrifices for other's misdeeds. One legendary goat was Marine Major Littleton Waller Tazewell "Tony" Waller. In 1901 he was the commander of 315 hardcore Marines serving under US Army command in the Philippines. His story will seem vaguely familiar. Historian Max Boot offers a carefully crafted account of Waller's travails in *The Savage Wars of Peace: Small Wars and the Rise of American Power*.[3]

Waller's boss was Army Brigadier General Jacob H. "Hell-Roaring Jake" Smith, the commanding officer of an ad hoc joint service unit called the Sixth Separate Brigade. American military officers of quality had snappy nicknames in the age before orders were whispered over fax machines and emails.

Waller and his Army counterparts based their operations on the fact that the majority of the natives were hostile to US actions and could not be trusted, despite pretenses by villagers of being pro-American. It was well known that many villagers were actually members of the insurrection.

President William McKinley sent the US Army's Company C, Ninth Infantry, commanded by Captain Thomas W. Connell. Boot reports that Connell was a strong advocate of McKinley's theory of "benevolent assimilation." The target was Balangiga, Samar, one of the Philippines' hundreds of islands. Samar was populated by an extremely violent, primitive society. (Dehumanization of opponents is not a twenty-first-century phenomenon.)

On September 28, 1901, the insurgents mounted a surprise attack on C Company. Led by town officials, the locals slaughtered the American soldiers. Only twenty-six of the seventy-four troopers in C Company survived. Most were tortured to death and their bodies mutilated.

On October 24 Waller's Marines were sent to punish the rebels. They held a less munificent view of the situation on Samar. Waller issued explicit orders to his officers concerning relations with the natives and the rules of engagement: "Place no confidence in the natives, and punish treachery immediately with death. . . . We must do our part of the work, and with the sure knowledge that we are not to expect quarter."

Waller's orders were within the limitations of General Order No. 100 of 1863 dealing with the rules of engagement with irregular warfare. The order stated that if enemy units "gave no quarter and became treacherous upon capture," it was lawful to shoot anyone belonging to that captured unit.

Hell-Roaring Jake told Tony Waller to kill everybody he encountered over the age of ten, including the women. Tony Waller didn't want to do it, and told his Marines not to. For the most part they complied.

After a short, glorious campaign that wiped out the insurgent's mountain headquarters, Waller inexplicably marched his men twenty-nine days and thirty-five miles through the jungle to the other coast. His men were reduced to eating roots. Along the way ten Marines starved to death. Upon relief they accused eleven Filipino porters who accompanied them of hoarding food. A delirious lieutenant claimed three of the porters tried to kill him with a machete. None of it was true. Waller, himself bewildered by jungle fever, ordered them summarily executed. He telegraphed Hell-Roaring Jake: "It became necessary to expend the prisoners."

Waller explained he had forty-five effectives to guard ninety-three prisoners and defend against three thousand restive natives. He simply couldn't afford the trouble the allegedly mutinous porters were causing.

Word of the atrocity got back to Washington in the dark days after President McKinley's assassination. It was all the war's legion of opponents needed to bash the unpopular campaign.

The story was all over the indignant New York and Washington press. Big newspapers were in an impassioned era of advocacy journalism in the wake of America's "new" imperialism. Before long, tales of water torture, beatings, and senseless murder emerged. Most of the atrocities were true; in this war, however, perpetuated by soldiers, not Marines. But then as now, the press often gets them confused.

At his court-martial Waller accepted full responsibility for ordering the executions. He naively believed Hell-Roaring Jake would do the honorable thing and admit he had ordered his favorite Marine to kill everybody over ten years of age who seemed belligerent.

Waller was wrong. Hell-Roaring Jake blamed his subordinate for everything. He testified he had ordered the Marine officer to treat everyone humanely. Enraged at his erstwhile superior's lack of honor,

Waller remounted the witness stand and recounted Smith's specific order.

Waller produced enough corroborating witnesses to convince the panel he was innocent. He was exonerated and restored to duty, eventually rising to the rank of major general. But he was never appointed commandant of the Marine Corps despite having aces like two-time Medal of Honor recipient Major General Smedley "Old Gimlet Eye" Butler in his corner. Historian Boot says it "put a pall over the entire US war effort in the Philippines."

APPARENTLY, THE LESSON in Waller's predicament was lost to the Marine Corps's institutional memory. The day Chessani and his subordinates were relieved, Lieutenant Lawton King, a First Marine Division PAO, denied a direct relationship existed between events unfolding in the Haditha investigation and the three officers' dismissals. The PAO claimed their relief was the culmination of a combat tour filled with failure. Chessani said it was rubbing salt in a wound. Worse, it was the second time a bogus press release had drawn blood.

"There was no one justification for the move," King said. "In fact many considerations factored into the decision to relieve the commanders. . . . It stems from their performance during the entire deployment."[4]

Kimber's relief the same day as Chessani and McConnell turned out to be more of a coincidence than anything else, although that didn't keep the voluble press from linking him to the alleged massacre for several more weeks.

Paul Hackett, Kimber's lawyer, a former Marine and at the time a Democratic Congressional candidate from Ohio running on his war record, said the thirty-three-year-old infantry officer was relieved because his subordinates used profanity and criticized the performance of Iraqi security services during an interview with Britain's Sky News TV.

Kimber should have never allowed that to happen. The Marines Corps comes down hard on commanders who can't keep their troops in line.

Chessani's relief was more difficult to comprehend. In Iraq, 3/1 was attached to RCT-2 as reinforcements instead of remaining with RCT-1, its parent organization. Schupp hadn't been Chessani's regimental commander long enough to objectively evaluate him. Until coming home, Chessani reported to Davis, the commanding officer of RCT-2, and indirectly to Huck, the Second Division commander while in Iraq. Davis rated Chessani superior in his February 2006 end-of-tour fitness report and Huck endorsed it. In combat, Davis claimed, Chessani could walk on water. Huck agreed.[5]

Buhl said the only way he could have screwed up enough to get relieved three weeks after completing a successful combat tour would have been to "crap in Natonski's mess kit." His scatologically euphemistic suggestion was not far from the mark.

Chessani's 2006 Combat Fitness Report (a required annual evaluation of a Marine officer's performance) from Davis described him as "A superb leader, who knows his men, knows the enemy, knows his business." Moreover, Davis recommended him for promotion and a Bronze Star. It is a rare honor in the medal-conscious Marine Corps.

Davis offered a veritable laundry list of Chessani's virtues:

Leads Marines from front in every operation. Demonstrates moral courage every day. Doesn't hesitate to report bad news fast or contest unrealistic plans/poor concepts. Despite the complexity and size of his AO [area of operations], he always maintains a calm, cool demeanor.

Always seeks advantage over complex, diverse insurgent enemy. Truly one of the finer thinkers in this COIN environment.

One of the top 3 infantry/Cav Bn cmdrs [commanders] of 13 who have served with RCT-2 [the regiment] during OIF. A superb leader, who knows his men, knows the enemy, knows his business. . . . Doesn't attract a lot of fanfare; just gets the job done to an exceedingly high standard.

Long ball hitter; recommend selection for promotion to Colonel and TLS [Top Level School].

Huck was equally effusive. In addition to agreeing with everything Davis claimed, Huck added a few lines of his own. Generals know how hard it is to break out of the pack of quality lieutenant colonels to cross the great divide to full colonel because they have already done it. So when they give a junior officer a superior rating they do it with the full knowledge of the weight of their words. Huck's endorsement was a report card on serious steroids. Chessani was headed for higher command.

Huck could have chilled Chessani's career simply by saying nothing. Instead, he chose to provide a kicker of his own: "Top notch officer with outstanding potential. Promote and select for TLS. Post TLS slate for Regimental command and subsequent joint tour. Unlimited potential and value to the Marine Corps. Capable of the most challenging assignments."

Eighteen months later, Huck claimed Chessani was a fraud who had intentionally deceived him both by overt lying and by intentionally omitting scandalous facts.

The general's contention that he was a victim of Chessani's intrigue-inspired negligence went to the heart of the charges against his former ace battalion commander. Chessani was accused of dereliction of duty for both failing to investigate and failing to adequately report to Huck what happened at Haditha. The charges centered around combat journal entries, called JENs, and commander's critical information requirements—CCIRs—that Chessani's superiors depended on for instant notification. When someone in the Defense Department leaked Huck's statement to the *Washington Post,* it added much-needed fuel to the waning fire.

Chessani's lawyers argued Huck's explanations were self-serving and tenuous at best. Faraj says it depends on what Chessani reported in his classified dispatches. Focused CCIRs are keys to harnessing the data essential to effective command and control power. Faraj argues Marine officers have both a specific and implicit duty to inform their commanders of potholes. Chessani's alleged failure to ensure that Davis was adequately apprised of the seriousness of the division's failure to accurately report what happened caused the problem to explode.

When the government "modified" Chessani's charges in 2007 to accommodate allegations his reporting was defective, his defense attorneys argued that his reporting far surpassed both the substance and the spirit of the orders and SOP pertaining to the manner in which he reported the events at Haditha. Perhaps he did follow guidelines, Faraj pointed out. But that wasn't enough. Chessani failed to personally inform Huck he had a potential problem. Faraj says he was trained to believe senior officers have a duty to do so.

The real issue is what Huck heard rather than what Chessani reported. Huge organizations depend on tiny cogs in big wheels that briefly mesh together before moving on to more facts and figures. There is far too much information for any one individual to hear about, much less absorb. Huck's defense was that Chessani hadn't made his information seem more important.

Whether Chessani was blameless or not is both a legal and a philosopical matter. Had he failed to adequately examine the facts of the incident at Haditha and pass his findings forward in a timely manner? If so, he was negligent, Faraj said. The chain of command is sacrosanct. Nobody except novelists ever overtly violate the chain of command. The first link in the chain is the private first class or lance corporal running a four-man fire team. The last link is the president of the United States. Marines that want to stay Marines don't buck the system. Nobody jumps links. In the Second Marine Division, there were no exceptions.

Faraj says that in the final analysis Chessani failed to keep his superiors adequately informed of potential trouble, a cardinal sin: "Command comes with affirmative duties that have no need of being spelled out because senior officers are supposed to know what they are."

Keeping the big bosses informed of potential trouble is at the top of the list.

"He didn't do anything terrible, but senior officers work in a political environment. They have to be aware of the potential for situations that require them to intervene."

There is clear evidence that the battalion staff certainly knew what had happened and was sharing it with all sorts of officers in various commands who had an abiding interest in what 3/1 was doing. That included the First Marine Division staff back in California. The battalion still belonged to the First Marine Division even though it was under the command of the Second Marine Division until it was released to Camp Pendleton in March 2006.

On November 29, 2005, ten days after the events on Chestnut, the senior commanders at Camp Pendleton had the story straight from the horse's mouth. That's when 3/1's operations officer Major Samuel Carrasco sent a sitrep to Major Jackson I. Reese, the officer running the G-2 Plans shop at First Marine Expeditionary Force (1MEF) at Camp Pendleton.

A G-2 is the expeditionary force intelligence officer. The 1MEF G-2 reports to the 1MEF commanding general, at the time LtGen Mattis, the officer who became the convening authority in the Haditha incident. That the report of such a large engagement did not reach his desk is inconceivable to the Marine officers who live in the esoteric world of Marine Corps commands and staffs.

Carrasco apologized to Reese for being late with his November 29 sitrep before providing a detailed briefing of what transpired ten days before at Haditha. It was written long before any outside influence was being felt by 3/1:

Things are tiring. We have been very busy in the Triad (Haditha, Haqliniyah, and Barwana). In the last two weeks we had 2 marines KIA by IEDs. One was killed in the ensuing wreck from a significant IED that flipped his vehicle. The other has a massive IED detonate directly underneath his vehicle. Miraculously no one else was killed in that. He was in an MAK Highback and it was so big it blew the doors off (ea. 400 lbs) 40 feet in the air and blew 100 feet on either side. The marine KIA was an immediate catastrophic loss. It was immediately followed by a SAF engagement on both sides of the road. The Muj were in occupied buildings (i.e. women and kids). The Marines did what the Muj had not seen before, they assaulted through the near ambush into occupied buildings. This action resulted in (8) EKIA and (15) NKIA. We then followed (7) more Muj on Scan Eagle UAV. Lost 2, but reacquired 5. They went into house, and I had the AirO [Air Officer] put (2) Hellfires into it, and then had rein Sqd immediately assault it. Our squad was immediately hit with SAF and over 15 enemy handgrenades [sic]. We pulled back and had our AirO drop (3) GBU-12s (one of which was a dud). 3 survived (Marines claim to have seen upward to 8 Muj in the house) well built, clean shaven, tight haircuts, leather chest rigs and loaded for bear . . . clear indicator of Foreign Fighters). The marines cut one guy in half with a 240G as two other fled into a copse of date palms. We hit them with a GBU-12 (dud) and then followed up with a LMAV [huge explosion]. Two minutes later one of the MAMs starts booking (unbelievable a man survived). We ended up detaining him. He was hiding with a family, holding a child in his arms. I guess he didn't think we would notice blood running out his ears. We confirmed 4 more EKIA, but speculate there is at least 4 more in the rubble. We couldn't count them, only smell them. . . . End of day tally (1FKIA), (11) FWIA, (13 EKIA), (5) EWIA, numerous detentions. . . .

They had a tough go of I [it], but they will be departing the AO before long. I watched on Scan Eagle as the squad I had assault the house a minute after TWO hellfires [sic] went in, got chewed up by AK, RPKs, and hand grenades. It resulted in us receiving (9) FKIA [typo—was actually 9 FWIA]. Fortunately the worst casualties was shrap [shrapnel] to the lower legs. Talk about feeling guilty. I should have put more bombs on it. I will lead with more air next time. . . . I won't make that mistake again. BYW our new Bn CO is doing awesome. Very even-keeled, and doesn't get overly excited. Exactly what the battalion needed. He isn't trying to prove anything and that is keeping morale high and the bn focused on the mission.

After 15 Jan. things are going to dramatically change around here. Our free reign of operations is going to come to an end. The locals here in Western Al Anbar hate us. It is very different that the Shia [sic] South as we experienced in Babylon.

Carrasco closes with some personal notes. Reese acknowledges the sitrep the next day.

Unless the division SOP for reporting enemy activity had somewhere broken down, Huck was apprised of the Haditha incident almost immediately. Whether Huck chose to do anything about the information or not was the issue before Marine officers who understand the subtleties of staff work. Former 3/1 battalion commander Bob Weimann, a retired lieutenant colonel, said it would be shop talk almost immediately. He opined that perhaps there weren't enough adornments to make Carrasco's sitrep stand out from a dozen other unfortunate situations emerging at the same time.

In the statement Huck offered to Ewers and Colonel Connell at Camp Lejeune, North Carolina, in April 2006, he could not recall being informed fifteen civilians had been killed. Huck reported he was overseeing several combat operations at the time, and that he had no reason to believe that the civilians killed in Haditha were not enemy fighters.

"I didn't know at the time whether they were bad guys, noncombatants, or whatever," Huck recounted.

Dinsmore testified that, two days after the incident, Carrasco and Dinsmore were dispatched to Huck's headquarters with a twenty-eight-slide PowerPoint presentation called a "story board" to brief him. The officers presented a formal, detailed brief that included the method and complexity of the attack and the Marines' response. In addition, they gave verbal explanations of how the Iraqis and Marines were killed and wounded, Dinsmore said. It was the same story Carrasco would later send to Camp Pendleton.

Both officers told Huck and Sokoloski that fifteen Iraqi neutrals (NKIA) and nine insurgents (EKIA) had been killed by counterattacking 3/1 Marines using their personal weapons. When they completed their presentations, each officer asked Huck and Sokoloski if they had any questions. Neither man asked any. Huck closed the briefing by congratulating them on a job well done. In the context of the moment their report seemed perfectly adequate.

Faraj used Huck's seeming indifference to the dead civilians to illustrate how easy it is for commanders and politicians to denude the victims of their humanity:

> The use of the terms NKIA and EKIA provides the strongest induce-ment of senior commanders and the politicians to fight their wars. Buried in those terms is a culture of ambivalence to accurate report-ing on human life that should leave no one wondering why the trig-ger pullers behave the way they do. In Iraq commanders used and condoned the term MAM. Every dead MAM automatically became an EKIA. It did not matter whether the MAM was an actual fighter or some poor schmuck who just happened to be at the wrong place and wrong time. Every Iraqi child and women were mere NKIA. The banality of the term "NKIA" to refer to woman and children served to dehumanize the person making the unintentional death a non-event in a war that was full of other similar non-events.

Although the news media wouldn't learn for almost a year that Huck was briefed immediately and that Sokoloski had approved Pool's erro-neous press release on November 20, the senior commanders in the Marine Corps certainly did. Sokoloski admitted as much to Watt in March 2006. During a later interview he told Ewers that he had decided to keep the truth from the media because of the negative "stra-tegic implications" such a revelation would have on the war effort in Al Anbar Province.

"We knew the, you know, the strategic implications of being per-manently present in Haditha and how badly the insurgents wanted us out of there," Sokoloski explained.[6]

When Pool put out the erroneous press release Sokoloski said he believed it was accurate enough. He thought it was more important to get out a story blaming the insurgents before the insurgents put out a fabricated story of their own. A year later, Sokoloski admitted he with-held the reporting error from Huck for two weeks after he discovered the report was wrong.

Davis was equally certain Huck made the right decision withholding the truth from the media. He told Watt that telling the truth publicly in February 2006 would have been a disastrous public relations move. He felt it was better to downplay McGirk's allegations by denying that the Marines had killed the civilians during a firefight than admit what actually happened. In his mind, Sokoloski's decision was part of the Marines' disinformation campaign to help win the hardened hearts and minds of the Iraqis in Haditha. "Frankly, what I am looking at is the advantage he's [McGirk] giving the enemy," Davis later said to Ewers.[7]

Two and a half months after being briefed by Carrasco and Dinsmore, Huck sent Chiarelli an email on the Haditha incident. At the time Chiarelli was in command of MNF–I and second in command in the Iraqi theater of operations. His boss was General George W. Casey Jr.

In his email, Huck advised Chiarelli that "I support our account and do not see a necessity for further investigation." In his sworn statement to Watt, Huck said he dismissed McGirk's allegations because he was basing his claims on the statements of a known insurgent proxy: "Allegedly, McGirk received his info from the mayor of Haditha, who we strongly suspect to be an insurgent."

In fact, the entire city council of Haditha had condemned the killings in a meeting with Chessani and other Marine officers in the area two weeks after the incident occurred. They even presented a letter written in English proclaiming their outrage. Chessani dismissed the allegations as extortion and insurgent-inspired propaganda. Huck said he was livid when he learned of the meeting after he had explained away the dead civilians to Chiarelli.

About the same time Huck was explaining himself to Chiarelli, Chessani was packing up to go home. He had either been in combat or training for combat for almost three continuous years. He was looking forward to a lengthy school break before moving on to higher command.

Six weeks after receiving his superb February fitness report and three weeks after reporting to Camp Pendleton, Chessani said he was officially relieved of command by Natonski, his boss at Pendleton. "It was just like the battlefield," Chessani explained.

> They [the Marine Corps prosecutors] wanted to isolate the force they wanted to destroy. That is why they did it. That is what Marines are taught. When I tried to explain, to put the ambush at [Routes] Chestnut and Viper in context they said, "I don't want to hear about that." All they wanted to know was what happened at the IED site. There were several significant incidents going on that day. We destroyed an insurgent safe house down the road with bombs the same morning, turned it into dust. There could have been civilians killed there. They didn't care; they didn't want to hear about that. We found insurgents buried in shallow graves still in their weapons and equipment. We had to bury dead insurgents wearing ammunition vests because they started to stink. They didn't want to know how it was related to what happened on Viper and Chestnut. I had a feeling there was an agenda.

Natonski was considered a hard-ass, but that didn't mean he was holding an agenda. He had assumed command of the First Marine Division in August 2004 while it was under fire in Iraq. He led the ground maneuver element under 1MEF through counterinsurgency operations, the Battle of Fallujah (Operation Al-Fajr/Phantom Fury), and the Iraqi National Elections in January 2005. He was one of the few American general officers who had actually led a division in a sustained, head-to-head fight since the Vietnam War. The Army generals who led Desert Storm planned the campaign for six months and fought it for one hundred hours. Natonski executed a month-long intense campaign he helped plan in six weeks.

Chessani said Natonski knew him professionally and personally. It didn't matter in situations of this magnitude. In the parlance of the Corp, 3/1's commander was "still pissin' Iraqi water" when Natonski ruined his career. Chessani's life as a Marine Corps leader was over.

His lawyers said Chessani could have walked away with a nonpunitive Letter of Reprimand for throwing his Marines under the proverbial bus. Instead he boarded it with them. He would endure a rough ride. Brian Rooney, one of Chessani's lawyers, opined that "somebody told Natonski and Schupp to fire Chessani, but nobody has yet to admit it."

While Chessani was in Iraq in 2005, Natonski was the commanding general of the First Marine Division and Camp Pendleton and not in Chessani's daily chain of command. The distinction is lost on most civilians but it is an important one nonetheless. The only way Natonski could have lost confidence in Chessani that fast was if somebody told him to, Rooney reasoned.

Chessani said he could read the tea leaves before he was dismissed.

"When I was in theater I heard they [the Marine Corps] were briefing the president of the United States. I knew I was going to be relieved and probably charged. I even told my XO [executive officer] to be standing by if I was relieved. But I didn't expect what happened. Some things I heard second-hand, like: 'Don't do anything to the Marines until after we [senior Marine Corps commanders] have briefed Congress.' I thought, 'What does that have to do with the Marine Corps? They are not in my chain of command.'"

In late March, Natonski summoned Chessani and several members of the battalion staff to his office. Chessani said he was expecting the call.

"They called me and told me to bring Captain [Lucas] McConnell, the CO [commanding officer] of Kilo Company with me. Then they called again and told me to bring Captain [James] Kimber, commander of India. I thought that was too much. I wondered what they wanted him for. I asked and they said they didn't know. I was also told to bring my XO and the Sergeant Major."

The next morning, after a terse meeting with Natonski, the three officers were relieved of their commands.

"It was the most devastating day of my life," Chessani recalled.

Rooney was enraged. Unlike most of his colleagues, Rooney left behind a family fortune in Pittsburgh for military service. He said he did it because he valued the Marine Corps's ethos of honor and fidelity. His critics say it didn't hurt his chances at a political career either. His family owns the Pittsburgh Steelers and his brother is US Congressman Tom Rooney from Florida. Brian would run for Congress as a Republican in ultra-liberal Ann Arbor in 2010 and lose.

Rooney was a junior member at the Thomas More Law Center, which defended Chessani pro bono. The law center's normal fare is legal issues affecting Catholic doctrines and mores. The other lawyers irreverently called it the "Pope's mouthpiece." Senior and managing partner Richard Thompson is best known for prosecuting notorious human euthanasia advocate and technician Dr. Jack Kevorkian.

When Rooney was hired by Thomas More Law Center, he asked Thompson to take Chessani's case for free. He told Thompson lieutenant colonels with twenty years' service make about $65,000 a year plus $800 a month for quarters when they live off-post. With five kids to feed and another on the way, there was no money for lawyers. The Marine Corps was jeopardizing his family, and protecting the sanctity of the family is what the Thomas More Law Center is all about. Morality is the issue, he said.

By 2009 Thomas More had spent more than $500,000 defending Chessani and the case never went to court-martial. Rooney estimated in 2008 that defending Chessani at court-martial would cost another half-million dollars as well. Most of that money was raised from sympathetic private donors appalled that the Marine Corps was willing to destroy his family as well as his career. Although Rooney did the talking, Thompson and litigator Robert Muise did the lawyering.

Muise is a former Marine Corps infantryman who left the Corps long enough to go to Notre Dame on his own dime before returning as a lawyer. He served more than thirteen years on active duty and has eleven children.

Pitted against them was a team of prosecutors led by LtCol Sean Sullivan. He was already the Haditha investigation's designated pit bull. On June 11, 2007, Sullivan set the tone for what was to come when he told the Article 32 pretrial hearing officer Colonel Christopher Conlin there was enough probable cause to court-martial Chessani for horribly botching the most important job he was ever faced with—deciding what to do about the fifteen dead civilians his Marines had undoubtedly killed.

Muise didn't respond. Occasionally, Thompson would lash out about principles. Muise usually remained buttoned up. He did his talking in negotiations and courtroom word fights. Rooney spun it out the courtroom door.

MURTHA AGAIN

On May 17, 2006, NBC reporters Jim Miklaszewski and Mike Viqueira aired the now-infamous remarks of Representative John Murtha on MSNBC. His heated rhetoric immediately raised the temperature another notch or two.

In its printed version of the report on MSNBC's website, Miklaszewski led with Murtha claiming US Marines "killed innocent civilians in cold blood."

"From the beginning," Miklaszewski reported, "Iraqis in the town of Haditha said US Marines deliberately killed fifteen unarmed Iraqi civilians, including seven women and three children.

"One young Iraqi girl said the Marines killed six members of her family, including her parents.

"'The Americans came into the room where my father was praying,' she said, 'and shot him.'"[8]

The only problem with the report was that the Marines Corps didn't have any evidence in June 2006. There wasn't any evidence to be had. There were allegations, innuendo, sworn and unsworn statements, and speculation, but there weren't any facts in evidence because no charges had been made. At best, there were indications that crimes might have been committed, although no prosecutorial effort was officially announced. Finding out what happened was supposed to be what the investigation was all about.

The evidence NBC's top Pentagon reporter had reportedly been apprised of included "Marine Corps photos taken immediately after the incident" showing that the victims were killed "execution-style."

One photo even "portrayed a mother and young child bent over on the floor as if in prayer, shot dead," said the officials who showed him on the "condition of anonymity because the investigation hasn't been completed."

The demand for charges against the Marines gathered steam over the entire long, hot summer. By then, Sharratt, Tatum, Wuterich, Salinas, Mendoza, and Dela Cruz knew they were major players. They were already on their second and third interrogations. Wuterich and some of the other Marines obtained civilian counsel. Their interrogations stopped. Most vocal among the civilian lawyers was Neal Puckett. The former Marine Corps judge was already garnering face time in the national press. On June 11, *Washington Post* reporter Josh White disclosed that Wuterich told Puckett he had done nothing wrong. Puckett denounced the charges in White's story.

"It will forever be his position that everything they did that day was following their rules of engagement and to protect the lives of Marines," Puckett told White.

IN EARLY JUNE, Hagee finally held his much-anticipated press conference that would undoubtedly clear up the allegations of Marine misconduct. New allegations were bubbling to the surface almost every day from leaks in Iraq and at the Pentagon.

Instead, Hagee talked about what it is to be a Marine. *Washington Post* reporter Dana Milbank claimed Hagee seemed prepared to "break into the Marine Corps Hymn" during his opening remarks at the Pentagon briefing. Perhaps he was. The Marine Corps's burnished image was showing signs of abuse, and no doubt he didn't like it.

Hagee remembered Belleau Wood and Iwo Jima and the "Frozen Chosin" without recalling what had happened at Haditha seven months before. The understandably perplexed press corps couldn't understand why he would brief Representative Murtha and not them. It didn't seem fair, Milbank sniffed.

It was well known that Chairman of the Joint Chiefs of Staff Marine Corps Gen Peter Pace was very unhappy as well. The sixteenth chairman of the Joint Chiefs of Staff and first Marine ever appointed to the United States' highest-ranking military office had only been in command six months when Haditha erupted in the headlines. Unsubstantiated rumors had it Gen Pace ordered thirty-fourth commandant General James T. Conway to clean up the Haditha mess when Hagee retired on November 13, 2006.

At least Hagee mentioned the case. In his opening statement, he said he was "gravely concerned" but that it would be "inappropriate" to comment.

"I refer all these questions to the operational chain of command for comment at the appropriate time," Hagee lamely explained.

He was still not saying anything when he retired. It didn't matter to Murtha. He had a direct line into NCIS through his executive assistant Gabrielle Carruth. She was on his personal staff as well as the appropriations associate staff. Carruth also served as Murtha's policy director. She had joined the congressman's staff in December 2001, following a one-year US Department of Defense fellowship from Georgetown University. Her credentials included a seventeen-year stint with the Navy, working around the world as a special NCIS agent, examining sexual assaults and white-collar crime.

At one point the defense attorneys explored whether there was a way to break Murtha's pipeline into NCIS. They decided it was a pointless exercise.

Meanwhile, NCIS was exploiting the growing rifts between the enlisted Marines facing murder charges. The NCIS special agents were telling them they could get the death penalty for intentionally killing women and children. It was time to divide and conquer and they were making the most of it. Chessani said it was the same tactics his intelligence Marines used to glean information from reluctant tribesmen.

The Thundering Third's problem was always too much or too little documentation. It was a problem of the ages. The ancient Roman legions in Vindolanda in northern Britain heated their winter encampments with bundles of the thin wooden plates they received their written orders on.

Nobody at 3/1 was burning anything, nobody was hiding anything, but they weren't writing it down either. During the November 19 fight things were hectic, to say the least. Chessani and his small staff had one infantry company in contact, several other companies on missions, and there was air support to coordinate, intelligence to evaluate, and brass to inform. The heat never came off. On July 9, 2006, then *Washington Post* reporter Thomas E. Ricks ran a story on page A13 claiming the Marines understood neither how to communicate nor how to fight a counterinsurgency campaign. He attributed the observations to Chiarelli, who apparently confided in those baffling unnamed "defense officials" always buzzing about.

In his report, Ricks said that Chiarelli found Huck, Sokoloski, and Davis "negligent" for relaying to his command poorly understood orders about how to treat Iraqi civilians. Ricks revealed that Chiarelli was concerned that the US military was "inadequately prepared to conduct an effective counterinsurgency campaign in Iraq." He didn't mention the two-year-old dispute between senior Marines and Army officers had actually started during the abortive first fight to take Fallujah in April 2004 that was still under way. At the time the Marines did not believe the ill-trained and unmotivated Iraqi National Guard was prepared to defend Fallujah from the insurgency. The Army generals thought differently.

Chiarelli came to Iraq in the waning days of the dictatorial Coalition Provisional Authority when Iraq was building a nominally sovereign government that had to be given at least lip service if not actual respect. The big unit slap-downs the Marines were conducting in Al Anbar Province in 2004 and 2005 were no longer appreciated.

Ricks said Chiarelli was particularly galled to learn that the local town council had complained in writing to Chessani about the deaths of two entire families without any positive feedback.[9] Chiarelli wasn't buying Huck's argument that the Iraqis were all insurgent sympathizers. In some respects the Second Marine Division was now paying the price for creating the Marines who had smashed the insurgency in

Fallujah in November 2004 and for trying to do it again in Haditha with Operation River Gate in November 2005.

"You've got to prepare for the fight you're in today," Ricks quoted "the second" unnamed defense official as saying. "It's totally different from fighting in Iraq two or three years ago."

At Haditha, the Marines didn't have enough firepower to dominate the countryside. RCT-2 didn't have nearly enough troops to even begin to pacify the 53,000-square-mile province. The insurgents at Haditha were still completely in control of the hearts, minds, roads, and rivers of the indigenous population.

Near the end of his scathing synopsis Ricks reported that Huck had "recently retired from the Marines and could not be reached for comment." No doubt Huck wished he had been allowed to retire. Huck was actually tucked away at the Pentagon in a disgraced general's non-job waiting to find out his fate.

Ricks saved his most damning indictment for last. Attributing the strength and depth of the Haditha investigation to Murtha's unfounded declarations, Ricks quoted the Beltway's favorite new mantra: The Marines at Haditha had "killed innocent civilians in cold blood." Ricks knew because Murtha knew, he explained; Murtha had "been briefed by a senior Marine officer on the probe."

On August 18, 2006, Rick's colleague David S. Cloud claimed unnamed Marines destroyed or withheld evidence in the case, at least according to "two unnamed Defense Department officials" who had already "been briefed on the case."

Kilo Company logbooks had been "tampered with," and an "incriminating video" taken by an "aerial drone" had been withheld from investigators from the day of the killings until Chiarelli "intervened," the two officials said. It sounded very sinister. It was the first time "details about possible concealment or destruction of evidence have been disclosed," Cloud said. "No charges have been brought yet."

A year later, after charges had been brought, the "missing" logbook pages turned up in evidence and the aerial drone's undisclosed video was discovered to have been beamed to the appropriate commands in real time. Cloud didn't know a stealthy Air Force "Predator" UAV was also beaming live pictures through operators flying it from Nellis Air Force Base in Nevada. Carrasco had already reported he used them to chase insurgents around the palm groves.

According to Cloud's unidentified sources, Kilo's imaginary logbook, "which was meant to be a daily record of major incidents the Marines' company encountered," was "missing every page for Nov. 19, 2005."

There were no conclusions about "who may have tampered with the log." Cloud added, but "SSgt Frank D. Wuterich, the leader of the squad involved in the killings, was on duty at the unit's operations center, where the logbook was kept, shortly after the killings occurred."

Cloud closed his report by describing how the "three-vehicle [there were four] convoy of marines was hit by a roadside bomb, killing a lance corporal. The squad then began going through houses nearby, killing Iraqis found inside in what defense lawyers have said was a justifiable use of lethal force by marines who believed they were under concerted attack by insurgents."

He concluded his voluminous indictment with allegations from the unnamed sources that the Marines "overreacted after the death of their fellow marine and shot the civilians in cold blood."

There it was—"in cold blood"—the capstone allegation that lay across the truth like a gelatinous red blanket of guilt. With that single unsubstantiated phrase Cloud managed to marginalize, repudiate, and then explain what actually happened at Haditha without an accuser who could be placed in the light of public scrutiny.

CHAPTER 11

HECTOR SALINAS—TRUMP CARD

Frozen in amber in 2008 was Sgt Hector R. Salinas, a twenty-three-year-old naturalized American citizen born in Spain. He was a corporal when he was a riding in the convoy going back to FB Sparta on Route Chestnut. Then twenty-one, Salinas was a fire team leader, an excellent grenadier, and soon to be taking over Wuterich's squad. He was in the lead vehicle that had a bird's-eye view of the road ahead. He believes his M203 was instrumental in breaking the back of the ambush that killed his buddy "T. J." Terrazas. The Marines who know him say he was very wary and taut, a sharp Marine who came from a security team in Kuwait. Like Mendoza and Dela Cruz, he would find himself a key witness in the events ahead.

Salinas was incorrectly named in the November 2006 NPR story as a potential suspect and never charged with a crime. Instead, he "voluntarily" stayed in the Marine Corps beyond his enlistment expiration date. He did so to avoid the legal entanglements the government offered as an alternative, his lawyer said. His usually silent Dallas-based lawyer, Daniel K. Hagood, a retired Marine reserve infantry officer, said his client was free to leave the Marine Corps about ninety days after receiving immunity in early January 2008, ensuring his availability for the scheduled courts-martial of Tatum and Wuterich. In the meantime, he went to Afghanistan as a contractor. He resurfaced publicly in 2012.

Three days after Christmas 2007, the Marine Corps acknowledged Salinas had been given "testimonial immunity" in return for the unvarnished truth about what happened on Route Chestnut. His immunity prevented the government from using Salinas's words against him in any subsequent proceedings as long as the sergeant testified honestly about his knowledge of events at Haditha.

In 2008, Hagood said his client was never coerced into staying at Pendleton involuntarily. In fact, Hagood said, Salinas "still hasn't decided" if he would leave the Marine Corps or reenlist when his options became available. Hagood's statement was contrary to contemporary wisdom in 2007 even before his client became a person of interest in the proceedings. Salinas couldn't wait to get out of the Corps.

In any event, early on Salinas was a government trump card in a hand of Texas Hold 'Em the government was running on Wuterich, Sharratt, and Tatum. The testimony of Mendoza and Dela Cruz was already uncertain. In the months since the ambush, it had been met with skepticism for being tainted with lies, questionable tactics, and bewildering motives. Salinas was legally pure. He was never charged with any crime and was merely a witness to the proceedings where the Iraqis died under Marine guns. By all accounts, he had fought honorably.

On February 19, 2006, Salinas gave a sworn statement to Watt about what he saw and what he did after the IED exploded. It was the first of three statements the government revealed to the defense in discovery. Before speaking to Watt, Salinas signed a Privacy Act Statement disclosure warning and a Rights Warning Procedure/Waiver Certificate that explained in micro-type all the rights and privileges he was waiving. Essentially, it was everything the Constitution holds sacred.

His voluntary participation in Watt's investigation was a matter of routine for Marines in 3/1 during February 2006. The form Watt presented to Salinas was ambiguous.[1] Instead of making a statement for a criminal investigation, Salinas was merely "assisting the appropriate authorities" in determining what they should do about the "Haditha complex attack" of November 19, 2005. The statement is signed by Watt as "investigator" in their cooperative effort. The witness signature block is blank. Salinas gave the statement to Watt on February 19 and signed his rights waiver on the twenty-first, a bit of a legal gaffe if the statement was ever intended to help prosecute him. Watt's informal investigation had the unintentional consequence of providing the future defendants some legal wiggle room to change their stories to more advantageous recollections without facing the onus of perjury.

Even the DA Form 2823 Watt used for his official instrument is a bit odd for the circumstances. According to Army Regulation 190-45, the form is intended for "law enforcement reporting" and designed for evidence collection in criminal offenses. The rights waiver that comes printed on it contains a line where Salinas and the other Marines had to initial to certify agreement to voluntarily discuss the "offense under investigation." The word *offense* is lined out, replaced by Watt with the word *events,* an innocuous description of what Salinas was agreeing to reveal. Some of the defense lawyers said that doing so made it clear that both Watt and Salinas thought Watt was a collector of facts and not a criminal investigator, something frequently forgotten in later recitations of the "Watt Investigation."

Salinas told Watt the usual story running up to the ambush. They had just passed Route Viper after turning on Chestnut from River Road when a large explosion erupted behind him and the convoy was hit by small arms fire. Simultaneously, Salinas noticed a white, four-door sedan stopped on a rise to his immediate left:

> It may have been observing the convoy. After the blast four or five MAMs exited the vehicle and started running south of Chestnut. We PID the MAMs so we all start shooting and they all go down.
>
> I did not see any markers to indicate that an IED may go off. LCPL Dela Cruz saw a white four-door sedan from the overwatch

position. I also saw the white four-door sedan up on the hill, at the front left of the convoy. It was located immediately to the left of our front vehicle. It may have been observing the convoy. After the blast, four or five MAMs exited the vehicle and started running south of Chestnut. . . .

We were taking SAF the whole time. We were possibly taking SAF from the north, but we were positively taking SAF from the south. I made it to the fourth vehicle and saw a casualty stuck under fourth vehicle and that 2xFWIA and 1xFKIA. I helped Doc Whitt work on FKIA and 2 FWIA. Doc was concerned and we continued to take SAF until the QRF showed up.[2]

In the unsworn statement typed on plain paper and identified as Exhibits 000159 through 000161 in the Bargewell Report, Salinas adds a signed, hand-drawn diagram depicting the ambush site as well as some descriptive analysis of his reaction to the white car that is not repeated elsewhere. In the unsworn version Salinas adds, "We PID the MAMs so, we started shooting and they all go down. *They kind of looked suspicious and I didn't have time to chase him*" [emphasis added].

That was the way he talked all the time: a firm recitation of the facts with just an edge of the disrespect shit-hot Marine grunts sometimes display. Faraj says a little bit too much attitude showed.

On March 18, 2006, Salinas gave a third voluntary sworn statement at Haditha Dam to NCIS Special Agent Mathew W. Marshall. The battalion was standing down for its imminent return to the States. The word was already out that some of the guys might have to stay behind. The investigation had narrowed to Wuterich's squad. The heat was on. Folks were dummying about Kilo's only moment in the sun during its long, tension-filled deployment full of IEDs, filth, and fear.

Marshall advised Salinas he was suspected of violating the Law of Land Warfare in the death of one of the non-combatants, therefore subject to criminal prosecution under the UCMJ. Salinas dutifully initialed the form in a dozen places to show he read it before signing it "Hector R. Salinas."

The carefully portrayed display of voluntary cooperation Marshall demonstrated by all the initial signing is an old trick that investigators use to show the suspect's willing state of mind and voluntary attitude in the face of losing their liberty for most of their young lives. Marshall kept Salinas in a basement room stinking of human excrement for twelve hours. Salinas waived his right to a lawyer and signed the form. There was no lawyer in the battalion. Capt Stone, the battalion staff judge advocate and Salinas's de facto lawyer, was in hock himself, so his advice didn't amount to much anyway. Salinas had nobody else to ask.

Salinas was facing his first combat engagement, the thing he had trained for for forty-two months, the moment a Marine earns the name. He responded accordingly and attacked the threat. The uninitiated can't appreciate an American infantryman's firepower until they have witnessed it. It doesn't erupt with the fury of the movies; there are no giant fireballs flinging cars and trucks through the air. Rather, there are huge bangs and immensely loud cracks accompanied by puffs of smoke and rising dust storms filled with invisible bits of metal that saturate bodies and punch holes in concrete. Death is sudden and devastating, rending bodies and buildings into parts. Blood and brains mix together in a bloody gruel. Nobody usually says anything cool.

Salinas could put out as much fire by himself as a fire team could in earlier wars. In addition to his fully automatic M16, he had an M203 grenade launcher attached under its barrel that fired 40 mm grenades four hundred meters with surprising accuracy and hand grenades to toss into confined spaces. He was covered in body armor that could stop at least one bullet hit, a ballistic helmet that actually deflected enemy strikes, and the similar firepower of his team. They had several types of lightweight radios at their disposal and reinforcements minutes away. The Roman Legions appeared equally invincible attacking Gaul.

Salinas was psyched up and ready to boogie when Kallop told him to clear south. He says as much in his play by play to both Watt and the NCIS special agents.

Salinas began his March 18 statement to NCIS with the usual preamble about where he was, whom he was with, and what was happening at the instant the IED exploded. Restraint showed up that wasn't part of his story until he started talking to Marshall at Haditha Dam.[3]

Faraj says it was both a good and bad ploy for Salinas to use. For one thing, it put him in a trick bag. He either helped kill the Iraqis at the white car or he knew who did because he said so twice. Additionally, he had been in on the attacks at Houses #1 and #2 and had subsequently searched them with Lt Kallop after Wuterich's fire team cleared the buildings. Finally, on the same day he talked to Marshall, Salinas signed an additional statement to an NCIS agent named Don A. Blane detailing just how much he understood the rules of engagement, the laws of land warfare, and the lawful application of deadly force. Doing so stripped him of all his wiggle room. Salinas was hooked on the barbs of the criminal investigation; he just didn't know it.

Marshal took Salinas's statement using notes and then typed it for him to sign. There appears to be nothing wrong with the practice on its face. The accused gets to review it and decide if they think it is correct. Even giving the benefit of the doubt to the NCIS agents that they tried to capture both the accuracy and spirit of Salinas's statement in its final form, what they write is not exactly what the accused says. At the time they were prohibited by NCIS regulations from recording the statements of the suspects.

In Salinas's statement, the subtleties of the remarkably concise language used in the sworn statement Salinas signed for Marshall is nothing like the way Salinas apparently writes or speaks. More importantly, it is a mini-indictment of the squad's actions that morning, something Salinas later claimed he never intended to do. Despite his best intentions, Salinas dutifully initialed the beginning and end of each page to acknowledge that he read and understood his sworn statement. No doubt Marshall was equally indulgent pointing out where Salinas needed to put his initials proving his free will in the matter.

Salinas's account for NCIS was far more muted than his early, exuberant recitation of events to Watt. In this version, as soon as the IED went off Salinas knew what it was, he said, so he dismounted from his Humvee and headed for the source of the blast: "I maneuvered toward the rear of the convoy where I heard the explosion. I also heard small arms fire coming from the east of my location. As I passed the rear of my vehicle I heard CPL DELA CRUZ giving orders to the occupants of the aforementioned cars. CPL DELA CRUZ repeatedly ordered the occupants to stop running by yelling '*qif, qif, qif,*' which means 'stop' in Arabic."

At that point, Salinas says he turned his head toward the commotion. He could see "4 or 5 MAMs" running southwest, which was away and somewhat diagonal from his perspective. "I could not tell if any of them had weapons," Salinas recalled, because his view was partially obscured by the white car. According to a notation on his hand-drawn diagram the MAMs "dismounted + ran." Next to the notation is a broken line indicating his line of sight to the scene. The Iraqis were "5 to 10 meters apart" (roughly fifteen to thirty feet) as they ran away, Salinas reported. Salinas recalled he was not "overly focused" on the MAMs or the white car because "CPL DELA CRUZ had them supervised."

He mentioned nothing about shooting anyone because he didn't have time to chase after them.

In his NCIS interview, Salinas said that seconds after he dismounted his vehicle and started toward the rear of the convoy, Dela Cruz opened up with his rifle. Salinas assumed "that he was engaging the MAMs from the white car."

"I do not remember hearing anyone other than Cpl Dela Cruz firing their weapon at this time," Salinas added, an observation in sharp contrast to Wuterich's admission that he "took a knee" and opened fire on the fleeing men. Perhaps it was more indicative of the fog of war than trying to tell a lie. Infantrymen sometimes only have a worm's-eye view of events boiling around them, much less a panoramic comprehension. People are shooting at them and they are trying to hide and shoot back at the same time.

Salinas said he arrived at the fourth vehicle to discover Terrazas dead and Crossan pinned under the vehicle by debris. Salinas removed Crossan's throat protector and back SAPI (small-arms protective insert) to let him breathe more comfortably and then retrieved Terrazas's casualty card to provide his number to Wuterich so he could report his death. Meanwhile, he helped Doc Whitt with Crossan while Guzman continued laying down fire. The ambush site was still being sprayed by SAF, Salinas remembered:

> I saw that LCPL GUZMAN, lying in a prone firing position, was engaging a house to the south of ROUTE CHESTNUT with Doc Whitt's rifle. During this period of time I could hear SAF impacting the wreckage of HMMWV #4. . . .

The SAF stopped just as the QRF led by Kallop arrived on the scene, an event Salinas attributed to the suppressive fire being laid down on House #1 by Guzman. Salinas told Guzman to climb aboard the Humvee for evacuation. Guzman told him he couldn't walk because his left ankle was broken. While a QRF evacuation team piled Guzman into the truck, Salinas said he formed up a team to engage the house the SAF was coming from. "I began forming a maneuver element to assault the house that LCPL GUZMAN had been engaging from the south of ROUTE CHESTNUT."

Not "Sgt Wuterich" or "we," but "I." Salinas believed he was in command. While Salinas formed his fire team, the insurgents began firing again. Salinas said he observed a MAM firing an AK-47 from the southeast corner of House #1, the house Guzman had fired on.

> I engaged the MAM with four or five M16 rounds and fired three High Explosive Duel Purpose (HEDP) M203 rounds at the two windows on the north side of the house and one at the roof top door. I used the M203 rounds as suppressive fire for a frontal assault on the house.

After firing the M203 for the last time, Salinas teamed up with Mendoza, Tatum, and Wuterich to assault the house. Unlike his platoon leader, Salinas never mentioned Sharratt laying down suppressive fire with his 240 Golf while the fire team advanced on the houses. He said Mendoza, Tatum, and Wuterich crossed Route Chestnut at a run, moving rapidly across the shallow wadi, a distance Sharratt testified was about two hundred meters. They weren't fired upon on the way, Salinas said. In later sworn testimony, Salinas claimed he took a different route across the wadi and met the still-forming team near House #1.

Salinas was leading the "maneuver element," with Wuterich "in tow" bringing up the rear, he said. The team stacked at the west entrance into the house with Salinas still in the lead, a classic combat formation loaded for bear.

Salinas was well drilled for what he was supposed to do; he was a FAST Marine, a specialist trained to roar into heavily fortified structures like a lightning bolt to take out anyone they find. Another Third Platoon FAST Marine corporal named Ryan Weemer found himself in another pot of boiling water for allegedly murdering an unarmed Iraqi prisoner at Fallujah a year before the Haditha Marines were charged. Weemer and Salinas both went to the same school to become members of the Marine Corps Security Force that guards the Navy's nuclear secrets.

Salinas kicked in the door. It was dark inside—no light except for the ambient glow of early morning coming from open doors at the end of the hallway. The house was full of "lingering smoke" from the M203 grenade explosions, he said. When Salinas turned into the hallway, he saw a figure running away. He could not "identify age, gender, or if the person was armed," he admitted to Marshall.

Without legal counsel, without any legal knowledge, and without being cognizant of what was in store for the Marines caught in the spreading NCIS net, Salinas started down a slippery slope telling Special Agent Marshall he just violated the ROE, the laws of armed conflict (LOAC), and a laundry list of standing orders and regulations that could land him in jail. His recollections would prove devastating to all the enlisted Marines who were there. Without knowing it, he was making the government's case:

> Although I did not positively identify (PID) the person as a threat for engagement, I had PID'd the house as "receiving contact" and when I saw the person running from the area that the contact had been received, I shot and killed that person.

Meanwhile, he could hear Mendoza engaging someone with his rifle on the other side of the wall. Then he heard an AK rack. Once heard, it is not a sound one easily forgets. Salinas hadn't:

> I was stacked on the hallway wall beside the kitchen door when I heard the sound of an AK racking at least two times in the room to the left of the staircase. I am very familiar with the sound of an AK racking as I have heard it several hundred times, from working around them to clearing them on patrols.

Deciding the sound represented a threat, Salinas and Tatum, who apparently perceived a similar threat, each threw a fragmentation grenade into the room where the AK was being racked. Instead of two distinct explosions Salinas said he only heard one loud bang. The explosion was so loud Salinas still had ringing in his ears when he gave his statement two months later, he said. "My team began clearing the rooms down the right side of the hallway on our way to the next house without further contact."

"My team"—there it was again. Salinas thought he was in command. Before his team could enter the room and clear it with a spray of automatic weapons fire, somebody—he did not know who—yelled that they had a runner bailing out of the back door.

Faraj believed this was a salient moment in Salinas's recollections. It was the basis for his belief that Tatum and Sharratt later returned to the houses to make sure they were cleared. Marines are trained to never leave their rear unsecured.

Salinas said that when he turned his attention to the fleeing figure, he could just make out a person speeding past the open doorway at the end of the hall. Several hours later, Salinas would reenter the room again, long after Tatum and he threw in their grenades, to discover the carnage they had wrought.

Conspicuous in its absence from Salinas's statement is any mention of the numerous casualties that filled the house. Even in the harshest combat arena, it is memorable to see so many dead civilians in a single structure, particularly children.

"When the Marines left the house, only Eman and her younger brother were still alive," McGirk had reported.[4]

In less time than it apparently took Eman and her younger brother to moan, Salinas moved his narrative from House #1 to House #2, where the squad was approaching its north face still in the combat stack the team had formed before entering House #1. Salinas later claimed he detached himself from the stack to provide overwatch. This is at odds with the recollections of the other fire team members, who said the team dashed toward the second house, spreading around it to cover both sides.

House #2 was surrounded by a patio wall that Salinas climbed. From his vantage point, he reported, he could see two entry points. There was no fire coming from the house, he said. While posted at the west side doorway he heard M16 fire coming from his right. Then someone—again he didn't know who—came up behind him and asked for "another" grenade. Salinas, backing up toward the voice, reached behind his back with his offering, never taking his eyes from his "own area of responsibility," he said. Immediately after handing off the grenade, he heard another explosion. Presumably, it was the same grenade he had just passed off, announcing the beginning of the team's second house-clearing operation.

Wuterich, Tatum, and Mendoza moved inside. Simultaneously, Salinas moved into the kitchen. A dead man was lying on the floor. Salinas told Marshall he couldn't see a weapon, "but I believe that I would have noticed a weapon if there had been one present."

"After the explosion in this house, I heard more M16 SAF inside the house, and then the team exited one of the rooms at the end of the hallway and went straight out," he recalled.

Scratched through in his written account with an ink line is the phrase "without clearing the remainder of the house." The excised words are neatly initialed by Salinas. His admission was another important stone in the foundation of Sharratt's version of events in which he claimed several fire team members returned to House #1 and cleared it again.

Faraj was quick to jump on it. Another reason to believe Salinas ordered Tatum and Sharratt to go back and finish clearing both houses, he said. Nobody else seemed to notice.

The squad moved on, outside now, between the houses in the neighborhood where empty windows stared back at them malevolently. *Where are the bad guys now?* they were wondering. Salinas knew there were already at least three dead MAMs, including the guy in the kitchen floor Mendoza had shot.

What was his state of mind? Marshall didn't ask.

The discipline Salinas and his team displayed at that moment is the Marine Corps's greatest achievement: training men to know the right answers when flight or fight demands an immediate response. Flight is the normal response. Walking intentionally into the very real possibility of immediate death simply isn't normal behavior. The prosecution wanted the jury to believe the men's motivation was murder rather than making war. In retrospect, it seems self-evident the Marines were responding to their training, but that wasn't so obvious in the statements the NCIS investigators had fabricated. Perhaps Marshall didn't know to ask and Salinas didn't know how to explain what it was like to try and make rational decisions under fire. Faraj said he didn't buy any of it.

"Salinas told Marshall during the many hours of interrogation. But like the senior officers who refused to consider Chessani's and Dinsmore's accounts of all the events of the day, Marshall was only interested in evidence that would advance his agenda and most certainly his career."

Faraj interviewed Salinas for the first time in 2007, eighteen months after the incident had passed. That interview lasted about an hour, Faraj recalled.

"Salinas described the SAF, the imminent threat the squad faced, the absolute lack of any intent to kill anyone who did not pose a threat."

Listening to Salinas's version of the events of November 19, Faraj came away convinced that the squad's actions were lawful, although with tragic results.

"The tactics used to enter the houses on November 19 were the very tactics taught at every MOUT course and combat town in the Marine Corps. If the Marine Corps and the politicians had a problem with the results, then either stop going to war or keep the infantry out of built-up areas that have any civilian populations. But the Marine Corps was not about to question the viability of MOUT tactics or to announce to the world that based on the training and the ROE briefed to the Marines, the squad's actions were lawful," Faraj argues.

"Prosecutors and NCIS were fabricating a case to challenge the basis for use of the tactics. They needed to minimize the perceived threat and claim that the situation required more of a knock and talk approach rather than the kinetic entry used in MOUT. And the way Marshall was going to do that is by writing statements that leave out any mention of threat against the Marines, hostile fires, or the active insurgent activity of that morning. To advance his agenda and career, a twelve-hour interview would be distilled to a handful of pages that could be read in twenty minutes talking about the killing of civilians."

In the quiet calm of a courtroom, perhaps it was possible to believe the defendants were capable of cool reason, debating the pros and cons of taking the civilians' lives, but not when the young Marines were stoked on fear and anger boiling together in the cauldron of fire on Route Chestnut.

HOUSE #3 TURNED out to be anticlimactic. Salinas remembered it being where Sharratt shot the lock off the door with his M240 Golf, as well as a good place to obtain overwatch on Route Chestnut. Sharratt's personal pyrotechnics at the door might have been the sustained machine gun fire Kallop heard and assumed was suppressive rather than intrusive in nature. Sharratt said it was the only time he fired the powerful weapon that day.

Kallop's confusion is understandable regardless of whether it was correct or a counter to a lie. Marines aren't trained to shoot doors open with medium machine guns. Too many bullets go flying around. Shooting a 7.62 mm machine gun into a door at close range without knowing what is behind it is dangerous—some might say stupid— especially when what is behind the wood may be hardened steel or concrete. Bullets tend to bounce all over the place, but it really does look cool! Again, it goes to state of mind. Marines don't normally shoot locks off doors with medium machine guns without somebody tearing them a new asshole, as Sharratt would say.

In any event, Sharratt's dramatic contribution was a pointless exercise. The building was under construction. Nobody lived there. Finding nothing, the four determined Marines moved north on Route Zebra, back to Chestnut where the fight had started. It was hard to believe it had been less than an hour since the IED exploded. Salinas was so drained he didn't even look at the dead men sprawled grotesquely by the suspicious white car.

"We passed beside where the white car with the downed passengers was," Salinas recalled, "but I did not pay much attention to the area."

Five dead guys sprawled in a grisly line with their heads blown apart and he scarcely gives it a thought.

Beyond the five dead men was the house on the rise where Sharratt and Wuterich first saw the Iraqis MAMs start turkey peeking at them from across the road. Salinas doesn't say Kallop told Wuterich to establish the OP on top of it. In his narrative they just did, after stopping long enough beside their Humvee to allow Sharratt to recover his SAW. Then Salinas and the rest of the team move to their overwatch location. After searching it they move onto the upper floor, establishing positions facing likely avenues of enemy approach. Tatum, with an M16, takes the north wall, Wuterich, armed the same way, goes to the southeast corner, Salinas with his M203, and Sharratt with his SAW, also cover the southeast.

Sometime later (there is no time lapse built into the narrative), Sharratt observes a running MAM exiting the east side of House #1, the building they had cleared with such ferocity at the beginning of the fight. That man was never identified. Sharratt and Salinas on the overwatch position, and Kallop behind the suspect, all shoot at him. He goes down hard. Nobody sees a weapon. A dead guy in a so-called ninja track suit worn by the Fedayeen Saddam was later found there. He was included in the insurgent count and never named. Faraj says that would make sense if he were a foreign fighter because nobody wanted his body. He joined eight other MAMs considered insurgents. Kallop tells the Marines "good job."

It is now about 1000 or 1030 hours, at least ninety minutes after the ambush was sprung. The MAM shot down was running from the same house where Salinas had seen a MAM firing after the ambush was initiated. It is from the same house where Tatum and he had double fragged a room, the same house where Mendoza shot a man in the face. And it was the same house where dead Iraqis were still leaking blood and brains on the tile floors. Only this military-age male had miraculously survived, unseen, unhurt. Salinas saw him running on a "ridgeline" dressed in dark-colored pants, "green or turquoise," he recalled, and "a tan-colored shirt":

> The MAM was not armed when I saw him. Both LCPL SHARRATT and I engaged the MAM with our respective weapons (M249 and M16). The MAM fell forward, face down, along the ridgeline.

Soon after the MAM on the ridgeline died, Kallop returned to the newly established OP for Salinas. He wanted to "do an assessment on House #1 and #2," Salinas said.

They approached the houses carefully, searching them "tactically," a euphemism for being very careful. A live MAM had just run out of it and a two-man stack has a hard time covering 360 degrees simultaneously. In the room where Salinas tossed his grenade with Tatum, he "observed something moving." It was nine-year-old Eman Waleed and her brother Abdul Rahman, eight, hiding from the unfathomable horror that had descended on their house, Salinas recalled:

> I observed a six-to-seven-year-old male and a ten-to-eleven-year-old female. The boy had shrapnel wound to his left upper back and the girl would not let us assess her injuries. As I tried to put a bandage on the boy's back, he and the girl began saying, "*Mujadine, Mujadine, Mujadine.*"

Two months later Eman Waleed didn't remember grenades exploding in her bedroom when she related her grim recollections to McGirk in Baghdad. She told McGirk she and her little brother were shot by Marines screaming in English. They were hiding in a doorway with just their rifle barrels visible.

"I watched them shoot my grandfather, first in the chest and then in the head. Then they killed my granny," she told McGirk.[5]

Four months later, she would tell NCIS investigators one of the Marines was armed with a pistol. So would her little brother, Faraj said.

Eman told *TIME* that the Marines began firing into the corner of the bedroom her eight-year-old younger brother Abdul and she were hiding. The other adults shielded the children from the bullets and died in the process. Eman says her leg was hit by a piece of metal and Abdul Rahman was "shot near his shoulder."[6]

Salinas explained what he did after finding the children:

> LT KALLOP and I left without doing anything with the children and they would not come with us. I returned to the OP and LT KALLOP returned to the OP, got LCPL Rodriguez then walked back to get the children from House #1.

Only Eman and her younger brother were still alive. Seven other members of her family were dead. A woman and a baby, probably Hiba Abdullah and her daughter Asia, escaped.

Nowhere in the Marines' narratives are the Iraqi soldiers that supposedly rescued the orphaned children. In the official version of events, the children were eventually evacuated to a US hospital after briefly being cared for by Iraqi soldiers. Kallop does remember at least one Iraqi soldier was there beating the locals with a stick. But the Iraqi soldiers played no discernible role, according to the Marines. They said Eman's story is a fabrication. That it did not happen. None of the Marines remember them doing anything but guarding detained civilians. More likely the children ended in the nominal care of the Iraqi Army soldiers because they spoke the same language. They eventually were evacuated to an American hospital. Two months later Eman Waleed would remember it was Iraqis, not Americans, who found them before tending their wounds.

Back at the OP, Salinas got no rest. Sometime after he returned, perhaps an hour, Wuterich saw another suspicious MAM, the one he reported turkey peeking at the Marines across the way. When he ran back in the house Wuterich got curious, Salinas said.

Once again, the team "gathered as a maneuver element to clear the house." Tatum stayed behind to secure the OP and maintain overwatch. Salinas led the team of Wuterich and Sharratt to the house. It was "occupied by an older man, a young boy, and approximately six women inside the house," Salinas said. The search revealed nothing. When the trio of Marines tried to leave to search next door, the women tried to follow them out, "so I tried to keep them inside in case there were any engagements in the area." His recollection of who was inside the residence differs completely from Sharratt, who didn't remember any MAMs in the first apartment.

Next door, Wuterich and Sharratt were already engaged. Salinas heard the gunfire erupt, "but by the time I got the women to stay inside," Wuterich and Sharratt were already walking out. Their encounter had been brief and deadly, Salinas later recalled:

I was walking to House #6 [also identified as House #4] and saw SGT WUTERICH walking out with an AK in each hand and LCPL Sharratt had a suitcase (Jordanian passports, etc.) in one hand and an AK-47 in the other. They told me they had entered the house, a MAM pointed an AK-47 at them and when LCPL Sharratt had a malfunction with the M249 [SAW] so he used his 9 mm to engage and kill the MAMs. I learned from HET later, that a MAM escaped out of House #6 and was detained by the IA [Iraqi Army] who learned the information.

Yousif Ayed told an entirely different story to McGirk. In his account, the Marines burst into the house of his father Ahmed Ayed (House #4/6)—McGirk calls it the third house—and killed four of his brothers. Yousif, who lived in a house next door, told McGirk that "after hearing a prolonged burst of gunfire," he rushed over. Iraqi soldiers keeping watch prevented him arriving.

"They told me, 'There's nothing you can do. Don't come closer, or the Americans will kill you too,'" Ayed reportedly said.[7]

Later identification, aided by DNA evidence and photographs, revealed that Marwan Aiad Ahmed, twenty-seven, Khatan Aiad Ahmed, twenty-six, Jasib Aiad Ahmed, twenty-eight, and Jarnal Aiad Ahmed, thirty-nine, fell before the Marines' onslaught. It was their misfortune to be MAMs with guns. The Marines identified them as suspected terrorists with strong ties to known insurgents and refused to pay their families *solatia* money. The families contended they were hard-working local folks trying to get by when they were executed.

Soon after the fight in Yousif Amed's father's house, Wuterich's squad was ordered to House #1, where a group of Marines from FB Sparta were picking up the bodies of the dead Iraqis. Salinas remained there as an observer, but did not participate in removing the dead, he recalled.

I entered House #1 and saw four bodies; one was an elderly man with his leg blown off and lying beside him. I did not enter each room and I did not load any of the bodies into the HMMWV. In House #2 I only observed a dead male in the kitchen area. I never went to other rooms in the house.

Nobody was apparently on fire in House #1 at that point; at least Salinas doesn't mention it. The burned torso would crop up several times later on without anyone ever wondering how it ignited. Ayad claims he returned to the scene of his brother's demise to discover the bodies were gone.

"But we could tell from the blood tracks across the floor what happened. The Americans gathered my four brothers and took them inside my father's bedroom, to a closet. They killed them inside the closet," Ayed told McGirk.[8]

Ayed was flat wrong—at least according the forensic reconstruction report of the scene made by Special Agent Michael S. Maloney, a forensic reconstructionist assigned to the Forensic Consultant Unit, Violent Crimes Division of NCIS.[9]

ON SEPTEMBER 1, 2006, Maloney completed his study of the events in the house where Yousif Ayed's four brothers died. Using photographs, bloodstain analysis, firearms/trajectory evidence, and a variety of other forensic clues, Maloney and Dr. Elizabeth A. Rouse, who had been assigned to the Office of the Armed Forces Institute of Pathology as a medical examiner, submitted their conclusions to NCIS. They are completely at odds with the account Yousif Ayad offered McGirk.

Their investigation and reconstruction of events, although limited by time, space, and sometimes conflicting accounts from Sharratt and Wuterich, revealed that there was indeed a fight in House #4 that Salinas described hearing in his statement. The NCIS investigators determined that Sharratt's account of shooting a man in the doorway was supported by "bloodstain patterns consistent with Man #2 being positioned in the open doorway to the bedroom." It could not be "determined if Man #2 was armed at the time he was shot."

Sharratt's contention that he shot a second armed man "is supported by bloodstain patterns consistent with Man #3 being positioned just behind the doorway to the bedroom.

"Man #4 was most likely located in the southeast corner of the room when he was shot," Maloney reported. "He would have been sitting or crouched down at the time and would have been obscured, partially or fully, from sight by the open closet door." This would contradict the statement that he was moving toward his "comrades" when he was shot.

Why Sharratt shot and killed the other two men is less than clear. Sharratt claims the other two men may have been moving toward hidden weapons when he shot them. Wuterich came into the room in time to finish off the fourth brother, although Sharratt said he was confident he had killed all of them by then. The evidence the NCIS investigators gleaned from the eight-month-old crime scene is less certain. Its value is further diminished because of the missing weapons that Sharratt, Salinas, and Wuterich all claimed were recovered from the house.

Without eyewitnesses other than the accused, without the three assault rifles and other material captured by Sharratt and Wuterich, Salinas's fate was sealed. He was going to be a witness—a trump card—in the game of life being played at Camp Pendleton.

CHAPTER 12

THE LEAKY BOAT—
THE "BARGEWELL REPORT"

U S Army Major General Eldon A. Bargewell cut his combat teeth as an enlisted man in the Special Forces—the mythical Green Berets who captured America's imagination in song and story. During two tours in Vietnam in 1968–1969 and again in 1970–1971, Bargewell was a Special Operations and Augmentation OP-35 MACVSOG operator in Northern I Corps, a super-secret Military Assistance Command Vietnam endeavor where dying was a distinct and frequent possibility. SOG troopers were legends in Vietnam.[1]

The men who dared to challenge the North Vietnamese Army on their home turf were indisputably among the bravest of the brave. Even among them, then staff sergeant Eldon A. Bargewell stood out, earning the Distinguished Service Cross—the decoration differing only in name from the Navy Cross—for leading a joint team of American and nominally South Vietnamese commandos in desperate combat.

After Vietnam, in 1973, Bargewell earned his commission as a second lieutenant and joined the fabled 75th Ranger Regiment. Following his stint with the Rangers, he disappeared for seventeen years into the chimerical Special Forces Operational Detachment—"Delta"—at Fort Bragg, North Carolina, where the murky operators who prefer a nameless, formless existence train to perform their clandestine black magic. Their lives depend on correctly deciding what a threat is and is not.

During his career, Bargewell received seven Purple Hearts, although legend says he accepted only four of them. Along the way, he reportedly earned the reputation for being both extremely blunt and superbly equipped to evaluate combat operations. Along with his colleague and friend General Peter J. Schoomaker, the thirty-fifth chief of staff of the Army and another spec ops stud, Bargewell was reputedly instrumental in shaping the special operations forces that destroyed the Taliban in Afghanistan in a few desperate months. No one who ever heard of Eldon Bargewell doubted his courage, honesty, or combat knowledge. By all accounts he was a brilliant soldier.

Bargewell would probably have remained in the shadows had Chiarelli not ordered him, on March 19, 2006, to pick up where Watt left off and pursue a no-holds-barred secret investigation of what happened at Haditha. Chiarelli wanted to know about the "training" and "command climate" the Marines were laboring under in restive Al Anbar Province. He wanted to know how the Marines were trained and whether they understood the ROE and LOAC that supposedly governed the way they fought.

Chiarelli did not believe the Marines were winning the hearts and minds of the Iraqi civilian population using the established techniques and doctrine of contemporary COIN operations. Too many civilians in the openly hostile Triad region were dead to sweep the question under the rug. Chiarelli told Bargewell to find out why.

Bargewell complied with alacrity. On the morning of June 15, 2006, Chiarelli got what he asked for, a 107-page review of what happened, when, and by whom. With his reputed bluntness, Bargewell laid it all out. It wasn't a pretty picture that he painted. Every disturbing, dehumanizing detail of insurgency and counterinsurgency warfare and the Marines' inability to effectively employ it was laid out without qualification in clear, concise English. On its face, Bargewell's report left little room for ambiguity.

His report was a devastating rebuke of both the Marines' behavior and the training, policies, and procedures they employed. At the heart of his criticism was Bargewell's determination that the Marines simply weren't equipped mentally to fight in a counterinsurgency environment. They had trained adequately for it, they were equipped for it, but their commanders' hearts were never really in it, Bargewell said. The Marines in Al Anbar Province didn't even pretend to fight the counterinsurgency war the "correct" way. Counterinsurgency operations are best conducted with a scalpel. The Marines preferred a hammer.

On July 7, exactly three weeks after Bargewell gave it to his boss, a spokesman said in a statement that Chiarelli had finished reviewing Bargewell's report before forwarding it to General George W. Casey Jr., commander of Multi-National Force–Iraq, with his own recommendations. In a brief statement issued from Chiarelli's headquarters, he said he had finished reviewing a lengthy investigation by Bargewell into the performance by Marine leaders in Haditha, as well as the training that Marines had received and the command climate their superiors had fostered.

The *New York Times* quoted a "senior Pentagon official" saying it "could" be several days before Secretary Rumsfeld would receive a complete briefing on the matter, and before a redacted version of General Chiarelli's findings "are made public."[2]

Both senior Army generals who reviewed Bargewell's finding were proponents of "conventional" COIN operations at odds with the Marine Corps's disposition for extreme violence when attacked. Casey received the report with much anticipation from the Baghdad press corps busying themselves inside the Green Zone speculating what would happen next. When nothing did, for a time the report disappeared from public view.

So did the NCIS investigation gathering steam in California and Iraq. Its investigation was still a low-profile, rarely mentioned event. Bargewell's report makes it clear the two were separate and distinct investigations. NCIS was looking for scalps, Bargewell was looking for operational realities, but ravenous reporters were unable or unwilling to make the distinction.

In the ten months between when Bargewell submitted his report and the massive leaks of April and May 2007, the report slowly ground its way around the Pentagon and into the offices of legislators and bureaucrats. Each stop produced a leak, tantalizing tidbits of disparaging observations provided by "they" and "them." Meanwhile, the report was withheld from the public, fueling more speculation about the horrors it held.

After leaking for a year, the report would pour into the laptop of the *Washington Post's* Josh White. White was the first reporter to take a whack at deciding what MG Bargewell said in his report to Chiarelli. White made his case for murder and cover-up on the front page of the April 21, 2007, edition of the *Post*.[3] From what he cited, it appeared White had either ignored or was not privy to the attached exhibits, statements, findings of fact, and details of physical evidence to flesh out the frame. Rather, White cherry-picked through enough critical observations in Bargewell's objective analysis to fill a bushel basket full of front-page, top-of-the-fold Sunday stories about dimwitted Marine officers running their own vicious war.

In White's view, the Marine Corps chain of command in Iraq ignored "obvious" signs of "serious misconduct" in the deaths of twenty-four civilians in Haditha that "fostered a climate that devalued the life of innocent Iraqis to the point that their deaths were considered an insignificant part of the war," he revealed. White also determined that the "officers may have willfully ignored reports of the civilian deaths to protect themselves and their units from blame.

"Statements made by the chain of command during interviews for this investigation, taken as a whole, suggest that Iraqi civilian lives are not as important as US lives, their deaths are just the cost of doing business, and that the Marines need to get 'the job done' no matter what it takes."

It was true, and it was indeed a callous view. White claimed that the enlisted Marines "at the squad level came up with a false story; that Kilo Company officers and the commander of the Third Battalion, First Marine Regiment, passed along insufficient information to the regimental commander; and that regimental officers and officers at the Second Marine Division ignored signs of a problem and believed the incident to be insignificant."

White's second allegation is an assumption, not an assertion. To this day, nobody except the First Squad, Third Platoon of Kilo 3/1 knows what really happened. There is plenty of evidence that shows confusion, severe anxiety, bad judgment, questionable behavior, and disingenuous reconstructions, perhaps even unintentional murder in some degree, but at that point in the investigation there was no acknowledgment crimes had been committed, much less concealed.

Finally, White accused the entire Second Marine Division chain of command in Iraq of failing to recognize the magnitude of the "inappropriate" civilian deaths instead of seeing an insurgent ploy:

> Bargewell found that Huck's division staff viewed the allegations of inappropriate killings as part of insurgent "information operations" and an attempt to make the Marines look bad.

White's disclosures were strong stuff that boded ill for the Haditha Marines. An ancient, leather-faced Marine once counseled, "Shit rolls downhill in the green machine." White's breathtaking front-page report triggered an avalanche of doo-doo that quickly found its way to the Marines standing at the bottom of the slope. Caught in the muck and mire that landed around the Haditha Marines were their suffering families, the kind of folks who put MY SON IS A PROUD MARINE stickers on the bumpers and rear windows of their cars. They were shocked into silence.

They didn't know White was gilding the lily in his sensational breakthrough report. Bargewell made many critical observations, and he did think the Marine Corps displayed a callous disregard for the lives of innocent civilians caught in the crossfire that erupted after Wuterich's squad was ambushed. All of that was true. What Bargewell didn't say was that the Marines were guilty of "inappropriate killing," or that the enlisted men and their officers in the Thundering Third had perpetrated a conspiracy so immense it threatened the very foundations of Marine Corps reverence for duty, honor, and country. White assumed all of that.

In essence, Bargewell said the young Marines, unclear about how they should fight, were led by seemingly callous, insensitive officers who were poorly equipped, trained, or inclined to conduct counterinsurgency warfare in the way the Baghdad brass expected them to. In addition, they were lousy report writers with no sense of good public relations. "Shut your pie hole and listen the fuck up" doesn't inspire a lot of goodwill among reporters. But Bargewell never said a word about murder.

His multifaceted report was both an indictment of the Marines' training and behavior and a subtle thesis for the Army generals who already believed the proper attitude and behavior for fighting counterinsurgency warfare was the Army way—for that matter, Bargewell's way. Equally important and far less acknowledged were his subtle laments that his hands were tied when he tried to look beyond MajGen Huck to the senior Marine and Army commanders running the show. For instance, why didn't Army LTG Vines insist on Marine adherence to policy?

The report lists the mitigating factors that limited Bargewell's complete collection of evidence, including the "effective" and "productive interrogation of witnesses" detailed in Sections l and 2 (U) and labeled "Constraints" and "Limitations." Bargewell was particularly galled by "Constraint (6)—restrictions on my authority to interview the three star MNC–I Commander [LTG John R. Vines] based on a provision in AR 15-6 that prohibits investigating officers from investigating the conduct of senior officers."

In a footnote Bargewell added, "As the investigation progressed, it became apparent that the higher echelon commanders, above MNF–W, needed to be interviewed to include the former MNC–I Commander. Once that became apparent, I determined our team would investigate through to the fullest permissible levels of command then recommend a senior ranking officer finish interviewing the remaining chain of command."

For some reason the press never clamored for either Vines's head or his appreciation of the events at Haditha. Limiting his access did demonstrate that Chiarelli or somebody higher on the food chain had no interest in determining what Army brass had to do with Haditha. Vines was the commander of the Multi-National Corps–I, or MNC–I, from January 2005 until January 2006, therefore was the senior officer in charge of the Haditha Marines.

Part 2.(U), called "Limitations," spelled out exactly what Bargewell's mandate was:

> At the outset of this investigation, the state of the evidence on the underlying events indicated that the Iraqi civilian casualties suffered near the intersection of Routes Chestnut and Viper in Haditha on 19 November 2005, were caused by a negligent or, at worst, reckless application of the ROE by Marines from Company K, 3/1. Our appointing order did not direct us to examine the killings themselves. The Watt investigation had made preliminary findings on those events and directly led to an NCIS investigation—which was in progress at the time of our inquiry. Therefore we intentionally did not closely examine the events that had resulted in the deaths of the Iraqi civilians, except as those events impacted the issues we were directed to investigate.

Bargewell's report was far more than a swipe at the Marine Corps, a claim several mid-level officers suggested when the report was leaked.

Just like two hardheaded mountain goats, the two outwardly friendly antagonists periodically slam their armor-plated heads together with thunderous claps and little permanent damage. In Iraq in 2005, the senior Marines and soldiers breathing the rarefied air of high command had been butting heads at least since the first occupation of Fallujah in the spring of 2004. That knee-jerk operation was triggered by the killing and mutilation of four Blackwater private military contractors hung from Fallujah's infamous "Brooklyn Bridge" like roast meat. Their argument was about tactics.

Mattis was commanding the First Marine Division in April, 2004 when rumors persisted that he and his boss Lieutenant General James T. Conway, then the commanding general of the First Marine Expeditionary Force, were butting heads with Army generals over the best way to soothe Fallujah before Operation Vigilant Resolve, the Marines' first attempt to pacify the ancient city. Conway reportedly argued that the insurgency wanted the Coalition to overreact in order to stir up the population.[4] Army Lieutenant General Ricardo Sanchez, at the time the head of MNF–I and Conway's boss, ordered him to do it anyway. It didn't work out too well.[5]

On May 1, 2004, US forces were withdrawing from Fallujah when Conway announced that he had decided to turn over any remaining operations to the newly formed Fallujah Brigade, which would be armed with US weapons and equipment. The group was trained by soldiers under US Army Lieutenant General David Petraeus, the first commander of the Multi-National Security Transition Command–Iraq and the NATO Training Mission–Iraq, which he commanded until September 2005.[6]

Petraeus's job was creating a competent, aggressive "new" Iraqi Army disabused of throwing its adversaries off buildings or beating the bare feet of recalcitrant soldiers with stiff rods to enforce discipline.

Despite the Army's best efforts, the "new" Iraqi Army folded its tents after turning over all the US weapons to the insurgency. At the beginning of the operation, 30 percent of the Iraqi contingent refused to go or deserted, and within days over 80 percent of the police force and Iraqi National Guard in Al Anbar Province deserted as well, gone by September 2004. Their departure prompted the bloody Second Battle of Fallujah in November, in which Coalition forces successfully occupied the city.[7]

Conway reportedly said of Al Jazeera's reporting at Fallujah, "Al Jazeera kicked my ass."[8]

The ensuing Operation Al Fajr/Phantom Fury in November turned into the fiercest battle in the Iraq War. Before it was over, 60 percent of the ancient city's 140,000 buildings were demolished and the insurgency in Fallujah was smashed. Somewhere between 1,200 and 3,000 Iraqi insurgents, sympathizers, and unfortunates died in the rubble of Fallujah. The Thundering Third alone claimed more than 1,000 kills and 1,200 captures.

The Fallujah fights and aftermath ensured relations hadn't improved by the time the Haditha incident emerged. Regardless, the Bargewell Report went a long way toward defining what happened at Haditha, but in the end eight ordinary Marines were left to explain why.

BARGEWELL SUCCINCTLY DETAILED his assignment in the first paragraph of his introduction:

> First, I was to examine the official reporting of the events of 19 November 2005 at all levels of command up to MNC–I and resulting follow-on actions. Second, I was to review the training the Marines received in the rules of engagement (ROE), the law of armed conflict (LOAC), and examine whether the command climate encourage the disciplined application of ROE and LOAC.[9]

Identifying "who" was the simplest part of Bargewell's effort. The Marine Corps chain ran from Major General Stephen T. Johnson, the senior Marine officer in Iraq at the time, to Marines like Tatum and Sharratt, two tired riflemen who thought luxury was a day without incoming.

Bargewell said he started his investigation with an open mind: "Accordingly, the investigation teams proceeded to collect evidence and interview witnesses based on the presumption (rather than a firm assumption) that the underlying events had occurred essentially as they had been described in the Watt investigation."

By April 2006, after NCIS investigators finished their initial interviews with what would become known as the "Haditha Eight," Bargewell stated his investigative team began receiving reports from NCIS indicating evidence some of the Marines under investigation lied to Watt and Bargewell's investigators about innocent Iraqi civilians being intentionally targeted.

"Forensic and testimonial evidence subsequently uncovered by NCIS, including incriminating statements from participants that were inconsistent with their prior statements, indicated that at least some of the killings may have been deliberate LOAC violations," Bargewell noted.

During their evidence collection efforts, Bargewell's investigators were able to obtain death house photographs denied Watt, leaving intelligence officer First Lieutenant Andrew Grayson in more trouble than he knew at the time.

"Upon viewing some of the photographs we were convinced that they were at least relevant to reporting and follow-on actions because we thought anyone viewing the pictures would be compelled to question the account of the killings that had been officially reported and conclude that further reporting and investigation was essential," Bargewell reported.

After receiving the alarming and potentially incriminating information and photographs, Bargewell ordered his team to "re-examine our investigative approach, our preliminary analysis, and our findings to determine whether they were flawed due to our working presumption about the underlying facts. We also had to evaluate the evidence of conspiracy to fabricate accounts of the killings at the squad level and incorporate the implications of the photographs in to our analysis."

In early June 2006, while the Bargewell Report was being final-ized, he received "the last of this new information from NCIS in the form of numerous statements and documents" it had compiled from March 13, 2006, through about June 5, 2006. Although it initially raised many red flags, Bargewell's investigators ultimately determined it did not change the basic premise of his report.

"In the end, we concluded that our investigative process was not fatally flawed and found that the newly provided NCIS evidence did not tend to impeach our overall findings with respect to reporting and follow-on actions or with respect to training," he wrote. "In short, our investigation indicated that the reporting of the incident was untimely, inaccurate, and incomplete and that the follow-on actions were less than appropriate."[10]

Despite the supplemental investigative reports from NCIS, Bargewell concluded that his team had not received any information that changed their opinion that proof existed of either intentional mur-der or a criminal conspiracy to hide the truth:

> Our interviews disclosed no evidence of a criminal cover-up . . . however, the preponderance of the evidence shows that the overall deficiencies in reporting and follow-on action—while sometimes perplexing—were not the result of an extensive and orchestrated criminal cover-up throughout the chain of command.

Bargewell was also tasked with discovering whether the 3/1 Marines' training was in compliance with the ROE and their associated under-pinnings. The notion that the battalion was going to Iraq to win hearts and minds had supposedly been hammered into place before arriving in theater, during transit, and upon arrival in-country. All of 3/1's training was duly documented and presented to Bargewell's investigators.

In 2006, Brigadier General John Toolen explained his appre-ciation of the training his Marines received to help them win the Iraqis' loyalty while he was the colonel commanding RCT-1 in the winter and spring of 2004, when Fallujah flared up like a rancid boil.

"Honestly, we didn't go in there with the intent on crushing the Iraqis," he said in an interview at his office in Marine Corps University at Quantico. "We went in there with the concept we were going to win them over with a patient, persistent, presence."[11]

In the end, RCT-1 and later RCT-2 did crush the Iraqis in Al Anbar, at Fallujah in 2004, and again in the Triad before, during, and after Operation River Gate in 2005. Both regiments tried restraint first, giving it an honest effort. LCpl Alex Nicoll groused that in 2004 Third Platoon was only killing barking dogs that gave away their positions at night. His buddy Joe Haman said the ROE in 2005 kept him from ever getting to throw a grenade into a room, something he had always wanted to try.

Brad Kasal, in November 2004 the first sergeant of Weapons Company, 3/1 and the former first sergeant of Kilo Company, said he used to carry candy in his pockets for the children. He told his Marines that every time they kicked in a door or roughed up an Iraqi they had created another insurgent. Unfortunately, the few Iraqis that responded with open friendliness were often threatened or killed. Kasal said the vast majority reacted with either feigned indifference or sullen hostility.

Kasal admittedly was operating in a paradox. At the same time he had to reinforce the notion his Marines were expected to eradicate antagonists. "Light the bastards up," he said. It was all part of General Mattis's well-publicized philosophy from 2003 that Marines in Al Anbar could either be the Iraqis' best friends or worst enemies; he left it up to them to decide. The al-Qaeda–led insurgency knew this and constantly tested the mettle of the Marines using pinprick attacks that mounted in ferocity until the Marines exploded in anger.

The young Marines going to Iraq in 2005 shared the same take on their mission. They were going to Iraq to win. They openly traded dead muj pictures and war stories like baseball cards and combat legends. Some guys even made music videos and slide shows on their laptops proudly recounting the Thundering Third's past performances. One enterprising young Marine from India Co made a rock video using combat footage, which was viewed on YouTube thousands of times.[12]

The video is a wonderful reflection of their mind-set. All their training was offensive in nature; take the objective, destroy the opposition. Don't look, aim for center mass, take them out, clean kills. MOUT is a perfect case in point. The Marines that went to Haditha were trained to refight Fallujah using tactics gleaned from "Lessons Learned" in 3/1's second deployment. "We fight as we train" was a creed they were expected to adopt. Aggression, not restraint, was their credo. The Thundering Third's training regime was intended to turn lion cubs into lions itching to hunt, a concept fostered by the senior Marine commanders. Bargewell noted that Major William J. Collins, the regimental staff judge advocate relieved by Davis, reported that his former boss referred to RCT-2 as his "Motorcycle Gang."

"That was right from Colonel Davis," the former regimental lawyer told investigators. "'[We're] going to take Viking (the call sign of RCT-2) on the road, and get the motorcycle gang together, we're going to go to these towns, we're going to clean them up and'—Basically that was kind of how he, kind of, described it."[13]

On April 22, New York Times reporter Paul von Zielbauer publicly introduced Capt Pool, the Marine PAO who set the Haditha situation on fire with his inaccurate press release more than a year before.

"The way I saw it was this," von Zielbauer reported Pool telling two colonels questioning him. "A bomb blast went off, or was initiated, that is what started the [attack], that is the reason they're getting this, is a bomb blew up, killed people. We killed people back and that's the story."[14]

The unidentified source—reputedly a lawyer—called it a "colossal blunder," sharing that Pool's thinking reflected that of his superiors, who believed that civilian casualties were an inevitable part of the Iraq war.

On May 6, von Zielbauer followed with a story that claimed senior Marine colonels and generals were preparing to throw Chessani and the other junior Marines under a train—a bus was not big enough—for covering up the twenty-four Iraqi deaths because it "was a potential public relations problem that could fuel insurgent propaganda against the American military."[15]

He revealed for the first time that Sokoloski, Huck's chief of staff, had approved Pool's erroneous news release. He claimed the investigators believed Sokoloski's action was "intentionally inaccurate" to cover up the civilian deaths although Sokoloski claimed the press release accurate at the time. Von Zielbauer's inference that Sokoloski intentionally lied to cover something up added more energy to the tsunami sweeping over the Haditha Marines.

In fact, Sokoloski said he wasn't even thinking about war crimes or covering up when he approved the new release for distribution—he was thinking about how he could beat the insurgents at their own blame game by using the Iraqi civilian deaths to benefit the Marines. Ditto for Davis, who still thinks McGirk's inflammatory reporting incited the Iraqis to further resistance.

"Frankly, what I am looking at is the advantage he's giving the enemy," Davis said of McGirk.

THE FOUR QUESTIONS

Much of the Bargewell Report was concerned with answering four questions Chiarelli ordered Bargewell to find answers for. Simple on their face, the questions proved to be complex, imprecise inquiries that raised almost as many other questions as they answered. On totality, however, the answers Bargewell said he discovered painted a poor portrait of 3/1 and RCT-2 command and control during events at Haditha. Although Bargewell and his team examined training and attitude rather than guilt or innocence, the answers they uncovered ultimately helped indict the Marines.

Question One: Was the training and preparation of the Marines (Company K, 3rd Battalion, 1st Marines) in the areas of rules of engagement (ROE) and the law of armed conflict (LOAC) adequate to prepare them for the combat operations experienced during a firefight with insurgents amidst several houses in Haditha, Iraq, on 19 November 2005?

Question Two: Did the Marines receive ROE and LOAC training in accordance with applicable training regulations or requirements prior to the 19 November 2005 engagement?

Question Three: Were house clearing and room clearing techniques adequately trained and followed by the Marines in accordance with controlling doctrine?

Question Four: Did the command climate within 3d Battalion, 1st Marines encourage disciplined application of the ROE and LOAC?

The answers in a nutshell:

Question #1

Findings: I determined that the training and preparation of the Marines in the areas of ROE and LOAC was adequate to prepare them for combat operations and met the Marine Corps standard for that training.

Sort of. Before deploying to Iraq, Bargewell discovered Marine Corps put the battalion through extensive training exercises at the squad, platoon, company, and battalion level. Of particular note was the Marines' emphasis on offensive maneuvers:

At that time, Marine units, to include 3/1, also attended SASO training at March Air Force Base which prepared Marines to deal with such current operating environment situations as Military Operations in Urbanized Terrain (MOUT), entry control points, vehicle checkpoints, counter-improvised explosive devices and application of the

ROE. Once 3/1 arrived in Iraq, ROE and LOAC were continually covered and emphasized in training on a weekly basis.

On page 70, Bargewell presents evidence from the deputy director for current operations, tactical training and exercise group, a Marine lieutenant colonel who trained 3/1 at the 29 Palms, California, training area. That officer said the Thundering Third had done quite well in the role-playing exercises developed to recreate as many scenarios as possible for the Marines charged with pacifying Al Anbar Province. Melded into his review was a barely noticed backhand slap that 3/1 "was an excellent unit that did many things well but needed to work on ROE and escalation of force." Such little factors collectively became a major problem for 3/1's Marines.

Several young Kilo Marines who attended the training at 29 Palms said that 3/1's Marines were chastised both there and at March AFB for being too aggressive in their responses. Joe Haman recalls a fight between some 3/1 Marines and a group of reservists at MOUT on March AFB who wanted to "do it right." At the end of a day the combat veterans told their less experienced charges that using restraint was a good way to get killed. Some of the Marines said the training was useful for the new men, but less so for the veterans who had faced down real Iraqis with real guns. It didn't have the same feel. "Never give them an opportunity to hurt you" was the battalion mantra in the months preceding 3/1's redeployment in late summer of 2005. Thirty-three dead men and five hundred wounded from a single battalion make for a lot of dangerous Marines.

Question #2

Findings: I determined that the Marines of 3/1 did receive the required training the law of war and ROE in accordance with MCO 3300.4 [Marine Corps Order 3300.4 regarding the Marine Corps Law of War Program].

There was no ambiguity. The Marines assured the inquiring brass of their constant vigilance. Being aware of the rules to fight by was always paramount. Wuterich, Mendoza, Salinas, Tatum, Sharratt, and Dela Cruz all agreed they had been well trained. Among the officers were LtCol Chessani, Maj Kevin M. Gonzalez, an ROE training officer, and Capt Stone, who taught laws of warfare to the line company Marines. They all agreed the men received constant ROE training, training updates, so-called resets in the rear. For backup they ensured every Marine carried an ROE card in case they forgot anything. It was pure CYA, so called because it means "cover your ass," something every service member practices early and often.

The ROE and LOAC in force at Haditha left no room for the bellicose behavior tolerated in Vietnam, Panama and Somalia, Desert Storm, even the "March Up" in 2003 when there was no ROE, and 2004 at Fallujah, when it was easy to "modify" the rules. It was time for the kinder, gentler war that allowed attack jet pilots to drop two-thousand-pound bombs from ten thousand feet and prohibited infantrymen engaging an armed enemy at ten feet without PID. Failing to adhere to the ROE was proving to be the single biggest insurmountable problem in the "new" war.

Question #3

Findings: I determined that house clearing and room clearing techniques were adequately trained by the Marines in accordance with controlling doctrine.

I determined that some of the Marines did not follow proper house and room clearing techniques by failing to PID (personally identify) combatants.

His analysis of PID understanding was completely the opposite of what the line grunts believed. Other than that, Bargewell discovered Kilo received its fair dose of training both before and after arriving in Iraq.

The report noted that training occurred primarily at the SASO exercise but was also taught at the home station MOUT facility at Camp Pendleton, California. "Several of the Marines involved in the incident had combat experience and had participated in house clearing and MOUT operations during previous combat operation in Fallujah."

Bargewell thought the men who had fought at Fallujah were a liability after the incident at Haditha. Their input, while useful for bucking up the spirits of the unblooded Marines, cast a bigger shadow on their subsequent behavior than the brass would have preferred.

Bargewell used Kilo Company CO McConnell to make his point:

> The Company Commander clearly understood and articulated house clearing concepts "positive identification" (PID) is supposed to be made on each target, inside and outside prior to engaging . . . Marines . . . to assess the target, backstop, and beyond. The point that "this is a different ballgame," from Fallujah was also frequently emphasized. The platoon leadership stressed PIDing of a target "before Marines engaged." Company K and the battalion had specific ROE during the deployment and the rules never changed with respect to Company K. Each time Marines left the base, they were reminded of the ROE by their leadership, usually a squad leader.

Pure bullshit, the young Marines responded. Despite the extensive training during their pre-deployment workup, the reinforcing shots they apparently got every time they sat down, and the ROE cards they carried, it was never perfectly clear what was right and what was wrong. When could they fire and when should they refrain? Their officers apparently expected that their extensive training to kick in during combat. Bargewell discovered that was not the case.

> Some of the Marines' statements appear to indicate a level of confusion over ROE, to include PID as it pertains to responding to the receipt of SAF from a house or building where there may also be noncombatants present. Specifically some of the Marines said that

if you are receiving SAF from an area or house, it can be deemed a "hostile house" and everyone engaged and killed.

Bargewell included excerpts from statements Marines made to NCIS interrogators during and after the Watt and Bargewell inquiries were under way. They underscored the contradiction he was discussing.

Salinas told NCIS investigators that "if he is receiving fire from an area that anyone in that area can be deemed an enemy and shot." On March 24, 2006, Salinas and Mendoza told NCIS interrogators they were taught that "if they received fire from a structure or area, that they could consider that place hostile and destroy it and any persons within."

Mendoza told NCIS agents that if an area was "deemed hostile, positive identification was not necessary and the house could be cleared room by room without positive identification of targets."

He added that "at the School of Infantry he was taught that . . . any males large enough to hold a weapon in the house are considered enemy and will be shot even if they do not have a weapon," adding "that because these were hostile houses he did what the Marine Corps taught him which was to kill anything in a hostile house."

Bargewell also noted the apparent perplexity of the Marines:

> Although the above statements seem to reflect some confusion, a few of these same and other 3/1 Marines, made differing statements that would support the notion that they did receive adequate training in house clearing techniques and understood the ROE and LOAC concepts as it pertained to house clearing.

He used a March 18 statement from Salinas to NCIS investigators for his example:

> In my training, I learned that if you receive contact from a house, the entire house is considered "hostile intent" and you can kick in the door and "frag" it, although you should still try to PID if

possible. . . . Just identifying a MAM is not sufficient to engage the person as a target and just being armed is also not a reason to engage a MAM. The MAM must present a threat to use deadly force. This has been my training here and in my past assignment.

Bargewell used Dela Cruz and his fire team to illustrate the correct manner for clearing the area:

After the IED explosion, one team headed south (led by Sergeant Wuterich), and Lance Corporals Graviss and Dela Cruz went north to clear houses. Lance Corporals Graviss and Dela Cruz encountered numerous noncombatants and MAMs while clearing houses at approximately the same time as Sergeant Wuterich and his men. Lance Corporals Dela Cruz and Graviss cleared at least seven houses, encountered numerous women and children, detained approximately 13 MAMs, and did not fire a single shot. Lance Corporals Graviss and Dela Cruz separated MAMs and women, found items of interest, and transported detainees. This action is in stark contrast to how Sergeant Wuterich and his team handled a similar situation.

Tatum offered a telling point of view when noting some Marines knew mistakes were made on November 19, 2005, "but they were putting it off on training, [and] not [taking] personal responsibility for their actions."

Question #4

Findings: I determined that comments made by the leadership to the investigating officers, from the Commanding General MNF–W down the chain of command through the Third Platoon Commander, reflect a mind-set and philosophy that are incompatible with a counterinsurgency (COIN) environment. The philosophy and mind-set reflected in these comments may have set the tone for a command climate that when and if communicated to the lowest levels, would discourage the disciplined application of ROE and LOAC, whether this result was intended or not. Based on available information, it cannot be determined whether this mind-set and philosophy was communicated down the chain of command to the lowest levels.

The answer to Question #4 is where the rubber meets the road. The Bargewell Report had already established the institutional attitude of the Thundering Third specifically, and the Second Marine Division generally. The division fostered an aggressive, power-on approach to eradicating the al-Qaeda–led and –bought insurgency. Discovering that Davis called his command the Viking Motorcycle Gang was a case in point. It is the kind of stuff young Marines love, the stuff that makes them want to go out and kill someone, but it was ever so politically incorrect in Iraq in 2006. In his discussion Bargewell dissects the casual revelations of callousness laid at his door and assigns the responsibility for it to each officer in turn.

He had already laid the groundwork in Questions #1 through #3, disarming, utilitarian inquires that merely established that the leadership of the Second Marine Division had ensured the Thundering Third filled in all the squares in their training and deployment cycle. He established that the trigger pullers were well aware of standing orders and regulations regarding the correct application of the ROE and LOAC.

Then he established that despite the repetitive, rhetorical show-and-tell training the enlisted Marines and junior leadership were receiving, the trigger pullers were ambivalent and confused by their indoctrination. Young Marines say they would rather face a court-martial than be too slow on the draw and die. An often-heard retort was, "I would rather be tried by a jury of twelve than buried by a detail of six."[16]

Although Bargewell stopped short of saying the enlisted men received their training with a wink and a nod, he did note that the Marines leading them learned how to survive at Fallujah and the lessons they offered their juniors were intended to make sure they did just that. Despite assurances from McConnell to the contrary, Bargewell demonstrated that the Annapolis grad's capacity to command could never be vigorous enough to overcome the pervasive mindset to survive that drove the Marines to train for another Battle at Fallujah.

BARGEWELL WENT TO US Army Field Manual 22-100 to establish the conditions he intended to examine at the pinnacle of the Second Marine Division hierarchy. The three officers at the top of the pyramid were MajGen Huck, the division commander; Col Davis, the RCT-2 commander; and Col Sokoloski, Huck's chief of staff. Bargewell called the conditions he expected them to disclose "climate":

> Climate refers to the environment of units and organizations. All organizational and direct leaders establish their organization's climate, whether purposefully or unwittingly. . . . An organization's climate is the way its members feel about their organization. Climate comes from people's shared perceptions and attitudes, what they believe about the day-to-day functioning of their outfit. . . . The members' collective sense of the organization—the organizational climate—is directly attributable to the leader's values, skills, and actions. In short, command climate is the atmosphere created by the chain of command within which the unit conducts its operations and training.

Bargewell started at the top with Marine Major General Stephen T. Johnson, at the time commanding general of MNF–W. He was the highest-ranking officer Bargewell was allowed to interview. MajGen Johnson was far from the action in Baghdad but had instantaneous communications with Huck and his staff. Bargewell also wanted to talk to Vines, the commander of the MNC–I until January 2006. Protocol stood in the way, however. The limits of Bargewell's mandate prevented him from interrogating anyone higher than his pay grade.

MajGen Johnson was a career infantry officer. He had served in command positions from platoon leader to Second Marine Division commander and had once been the inspector general of Central

Command. In November 2004 he took command of II Marine Expeditionary Force (Forward), deploying to Iraq for Operation Iraqi Freedom, and remained in that capacity under a few different titles until January 2006.

TIME magazine revealed what Bargewell was reportedly saying about Johnson. According to a November 14, 2006, story by Sally B. Donnelly in Washington, Johnson's "failures" had raised "red flags" so high that the Marine Corps had asked NCIS to step in and investigate him. His case was "further complicated by the fact that the Bargewell report was quite vague in parts," according to "a source who has seen it."[17]

Johnson—in an unsworn statement simply called the "Johnson Statement," taken after he returned to the United States in late January 2006—was anything but vague. The career infantryman spoke to Bargewell's investigators with revealing candor. His transparent disregard for Iraqi civilians caught between his Marines and insurgents is evident.

Bargewell selected a few of the comments from Johnson's statement to illustrate the climate he helped to foster:

> I suspect that the way I looked at it was that they were killed as a result of this assault. Now, whether I was thinking because of an IED or because of the subsequent firefight, I knew that the Marines had been attacked by people from other—by the enemy from other locations. And so I think in my mind it was simply a cost of that battle because civilians had been caught in that. . . .
>
> I think that the way this is laid out is that the impression that we were dealing with is that these folks were hit as a result of this coordinated attack that occurred there in Haditha, in that particular incident. That it was reported and that while it is regrettable, I think it was probably considered that at that time an element of the circumstances; and that our thought process would have been that, hey, if the enemy hadn't done it, those people wouldn't have got killed. That's how I would have—how it shapes up in my mind. . . . I mean

we had a number of different things over the time that we were there that really brought us out of our seat as far as following up and asking questions and monitoring it closely. And the fact that this didn't do that is an indication to me that at least that I was looking at it as the cost of doing business.

On September 12, 2007, the Marine Corps issued a press release indicating that MajGen Johnson had "been fully exonerated of any culpability related to the events of Nov. 19."

Bargewell's selection of quotes from Col Davis, a hard charger who didn't mince words, was even more revealing. His honesty cost him his career:

So, yeah, I mean what triggers it is a complex ambush, that is the first thing that jumps your mind. You've—I've got a KIA. I've got a complex ambush. Okay. Get back to me. That civilians are hit in that—I hate to—I mean, I am not trying to be cavalier or callous about this, this is not an uncommon occurrence when you get ambush like that. Those type of numbers when you start seeing them, yeah, I mean, we paid attention.[18]

And it is regrettable and I mean it is truly and genuinely regrettable that these people are dying like this and they are dying by the dozens every day for any number of reasons, everything from health, impure water, things like that, right to acts of war, acts of terrorism, routinely. But, where clearly it would be nice to make that link if we didn't have to kill any of them, that's fine. They will respect strength, they will respect power, and that's how you start bringing security and stability to that AO.[19]

Chessani was his usual undemonstrative self. Without trying to qualify his own action, or putting the responsibility on the civilians for trying to survive their chaotic world, he simply shared his perspective. He believed his Marines had reacted appropriately to a deadly threat and civilians unfortunately had died:

The initial reports were that they had taken an IED and then small arms fire. The actions of the day, I believed the enemy picked the ground, where he wanted to attack us.

They were—they had set this up so that there would be collateral damage. They had fired from buildings at us, drawing fire back. So I did not have any reason to believe that this was anything other than combat action.

I saw it as a combat action. Enemy had picked the place; he had picked the time, and the location for a reason. I didn't know what his reasons were, but I believed he made a definite choice in where it was and thought that, you know, he wanted to make us look bad.[20]

Kallop, the Third Platoon commander, displayed his youth and inexperience during his interview:

Yeah, I mean, the enemy—the enemy chooses places to engage us that, I mean, you know, Sir, that—where they can hide—where they can hide fast, they drop their weapon and be another person on the street. And unfortunately, that day I thought that the fire was coming from that house. I thought that that house was an enemy house; and when we started to clear it—after it had been cleared, I was like, well, crap, either they're here or they got out back, but they used these civilians—they use these civilians to cover their movement or to—so we wouldn't engage them.[21]

Bargewell ended his report with finding and recommendations. It is an ominous note, a final shot at where he thought the problem lay:

I determined that the comments made by the leadership to the investigating officers from the Commanding General MNF–W down the chain of command, through the 3rd Platoon Commander, reflects a mindset and philosophy that are incompatible with a counter-insurgency (COIN) environment. The philosophy and mind-set reflected in these comments may have set the tone for a command climate that, when and if communicated to the lowest levels, would discourage the disciplined application of ROE and LOAC, whether this result was intended or not.

Despite his findings, the three officers with whom Bargewell laid the most blame escaped criminal prosecution. In spite of a reported recommendation to Secretary of the Navy Donald C. Winter from then lieutenant general Mattis that they receive nonpunitive letters of caution, Huck, Davis, and Sokoloski all received Secretarial Letters of Censure. Winter's knife stabbed as hard and deep as any court-martial could.

In his September 5, 2007, letters of censure, Secretary Winter said the three senior officers had "betrayed the trust" of the Marine Corps for not investigating and reporting the Haditha matter appropriately.[22] The officers declined their right to trial by general court-martial to clear their names.

The contents of those letters remained secret until revealed by the blog *Defend Our Marines*. A couple of PAOs said the letters were a "personnel matter" not open to the public.

Winter was particularly critical of the three senior Marines' apparent reluctance to respond to multiple requests by *TIME* magazine to reveal what happened at Haditha after McGirk began his inquiry. Winter is apparently very sensitive to media inquiries and made the senior Marines' failure to adequately inform the press the central theme of his criticism. He told all three senior officers that their failure to submit to media interrogation was indicative of their inability to understand and fight a counterinsurgency war.

"Even when made aware of the serious allegations raised by the *TIME* magazine journalist, your response to higher headquarters was to forward incomplete, inaccurate, and inconsistent materials provided by a subordinate unit, rather than to initiate a thorough inquiry into the incident," Winter said in his rebuke to Col Davis.

Two days after being revealed in the blog, a spokesperson for Secretary Winter told *Defend Our Marines* that "*TIME* magazine was mentioned as an example of an incident which garnered significant, national media interest; and yet—initially—was not thoroughly investigated. The Secretary was not giving *TIME* magazine special consideration, nor was he suggesting that media have a specific right and/or need to know."

Winter singled out Sokoloski for failing to append the erroneous news release that instigated the furor. The press report inaccurately claimed that fifteen Iraqi civilians had been killed by the same roadside bomb that killed Marine Lance Corporal Miguel "T. J." Terrazas. Winter accused Sokoloski of intentionally withholding the error from MajGen Huck, thereby undermining his ability "to respond to the incident."

Winter repeatedly mentioned the efforts of the unnamed *TIME* magazine reporter in his condemnation of the Marine officers. Winter told the officers they had "failed the Marine Corps" for doing nothing when McGirk claimed infantrymen from Kilo Company had slaughtered innocent women and children.

Maj Dinsmore testified about McGirk's involvement in revealing the fictional allegations while he was the battalion S-2 (intelligence officer):

> In late Dec05, we also heard a reporter identified as Tim MCGIRK was scheduled to visit our Battalion. Based on what I was told I believed he was going to visit us to refute the press release that attributed all the deaths on 19Nov05 to the IED blast that killed LCPL TERRAZAS. I and the rest of the Battalion staff had been puzzled by the inaccurate press release but did not formally protest the inaccuracies because we were busy and it did not seem important. I was tasked by COL CHESSANI to develop an unclassified brief for Tim MCGIRK regarding the events of that day. Tim MCGIRK did not show up and I never gave my brief to him. I do not know the reason he did not show up, my assumption at the time was he had found another source of information which gave him the story he wanted to report. I did not give his visit anymore thought until I read the article in a Mar06 issue of *TIME* magazine.[23]

Winter chastised Davis further for failing to adequately investigate the deaths of the fifteen civilians whose families later received *solatia* payments from the Coalition government. The money was intended to be an apology for the loss of innocent family members. In total the Marines at Haditha paid about $38,000 in *solatia* payments authorized by Davis. *Solatia* payments to seven Iraqi families who lost family members were denied because the decedents were known insurgents. How it was known they were insurgents in February 2006 was never explained. Winter told Davis "you approved an unusually large payment of $38,000 to the victims' families, yet failed to recognize the seriousness of this incident and direct an adequate investigation."[24]

Evidence subsequently revealed during the summer-long investigation showed that everyone in the battalion's chain of command, from squad leader to Chessani, reported the number of civilian deaths almost immediately after they were discovered. Two Marine officers accused of failing to do so had already been exonerated when Winter dropped his hammer.

What the officers didn't do was display an ounce of curiosity about the reason for the deaths of the little children and their mothers. Off the record they said that as callous and disgusting as it seemed in middle America, Haditha wasn't a big deal in the shredded fabric of war-torn Iraq. Death was everywhere.

Winter blasted Huck the hardest for failing to provide leadership because "despite the high numbers of civilian deaths in Haditha, subsequent inquiries about the nature of the incident from news media and your commander [Army LTG Peter W. Chiarelli], and the likely counterproductive effects these deaths would have on your mission, you failed to ensure that the circumstances surrounding the Haditha engagement were investigated thoroughly."

Huck testified he told Chiarelli and Army General George W. Casey—the overall commander of MNF–I from June 2004 to February 2007—that he was satisfied the civilians died as a result of collateral damage incurred during the firefight. He lamely explained that his initial impressions didn't change until McGirk began asking damning questions in January 2006. The resulting pressure from senior commanders in Baghdad led to his belated decision to more thoroughly investigate the allegations of murder and misconduct.

Winter apparently wasn't satisfied with the speed of Huck's decision to bow to media pressure. He tongue-lashed Huck for failing "to ensure that the circumstances surrounding the Haditha engagement were investigated thoroughly. . . . Your advice to your immediate commander, Lieutenant General Chiarelli, regarding no necessity for further investigation conveyed a cavalier attitude towards the gravity of these allegations."

Winter went on to tell Huck he should have ordered the investigation "at least to ensure the rules of engagement and the rules of land warfare" had been followed.

Winter never offered to explain why he ignored indisputable evidence that the "facts" revealed by *TIME* magazine were the fabrication of two Iraqi insurgent operatives who duped McGirk. Two exhaustive investigations and a summer-long inquiry that called upon dozens of witnesses who were there revealed the only absolute "truth" in *TIME's* heart-wrenching account was that twenty-four Iraqi citizens were killed during the day-long melee.

Winter's critics call his decision not to prosecute the senior commanders a flawed one. Most of them were the defense attorneys, the families of the defendants, and a small but growing group of people enthralled by the case suddenly showing up on a bulletin board run by an ultra-conservative website called Free Republic. They were upset that Huck and his senior subordinates were deemed immune from prosecution when the line officers and enlisted men who were getting shot at almost daily were charged with massacre and cover-up. The mainstream press scarcely gave Winter's rebukes any play at all.

Marine Corps Major Eric Dent, a spokesman for Headquarters Marine Corps at the Pentagon, told *Defend Our Marines* that "the Secretary's letters of censure do not prevent the Marine Corps from taking punitive or administrative action against the three censured Marines."[25] It never happened.

Although Winter's action effectively ended their careers, it did not require them to prepare for trial. The role they played in the incident at Haditha was over, a footnote in a sordid history.

CHAPTER 13

WHAT DO WE DO NOW?

Bargewell's report provided Chiarelli what he wanted to know about the "training" and "command climate" the Marines were laboring under in Al Anbar Province. Chiarelli knew how Marines were trained and whether or not they understood the ROE and LOAC.

The first thing the Army general probably noticed was something any boot Marine is sure of almost as soon as they join the Corps. Marines are different than other American warriors. They think and fight differently; they have a different ethos, and different orientation than members from other branches of US military service. Every Marine is considered elite: it's the reason they don't plant gardens of adornments on their uniforms, or wear snappy berets to remind them they are special. The mission always comes first. High diddle-diddle, right up the middle. Get it done. They are America's Legion.

The Marine Corps unabashedly sees itself as an instrument of incredible force—a spare, lean, killing machine with the ability to strike hard, alone, almost immediately, a self-sufficient package of power projection that has little in common with the slow-moving, elephantine US Army. It is a myth, of course. The Marine Corps is equipped and trained to take and hold objectives near beaches until relieved by conventional land forces. Overwhelming firepower on a specific target for a specific time is both the key to their success and their Achilles' heel. The Marine Corps has limited staying power fighting by itself. Afghanistan is the farthest the Marine Corps has ever gone afield. It is by design an amphibious fighting force. It doesn't have enough strength or depth to take and hold land objectives forever, although that is what its mission eventually morphed to in both combat theaters of the Global War on Terror. Within their normal mission parameters, Marines know if relief is not forthcoming they must either withdraw or be sacrificed. In the meantime, they are alone on the battlefield. And because Marines fight alone, they believe they are entitled to be their own final arbiters inside the crucible. The more Bargewell probed this phenomenon, the more evident it became that Marines marched to the beat of their own drummers.

Chiarelli correctly believed the Marines were not winning the hearts and minds of the Iraqi civilian population using techniques and doctrine acceptable to the architects of the "new" Army-inspired COIN effort. In fact, they weren't implementing much technique at all beyond what MOUT brought to the table.

The why is found in the "5-3-5 Tenets of Force Protection."[1] The term 5-3-5 refers to the fundamental elements of force protection taught to 3/1 at 29 Palms as "pre-combat actions" and covered at the Basic School and Infantry Officers' Course as well. The thirteen tenets of force protection were the bedrock of Marine infantry patrolling skills in Iraq in 2005 and included "legal and ethical habits of action and habits of thought that illustrate the fact that combat activities must be considered in light of laws of war, ROE, and ethical conduct."

The 5-3-5 rules were simple enough to fit on a card carried by 3/1's Marines:

Pre/Post Action:

1. Precombat checks/Precombat inspections
2. Rehearsals
3. Confirmation briefs
4. After-actions report
5. Debrief

Habits of Action:

1. Guardian Angel—a designated marksman
2. Geometry of Fire—know where to shoot
3. Unity of Command—know who is in charge

Habits of Thought:

1. Sturdy professionalism.
2. Make yourself hard to kill.
3. No better friend, no worse enemy.
4. First, do no harm.
5. The Iraqi people are not our enemy, but our enemy hides amongst them.

Corollary 1: You have to look at these people as if they are trying to kill you, but you can't treat them that way.

Corollary 2: Be polite; be professional; have a plan to kill everyone you meet.

Traffic checkpoints were a case in point. Folks died at them all the time. Even MajGen Johnson said so. And now too many civilians in the openly hostile Triad region were dead to sweep the questions about what was going on under the rug. It didn't take a genius to figure out the Marines at the pointy end of the stick were in a precarious position. Somebody was either going to fall or get impaled.

The March 31, 2006, interview of Col Davis, the CO of RCT-2, offered some insight.[2] He had tactical responsibility for pacifying the

Triad region. Casey and Chiarelli saw his job as convincing the locals to change sides by giving them aid in exchange for help subduing the insurgents. Davis did it by locking down the Triad so tight a terrorist couldn't spend two days in a row somewhere without a RCT-2 knock-and-talk squad showing up in the neighborhood. When it wasn't line Marines it was HET, or recon, or snipers, or civil affairs officers driving around essentially buying the peace from the sheiks who needed money to remain in power.

Only when the insurgents fought back were the Marines supposed to kill them. They tried it the "right way" first. Chessani said 3/1 alone found over four hundred arms caches and propaganda mills in Haditha. Tons of ammo and weapons were blown up in the desert; tons more were being found every day. Soon, it was peaceful enough that oil again started flowing into Syria.

Chessani credits Davis with the turnaround. He says Davis was a fine officer, a great regimental commander, and a tough Marine. He says he holds no animus and lays no blame on Davis for relief. Chessani saw Davis as a hard-fighting combat commander on a mission. He was hard only on those who disagreed with him. He relieved his staff judge advocate Major William J. Collins for thinking and eventually saying he was playing fast and loose with the ROE and LOAC.

Davis recommended Chessani for the Bronze Star medal for the way he handled himself at Haditha. Chessani said it was the aggressiveness inspired by Col Davis that fired his Marines to seek out the enemy.

"We worked closely with our Human Exploitation Teams (HET) and my S-2 [Captain, later Lieutenant Colonel Jeffrey Dinsmore] was a bulldog. I was so lucky to have him. He knew what was going on. We got those weapons. We took away the enemies' ability to attack my Marines and civilians. The people were safer. Not even the insurgents wanted to kill civilians if they didn't have to. We took away the means."[3]

Chessani says if he had balked at following Davis's orders it would not have happened. Davis reciprocated by rating Chessani among the best of his officers, ready for higher command.

Ewers and Col Richard A. Connell discovered what he was thinking when they questioned Davis on March 31, 2006:

Q. But here you've got specific allegations, whatever the source, however suspect—however suspicious you are of the source, that your
Marines killed guys in ways that they shouldn't have killed them.
A. I asked my [S-]3, my Judge Advocate, my P.A.O., "Okay, what do
we have here? All right. Let's go back and review the story boards."
We reviewed the story boards, talked to Chessani, there is no meat
here. If I am not mistaken, McGirk's allegations are that he had
been contacted by the Mayor of Haditha that the Americans had
slaughtered people and that there was a video of that. Now I have
never seen this video but I've been told it's films of the deceased in
a morgue or something along that line. Haditha is a special place
for the insurgents. It was the center of their information operations.
When we did Operation River Gate we overran a facility, captured it,
ten stack computers, each one capable of producing ten CD's simultaneously. So if you have a beheading, an IED incident, within ten
minutes you get 100 CDs out. . . . And this is all part of the murder
intimidation campaign. We to this day don't know why, outside of
the obvious strategic nature of Haditha, why Haditha is so important to the enemy. . . .

    In my mind this was all part of a play. They could not get what
they wanted through Chessani, this was never hidden, this was never
covered up, so they go outside to let the press come in and try to
work it as an angle to move us out of there.[4]

His candor was a self-inflicted dead check on his once promising
career.

    SgtMaj Edward T. Sax was no more circumspect than Davis when
he was interviewed by Ewers and Connell a few weeks after the battalion returned to Camp Pendleton. Sax and Davis were hard-chargin'
combat Marines of the same mind.

Sax candidly admitted that civilian deaths occurred with far more frequency than US military strategists preferred. Sax had just finished two hard combat tours in a row and had seen more death than human beings ought to.

Sax admitted he was opposed to the investigation and prosecutions from the start. By the time he was interviewed in the Bargewell inquiry he had a good idea what lay in store for the young Marines who were going to be prosecuted. He'd figured Chessani was going to get relieved as well. Chessani said he told Sax it would probably happen soon and briefed him how to smoothly transition command to the battalion executive officer.

Sax knew why. Even some of his own Marines thought the trigger pullers should go down. The scene at Chestnut was ugly. First Sergeant Espinosa said so. More Marines thought First Squad and the incriminated officers were just more victims of the war.

Sax was getting blow-by-blow accounts of how NCIS was treating his young Marines every day. It upset him. Brad Kasal called him "a great sergeant major." Sax is one of those bigger-than-life characters Marine legends seem to grow. The men responded with fierce loyalty to him. He knew that with the battalion and regimental staff judge advocates on the defensive, the Marines were essentially on their own. Sax stuck his neck out anyway.

Just before the battalion left for Kuwait, Sax warned the NCIS special agents interrogating his Marines to lighten up after he discovered they were conducting nonstop interviews. He testified the badge-heavy interrogators were putting in double time double-teaming First Squad in the bowels of the dam, forcing them to urinate on the floor of the interrogation room instead of letting them use the head. The technique came from the same textbook interrogators used while conducting "enhanced" interrogations of captured insurgents in the same room. When Sax heard what was happening to his Marines he went to the NCIS special agents and told them, "If one of my Marines had to urinate they were to take their penis out and pee on the table," he testified.

A month later he was visited by lawyers Colonel Ewers and Connell. Apparently the stress of so much combat had clouded his usually sharp memory. Ewers, who knew Sax, questioned him first.

Q. Okay. Do you recall—or when was the first time you recall hearing that there had been non-Marine casualties?

A. Before we went out in town, if I remember correctly, sir. I know for sure when we got out in town we heard about some non-Marine dead. Specifically, females and children and that's obviously a big concern.

Q. Okay. And did you discuss it with the Battalion Commander?

A. We did talk a little bit about it. I'm sure, sir, at some point, you know talking about—both of us were in Fallujah. He obviously spent some time at the regiment and my last tours I was at the at the regiment in Al Qarma in Fallujah and we kind of talked along the same lines of some of the kids and women we ended up shooting in ECPs [entry control points] and VCPs [vehicle control points] pull up in the car at night—I hate to use that example but when a car doesn't stop, it crosses the trigger line, Marines engage and, yes, sir there are people inside the car that are killed that have nothing to do with it.

Q. Were any of those discussions, do you recall, concerning what happened on 19 November?

A. It either happened later on that night, sir, or probably the next day, I'm sure.

Q. Did you hear who reported those casualties as KIA, and EKIA, to the Battalion Commander?

A. No, I don't, sir. I don't remember who reported it or hear that reported to him via radio.

Q. Was there any issue as far as you can see with, was there an RFI [request for information] sent down from Battalion Commander to company asking what was going on with the civilian casualties?

A. No, I don't remember an RFI going down to company, sir. I probably should have stayed in the COC and probably obviously know a lot more [about what happened on Route Chestnut] than I know at this point. I automatically assumed if any casualty was called over that was friendly KIA or friendly WIA or neutral KIA or neutral WIA, the CO at some point is going to start asking questions. No, I don't, sir. I don't remember who reported it or hear that reported to him via radio.[5]

The sergeant major's polite interview was a far cry from the examinations his Marines endured at Haditha Dam. They were held incommunicado while they were being questioned, unwilling participants in a good guy–bad guy routine Sharratt described as "stupid" and madly predictable after hours and hours. Tatum said he had to urinate so badly he signed the last statement NCIS typed for him without reading it so he could get to the head. The incident changed the entire complexion of the case against Wuterich. Up until Tatum had to urinate, he repeatedly insisted he did not know who was alongside him firing into the back bedroom of House #2.

Salinas called his interrogation "a real long day." The men being questioned were escorted to chow by NCIS agents and forced to eat with them as well, a show of power that didn't go unnoticed. Once the battalion returned to Pendleton, individual Marines and sometimes entire squads were called to NCIS headquarters for more interviews.

GETTING DOWN TO BUSINESS

There was a method in the NCIS agents' apparent madness. LtCol Vokey said in 2007 somebody high in the Department of Defense told NCIS to get the goods on the Marines who did the killing, fry their young asses, and move along.

On November 11, 2006—Veterans Day—LtGen Mattis issued a memorandum intended solely for Vokey's eyes, ordering him to detail only one defense lawyer to each defendant. Somebody leaked the letter to *Defend Our Marines*. The civilian defense lawyers protested his order so vehemently Mattis later quietly rescinded it.

At about the same time, Secretary Rumsfeld formed a study group to deal with the situation. Chessani's lawyers at the Thomas More

Law Center revealed that this shadowy legal body was set up by the DOD to manipulate the prosecutions of US Marines charged for the Haditha killings. The DOD repeatedly refused to comment on the allegation.

Vokey said the quasi-official shadow council included the senior official or a representative from the offices of the under secretaries of the Army and the Navy, general counsel to the DOD, and the staff judge advocate of the Marine Corps. Headquarters Marine Corps separately set up "Legal Team Charlie" to prosecute the Haditha cases, bringing in desperately needed lawyers exclusively for the team.

Team Charlie used the DOD study group's analysis of the political and legal situation to help decide what course of action to take against the eight Marines awaiting their fate. The group was briefed by high-ranking Marine Corps lawyers sent by Brigadier General Kevin Sandkuhler, staff judge advocate to the commandant of the Marine Corps. Also in the mix was Peter M. Murphy, former general counsel to the Marine Corps—a civilian. He counseled commandants and their lawyers for twenty years. Murphy and Sandkuhler retired before the Haditha case was adjudicated.

As soon as the DOD's study group was formed, Marine Corps lawyers began trooping into Rumsfeld's office at the Pentagon while Commandant General Michael Hagee climbed up Capitol Hill to brief the moneylenders on the progress of the investigation.

"The prosecution actually believed—and still believes—it can win a conviction. It oversold that to General Sandkuhler and he believed it," Vokey recalled in September 2008.

The Marine Corps and the DOD never responded to numerous requests for clarification.

NCIS Director Thomas Betro acknowledged sixty-five field agents were involved in the biggest investigation in the agency's history. Despite what is currently offered on TV, NCIS is best equipped for ordinary crimes: dope and indiscreet sex, occasional garden-variety homicides, and the cheating and stealing that goes on everywhere in life. This time they were ordered to go onto the Haditha battlefield and reconstruct the alleged crime scene, find out how twenty-four Iraqi people died there, and identify who did it.

NCIS forensic specialist Michael S. Maloney was an important member of that team. Along with four colleagues called in from around the world, he was tasked with discovering the so-called ground truth of the incident. Ground truth is not the same thing as whole truth. Generals and admirals need to know what happened so they can tailor the event to meet political and legal expectations consistent with good order and discipline. Maloney was informed he was participating in the biggest military criminal investigation since the infamous My Lai massacre turned middle America against the war in Vietnam. Implicit in his directive was to find enough evidence to obtain convictions.

Maloney was told by his superiors that the objective of the team was to ensure the forensic evidence they uncovered was presented the way the government wanted it revealed. His instructions show just how far the government intended to go to ensure the public and political perception of the truth conformed to the desires of the Pentagon brass seeking a pound of flesh.

When the special agents grumbled, the forensic team was told to "get with the program," according to Maloney, by "providing evidence the supported the government's theory of prosecution." The NCIS special agents were not to concern themselves with exculpatory evidence unless it was beneficial to the prosecution.

Fact finding and truth telling are not necessarily the same thing either, Maloney explained.

"I received an email communication from lower headquarters—a mid-level manager—how did he put this—I needed to 'recognize what version of events the prosecution was supporting and that I was to make certain it (our findings) didn't go any further.'"

NCIS director Thomas A. Betro was getting briefed every week or two, looking for clues the NCIS agents developed in order to skew the circumstances until they conformed with the evidence the government desired to discover, Maloney said.

"Clearly the senior management was not happy with the facts we were uncovering. Our findings did not follow the preconceived notion of events."

It was apparent by mid-2007 that Wuterich was going to take the fall for the enlisted men. It was pre-ordained by the "theory of prosecution" Maloney's superiors at NCIS headquarters in Washington, DC, ordered him to prove. His orders came "straight from the top," Maloney was told. The NCIS agent's evidence was never revealed in open court and remains locked away to this day. A video resconstruction of the shooting being produced at the Illinois State Police Criminal Laboratory in Springfield was killed because it showed events could not have happened the way the prosecution wanted it to.

Proof that this entire investigation was a politically motivated quest for a prosecution of specific individuals rather than a search for justice is supported by several details of the investigation, Faraj believes.

The evidence NCIS investigators turned up showed at least two and probably three Marines had shot into the group of women and children there at very close range, yet only Wuterich still faced prosecution. Among his accusers were four Marines who admitedly gunned down unarmed civilians in two separate houses in which no weapons were recovered. Their admitted behavior was dismissed as either lawful or irrelevant.

Except for the five men by the white car, Wuterich was never seen shooting anyone. How an entire fire team could clear two houses full of civilians without knowing whether Wuterich fired his weapon is more unlikely than winning a lottery. Warriors in combat are very situationally aware in close quarters; otherwise, they might get killed. Despite Maloney's recommendation for further ballistic and forensic testing to identify how the victims were killed and by whom, his NCIS bosses prohibited his team from conducting any further investigation.

Two years after they made them, Sharratt's and Tatum's self-incriminating statements were dismissed by military judge LtCol Paul Ware for being inconsistent with the evidence the prosecution presented. Ware said Sharratt's and Tatum's statements to NCIS admitting they returned to Houses #1 and #2 to clear them a second time was the result of confusion and reaction to psychological trauma. Sharratt's own lawyers claimed Sharratt's admissions were the fantasies of a "great spinner" of sea stories.

The forensic evidence never introduced in any hearing was equally damning, Maloney said. The NCIS reconstruction showed that after attempting to kill everyone in House #1, Wuterich's entire fire team had moved to House #2 and killed everybody there. Those facts alone should have convinced the brass that all was not right at Haditha, Maloney said.

The conventional wisdom reportedly leaking from inside NCIS into Murtha's office was "How hard can it be to get a conviction?" Faraj and several other civilian defense attorneys said the prevailing attitude among the NCIS agents and prosecutors was upbeat. The suspects were teenagers and cocky young officers. Usually, they went down hard on a bluff. The battalion commander would roll over to save his career. Nobody at NCIS apparently expected a problem.

Honest people are much easier to break than crooks. They have a conscience and a moral code. It didn't help that the defendants were led by the senior Marine left holding the bag when he wouldn't throw his subordinates away. Nothing screws up a preordained investigation worse than somebody with principles.

The NCIS decided to tackle the investigation incrementally. It started with the rules. Warfare actually has rules, promulgated by well-intentioned individuals to be mandated and enforced by legal and quasi-legal institutions ranging from world courts to nongovernmental organizations. The laws are intended to minimize unwarranted death and destruction on the battlefield. History has shown repeatedly that laws of warfare are always a tool for the victors, never the vanquished.

THE RULES

There are lots of rules for war fighters. They are intended to place checks and balances on mayhem. The first thing the Navy investigators had to prove was the enlisted Marines broke the rules of escalation of force (EOF), the lowest bar the defendants had to stumble over to commit war crimes. It was spelled out in the "secret" frag order detailing the ROE in February 2005—cryptically spelled out in red ink as "SECRET//REL TO USA, IRQ, MCFI//20151003—DISPLAY ONLY TO IRQ"—and included "General Guidance" for "US National Policy, Military Policy, ROE Policy, and Applicability."

Included on page E-1-20 is the section detailing the use of force on individuals who posed a threat to Coalition Forces "by committing a hostile act or demonstrating hostile intent," the key to determining if the Haditha Marines committed war crimes. The instruction said US Forces "may use force, up to and including deadly force, to eliminate the threat." When time and circumstances permitted, graduated degrees of force were mandated:

- Verbal warnings.
- Show weapon and demonstrate intent to use it.
- Physically restrain, block access, or detain.
- Fire a warning shot (if authorized).
- Shoot to eliminate the threat.

The men in First Squad argue they did all those things, although in a more compressed and accelerated fashion than the spirit of the rule suggests.

Complicating the issue further was a Secretary of the Navy directive titled "SECNAVINST 5500.29, OPNAVINST 5580.14C" that defined EOF as "taking means appropriate to the threat or equal to the threat." That directive said escalation moves upward in eight stages of violence from least severe to most severe.

Verbal persuasion was step one; simply persuade the Iraqis to cooperate using a language most didn't speak. The SECNAV directive said there were two basic levels of verbal persuasion:

1. Light Control. Giving friendly directions and advice.
2. Heavy Control. Using voice inflection to give stern warnings.

When that didn't work:

Physical confrontation: Application of unarmed self-defense/appre-hension techniques and take down holds using the ASP baton, PR-24, riot baton, etc. This included three color-coded stages of escalation:

1. Green—Beating on shins, instep, Achilles' tendon, upper arms, forearm, buttock, thigh, and calf.
2. Yellow—Secondary strike zones including collarbones, knee joints, shoulder blades, elbows, back of hands, upper arm, shoulder, and upper abdomen.
3. Red—Potentially lethal strike zones including temples, ears, eyes, the bridge of nose, upper lip, jaw, throat, solar plexus and groin, back of neck, behind ears, kidneys, tailbone, rib cage, and spine.

The next step up the stairway to heaven is releasing military working dogs alone or in conjunction with DOD-approved nonlethal weapons like tasers, beanbag rounds, noise devices that overpower protestors, and microwave heat projectors that make the victims feel like they are being roasted.

If that fails, the last resort is individual firearms. The SECNAV directive warned that a firearm "shall never be drawn unless its use is deemed necessary by the sentry and the situation which caused you to draw would be proper under the use of force guidelines." Firearms could, however, be drawn in situations "where it is anticipated that they may actually be required."

In Iraq in 2004–2005, EOF moved a bit swifter than the direc-tive suggests, according to the Marines who lived it. They never had war dogs or noisemakers or microwave people cookers. EOF usually jumped from verbal commands to occasionally shooting warning shots, or skipping the warning shots and just taking them out. The short name is the familiar refrain "lighting them up."

By 2005 there was entirely too much "lighting up" going on in Al Anbar Province, according to the Army and Marine Corps generals under the growing influence of the COIN proponents. Army General David Petraeus, then an ambitious lieutenant general and rising star, was noted for saying, "The idea is to end each day with fewer enemies than when it started."[6]

The Marines weren't doing that. Haditha was a great example for the new thinkers. The notion that collateral damage was simply an unfortunate part of combat no longer washed in Washington.

On September 24, 2007—almost two years after the incident at Haditha—the Marine Corps released new rules for war fighting in the *Law of War, Rules of Engagement, and Escalation of Force Guide* from the Marine Corps Center for Lessons Learned. The first new lesson in it was "First, Do No Harm."

The epitaph of the Third Battalion, First Squad Marines was written on page one, contained in the epigraph attributed to LtGen James N. Mattis: "Marines keep their honor clean. Doing the right thing must guide our conduct in all operations, at every level, and in every application of tactics, ROE, LOAC, and EOF procedures."

It was an astounding turnaround for the general who in 2004 warned Arab sheiks in Al Anbar province, "I come in peace. I didn't bring artillery. But I'm pleading with you, with tears in my eyes: If you fuck with me, I'll kill you all," according to author Thomas Ricks.[7]

THE AUTHORITIES WISHING to see the Haditha defendants disposed of as quickly as possible had another problem as well: the broad operational order that specifically addressed what was hostile enough to kill.

Called "ANNEX E (CONSOLIDATED ROE) TO 3-187 FRAGO 02, OPORD 02-005,"[8] the aphoristic acronym straight from the eight-sided Puzzle Palace was part of the secret operational order for conducting war in Iraq. The defense intended to drag all twenty-seven pages out at the appropriate time to illustrate the conflicting rules and regulations Marines at Haditha were supposed to consider while getting shot at.

The prime directive concerning the Marines' use of force is found at paragraph 3.G.(3) (S//REL) PROTECTION OF DESIGNATED PERSONS AND FORCES on page E-1-21. In the old Corps, there was a guiding dictum for handling imponderables: "When unable to dazzle them with brilliance, baffle them with bullshit." The FRAGO, or "frag order," was a case in point.

[N]ecessary force, up to and including deadly force, is authorized to protect designated persons and military forces. . . . The following designated persons may be protected with necessary force, up to and including deadly force:

- All US persons.
- Detained persons, POWs, and criminal suspects under MNF custody *must* be protected at all times.
- Coalition Forces, Iraqi Forces, and/or personnel participating in military operations with MNF and the Iraqi government, and their associated mission.
- Essential equipment and supplies.
- Nongovernmental organizations (NGOs) and international organizations (IOs) providing humanitarian assistance and/or relief in Iraq, Saudi Arabia, Jordan, Kuwait, Syria, and Turkey, and their associated mission essential equipment and supplies. Specifically, necessary force, up to and including deadly force, may be used to protect the International Committee of the Red Cross (ICRC).
- United Nations (UN) relief organizations, such as the United Nations Assistance Mission to Iraq (UNAMI), and any United States or United Nations supported relief organizations and their mission essential equipment and supplies.
- On a case-by-case basis, the OSC may designate certain persons or forces as essential to the restoration of order and security.

- CDR, CENTCOM may designate additional persons and military forces for protection.
- Within Iraq necessary force, up to and including deadly force, may be used against individuals or groups of individuals who commit, or are about to commit, an act that is likely to cause death or serious bodily harm to another.

FRAGO 02 was a tall order. Did Wuterich and his diminished squad intend to commit murder, or were they using deadly force just like it said in the rule book? If the former, Wuterich was a criminal. If the latter, no crime had been committed and a grave injustice was being done. But to whom? There were still fourteen innocents to atone for.

CHAPTER 14

THANK YOU FOR YOUR SERVICE

On May 31, 2006, two days after the Monday celebration of Memorial Day, President George W. Bush spoke publicly for the first time about the Haditha incident. He wasn't happy. In case anyone had missed his message, the next day Bush reinforced his displeasure by calling the allegations "very troubling for me and equally troubling for our military."[1]

The Marine Corps had the undivided attention of the president of the United States. His unspoken message was not lost on the brass. The Pentagon poured millions of dollars into the Haditha investigation in response.

A Marine isn't expected to improvise, adapt, and overcome for nothing. The Corps quickly announced it was building a multimillion-dollar media center and courtroom at Camp Pendleton. Called the Justice Center, it was staffed with reservists and enlisted Marines recalled from the roles of the Individual Ready Reserve. Situated deep inside the sprawling base, it was perfect for controlling public access to the defendants and their lawyers. That was the point. The only question still unanswered was who would ultimately be charged.

On December 12, 2006, speculation reached its zenith when ABC News reported that eight Marines would face criminal charges in connection with the alleged murder of twenty-four civilians in the Iraqi town of Haditha. The most serious charges were expected to be filed against six Marines who were on the scene of the killings, including squad leader SSgt Frank Wuterich, ABC reported.

The sources would not specify what charges the Marines would face, but they were expected to be either murder or manslaughter.

An ABC reporter covering the story added that "two senior Marine officers who were not on the scene at the time of the killings will also be charged," according to "sources familiar with the case." That proved to be a relatively rare understatement. There were in fact four officers charged.[2]

Nine days later, on December 21, the eight Marines from 3/1 that had been selected for prosecution were publicly indicted for murder, assault, and cover-up. Senior among the Haditha defendants was LtCol Jeffrey Chessani, who still refused to barter with the prosecution. Chessani was charged with one count of violating a lawful order and two counts of dereliction of duty. That would later change.

Standing with Chessani was McConnell, the Annapolis grad who had competently commanded Kilo until he was relieved. McConnell was charged with two counts of dereliction of duty. During the actual incident he was personally directing an attack by another Kilo platoon in which eleven Marines were wounded, coordinating aerial and ground surveillance at multiple sites, calling for air strikes, and keeping tabs on casevacs (casualty evacuations) getting his wounded out of the battle zone.

The government claimed McConnell had inadequately investigated and reported his company's circumstances to higher headquarters after the fact. He retained Orange County lawyer Kevin D. McDermott, who was quick to jump on the government's case with both feet.

On December 7, two weeks before McConnell was formally charged, McDermott told the *Napa Valley Register*, "I have not received any word that Capt McConnell is in the firing line at all anymore. Even with all the rumor mills going on, he is not being looked at for the events that day."

Stone was charged with two counts of dereliction of duty for not adequately investigating the incident and an additional count of violating a lawful order for not conducting a war crimes investigation. He hired civilian attorney Charles Gittins, another former Marine.

The acerbic Virginia-based lawyer told *Defend Our Marines*, "General Huck did not believe there should have been an investigation, nor did the staff judge advocate for the regiment. My client was the lowest-level guy and he reported everything that he had been told. There was no requirement that he should have done more. I don't think the people who made the charging decision thought it through—it seems like they just threw everything at a dartboard," and then Gittins shut up.[3]

Less than three months before the Haditha killings, President Bush had recognized Stone for his patriotism and following the family tradition. Bush praised the young officer during a 2005 visit to San Diego to rally support for the Iraq war. Bush noted that Stone's grandfather was a sailor who had supported the Marines in World War II's battle for Iwo Jima.

"And today . . . Capt Randy Stone carries on a proud family tradition," Bush was quoted by reporter Mark Walker in the *North County Times*. "Capt Stone is a Marine officer now serving in Iraq. He knows that he and his generation are doing the same vital work in this war on terror that his grandparents did in World War II. He also knows how this struggle will end."

Bush quoted Stone as saying: "'I know we will win because I see it in the eyes of the Marines every morning. In their eyes is the sparkle of victory.'"[4]

Andrew Grayson, the intelligence officer whom Watt thought was too cocky, was charged with obstruction of justice for allegedly telling his subordinate SSgt Laughner to destroy at least seventy-nine digital images of the dead civilians, dereliction of duty, and making a false statement to Watt. He was the last of four Third Battalion officers who were charged with dereliction of duty at Haditha to have his case aired. Grayson retained Joseph Casas, a former Marine enlisted man and Navy lawyer in solo civilian practice. Casas maintained that his client got into hot water because he impetuously decided Army Colonel Watt didn't have "a need to know" about the classified intelligence material—including the photographs of the dead Iraqis—which Grayson was obliged to protect. Jeff Dinsmore later defended Grayson's attitude, citing a widely held belief among intelligence officers that "need to know" means need to know, and Watt didn't have a need, only a desire.

Marines who were there say Grayson's real crime was being "slick," one of those indefinable military pejoratives best understood by those making the rules at the moment. The government claimed Grayson had somehow hoodwinked the entire chain of command to fraudulently obtain his discharge from active duty. That charge was tacked on later when the Marine Corps mistakenly discharged Grayson and then hauled him back to active duty after giving him his discharge papers. His court-martial would take on an air of desperation sometimes masquerading as lunacy.

Among the enlisted men charged the same day was meritoriously promoted SSgt Wuterich, the leader of the ambushed squad. Wuterich was charged with twelve counts of unpremeditated murder against individuals and one count of murder for the deaths of six people "while engaged in an act inherently dangerous to others." He was also charged with making a false statement and obstruction of justice for allegedly causing Dela Cruz to lie. His original complaint would be changed several times to accommodate the shrinking pool of evidence against him.

Dela Cruz was charged with five counts of unpremeditated murder for killing the five Iraqi men by the white car. He would later admit he urinated on one of them in the heat of the moment.

Dela Cruz was a corporal at Haditha and an infantryman with considerable combat experience. Bargewell would use his behavior after the ambush as an exemplary model of restraint. It was later revealed Dela Cruz is a vicious man with a penchant for striking and otherwise abusing Iraqis and fellow Marines. He was also charged with making a false official statement about shooting the five Iraqis by the white car.

At the bottom of the heap were Lance Corporals Stephan Tatum, the quiet rifleman from Oklahoma, and Justin Sharratt, the boisterous lad from Indiana who had always wanted to be a Marine. They were accused of intentionally killing or wounding civilians during their assaults on the contested houses. Their behavior after the initial sweep of the houses would have come into question if the trial had continued. Faraj was prepared to elaborate on Sharratt's recollections of what happened at Houses #1 and #2 after the first sweep partially cleared them. He wanted to know how expended 9 mm rounds were discovered in both houses when Sharratt, who officially wasn't ever there, was the only Marine so armed at the time.

The enlisted men faced life sentences if they were convicted. The officers faced much shorter prison terms and dismissal from the service with the loss of all pay and privileges. Chessani had six children, and a seventh would be born before his tribulations ended. His life hung in the balance. Everyone else involved with Haditha was granted immunity, taking the Fifth or heading for safe harbor. Leading the flotilla was MajGen Huck and his executive staff.

ENTER THE CONVENING AUTHORITY

Luckily for the defendants, military justice has a designer component built into it. It is called the convening authority. The convening authority, in this case a three-star general, can do all kinds of things to manipulate who the defendants are and where and when they can be tried, by whom, and why—discretion federal law enforcement officials and jurists don't have. That is because military law, in the final analysis, is about maintaining good order and discipline. Good order and discipline is subjective by nature and is sometimes unpredictable. What is good for the goose in not necessarily always good for the gander in military service.

Service members take an oath to lay down their lives if ordered. It is taken lightly in a big room full of tired-eyed recruits and very seriously when someone fails to comply. American history is relatively free of grave markers for those shot for their failures, but it has happened.

For a time the press bandied about the death sentence for some of the Haditha defendants until the Marine Corps came out publicly to say it wasn't going to happen.

Nonetheless, the Marine Corps is a society where hands in pockets and being outside without a cover are serious crimes because they go against the good order and discipline of the service. Discipline is the rock everything else is built on. Haditha was shaking the rock like nothing before it ever had.

By the time the indictments were revealed, those who managed to afford it had already obtained civilian counsel. Wuterich, who had the most to lose, had obtained the services of Neal A. Puckett. Puckett briefly partnered with a lawyer named Mark Zaid, a self-promoter working primarily for plaintiffs and defendants embroiled in disputes within the intelligence community. Like Zaid, Puckett also has a penchant for publicity. He likes to say he "never lost a case" in his military career.

In August 2006, Puckett and Mark Zaid sued Representative Murtha on behalf of Wuterich and threatened to sue Minnesota Representative Joe Kline if he didn't apologize within thirty days for calling Wuterich a "cold-blooded murderer." Kline, a Republican, apologized. It was the first act to play in their unique form of theater. The beltway pair's proclivity for publicity pissed off the other attorneys who either couldn't get it or didn't want the attention the news media was lavishing on the war's biggest war crime investigation. All the attorneys talked, although the Marine Corps lawyers officially didn't say anything. Despite their usual reticence, offhand comments and oblique references passed in hallways sometimes led to breaking bits of news.

The biggest issue wasn't talk—it was money. Most of the money to defend Wuterich was raised by the ultra-conservative news magazine *Newsmax* and United American Patriots, a group that worked hard to raise money to defend the Haditha Marines. Before finding friends, the defendants' families were mortgaging their lives to get competent civilian counsel. None of the lawyers made a profit, although Puckett would bring in hundreds of thousands of dollars in donations during his six-year defense of Wuterich. The big winner was CBS television, which earned untold advertising dollars when Wuterich told the nation what happened on *60 Minutes*.

On March 18, 2007, it was showtime. Puckett told Wuterich to hang it all out on national TV. Some of the other defense attorneys were appalled, thinking Wuterich dug himself into a hole so deep even Puckett couldn't protect him. Others thought it was good theater. Faraj thought it was bad tactics. The interview created new legal vulnerabilities, he said.

The young sergeant's straightforward honesty didn't drive well on a road full of twists and turns, and his uncomplicated answers to questions filled with nuance made him sound cold and flat. To many he appeared a well-controlled heartless killer rather than the misunderstood warm-hearted father of three little girls Puckett wanted him to play.

He was a killer, a sergeant of Marine infantry. He was trained to be controlled, and that was how he came across. War is directed violence. It takes controlled people to pull it off. He had probably sounded the same way when he told Kallop what had happened to Terrazas while he was still on the road. Sharratt said he always stayed cool and collected.

The interview would have repercussions far beyond what Wuterich said. It would evolve into a constitutional issue to decide if and when the military has a right to a news entity's private stock, in this case the video of Wuterich that CBS shot and then didn't air.[5] Such video is called "outtakes" in the industry. In the interim, Puckett kept up a full schedule making statements in the *New York Times* and *Washington Post*. His assertive performance in front of the cameras gave him an air of authenticity that lasted until the Article 32 preliminary hearings finally began.

Puckett found that it was impossible to separate Wuterich from Tatum and Sharratt and the rest of the squad without sounding disingenuous. They were a collective. Some were Fallujah vets. That meant a lot, probably a disproportionate amount in the scheme of things inside that squad of Marines. They'd been there and done that before. Graviss,

a stand-up Marine who avoided the entire incident at Haditha by moving north from Route Chestnut after the ambush, would get caught up
in several webs spun during the unrelated murder trials of Kilo Marines
that followed the luckless company like a black cloud for four years.
Haditha was just the most famous.

Both sides used him as a witness to reveal the intersquad politics,
the squabbling, the weaknesses otherwise never revealed. He wasn't a
snitch by any means, but he wouldn't lie. In statements and hearings,
Graviss was direct, clear, and unyielding in principle. Many Marines
are.

Stephen Tatum was another case in point. He was also considered
a straight-talking, uncomplicated Marine who quietly did his job well.
His family hired no-nonsense Houston attorney Jack Zimmermann,
a decorated combat Marine officer from the Vietnam War, to defend
him. Zimmermann shared Tatum's propensity for not running off at
the mouth. Tatum had seen a lot of war as a rifleman at Fallujah, where
he distinguished himself at the infamous Hell House when Kasal and
Mitchell earned their Navy Crosses. Sharratt was with him. He was one
of the Marines from Third Platoon who braved intense enemy fire to
help bring the wounded out on November 11, 2005, after the squad
got pinned down in a Chechen kill sack. Those kinds of bonds can't be
broken.

A native son of Edmond, Oklahoma, Tatum was a good enough
Marine to earn honorable mention in several books and magazine
articles for his quiet bravery under intense fire. Along with his soldier
brother, he made his family proud back home. Even the prosecution
described him as a dependable, undemonstrative Marine infantryman.
His buddies say he is by nature a quiet man who doesn't involve himself with the histrionics of some Marines. His former squad leader and
Navy Cross recipient R. J. Mitchell said Tatum was one of the best
Marines he fought with at Fallujah.

Tatum's answers to Watt, Bargewell, and NCIS at Haditha Dam
and later in the States were clear, reasoned, and concise. He clearly
knew right from wrong, and he had a conscience. He never tried to be

evasive and repeatedly fell back on the position that he had relied on his training to bring him through that morning. Nothing in Tatum's manner suggested he was ever out of control. That made it all the more confusing in 2007 when his lawyer, Jack Zimmermann, cut a deal with the prosecution to give Tatum testimonial immunity.

Tatum's case defined as well as anyone caught in Haditha's web the real cost of the prosecution. His family was financially threatened and spiritually battered long before he stood in front of hearing officer LtCol Paul J. Ware. Their world came crashing down in June 2006, when the Marine Corps told Tatum he was suspected of murdering elderly men, women, and children.

Without hesitation his parents cashed in their life savings, took a second mortgage on their home, and started looking for a crackerjack civilian lawyer. They knew that was what it was going to take to get their son all the way home.

At the end of June, Tatum learned he was going to be charged with murder. On July 12, 2006, his family hired Zimmermann. The Texan came with good credentials and a sterling reputation, but he didn't come cheap. He immediately needed at least $50,000, and that was just for starters. If he went to court-martial, Zimmermann told them, their son's legal costs were expected to reach half a million dollars. The solution was not having one.

The first thing Zimmermann did was put his client behind a wall of silence. It wasn't Zimmermann's style to churn the water with tantalizing tidbits of misinformation to cloud the real issues. He was still waiting to discover exactly what his client allegedly did. Until he knew, he wasn't going to comment. He said so.

Zimmermann also put an immediate halt to reporters' efforts to get something revealing from Tatum or his family. He tried to refocus their attention on the horrendous burden the government was placing on his family's shoulders. Zimmermann told Tatum's family the only place they would find money to pay him was the public.

It was tough on Tatum's parents to ask for help. Despite their obvious reluctance to publicly ask for assistance, their simple, honest plea in an open letter captured the pain that was palpable in their hearts when they wrote it. Implicit in their letter is a huge question: How could our country, and the Marine Corps, do this to our child? He did everything he was supposed to, it seemed to say, and this was his reward:

> Of our four sons, one is in the Army and one is in the Marines. They both have served two tours of duty in Iraq. Stephen, our Marine, is a Lance Corporal. He and his units have served in two of the toughest assignments. One was in Fallujah in 2004, and the other in Haditha in 2005. He has served his country and flag with great honor and pride. He was well led and well-trained to fight foreign Islamic terrorists and Iraqi insurgents.
>
> We are hard working people, and so do not like to ask for help. The Marine Corps cannot pay for civilian lawyers, but we have taken out a second mortgage on our home and used our savings to defend our son. We need help for expert witnesses, from pathology to scene reconstruction, to ballistics, and others. It is very important that we have our own witnesses and experts.[6]

The letter touched the hearts and purse strings of America.

Zimmermann by reputation was among the deans of the civilian attorneys representing the Haditha Marines. He had the most combat experience, the most time in uniform, and the most time in command. In the civilian world, he was a high-profile Houston criminal attorney in a city that likes its crime news as raw as it likes its meat. From the rake of his expensive gray Stetson to the concise way he speaks, he is all about the Marine Corps. It isn't a front.

In addition to graduating from the University of Texas School of Law in Austin in 1975, Zimmermann graduated from the United States Naval Academy at Annapolis, Maryland, and the Krannert Graduate School of Management at Purdue University in West Lafayette, Indiana.

Zimmermann had earned his combat diploma at Vietnam U, serving as commanding officer of two artillery batteries and earning two Bronze Stars and a Purple Heart in the process. After fourteen years of active duty, he moved to the Marine Corps Reserve for sixteen years, serving as the commanding officer of the infantry battalion headquartered in Houston as well as being a reserve Marine Corps judge.

Zimmermann ran his defense a lot differently than some of the other attorneys. Instead of seeking out reporters, he used his position like a scrubbing board for washing their dirty laundry. Zimmermann turned his guns on the reporters condemning Tatum and the other Marines. Before pulling up stakes, he took particular umbrage with reporters who relied on unnamed sources to convict his client in the court of public opinion.

He made his position clear to John A. Williams, a reporter for the *Edmond Sun*, Tatum's hometown newspaper.

"I don't have any information that the story is correct or incorrect, but it's possible that that might happen," Williams reported Zimmermann said when asked whether his client was going to be charged. "I have no information that would confirm that. There were thirteen people in that squad, including the individuals (who) were wounded. But I don't know where this reporter got the fact that only five of the remaining people would be sent forward."

Zimmermann blasted Murtha as well for his famous claim that the Marines "killed innocent civilians in cold blood." Both as a Marine and an attorney, he found his brother officer's irresponsible indictment reprehensible.

"He should have known better," Zimmermann told *Defend Our Marines*. "Especially being a former Marine. He shouldn't have made those comments. He makes it sound like he has accepted the insurgents' view of what happened and the facts don't support that."

THE PRE-PROCEDURE SPARRING went on from the announcement of the charges in December 2006 until early spring 2007, when the government sprang what seemed a surprise on the defense by granting Dela Cruz immunity in return for his testimony. LtCol Sean Gibson, the Pendleton spokesman, said Mattis announced he had dropped murder and lying charges on April 17 so Dela Cruz could testify for the government.

Former Marine Daniel Marino, for a while Dela Cruz's DC-based attorney and a partner in Sutherland, Asbill & Brennan, confirmed his client's new status and refused further comment.

Dela Cruz joined seven other enlisted and commissioned 3/1 Marines the government had already given immunity to. Few of them contributed any testimony. The immunized Marines now outnumbered the accused enlisted men. Dela Cruz, however, was the only witness admitting to shooting five unarmed men. Before being immunized, Dela Cruz had faced up to life in prison for the unlawful deaths.

His sidekick, Mendoza, was never charged. The kid with the gelatin-thick Spanish accent gave a marvelously worded and concise statement in English to NCIS investigators during the time he was apparently fluent in his second language. On March 19, 2006, when he gave his first statement, Mendoza could think clearly enough in English to say things like, "That training, as it pertains to the events of November 19, consisted of the instruction of clearing a house."

He laid out his entire story in six pages of single-spaced narrative. In the years that passed, his fluency lapsed considerably. Mendoza dutifully initialed the beginning and end of each paragraph to show he read and understood what he said to the helpful NCIS special agent.[7]

Like Salinas, the twenty-year-old from Guri, Venezuela, remained hidden in the government's deck of cards, in his case going all the way to Chicago, where he found himself in the same reserve outfit Sullivan came from. No sooner had he gotten there than he was in trouble with Immigration & Customs Enforcement (ICE). Why he was in Chicago in a reserve outfit and how he got there was never revealed by the prosecution. ICE said he did nothing wrong. The defense intended to make his circumstances a point of serious contention at Wuterich's court-martial.

Mendoza admitted killing two Iraqis, one MAM in House #1 and another in House #2. Sharratt said the first man Mendoza shot had an AK lying next to him when Sharratt gave him a dead check before taking it from his side. Nobody else remembered that happening. It was during one of those outbursts that questions rose about the machine gunner's whereabouts. If he didn't go in either house, how could he recover an assault rifle? Then the dead man somehow burned up. Mendoza seemed as confused as Sharratt. Their inconsistencies provoked a lot of uncertainty before the courts-martial began and even more when they concluded six years later.

By his own admission Mendoza's two victims were unarmed. The first one to die was the Iraqi male in his twenties. He died when Mendoza opened the door to a room after coming inside House #1. In one account, Mendoza said he didn't know what to do in House #1 so he asked Tatum. He claimed Tatum told him to shoot the man. Tatum always denied it. In another account, Mendoza said he shot the man several times after the man appeared to reach for a weapon. The second man he shot through a glass door from twenty-one feet away. His victim was answering the door when he died.

Mendoza said he did it because the house was declared hostile and Marines killed everybody inside hostile houses. Faraj thought Mendoza was so riddled with guilt he convinced himself he had committed a crime.

Mendoza said he learned the procedure in School of Infantry and practiced it over and over during 3/1's work up for Iraq.

"Again, I fired because I had been told the house was hostile and I was following my training that all individuals in a hostile house are to be shot," he later testified.

That afternoon, Mendoza was detailed to go back into the two charnel houses to tag and bag Iraqi bodies. He remembered seeing at least two bodies in a back bedroom in House #2. He was also on the detail that picked up the dead MAMs still lying in the sun by the white car.

On April 2, 2006, Mendoza failed a polygraph examination when he was twice asked whether the first man he shot had actually reached for a weapon. The examiner said his response was evasive. In Haditha logic, it made sense. Both dead men were MAMs, and MAMs were always suspect; therefore, they were counted as insurgents. It wasn't totally improbable. Mendoza was deemed the government's second-best eyewitness after Dela Cruz.

It was almost time for the courts-martial to begin.

CHAPTER 15

WUTERICH/CBS/
COURT-MARTIAL

By the time LtCol Jones convened Wuterich's general court-martial on January 5, 2012, those who cared had already heard from the defendants and witnesses several times. The experts' evidence and testimony was still interesting and inconclusive. That never changed. The former defendants' recollections were still evolving. The witnesses who had been immunized in 2007 had spread to the four winds. So had the evidence. Wuterich's controversial interview with Scott Pelley on *60 Minutes* had already aired three times. There was nothing new to add. Interest in the sensational allegations had peaked years before.

Wuterich's anticlimactic Article 32 hearing in September 2007 was scarcely a mindful recollection in the public domain by January 2012. Although hearing officer LtCol Paul Ware recommended the murder charges against Wuterich be dropped—changed to a lesser offense of negligent homicide—it never happened. In 2010 prosecutors reduced his charged to nine counts of involuntary manslaughter for the deaths of nine of the twenty-four Iraqis killed at Haditha. He was let off the hook for the others, although he was still faced charges of aggravated assault, reckless endangerment, dereliction of duty, and obstruction of justice as well. Eventually the government threw out charges that Wuterich conspired to cover up what happened. By the time he reached court-martial in January 2012 the charges had been changed to three counts of willful dereliction of duty, nine counts of voluntary manslaughter, and two counts of assault with a dangerous weapon or other means likely to produce death or grievous bodily harm (his M16). How those particular charges and numbers were settled upon defied even the public affairs officer's ability to explain.

Meanwhile, the moral questions raised by the former squad leader's guilt or innocence still lingered unanswered in the institutional conscience of the Marine Corps. While those principles waited to go to trial, the war in Iraq ended, as did the battle between government prosecutors and CBS over the video outtakes the government remained certain would show that Wuterich was a murderer. The government had demanded to see them and CBS said no. For almost three years the tasteless fodder ground through the courts being slowly digested by legal scholars who like to chew on knotty issues. In the end the Marine Corps won that skirmish. The prize was a worthless DVD detailing how the big boys do on-camera interviews. On the unexpunged version, Pelley is seen going through the machinations broadcasters perform while preparing an important interview for a popular television news magazine. Wuterich is shown eagerly cooperating, answering the same questions with the same answers until Pelley and the producer are satisfied the shot is right. No desperate secrets were revealed; no smoking gun fell on the floor.

After the CBS outakes proved to be a flop, the only scintillating piece of the case still awaiting detailed examination was what really happened that day. Despite all the inspections of the evidence, all the interrogations, all the lying, speculation, and sheer presumption, the guilt or innocence of the Marines accused of massacre was still in the air. After millions of dollars spent and thousands of man-hours burned, the only evidence the government submitted was contradictory, confusing, and more and more irrelevant. There were newer and greater war crimes in both Iraq and Afghanistan to exploit. When measured against the scale of death and destruction the Global War on Terror brought to the world, Wuterich's alleged crimes seemed almost minuscule. By and large, the reporters who had sensationalized the incident beyond recognition had moved on. Hidden in the rubble was the hearing officer's opinion that the case was fraught with dangerous rocks and shoals. Wuterich wasn't in sheltered waters yet.

ENTER FARAJ

Major Haytham Faraj was still just a name on a roster in the Haditha matter when Ware opened Wuterich's Article 32 hearing. Wuterich's detailed Marine defense counselor had done a fine job defending a different Marine in the courtroom next door. He wasn't a stranger to the Haditha scene in 2007, merely an unknown quantity. Faraj had been assigned as defense counsel for Wuterich on January 11, 2007. He was joined by his former boss LtCol Colby Vokey on January 17. At the time there were no indications that suggested their pairing created a dynamic duo that would plague the Marine Corps legal apparatus at Camp Pendleton until both men retired.

Vokey was already well known by the press and court watchers because he was the big enchilada for all the Marine defense attorneys on the West Coast. In some senior Marine circles he had a reputation for being a shit disturber as well. Besides demanding at least a modicum of justice for the alleged terrorists concentrated on an island prison in Cuba, he wasn't shy about saying so in the press. Nor did he toe the company line when it came to defending his Marines.

Faraj was fresh from defending Corporal Thomas, convicted of kidnapping and conspiracy and acquitted of other charges, including premeditated murder at Hamdaniya in a case prosecutors called "an old-fashioned, premeditated conspiracy to kill." It was a major trial for the rookie lawyer. Although that scandal had been eclipsed by the Haditha probe, it was still an important news story, a great foil for news organizations when there was nothing new in the Haditha investigation. For many pundits and politicians, the sordid tale of Hamdaniya was proof the Marine Corps was running amuck.

While Faraj waited for *US v. Wuterich* to percolate, he stayed busy defending Thomas. It was a tough one. The government said that during a nighttime patrol in on April 26, 2006, Thomas's squad intended to kill a suspected insurgent after kidnapping him from his home. When they couldn't find the insurgent, they kidnapped Hashim Ibrahim Awad, a retired policeman who lived nearby. Thomas, the senior corporal in the squad and a fireteam leader, led a four-man team that seized the father of eleven.

During the eight-day court-martial, civilian attorney Victor Kelley and Faraj argued that the twenty-four-year-old Marine was following the orders of his squad leader. It proved an effective pairing.

"Kelley was a true gentleman who cared about the client more than himself. He was the actual lead counsel but never said so. He called us a team."

Faraj wouldn't be so gracious after his next defendant's court-martial.

The defense presented evidence that Thomas's judgment was clouded by concussive brain injuries from more than nearby twenty-five bomb blasts during his three tours of Iraq. Thomas said the only thing he was ever good at was being a Marine. His defense team did a convincing job warding off what seemed like a dead bang conviction when Thomas pled guilty on January 2007 only to withdraw his plea in February.

Faraj believed Thomas had a sympathetic panel: officers and NCOs who had been there and knew how the Marines fought.

At the end of his court-martial, prosecutors told the court Thomas deserved fifteen years in prison with a dishonorable discharge, reduction in rank to E-1 (private), and a fine. He had already served almost eighteen months in the brig. Kelley said the pretrial agreement Thomas rejected called for twelve years in prison.

The defense asked the court that he be credited for the 519 days he had already served in the brig and be returned to active duty. It didn't happen. The kid who had found a home in the Marine Corps was booted out.

"We failed him as a Marine Corps, because under good leadership, this Marine would not be here today," Faraj told the court during his close. "Consider where the responsibility lies."

Apparently, the military jury of three officers and six enlisted Marines agreed. They deliberated Thomas's sentence for less than an hour before returning their decision to recommend Thomas be sentenced to a bad-conduct discharge and a reduction in rank to private. Marines expect their leaders—even their junior leaders—to lead correctly. They don't like to be disappointed.

Neither does the Marine Corps reward failure. Thomas's squad leader, Sergeant Lawrence G. Hutchins III, was not afforded the same consideration as Thomas. He was found guilty of murder, conspiracy to commit murder, and making a false official statement and larceny, and was acquitted of the greater charge of unpremeditated murder. He got fifteen years. It was a huge hurdle that Faraj already knew Wuterich would have to overcome.

Following Thomas's court-martial, Faraj began taking a more active role in Wuterich's defense. He was inside the courtroom more often, occasionally appearing in impeccable utilities, a poster Marine with a face set in stone. His demeanor didn't encourage intimacy. Unlike the civilian attorneys, he was not warm and fuzzy, not even among the Marines on the defense team. Faraj was old school among the bright young attorneys the Marines put up to defend the Haditha Eight. He was humping a ruck across the Horn of Africa when most of them were still wearing Captain America pajamas to bed.

Faraj's remoteness was intentional. He thinks informality in the workplace, particularly in the courtroom, breeds disrespect. He stressed that in his dealings with his colleagues, most of whom were fresh out of law school and even fresher in Faraj's Marine Corps. He was appalled the way his junior colleagues were being treated; like "lance corporals" despite being "brighter than average junior officers and more mature, thanks to three years in law school." Education and title, however, didn't earn them the respect junior officers in other branches were accorded by custom and tradition. Grunts see lawyers as another impediment in their path to survival. The career Marine lawyers equated the rookies with the less endowed troops. To get more than the trapping of military courtesy they had to earn it, as begrudgingly as it was offered by senior Marine lawyers who rested on their prerogatives and junior Marines who thought they were pogues.

Faraj was steeped in nineteen years of formality intrinsic to infantrymen, who cannot afford to let intimacy interfere with the mission. He believed in the formalities and prerogatives of rank that he saw as a two-way street. His remoteness was at odds with Puckett's freewheeling, shoot-from-the-hip style. His knowledge of the Marine Corps and how it operated gave him an advantage the rookie lawyers didn't have and never would.

Although he didn't know it at the time, Faraj had plenty of time to learn the facts and prepare the case. In 2007, however, he figured he would have to work twice as hard as he already was to get ready for trial in time. With the Hamdaniya war crime trial over and the Wuterich Article 32 hearing set to begin August 30, 2007, it was time to get ready for some serious lawyering.

The Wuterich examination was expected to take two weeks. Faraj fully anticipated the hearing officer would find enough evidence to recommend the case for trial. It happened to be the opinion of Neal Puckett as well. Regardless, it didn't seem to matter. The intense news coverage that preceded the hearings for Sharratt and Tatum had waned. They had been exonerated. Sharratt had even been commended by LtGen Mattis. The elusive smoking gun was still undiscovered. Without anything scintillating, the Haditha massacre got tucked away on the inside pages of the nation's big daily newspapers.

Puckett was strangely silent. He'd made big news the year before when he joined forces with Mark Zaid to sue Representative Murtha on August 2, 2006, for libel and invasion of privacy on behalf of Wuterich. The lawsuit alleged Murtha "tarnished the Marines' reputation" by telling news organizations in May that the Marine unit cracked after a roadside bomb killed one of its members and that the troops "killed innocent civilians in cold blood." The suit alleged Murtha repeatedly said the incident was "covered up." Nobody except Puckett and Zaid thought it would go anywhere. Murtha was protected by the color of his office. There wasn't much chance Puckett would ever get his hands in the Pennsylvania Democrat's deep pockets. More likely he was looking for face time.

His effort kept Wuterich's name in the news for a while before it slipped off the radar screen, lost in the clutter of new allegations of misdeeds and political scandals. Faraj didn't mind the respite from all the scrutiny. He had his hands full with the minutiae of the prehearing preparations. He said he was alarmed to discover much of the essential scut work needed to flesh out bare-boned hyperbole already offered by the defense was not in the kind of order it took to get ready for an evidentiary hearing. He did not anticipate more than a few months for pretrial bargaining after the evidentiary hearing, a flurry of pretrial motions, shuffling dates, and putting the witness list together, and then it would be time for court-martial. He expected to stay fully engaged until well after Christmas. And he still had other cases to address at the same time. It was not to be.

Wuterich's Article 32 hearing started on time. Puckett was there every day sitting next to Wuterich, with Mark Zaid, Vokey, and Faraj jammed in beside them. The civilian lawyers always looked slightly out of place, their conservative blue and gray suits almost gaudy next to the Marines. Puckett relinquished the interrogation of Dela Cruz and Mendoza to Vokey and Faraj. Both men were dressed in regulation computer-designed camouflage utilities. It was the uniform of the day, a signal of sorts that seemed to say whatever went on here didn't carry the full weight and solemnity of a court-martial. It scarcely made a difference to the formalities. Other than the uniforms and somewhat more flexible rules of evidence, the procedures for conducting the business of the hearing aped the protocol observed in a general court-martial. There was no relaxed posturing, no one casually leaning on the examiner's podium exchanging barbed repartee with the opposition.

Ware ran the proceedings in a friendly, competent manner, ever mindful of who was watching.

Wuterich did his communicating through Puckett unless Puckett was questioning a witness. The pecking order was Puckett, Zaid, Vokey, and Faraj. By the end of the hearing it was mostly Vokey and Faraj. Neither of the civilians appeared to have a convincing grasp of the subtleties of infantry life. Faraj says his biggest regret in representing Wuterich was never establishing the intimate bonds of trust and mutual support defense lawyers strive to achieve with their clients. He was the technical expert, Puckett held the reins. After the trial, the two ended their partnership and have not spoken since.

Nine witnesses testified under oath. They had all been seen or heard from before. Ware considered 215 exhibits. All eyes, meanwhile, stayed on Mendoza and Dela Cruz, who had been promoted to lance corporal while waiting to testify against their former squad leader. Their time was being wasted. Dela Cruz was in a casual status, marking time until he could get back to the fleet. Mendoza had been spirited from Pendleton for safekeeping to drive at the headquarters for a Chicago reserve battalion. At the time, Mendoza's transfer seemed frivolous, a lucky venture for Sullivan, who just happened to live there as well. Remarkably, so did Dela Cruz. Sullivan would return to his hometown on America's dime several times to question his carefully shielded witness before the Wuterich court-martial began. At the very least it seemed to Faraj that Sullivan was playing fast and loose with the rules. The irony was wonderful. The Marine Corps attorney travels from Camp Pendleton to Chicago—where he lives—to visit a witness who lives at Camp Pendleton. Faraj intended to make an issue out of it.

In the meantime, the Marine Corps was saying not so fast. It wasn't always obvious. The message was faint, restrained, hidden in a flurry of sinister pronouncements. At first it seemed obvious the Corps intended to throw the enlisted Marines under the first available bus, except it wasn't working out that way. Despite the hyperbole, it was looking more and more like the work of an artful dodger dancing in a hall of smoke and mirrors. The Marine Corps was slowly throttling its own prosecution.

Wuterich's court-martial never had much to do with right and wrong. In the civilian understanding of the words, they are relative terms that have little correlation to combat situations. Wronging someone or something in civilian life bears almost no relationship to wronging someone or something on the battlefield. The most sinister, heinous crimes in the relatively tranquil world of ordinary society are routinely perpetrated on the battlefield. Premeditated murder, ambush, long-range random killing, and general slaughter were all part of the day in the life of a junior Marine in Iraq in November 2005.

That alone made Wuterich's situation unique. He was being court-martialed for doing what he was trained to do. Marines are taught that killing is good. They are inculcated with the notion. Before going to Iraq, Wuterich taught other young men that killing was good, the measure of a Marine. Squeamishness isn't allowed. Nothing had changed in the seven years that had passed since he was training boots. Young men, barely more than boys learning to be Marine infantrymen at nearby Camp Pendleton, flooded next-door Oceanside every Saturday to scan the scalping knives and killing hatchets offered by local vendors to supplement their military hardware. Their conversations routinely turned to the best ways to kill someone, as if they already knew the black secrets they would eventually be expected to learn.

Military law doesn't concern itself with the morality of death and destruction on the battlefield, only its lawful implementation. Faraj intended to capitalize on that bleak reality. He intuitively understood that the real purpose of the military justice system is to maintain good order and discipline. Faraj says he was equally certain a realistic good jury would feel the same way:

> While the military justice system has evolved in the two centuries
> since it was created, it remains primarily a tool for the commander
> to ensure readiness. When someone in the military is accused of a

crime, it is that person's commander that convenes that court-martial. The commander charges the accused, assigns a prosecutor, and decides what if any resources the defense will receive.

Frank Wuterich had gone through a number of different convening authorities. They began that case with Mattis, then got LtGen Samuel Helland, followed by LtGen George Flynn, and finally Waldhauser. All four generals were generous with providing resources to the defense in terms of funding to pay for experts for the case, but then they were required to by law. The law says that any expert the government gets, the defense also has a right to get. But that's about where equity ends.

The convening authority and his legal advisor pick the jury. The convening authority's legal advisor—known as the SJA [staff judge advocate]—is nothing more than a senior prosecutor. SJAs have a duty to be neutral advisors to the commander. In theory, the commander appoints the various players in a court-martial guided by his supposedly neutral advisor and excepts the outcome. In reality, most SJAs assume a prosecutorial function; they assist the prosecutor and rarely advise the commander in a way that incorporates the much cited but rarely applied presumption of innocence. The law tells the commander and the SJA that the accused is presumed innocent. Yet neither the system nor the law treats an accused that way.

The law authorizes a commander to put an accused in jail, remove him from his job, restrict him, and subject him to invasions of privacy that no American civilian would ever accept. The same commander who charges the accused, restricts his liberty, determines what resources he gets to defend, decides what witnesses the defendant will be allowed to call, also picks the jury. The selection process is supposed to be random and calls on the commander to select the best qualified based on education, experience, maturity, and knowledge. But regardless of randomness, the jurors work for the commander and will always return to the command of the person who decided to charge the accused.

Marine recruits receive their first briefs on the Uniform Code of Military Justice almost as soon as they get their heads shaved. They can't be charged with violating the UCMJ until they are instructed on it. Lectures on the subject are routinely offered by military lawyers, company and battalion officers, and service-wise NCOs, whose perspective is from the bottom of the pile. The NCOs' down-to-earth lectures are the most revealing because they are the easiest to understand.

When Faraj joined the Corps at seventeen, he said he shared essentially the same lecture that recruits got in my generation and recruits in all branches still get today. It goes something like this:

> The Uniform Code of Military Justice applies to you. Under the UCMJ you can be charged and sent to NJP [non-judicial punishment] or court-martial for violating orders, failing to be in the proper uniform, failing to adhere to standards of appearance, going UA [unauthorized absence] and by failing to give instant, unquestioning obedience to orders. You *will* learn the eleven general orders. If you violate any of those orders you will be charged and go to the brig. If someone in a higher rank or billet gives you an order you follow it. How many of you here believe you are smart? You will be the first ones to get into trouble. This is not the fucking Navy or Army and definitely not the Air Force. Nobody gives a fuck what you think and no one is interested in your opinion. Keep your mouth shut and do what you're told. You're not paid to think, you're paid to obey. Are any of you confused?

It has to be that way to ensure discipline. Although the military's appellate courts in the past few decades have put some barriers in place to protect the process and eliminate improper influence of the military justice process, generally speaking the convening authority has all the power and the defense none. A military defendant can file a motion through a lawyer to get a military judge to consider a matter, but the judges are military officers who have career objectives of one day being promoted and perhaps becoming senior judge advocates. Even the most courageous military judge must undoubtedly consider the impact of controversial decisions on future career prospects.

The only way to overcome such a huge disadvantage is by using the system as a defense rather than arguing against it, especially when the defendant is accused of committing deeds so horrific as to defy the very concept of justice. War is a dirty business. Faraj knew the only way Wuterich's behavior could fairly be judged was by placing it in the context in which it occurred. He said he already sensed the combat-hardened senior NCOs and officers who would one day sit on the panel thought the same way he did. The real question they wanted to know was whether Wuterich had intentionally or negligently incited his squad of roughnecks to commit murder. If his omissions were intentional, he was guilty. If he led his squad into combat expecting the worst while acting in accordance with accepted doctrine and tactics of urban warfare, he was innocent. At stake was the honor of the Corps.

HEARING OFFICER LTCOL PAUL WARE

By the time 2012 rolled around, many Marines wondered why Wuterich was even going to trial. It should have been obvious. In his October 2, 2007, final report, hearing officer LtCol Paul Ware took great pains to explain to the convening authority why.[1] Ware made clear that, although the government's case was seriously flawed, it was not without merit. He never exonerated Wuterich. He argued instead that pursuing Wuterich for murder and cover-up was a waste of time. Although the facts he chose to consider were much the same as the evidence disclosed in the hearings of Lance Corporals Tatum and Sharratt, Ware strove to give his decision regarding Wuterich a unique flavor.

His first finding and recommendation concerned the five men who were shot to death near the white car: Charge one included five identical specifications claiming Wuterich, "with the intent to kill or inflict great bodily harm," had murdered the five dead men. Ware unquestionably didn't agree.

In a lengthy dissertation, he told Mattis the issue "turns to whether the ROE allow for deadly force to be used under the circumstances described by other evidence" regarding the way in by which five Iraqis died.

"Although it is easy to second guess his decision to respond with deadly force as the best option, not choosing the best option doesn't make other decisions illegal," Ware opined. "On the whole of the evidence, I believe the actions of SSgt Wuterich were 'reasonable and lawful' under the circumstances presented to him." Ware declared there was insufficient evidence to prosecute him for shooting the decedents.

Ware disposed of the charges of murder and assault in House #1 and House #2 in similar fashion. The charge sheet claimed that Wuterich did, with "wanton disregard for human life, murder six persons inside a House identified as House #1, by: advising the Marines under his charge, prior to the Marines' entry into House #1, to 'shoot first and ask questions later' or words to that effect, thus disregarding the requirement to have positive identification prior to engaging a target." He compounded his crime by using "deadly force without conducting positive identification prior to engaging individuals within House #1."

After a careful review of all the allegations point by point, Ware told Mattis "that the Government has failed its burden to demonstrate reasonable grounds to believe SSgt Wuterich committed a crime within House #1."

Ware held a more jaundiced view about the seven identical charges of assault with intent to kill in House #2 that Wuterich denied knowledge of. He said Wuterich was a liar. The charge said Wuterich acted "with the intent to kill or inflict great bodily harm, murder a person . . . by means of shooting that person with an M16A4 service rifle." Ware believed Wuterich had intentionally participated in the deaths of the seven innocent victims by shooting them:

> It is SSgt Wuterich's insistence that he did not participate in shooting inside House #2 that causes great consternation. I am left with two alternatives. He either did fire inside House #2 and the trauma of the event and through denial has convinced himself that he didn't or

he was woefully derelict in his duties. If SSgt Wuterich fired inside the room, the evidence demonstrates that there was sufficient lighting to see the occupants. Unlike in House #1, there is no evidence that a grenade exploded which would have caused decreased lighting. Perhaps SSgt Wuterich perceived a threat inside the room after hearing the Aunt scream. There is simply no evidence to support any conclusion other than he entered the room, saw the occupants and fired away.

Ware left little room for ambiguity: "I believe that SSgt Wuterich's statement that he did not fire in House #2 is false, and absent a fanciful conjecture, the government has reasonable grounds to proceed with referral of this charge."

Faraj was flabbergasted by the government's claim that Wuterich conspired with Dela Cruz to cover up the shootings at the white car. There was nothing to cover up, he argues. The five men were inside the so-called "security zone" at a moment when the Marines were under attack and had inexplicably exited the car for whatever reason. Under the existing ROE, they were lawful targets. If the men had held murder in their hearts, the entire squad had been in grave danger. Wuterich and Dela Cruz and maybe Salinas did what Marines are expected to do and shot them down, eliminated the threat, and secured the exposed flank. It was ugly because it was war.

The government charged that Wuterich solicited Corporal Sanick P. Dela Cruz to "lie and state that Iraqi Army members shot the male passengers and that the passengers were running or words to that effect." Again Wuterich compounded his crime by conspiring with Dela Cruz to claim he ordered the car's occupants to "*qif, qif* [stop, stop] or "words to that effect" when they reportedly began to flee before Wuterich began shooting them.

Ware wasn't buying it either. He didn't believe anything Dela Cruz said and went out of his way to make apparent to everyone in the courtroom his distaste for the little man with the mean reputation. He told Mattis the government had "failed to provide sufficient evidence to establish reasonable grounds that the statement was official or made with the intent to deceive."

Having disposed of the government's case, Ware recommended a new set of charges against Wuterich. They weren't so serious as to put his life in jeopardy, but he still faced the balance of it behind prison walls if he were convicted.

Instead of murder, Ware recommended that Wuterich face general court-martial for seven counts of negligent homicide for killing Aida Yasin Ahmed, Mohomed Younis Salim, Aisha Younis Salim, Zainab Younis Salim, Sena Younis Salim, Noor Salim Rasif, and Yuda Hasin Ahmed and one specification of negligent homicide for killing Mohomed Younis Salim:

> There are reasonable grounds to believe that SSgt Wuterich commanded or approved of LCpl Mendoza shooting Younis through the front door. LCpl Mendoza's testimony that either Sgt Salinas or SSgt Wuterich were knocking on a door is corroborated by Safah who describes hearing a bell or door knocking. This logically would cause Younis to approach his front door. LCpl Mendoza shot the man through the door with no display of hostile act or intent. His testimony is that SSgt Wuterich told him to shoot. If true, SSgt Wuterich is liable for the negligent homicide of Younis.

Ware didn't stop at seven counts of negligent homicide. He tacked on a long laundry list of lesser included offenses that replaced rather than ameliorated the charges against Wuterich. In essence, he told Gen Mattis the prosecution didn't think things through too well when making the list of complaints that preceded the indictment. In Ware's view, the government had a reasonable criminal case against the staff sergeant if only the prosecution knew what it was doing.

He recommended that Wuterich also be charged with two counts of assault, a violation of Article 128 of the UCMJ, for participating in and ordering the wounding of Abdul and Eman, the two children who survived the ravaging of House #1. Article 128 says the assault was "likely to cause death or great bodily harm" to whomever it was inflicted upon. He also thought Wuterich should be charged with obstruction of justice, two counts of willful dereliction of duty, and two counts of violating a lawful general order.

The first count of willful dereliction was for failing to report a violation of the ROE after witnessing Mendoza kill an unarmed man through a door and a second for failing to report a suspected violation of the ROE when he "learned or witnessed" Marines under his command "killed unarmed women and children inside House #2."

To make sure everyone understood he was after Wuterich's hide, Ware recommended Gen Mattis charge Wuterich with being an "accessory after the fact to negligent homicide" who did "in order to hinder punishment of the said PFC Mendoza and LCpl Tatum, assist the said PFC Mendoza and LCpl Tatum by concealing and not reporting up the chain of command accurate details of the events that transpired in House #2."

Coupled with that, Wuterich committed the offense of "misprision of a serious offense" for concealing relevant incriminating information. The unfamiliar term *misprision* means Wuterich hid a crime when he failed to reveal Mendoza and Steven Tatum "had actually committed serious offenses to wit: negligent homicide of seven individuals within House #2" by not reporting the "circumstances, number and nature of casualties inside House #2" and failing to pass it up the chain of command as "soon as possible." When all was said and done Ware recommended a new laundry list of charges that included: seven specifications of negligent homicide, one for each victim within House #2; two specifications of willful dereliction of duty; two specifications of violating a lawful general order; one specification of accessory after the fact for negligent homicide; and one specification of misprision of negligent homicide.

Ware concluded by reiterating why he thought Wuterich was guilty of intentionally killing fifteen men, women, and children without premeditation:

> I am recommending that the Government pursue the lesser offense of
> negligent homicide and not murder because I believe after reviewing

all the evidence, no trier of fact can conclude SSgt Wuterich formed the criminal intent to kill. The evidence is contradictory, the forensic analysis is limited and almost all witnesses have an obvious bias or prejudice. The case against SSgt Wuterich that he committed murder is simply not strong enough to prove beyond a reasonable doubt. What the evidence does point to is that SSgt Wuterich failed to exercise due care in his own actions or in supervising his Marines. When a Marine fails to exercise due care in a combat environment resulting in the death of innocents, the charge of negligent homicide, not murder is the appropriate offense. Accordingly I believe the elements and theory of negligent homicide best fits the evidence of what occurred inside House #2.

Finally, although I believe the Government will fail to prove beyond a reasonable doubt that SSgt Wuterich committed any offenses other than dereliction of duty, due to the serious nature of the charges, I recommend referral to a general court-martial.

CHAPTER 16

TRUTH ON TRIAL

When Wuterich finally went to court-martial in January 2012, his situation was confusing in many ways. It had been five years since the evidence in his case had been reviewed. Much had changed in the world while the case moldered. It was understandable why many people confused Wuterich's Article 32 investigation with his court-martial and thought it had passed. Meanwhile there had been new scandals to report, each more horrific than the last.

Among the enlisted suspects, Dela Cruz was immunized and Salinas and Mendoza were never charged. The charges against Sharratt and Tatum had been dismissed, and all the officers had been cleared. Everybody else who knew anything about what actually happened on Route Chestnut was immunized, removed from consideration, ignored, or discharged and out of reach. Even the Marines still dangling on the government's hook had already testified nobody did anything wrong. It would seem that alone was enough to set Wuterich free.

Puckett didn't see it that way. He is a deal maker. Faraj says Puckett didn't like jury trials that actually went to the jury for a decision.

Throughout the trial he was worried that the case would find its way into the panel's hands for a decision. Faraj said he thought Puckett lacked self-confidence. It was a bold statement.

Self-confidence has never been a problem for Faraj. Knowing him, one quickly discovers he prides himself on being able to connect with fellow infantrymen. He believes the infantry is the epicenter of Marine Corps legends and traditions. By the time of trial, Faraj was out of his immaculate uniform and into a suit, but he still walked and talked like a hardcore Marine. Puckett, on the other hand, walked and talked like a lamb in wolf's clothing. The jury didn't connect to him. Faraj thought it was up to him to be the wolf.

Faraj geared his presentation to make sure the jury understood it was talking to a peer. His suits and his position at the defense table said he was a civilian lawyer, but inside he was still a grunt. The personification radiated from him in the cramped courtroom where a mere few feet separated the accused from the jury. Their proximity didn't bother Faraj. He wanted the men of the jury to sense his intensity. He spoke a language they understood. His formality, directness, and stone face all suggested he was still a Marine officer on the hunt. The jurors liked that. It was something they could relate to.

Even before the process began, Faraj said he had identified a number of issues that needed to be presented to the jury so they could be discussed before the trial began. Although Puckett had already submitted questions for potential panelists to the military judge, they did not address the substantive issues and danger points in the case the way Faraj said they should.

Faraj believes the best way to convey a message of the defense is during the *voir dire* process that precedes the selection of the jury, or "panel" in military parlance. Voir dire is a French legal term that loosely means to speak the truth. Juries selected in all but very few US trials undergo the process. It is a way for the lawyers and judge to vet the prospective jurors to ensure they are up to the standards required of persons making momentous decisions. In military courtrooms, voir dire is also a mechanism for the convening authority to discover which way the wind is blowing. More than one criminal prosecution has suddenly changed course after the convening authority realizes the government's case—in effect his case—is a loser. At worst, a good voir dire examination will plant seeds of doubt. Faraj intended to start cultivating them immediately.

"During the voir dire, the lawyers are supposed to ask questions of the jurors to ensure discover any biases they might have. Jurors that have any kind of bias, know the witnesses or lawyers, or know something about the case may be challenged and eliminated from the jury."

Faraj held that a good voir dire examination and opening statement were essential to winning the case. He believed he was good at both. When Puckett and he discussed the various roles and responsibilities, Wuterich had five lawyers in his corner. With so many, Faraj offered to take a backseat and focus on writing and research in support of the team. He argued that the lawyers' egos needed to give way to what was best for the client.

None of that mattered on January 4, 2012. By then, almost everyone who had started the case in 2007 was gone. Puckett, Faraj, and a new Marine lawyer were it. Mark Zaid stepped aside early on. Wuterich lost Vokey after he retired, the result of a complicated conflict of interest situation with one of the key witnesses represented by the law firm he joined. When Vokey left the case in 2009, the voir dire procedure went unassigned.[1]

Faraj was aware of the questions Puckett had submitted to the judge in July of 2010, when the case was set to start sometime in that year. On the morning of January 4, 2012, however, it was Faraj who would be doing the voir dire. That was decided in November of 2011 when Wuterich once again appeared to be heading for court-martial. Faraj says he failed to review the questions submitted by Puckett at that time, assuming that they would be a good starting point.

When he finally got around to reviewing Puckett's work, he says, he realized that the questions intended to be asked were of no value to the case. They were bland questions—"meaningless softballs"—that failed to present the fundamental issues to the jury. Faraj wanted to get into the subtle nuances of this case. He wanted to know if the jury panel was capable of understanding the difference between a negligent act and an intentional one. He wanted to find out if these officers and staff noncommissioned officers adhered to the principle that a Marine Corps leader is responsible for everything that his unit does or fails to do, that they "would not sever the chain of responsibility to Wuterich" if they found a crime was committed. Faraj knew that there was no direct evidence showing that Wuterich shot anyone. The only way Wuterich could be found guilty of wrongfully killing someone was if the jury attributed unlawful deaths committed by someone else to Wuterich. Faraj needed to understand where the dividing line of responsibility lay in the minds of the jurors. Would they automatically hold Wuterich responsible for everything his Marines did, or would they sever his responsibility from acts that he could not control or foresee? Faraj had no desire to kick anyone off the jury; his was the style of inclusion. He intended to have a conversation with every juror to discuss the nuances of these issues.

On January 3, the day before court-martial was scheduled to start, Faraj submitted a new set of questions to Judge Jones. By now, Faraj said, he detested the man with the sonorous voice and paternal manner who held the keys to Wuterich's kingdom. Faraj thought he was a shill working on behalf of the convening authority. He informed Jones he would not be asking the questions previously submitted by Puckett.

When the questions of the prospective jurors began January 4—more accurately, when the conversation between individual jurors and Faraj began—it became clear that Faraj wanted the jurors to reflect on their leadership experiences and "share circumstances when one of their Marines committed a wrong they had no direct responsibility for." All the examples, whether they thought of them on their own or were offered by Faraj, were circumstances that would be considered criminal in nature.

Faraj said that when he sat down after the last question was asked, he was confident that "if the jury comes to the conclusion that an unlawful killing was committed, they would not hold Wuterich responsible for it." And if they believed his Marines had violated the

ROE, they would at worst find Wuterich guilty of negligent dereliction of duty, which carried a maximum sentence of three months in jail.

"That would be a win because it bested the government's best offer by fifteen months."

PUCKETT AND FARAJ met that night at the beachside condo they had rented for the trial. Tensions between the two lawyers were beginning to mount. For one thing, Faraj was unhappy with the living arrangements. He was a bachelor. He liked his quiet solitude. Puckett had brought his wife with him. She would remain there for the length of trial. Her presence was a distraction for Faraj that he did not appreciate. She had become the de facto business manager for the business partners, and business was not going so well. Her presence was a daily reminder things weren't as they should be. The irritation did nothing to better the relationship between the two men.

The first morning of Wuterich's court-martial began with an abrupt wake-up call. Before the voir dire proceeding began, LtCol Jones offered a bit of news that set the reporters in the courtroom buzzing. "Chessani will not be a witness," Jones intoned almost matter-of-factly. The officer who categorically stated that his men were not murderers, the lieutenant colonel who threw away his career to defend his enlisted Marines, and the highest-ranking Marine to be criminally prosecuted for the incident, was not going to appear.

"We lost that battle," Puckett said during the morning break.

Puckett said Chessani was one of the witnesses the government objected to during pretrial negotiations to determine who would and would not be called to testify. When asked if the defense was disappointed by the decision, Puckett said his defense team had "tried vigorously" to bring Chessani back to Camp Pendleton one last time.

Chessani was important not only because he commanded 3/1 Marines at Haditha, but he also was frequently quoted during the reporters' feeding frenzy that followed the alleged massacre as vehemently saying, "My Marines are not murderers," when apprised of massacre allegations.[2]

He was referring, of course, to the March 2006 cover story by Tim McGirk. Chessani had already retired from the Marine Corps with his rank and retirement privileges intact after being exonerated of all criminal charges. His testimony was not essential, but it made very nice frosting. Everyone thought he would be missed.

The business of the day, however, was not disposing of the charges. It was merely voir dire day, the first of two days the lawyers needed to decide who would be seated on the panel. The convening authority, LtGen Thomas D. Waldhauser, had authorized a pool of eleven senior Marines, five officers and six NCOs, to determine the guilt or innocence of SSgt Frank D. Wuterich. By law, Wuterich was entitled to a panel in which one-third of the members were enlisted men. His pool included a full bird colonel, two lieutenant colonels, a major, one captain, a master gunnery sergeant, a first sergeant, two master sergeants, and two gunnery sergeants. Not all of them would serve.

According to testimony offered before the voir dire process began, the potential panelists were given a questionnaire to complete during the Christmas holiday season that was handed out by the chief of staff of the First Marine Division. A week before the court-martial began, the panelists being considered for selection were notified they would be part of the pool of potential jurors to be quizzed in the cramped courtroom at Camp Pendleton the following Wednesday. Most of them said they did not know they would be involved in the Haditha matter until they were selected for the panel pool.

Lawyers from both sides of the courtroom spent most of Thursday tediously and repetitively grilling the potential panelists to determine whether they would ultimately decide Wuterich's fate. First lead prosecutor Maj Nicolas Gannon and then Faraj asked the entire eleven-member pool general questions. Once that was accomplished, the courtroom was cleared so each individual in the pool could be summoned for personal interrogation.

"I can't think of a single witness desiring of being helpful to the government," Gannon complained to LtCol Jones at the conclusion of the tedious two-day proceeding.

At the close of the voir dire process, as few as five or as many as all eleven of the potential panelists would be seated, according to PAO LtCol Joseph Kloppel. In the meantime, the attorneys tried to divine from the answers of the jury pool whom they wanted on the panel.

The potential panelists already knew Wuterich was charged with violations of the UCMJ for his role in the deaths of fifteen Iraqi citizens who were killed. Who they were apparently didn't matter. Instead of a name, each Iraqi victim was assigned a number. It was supposed to be less inflammatory that way. During the proceedings, the potential jurors did hear a laundry list of familiar American names, all players in the six-year investigation of the alleged massacre who briefly captured the attention of the world when they were revealed in early 2006. Few of the names would be heard again.

On Thursday morning, Jones asked the prospective jurors whether they could give "fair consideration" to sentencing Wuterich to a dishonorable discharge and more than 157 years in prison for his role in allegedly killing the civilians more than six years before. The entire pool of potential jurors raised their hands in affirmation. That was good enough. On Thursday afternoon, eight of the Marines, three officers and five noncommissioned officers, were selected and the trial began.

PAO Kloppel—the only Marine officer allowed to be either approached or questioned by the press—told assembled reporters the government was expected to call at least forty prosecution witnesses, including several Marines who were granted immunity in exchange for their testimony. Subsequently, Jones told the potential panelists they should expect to be in the tiny, austere courtroom at Camp Pendleton for as long as four weeks. More than seven years after Wuterich fired his rifle in anger for the first and only time, his court-martial was about to begin.

RIGHT ON TIME the following Monday morning, the eight-member panel trooped in and the general court-martial of SSgt Frank D. Wuterich began in earnest, with Gannon introducing the government's case. He was subdued, reserved, and brief.

Sitting next to him was LtCol Sean Sullivan, the still-paunchy Chicago reservist who was called to active duty six years before to augment the prosecution team the government was assembling. It was supposed to be a temporary detail. He was thinner now and quieter; more of his short hair had departed. Some of the steam had left his demeanor.

Across the aisle, wearing airs of pleased expectation, were Puckett and Faraj. Assisting them was detailed Marine counsel Major Meredith Nelson, a relative newcomer to the Haditha imbroglio. She rarely said anything during trial.

Gannon gave the opening statement for the prosecution. Faraj thought he took the right path:

> Unlike most prosecutors who stood in that same courtroom promising to deliver powerful evidence of guilt only to fail, Gannon was precise and measured. He did not overpromise. He learned from past mistakes. He argued that Wuterich made a series of fatal assumptions and finished with his ace card, the trusted Army Colonel Gregory Watt who would tell them that Wuterich admitted to him he told his ad hoc fire team to "shoot first and ask questions later." Those six words defined seven years of litigation and tens of thousands of documents.

Wuterich's now famous "shoot first and ask questions later" statement came in almost immediately. Gannon let the jury hear it in his opening and promised it would be repeated again by Watt. It was the highlight of his introduction. Expecting much worse, Faraj decided he should be thankful *if* that was all the government had. For a second he really believed Wuterich was going to walk. Then he shook it off. Misplaced optimism was dangerous. He had to assume the worst.

It was obvious long before the trial began that the phrase rankled Faraj. In August 2010, he unsuccessfully filed a motion to suppress it from evidence. He relied on a law that says if a defendant makes a statement or admission that is not corroborated it cannot be used against him.

"None of the Marines Wuterich supposedly said this to heard it; nor should they have," Faraj complained. "When Salinas, Mendoza, and Tatum advanced against the first House to the South, Wuterich went around the giant ditch that separated the road and the houses. There was no one with him to say it to, and more importantly, no one to hear it."

It was an important point of law clearly pregnant with profound implications. Unfortunately for Wuterich, Jones did not agree with his argument. Jones decided that the corroboration the government needed to introduce the statement into evidence was found in the aftermath—in the many deaths that Wuterich's alleged statement caused. Never mind whether he never really said it. Jones noted that Wuterich told Watt he said it and then repeated himself on *60 Minutes* for the entire world to hear. It was close enough. His qualifying "or something like that" didn't mean doodly. Wuterich was stuck with it.

Faraj was beside himself when he heard about the unfavorable ruling. His dissatisfaction was evident from the dark thundercloud that hovered over him the entire afternoon.

"Jones must have concluded that except for Wuterich's statement the killings would not have happened. To reach the decision Jones would also have to conclude that all the Marines were lying." Faraj was not only disappointed, he said, he was furious. In his opinion the words, even if uttered, were meaningless: "Anyone who's ever cleared a room or structure in a MOUT environment knows that you shoot going in and you don't ask questions. What Wuterich told his Marines is what the Marine Corps teaches anyway. And here was this judge who could not see it."

This would be the first of many skirmishes Faraj would have with Jones and lose. Jones's decision to let those seemingly innocuous words come in as evidence would have profound consequences on the entire trial and the closing of the Haditha chapter in the Iraq war narrative.

After Gannon concluded his brief introduction it was Faraj's turn. He strode to the podium, covering six or so feet in two strides. He was like a racehorse in the starting gate, fumbling with paper and microphones while he gathered his wits. Faraj's disappointment that Jones let in the fictionalized account of Wuterich's actions fueled his fury. Unlike Gannon, his opening was passionate and animated. He began by taking the jury to bleak Route Chestnut on the morning of November 19.

Faraj detailed how the four-vehicle convoy turned onto Chestnut, the explosion, death, and response. According to the evidence "30 percent" of the expended cartridges found in what was now called House #2 where eight people died were expended AK-47 cartridges and 9 mm pistol rounds that weren't accounted for by the attacking Marines.

"The government ignored it," Faraj added incredulously. "Where did this come from, where did the 7.62 (AK) come from? Who was in the back bedroom; who shot the 9 mm rounds?"

He showed the jury the squad's actions at roadside: Wuterich taking a knee and shooting in the direction of the five men who stepped out of the white Opel while Dela Cruz engaged from the north before walking up and executing them one by one. Faraj demonstrated how the government's best witness stood over one of the men he shot, took out his penis, and urinated into his exposed skull. Dela Cruz had said his emotions got the best of him. They probably did. Killing five men execution style tends to do that; at least that was how Dela Cruz remembered it. Faraj wanted to put the vicious little man on ice before the trial even began. The listening Marines didn't seem either surprised or upset Dela Cruz could be so cold.

Gannon was just as aware of Dela Cruz's reputation as Faraj. Only weeks before the court-martial began he had been forced to disclose to the defense that while still in Iraq Dela Cruz had threatened to kill a fellow Marine named Andrew Wright over his opinion of what happened there.[3] The Notice of Disclosure said Dela Cruz "'Struck him in the face with his closed fist,' and promised 'if I ever see you on the street I'll kill you' or words to that effect." Faraj welcomed the news. It was another nail in the coffin of the government's best eyewitness.

Gannon countered by deciding to hold Dela Cruz for a few days before presenting him to the jury. Gannon wanted the effects of Faraj's brutal exposé to wear off some before he brought the culprit to the panel to explain why Wuterich was guilty and Dela Cruz wasn't. Gannon chose to lead with Tatum instead. Sullivan would do the examination. Puckett would take the cross.

Former Marine rifleman Stephen Tatum took the stand Tuesday morning on the second day of witness testimony. Sullivan asked him to recount his actions after his twelve-man squad was ambushed on the way back to its firm base after resupplying an isolated combat outpost south of the city. The facts had been hashed over so many times they were a rhythmless mantra.

Tatum didn't volunteer to testify. He was ordered to testify as part of a testimonial immunity agreement his civilian lawyer Jack B. Zimmermann struck with Marine prosecutors and the Department of Justice.[4] The government said "it was done to further the truth seeking function," Zimmermann said at the time. Upon reaching the agreement on March 28, 2008, the Marine Corps dropped the charges of involuntary manslaughter, reckless endangerment, and aggravated assault in return for Tatum's future testimony.

The Oklahoma native, accompanied by Zimmermann, spent three dull hours on the stand. The government got him first. Sullivan began his interrogation by asking Tatum to recount the events of November 19, 2005, before the IED exploded. After detailing just how the convoy found itself on Route Chestnut, Sullivan got down to cases. His apparent intention was to prove that Wuterich failed to follow the ROE when he ordered Tatum and two other Marines to "clear" two houses suspected of harboring insurgents who were shooting at the decimated squad with small arms. The Chicago reservist was trying to pluck from Tatum evidence that Wuterich had acted in a manner contrary to his training and responsibilities when his Marines stormed two houses, resulting in the deaths of fifteen civilians. Sullivan particularly wanted to prove Wuterich was the Marine Tatum followed into the back bedroom of House #2. Wuterich maintained he never fired his weapon there. Tatum was resisting him. In his mind, he was in combat. He was doing his duty.

The day before, during opening statements, Faraj had revealed that 30 percent of the expended cartridges found in the second of two house cleared in the Marines initial attack were apparently fired by insurgents. It was a piece of the puzzle that suddenly came into play. His revelation was the first evidence that insurgents might have used the houses as strong points. During Sullivan's interrogation, the importance of the startling new evidence was revealed. How and when that ballistic evidence was discovered and revealed was never explained. NCIS never presented any crime scene reconstuction that mentions the finding. The swollen brass cartridges would have been a game changer in 2006.

Ever since he was indicted in 2006, Tatum had never wavered from his position that he was part of a fire team engaged in lawful combat with an armed enemy. Tatum told Sullivan that he was unable to tell the age, gender, or sex of the people the counterattacking Marines encountered inside the almost dark houses. In his mind, they were the enemy, certainly not victims. Finding expended enemy shell casings inside the victim's homes strongly suggested insurgents had been there.

Sullivan inadvertently helped the defense when he asked Tatum why he had joined Wuterich's ad hoc team ordered to "clear south" by his platoon leader Kallop. Faraj thought it was a stupid question that revealed to the jury how little Sullivan understood about the infantry. Perhaps he was hoping Tatum would say Wuterich told him to kill everyone they found. His answer was not what Sullivan wanted to hear.

"I had served with them for a long time. I proceeded to join the group going toward House #1. The house had been declared hostile. Any individual there was hostile," Tatum told the court. Implicit in his response was his unwavering sense of duty toward his brothers. Sullivan still didn't get it.

Much of Tatum's testimony was equally familiar, following closely the statements he voluntarily gave to Watt in February 2006 before a far more damaging recollection was pried from him during fourteen hours of interrogation by NCIS special agents in the bowels of Haditha Dam the following March. Sullivan couldn't shake him from his familiar story.

During cross-examination by Puckett, Tatum repeated several times that he felt neither he nor Wuterich had done anything wrong when they swept through two darkened houses shooting and throwing grenades as they cleared the structures one room at a time.

At one point Tatum told Puckett how he heard an AK-47 being "racked," a sound he recognized instantly.

"Once I heard that AK-47 racking, I wasn't going in that room to endanger myself or my Marines. At Fallujah we learned we never went into a room without throwing in a grenade," he said.

Later in his testimony, Tatum explained how hard it was to distinguish targets, much less legitimate combatants, in contested houses.

"You can barely see anything because of dust and plaster; dust fills the air. You could see targets. Our job was to take out every target," Tatum testified.

During Puckett's cross examination, Tatum told the court the zealous NCIS special agent had forced him to urinate on the floor of the room where he was questioned during his marathon interrogation rather than allow him to use a latrine. Their interrogation went on so long he could not remember what he had said or whether or not he had actually signed the statement obtained by the NCIS special agent.

"You spent twelve to sixteen hours trying to answer the NCIS the best you could," Puckett said toward the end of his examination. "Sitting here today, you know you did the right thing—don't you?"

"Yes, sir," Tatum answered emphatically.

After encouraging Tatum to tell the panel about his encounter with the NCIS special agents at Haditha Dam, Puckett inexplicably changed subject without establishing clearly that Tatum's statement to NCIS was coerced. It was a small but important point of fact. Faraj was astounded. Instead of beating that drum, the former military judge moved on to what Tatum and the other Marines knew before they left FB Sparta to resupply the isolated outpost. The critical moment was lost in the ensuing maelstrom—ultimately a tempest in a teapot rather than a storm.

Puckett's innocuous question drew an immediate objection from lead prosecutor Gannon. He claimed Puckett was entering into the no-man's-land of classified activity. Faraj, sitting helplessly at the defense table, immediately questioned Gannon's motives. With a single word Gannon had redirected the course Tatum's testimony was taking, and it wasn't heading back to Houses #1 and #2. The court recessed for about twenty minutes while the attorneys argued before Judge Jones whether any classified information was going to be revealed.

"There is nothing that was discussed that was classified, and if it was, it was declassified," Faraj argued with evident anger during the ensuing sidebar. He thought they should be talking about who Tatum followed into the killing room in House #2. In his view, that was the most important issue in the trial.

After overcoming the prosecution's strenuous objections about classified documents, Puckett was allowed to proceed. The question of whom Tatum followed into the death chamber in House #2 was tabled indefinitely.

The "secrets" Gannon was ostensibly trying to protect were revealed in 2007 during the long months of pretrial Article 32 investigations. Tatum acknowledged the night before the convoy his squad had been briefed to expect trouble. They were warned to watch out for snipers active everywhere in Haditha and the infamous white cars that insurgents were using as VBIEDs. Jones overruled Gannon's objection and let everything in.

"You were told about that because of certain types of complex attacks involved white cars. You were aware that a number of these incidents [occurred in Haditha], is that right?" Puckett then asked. "You had been told Iraqis hid weapons and then pulled them out and fired at you after you thought things were clear."

"Yes, sir," Tatum responded.

Faraj fumed from the sidelines.

"It was great theater without doing anything to further Wuterich's defense. Regardless, that is what happens when defense attorneys rely on established facts rather than exploring new territory," he later said.

After one more witness, the first week of trial ended inconclusively. Except for the revelation by Faraj that 30 percent of the expended brass found in the killing zone was Soviet-style 7.62 × 39 mm AK ammo, nothing new had been revealed.

Faraj used part of the weekend to analyze what had already happened. Leading with Tatum made sense tactically, Faraj decided on reflection, although he was disappointed he hadn't been able to tear into Dela Cruz first. Tatum, like Dela Cruz and Mendoza, had received immunity, but unlike them Tatum had never admitted to lying under oath. Faraj figured the jurors respected that. Tatum had maintained the same story throughout the process, even though part of the story was penned by NCIS and reluctantly signed by Tatum after an arduous day of interrogation in the Haditha Dam.

Puckett had managed to diminish the impact of the NCIS statement when at his urging Tatum told the court he signed the damning account so he could urinate in peace. If saying that going into the back bedroom of House #2 and opening fire as the second man afforded him the opportunity to pee, he would have signed anything. It was a smart move. No matter how NCIS sliced the pie, Tatum was duty bound to follow the first shooter.

Puckett's cross-examination planted other seeds of doubt as well. Initially, in Tatum's statement to Watt, he said he did not know whom he followed into the back room because of the smoke, debris, and low visibility in the house after the fragmentation grenade had gone off. He could tell it was a Marine because of the Kevlar helmet and body armor, but that was all. Therefore, he was unsure who was in the lead. Faraj hoped the Marines on the panel who had faced similar challenges would relate to the chaotic moment. Tatum's account to Watt had the same ring of authenticity.

However, after fourteen hours of interrogations by NCIS, Tatum's lack of certitude morphed into unquestionable conviction that Wuterich was the shooter. How his situational awareness and vision both improved so remarkably under intense questioning was not explained. His statement to NCIS, which was transcribed and handed back to him for signature, was certain, well written, and unadorned by Tatum's characteristic Oklahoma homilies. After hearing Tatum speak, there was little doubt the all-important NCIS statement was a product of the NCIS, not Tatum.

Conversely, in the dodgy event the jurors believed the NCIS version of the facts, Tatum's statement provided Gannon with important evidence that Wuterich led the way into the room where six children and two adults appeared to have been ruthlessly exterminated. It would be a significant victory for the prosecution. Puckett had failed to pin it down. Faraj thought it was a strategic blunder in light of the evidence each juror was holding.

The high-velocity bullets the two Marines fired had literally shattered the tiny bodies of the children who lay in their mother's bed, comforted by the false sense of security every child finds in the protective embrace of a parent. Gannon used Tatum to send the jury a message that neither Marine who went into that blood-spattered bedroom understood or respected that sacred boundary. Five children and two adult women died where they lay, on a bed in a back bedroom that the Americans had told them they should use to remain safe and out of the way in the event its soldiers ever came to search. The admission provided a victory for the insurgents as well: Americans didn't keep their word.

The realization momentarily stunned Faraj. The pain was in his voice when he retold the story months later. It wasn't just about who did it. It hurt to see what Americans—especially American Marines—were capable of doing with the firepower Uncle Sam puts in the hands of its young men. If the realization wounded him, he knew it was going to pain the panel as well. Macabre scenes of death have a way of stepping out of the dark recesses of combat veterans' minds to remind them what war really is. Gannon had placed a big obstacle in Wuterich's path and Faraj wasn't certain Puckett had removed it.

There was no doubt Tatum fired inside that room. But was he number two behind his squad leader Frank Wuterich or somebody else? It was an important distinction that Gannon thought he had nailed down. Despite Tatum's damning statement to NCIS, Faraj thought otherwise. He could establish the methods NCIS agents used to coerce him. He could make a big deal out of piss-soaked basements and disrespect to combat vets by pogues—they were both effective tools. His problem in the meantime was willing Puckett to ask the right questions. He was at the defense table, and Puckett was at the podium. He felt helpless. Puckett conversely seemed in his element. Unfortunately, his comfort zone might as well have been Mars as far as Marines who have been in a fight were concerned.

Every infantryman knows that when you follow someone into the room and that person is shooting, you go in shooting as well, Faraj impotently fumed at the defense table. Tatum could never be found guilty on those facts. He followed the lead man, who went in shooting. He was required to do so. The forensic reconstructionists confirmed that there were at least two shooters. What they could not do was identify who those shooters were. No autopsies were ever conducted, no conclusive ballistics tests were ever conducted, no forensic evidence was available, and there were no eyewitnesses who could testify. Unless Tatum admitted to deliberately shooting at innocent children he would never be convicted of anything. He was a good guy, a standup Marine, and an unimpeachable source. In Tatum, Puckett had a witness with currency to spend. He needed to get back to Tatum's original account. All Puckett needed to do was shake Tatum's conviction that it was Wuterich he followed. It was hard, but doable. In his statement, Tatum had even counted the shots Wuterich fired. That was about as close to certainty as it gets in a firefight. Faraj expected Puckett to keep hammering Tatum until he admitted he didn't know whom he followed into the room. It didn't happen.

While it may have been comforting for Tatum to know he was judgment proof, it wasn't doing Wuterich any good. Wuterich, apparently unperturbed, was calm next to him. Maybe he figured Tatum had his back. Faraj wondered if Wuterich understood the implications of Puckett's performance. If Gannon managed to convince the jury Wuterich was the Marine Tatum followed into the room, his testimony alone—buttressed by the gory pictures of the carnage—would probably secure Gannon some sort of conviction. At a minimum, Gannon would shift the burden of proving otherwise to the defense. Puckett's job was to make sure that didn't happen.

Ultimately, Tatum's cross-examination—awaited with such great anticipation—was, in a word, "underwhelming," Faraj later said in private. "Puckett stood up with his omnipresent Mac Air in his hands and asked Tatum questions that were based on his direct examination by Gannon."

Missing was something new, an idea, a notion perhaps that suggested Puckett, too, was in pursuit of the elusive Holy Grail. Eventually, Puckett managed to get Tatum to admit that the statement he gave to NCIS was a little different than what he was testifying to now. It was an important admission, perhaps a row of bricks in the foundation of the defense's case, but nothing more. It certainly wasn't enough to build the entire defense on.

Faraj immediately realized something was missing. The realization hit him like a ton of bricks when it occurred to him Puckett didn't ask Tatum about his previous statements to Watt and NCIS. He didn't ask the lanky Oklahoman why he initially claimed he returned to Houses #1 and #2 with Sharratt. Why had they gone back? What had they done? Who gave the okay for doing it? The answer was obvious to a combat-savvy Marine but not to people who didn't know better. Marines never, ever left potential enemy threats to their rear. It was stupid. Live insurgents of any stripe posed a real threat. The lessons learned in Seoul, South Korea; Hue, South Vietnam; and Fallujah were in play. Where was Wuterich while this was being decided? Did he even know? Had Tatum fired into the houses again? Who was with him? Who told him to change his story? All were legitimate questions still hanging fire when Puckett smiled at the panel in his charming way and sat down. Puckett's performance raised far more questions for Faraj than Tatum answered.

Tatum was a key witness. Faraj had hoped Puckett would take him through the interrogation by NCIS and have Tatum explain in detail what 'fourteen hours of harsh questions felt like, how they broke him down until they got him to begin to doubt himself about two key issues: (1) the identity of the first person in the back room of House #2, and (2) going back through both buildings with Sharratt to clear them again.

At best, Puckett's cross of Tatum was a lackluster performance, Faraj says. The panel didn't seem moved. Faraj gave it poor marks. A premier witness, a key to Wuterich's defense, had walked out of the courtroom with a smile. He shouldn't have been smiling; he should have been worried. He had sworn to tell the unadorned truth. Tatum was still immunized. He'd made a deal with the government. Behind him was his defense attorney, Jack Zimmermann, who was no doubt equally pleased his client had managed to walk out of the courtroom without ever mentioning what the whole truth was.

Faraj went back to the beachside condo seething. He was unhappy, grouchy. He was still irritated by the unnecessary presence of Puckett's wife. Her constant company exacerbated his already uneasy feeling that Puckett was unprepared for trial. His partner's domesticated habits were a constant reminder Puckett wasn't pounding down the case file instead of commiserating with his wife. Faraj didn't tarry. He liked to get going with his day as soon as possible, Puckett and his wife were far more urbane.

"They practiced a standard morning routine that they rarely betrayed. They awoke around six o'clock, went for a thirty-minute walk, ate a cheese omelet, and drank one cup of cappuccino that Puckett personally brewed on small portable espresso machine. Sipping their espresso, they would then move to their respective Mac laptops to review case materials that should have been examined long before."

Living in such close quarters was enervating, Faraj groused.

"Puckett is *Drudge Report* and I am NPR. Puckett watched Fox and I watched MSNBC. Just knowing where we got our news was an indicator of the true gulf growing between us."

Wuterich was stuck in the middle.

SALINAS

Faraj wasn't feeling any better the next day when former sergeant Hector Salinas took the stand. The government witness and former fire team leader was finally getting his say after being incorrectly identified as a prospective defendant before the real defendants were indicted.[5] The government had played him like a wild card for more than a year before letting him out of the Corps. Without ever charging him with anything, they granted him testimonial immunity. Then he had dropped from sight, a hole card Gannon, Sullivan, and his civilian attorney Daniel Hagood kept close to the chest. He was in Afghanistan part of the time, a civilian doing war work. Faraj thought he knew what Salinas was going to say; however, he wasn't sure how he would present himself. His demeanor was important.

Salinas is a big man, well spoken, and seemingly sure of himself. He likes the limelight. He walked into the courthouse on Wednesday afternoon, the seventh day of the trial, mugging for the cameras. He intended to be outspoken and memorable. Nobody was disappointed.

Salinas was supposed to be a prosecution witness. He had been immunized a year after Wuterich was indicted. His testimony was untarnished by criminal charges. Even so, the Marine Corps kept him on ice at Camp Pendleton long past his discharge date, letting him simmer until somebody realized they wouldn't break him, or decided not to. Shabby treatment left a bad taste in his mouth. Unless the government wanted to use Salinas to illustrate the young Marines' state of mind the day of the incident, he was a terrible prosecution witness. All the defense had to do was listen.

Salinas, among other things, was expected to refute testimony offered by Dela Cruz, who once claimed Wuterich told Salinas and him "that if we ever got hit again, we should kill everybody in that vicinity to teach them a lesson." Dela Cruz told NCIS the conversation with Wuterich and Salinas occurred before the ambush, after a roadside bomb had gone off that injured several Marines. As expected, Salinas said it was a lie. So did every other Marine who supposedly heard about the conversation.

Later in his testimony, Salinas threw the government's entire case against Wuterich into question when he told Sullivan that he—not Wuterich—was in command when they swept the first two houses. Faraj knew it was coming. It was only part of his dramatic testimony, recollections that included running through automatic weapons fire and searching for Crossan's missing fingers while occupied suppressing small-arms fire with his M203 grenade launcher.

"Rounds were impacting on the fourth vehicle. I went back to render aid to my Marines that were wounded. There was destruction everywhere. There was a fog, a haze. When the smoke was clearing out, I could see an object. It was LCpl Crossan. He was missing a couple of fingers. His body armor was obstructing his airway. . . .

"I got as low as I could because I heard rounds coming. It was the impact of the rounds hitting the high back. I got low on the deck."[6]

Salinas is a good storyteller.

Instead of incriminating Wuterich, Salinas described an ugly, bitter war in a no-quarter wasteland after two bloody years of internecine warfare. He told the jury what an infantryman sees in a firefight.

"On the outside of the house, on the east side of the house, I saw a small silhouette. Things look small that far away. It was a tall man. There was rounds impacting around me, so I engaged him. I used my M16. I shot more than twice but not the entire magazine," he told Sullivan.

"Then I took my 203 [M203 40mm grenade launcher attached underneath his rifle] and fired rounds on the house—fired two or three."

The big Texan's voice filled with the pain when he remembered his buddy T. J. Terrazas. For an instant, he actually sounded sincere. There's a saying in the Marine Corps about "getting payback." The notion is plugged into young Marines' heads in boot camp and force fed into them in the School of Infantry at Camp Pendleton, where Wuterich used to teach, until they don't even know it sounds startling. Salinas wanted payback.

Salinas was the First Fire Team leader, a sergeant-in-waiting, champing at the bit to take over the squad as soon as Wuterich took over as Third Platoon sergeant. That's a big deal in the Marine Corps. Salinas claimed he was in charge when an insurgent triggered the IED that reduced his command by three.

"I believe I was the convoy commander," Salinas testified on January 19. He added he didn't remember Wuterich giving an order the entire day.

While tending the wounded until the QRF arrived, Salinas noticed that Wuterich and two other Marines were heading south, where Salinas had seen a silhouette at the same time bullets splattered into the armor of the wrecked Humvee that he pulled his friends from. He chased after them by a different route, he said. He was the first Marine in the door, he claimed, the first guy to throw a grenade, the first guy to see the product of his handiwork.

"There were women and children in the house," Sullivan exclaimed.

Six people died in House #1.

"But I didn't know that," Salinas snapped back, "and I wasn't going inside that room without throwing in a grenade."

During his testimony, it was often hard to distinguish whether Sullivan or Salinas was in control of the examination. No matter what Sullivan asked him, Salinas parried with a quip or a notable quote that kept the jurors' attention. Not only was he a good storyteller, Salinas was an artful dodger, at least that day. Sullivan simply could not pin him down when he tried to make Salinas appear uncertain. Instead, he sounded like an evasive braggart. Puckett and Faraj were concerned he would appear a buffoon.

Several dozen fruitless questions later, Sullivan asked Salinas what he would do differently if he could have.

"I would have called in an air strike," Salinas replied. That got everybody's attention.

His testimony was as dramatic as it seemed staged. Salinas made the headlines in *Al Jazeera*.[7] Faraj was not happy with Salinas's performance in front of the jury. He suspected they thought Salinas was being slick. His instincts were correct. After the trial, Faraj would learn at least three of the jurors, the lieutenant colonel who chaired the panel and at least two senior NCOs, found Salinas's testimony contrived. They suspected he was glibly trying to hide something. The only redeeming value his testimony produced on Wednesday afternoon was that his demeanor brought into question why the prosecution brought Salinas into the courtroom instead of the defense.

Faraj and Puckett thought Gannon made a tactical blunder doing so. Faraj conjectured Gannon hoped to show the jury how hopeless it was trying to get the truth from the squad of murderous conspirators who had managed to stymie justice for so long. Faraj called it a vain attempt to garner "sympathy" for the prosecution. Whatever Gannon intended, it was bad tactics.

The defense hoped to capitalize on Gannon's badly framed ploy, although it was obvious Salinas was still a bit of a wild card. He needed some toning down. The next morning before trial resumed, Faraj and Puckett sat down with the big-talking Texan for a bit of discussion before he took the stand for cross-examination.

Faraj was certain Salinas both liked and respected him. Faraj had treated him like a fighting Marine instead of a leper in 2007 when he interviewed him the first time. They had established a rapport. After his interview Faraj suspected Salinas hoped to help Wuterich by trying to outfox the foxes. He was smart, but he wasn't that smart:

> Salinas came in with an agenda, at its core an attempt to assist Wuterich by either creating or omitting facts without admitting any culpability. When we talked to him he asked us "how he was doing." We didn't want him helping us. I told him his truthful testimony was the only thing helpful. We didn't need any dishonesty to prove what happened. Wuterich hadn't shot anybody in House #2. We knew who the shooters were. Mendoza and Tatum had cleared the room.

Then Tatum and Sharratt returned. That is why there were so many head shots. When it came to actions that may be questionable he tended to disassociate himself from it. Jurors have a way of detecting deviousness.

It wasn't about what he said as much as how he said it. Salinas's testimony before Sullivan often teetered back and forth on the edge of insolence. Although he was never openly disrespectful, he was playing to the jury instead of the truth. He came across as being arrogant and disrespectful. Faraj told him to knock it off.

Faraj said he was prepared to skewer Salinas if he had to. The former Marine was a prosecution witness and therefore expendable. For instance, Salinas testified he never went into House #2, that he never witnessed the carnage until later. That defied his training, ignored battle doctrine, and was plain bad tactics. Faraj knew Salinas was a better Marine than that.

Salinas told Sullivan he was outside providing security. Wuterich thought otherwise. It took the former squad leader a while to remember why; the killings in House #2 had traumatized him to the point he wasn't certain what happened at first. He needed time to piece everything together. One of his recollections came out of the blue in 2008 while videographer Michael Epstein was filming a discussion he was having with Vokey, Faraj, and Puckett.

"All of a sudden Wuterich asked, 'There weren't any insurgents in the back bedroom?' He had suddenly remembered why he didn't know that. He had never entered the back bedroom. He was behind Salinas in the stack when they went into House #2. Toward the back of the building, Wuterich and Salinas turned left to clear a room that turned out to be empty. Mendoza and Tatum turned right. All the shooting happened later," Faraj remembered.

Faraj believes that after Tatum fragged the bathroom of sorts, Mendoza moved to the back bedroom and tossed in his grenade without removing the tape around the arming handle. When the team realized what he had done, they bailed out of the house because they weren't sure whether or not Mendoza had just supplied an insurgent with a live grenade. Mendoza, left by himself, took refuge behind the refrigerator in the kitchen. The Marines who had bailed out yelled for him to keep a close eye on the door while they decided what to do next. What really happened next remains speculation.

All of the Marines and the little girl from House #2 that survived remembered a woman—Safah's aunt—opening the bedroom door and screaming. Faraj surmised her screams startled Mendoza so badly that he shot her. Then he charged into the room and began firing, Tatum at his heels. In a 2008 deposition never revealed to the jury, Mendoza explained that the rest of the team bailed out of the house while he took refuge behind a refrigerator in the next room because he would have to expose himself if he followed the rest of the team out the door.

They didn't bail out of the house because the grenade didn't go off. Unexploded ordnance is scary, but it is also anticipated. If a grenade fails to blow after a minute or two it probably isn't going to unless it is disturbed, and probably not even then. But when it doesn't go off because the arming handle is still attached, that is a big problem. Thanks to Mendoza, the enemy might have just acquired a deadly weapon. That was why Mendoza was hiding all alone. Faraj intended to put that scenario before the jury at the appropriate time, whenever that turned out to be. It was less than two weeks into the trial and the government was destroying its own case. Faraj thought there was plenty of work ahead, but he was certain the defense would ultimately prevail. It didn't have to win, it just had to not lose. The only way that could happen was if somebody screwed the pooch. Faraj didn't intend that person to be him. His optimism evaporated exactly one week later.

DEAL MAKERS AND WARRIORS

When Faraj changed clothes at lunch for his daily run on Wednesday, he was almost certain the defense would prevail. Running the hills of Camp Pendleton gave him lots of time to think. Soldiers and sailors who've experienced the pleasure of Camp Pendleton's terrain claim the dusky hills only go up. When Kasal was pushing troops at the infantry school, he ran up them so eagerly his dog-tired boots called him "Robo-grunt." They had broken more than one young Marine warrior who went a-harboring visions of conquering another Mount Suribachi. The hills were unavoidable, imposing, and majestic. If Faraj could conquer them, he could conquer anything. He says it goes to attitude.

On January 18 at about 12:40 p.m., Faraj was returning from his daily run, engrossed with his ongoing cross-examination of Humberto Mendoza. The Marine from Venezuela had already spent two grueling hours on the stand before lunch. Faraj had him so flummoxed he didn't know whether he was coming or going. Mendoza had endured a series of verbal slaps before the lunch break and was still reeling a bit from the blows when court adjourned.

Faraj was met at the courthouse parking lot by Puckett, Wuterich, videographer Michael Epstein, and Puckett's wife. Epstein had become an indispensable part of the defense team since he had joined Puckett in 2006. Faraj thought of him as his friend and confidant. He was watching when Puckett went to Faraj and declared that Sullivan wanted a deal.

"He's talking about negligent dereliction, confinement, no discharge," Puckett said.

"Fuck him," Faraj answered. "They were offered that two years ago. Now that their case unraveled, they want a deal? We told them this would happen. In fact, you told them this would happen and that they're going to be embarrassed. Remember?"

Puckett was adamant. He replied that Wuterich was interested in a deal. The rapidly aging young Marine wanted out. Seven years of getting beaten on was all he could take. Surrounded by his parents and children, all he could think about was his family's welfare. He had fought the good fight longer than any other Marine charged in the Haditha affair. Knowing Sharratt was waiting in the wings, knowing Faraj was going to rip open the scab that had concealed the festering wound for six years was unnerving him. Faraj knew that.

"It's his decision," Faraj answered.

Faraj stalked toward the showers before any more discussion ensued. Inside, he was boiling. He began wondering if he should resign in protest. He even considered going to Jones and asking to be recused. Doing so would certainly make a splash, he reasoned, but what would it really accomplish? He was still in that state of mind when he reentered the crowded courthouse. His shower had done little to cool him off.

Everyone on the defense team had already moved back to the so-called defense room. The ostentatiously named second-floor cube was in actuality a ten-foot-by-ten-foot enclosure usually used as a lunch and break room more than any kind of meeting room. But for this occasion it was ground zero. Faraj, still mightily perturbed, walked in and declared "no talking until they get us something on paper and approved." Puckett surprisingly agreed. Faraj remained doubtful and suspicious.

He felt better when he got back into the courtroom. In the quiet moments before the storm, he had focused his discontent. He went back into the courtroom with a plan. After the panel marched in and took its seats, the trial resumed as if nothing out of the ordinary were going on. Faraj seemed intense, perhaps even seething, but there was nothing extraordinary in his manner. He was a daunting figure when he went on the offensive. He didn't throw softballs that floated in from left field. He threw fastballs, burners that zinged past Mendoza with relentless assurance.

Mendoza turned out to be a disaster for the government. The rattled former infantryman agreed that he had lied before the court-martial and was lying now as well. Faraj had skillfully walked him through those actions that very day. He went so far as to have a door built and brought into the courtroom to demonstrate how Mendoza claimed he had opened the door and looked into the room containing women and children in the back of House #2. He had opened it before in other proceedings. It was a useful tool. The moment was climactic. Mendoza testified that he opened the door to that bedroom, walked in a few feet with his rifle hanging in its three-point sling, and then did nothing.

"I looked around the room and saw women and children," he said. "I then walked outside and saw Tatum. I told him it was only women and children. He waved me with his head to go away."[8]

Although electrifying testimony, Mendoza's narrative made no sense to Faraj. The house was still considered hostile. It had not been cleared. Mendoza had started the carnage with his shooting of an innocent man who came to open a door after they had either knocked or rung a bell. Even that minor little point was still not clear. What kind of Marine rings a doorbell while sweeping through hostile houses?

"It was nonsense. The whole story was nonsense. Mendoza was high on adrenaline, he was a boot, and he was scared. He did not have to shoot anyone in the back room; however, it strained all tactical and common sense to walk in the back room with a rifle hanging from the sling."

Mendoza was hiding a secret and Faraj knew it. Faraj also knew that Safah Younis Salim, the sole survivor in the back bedroom, testified that someone opened the door to the back bedroom and tossed a grenade that hit her dress at her legs. The terrified kids immediately huddled on the bed for safety. The grenade, or "bomb" as she called it, did not go off. It did not go off because the arming handle that released when the pin was pulled was secured with a wrap of electrical tape as an added safety mechanism. The added safety was taught to junior Marines to ensure they didn't inadvertently yank out the safety pin on the grenade and have it go off. The additional safety worked because Mendoza forgot to unwrap the grenade. Safah also said that the same Marine who threw the grenade came back and shot at them.[9]

Safah's testimony was key evidence. Her testimony, when considered along with Mendoza's story, proved that Mendoza was the one who threw the grenade into the room and the first Marine to shoot at them. The door to the room was opened only once before the family was shot, Safah said. Mendoza testified that he opened the door, walked inside, backed out, closed the door, and then after a conference went somewhere else. Little Safah strongly disputed him. She was certain he was the little man who threw the grenade; he was the only American smaller than she was.

A miniature Marine walking nonchalantly into a room full of possible insurgents immediately after tossing in a dysfunctional grenade defied logic. Nobody who has a will to live walks immediately into a room after a grenade fails to explode unless they intend to do harm. It would be suicide to give the grenade's recipient time to arm the device. Faraj hoped the jury intuitively knew that already, but he intended to be sure.

When Mendoza demonstrated his actions in front of the jury, not one of them appeared to believe him. The enlisted Marines seated in the back row of the jury box had quizzical looks; a couple whispered to one another. The officers in the front row of the jury box were more stoic, but they clearly rejected Mendoza's testimony.

And the jurors had not even heard from Safah yet. Nor would they. Gannon did not want them to. He made his objection clear when Faraj told Jones early in the case that she would be one of the witnesses. The government said they could not bring her to the United States, but that she could be deposed and her video deposition played to the jury. It was a ploy, a nice name for a lie. The government had no intention of admitting the survivor's testimony. On the first day of the trial, Gannon declared that the government would object to any testimony from the one surviving victim of House #2. She would implicate Mendoza in murder and that would never do for the government's second-best witness.

Gannon's objection made no sense to Faraj at first. The government, which had spent seven years prosecuting Wuterich to bring so-called justice to the victims of Haditha, did not want the lone surviving child from the bloody bedroom of House #2 to be heard from. Gannon did not want her to tell her story because he knew that her story would be believed. She would contradict the government's theory in its case against Wuterich. Therefore, Safah's testimony was key evidence—for the defense. Her story would reveal that the government gave immunity to the real shooters after they had evidence of who those real shooters were. The government knew Wuterich wasn't one of them and had charged him anyway. Her testimony would be explosive. Faraj was certain it would raise far more issues than merely embarrassing questions about the prosecution's mishandling of the case.

Safah's testimony, when considered along with Mendoza's story, provoked reasonable suspicion that Mendoza was the one that threw the grenade into the room and was the first Marine to shoot at them. The door to the room was opened only once before the family was shot, Safah said. Mendoza testified that he opened the door only one time. Safah said that was when the grenade arrived. Then there was an interminable wait before the same man rushed in shooting after killing her aunt when she opened the door and screamed at the sight of Safah's prostrate father.

IT DIDN'T TAKE a genius to figure out the government's case was dying of self-induced asphyxiation. But why? It seemed that every witness the government had produced since the hearings began in 2007 had choked on the prosecution's version of events. It snagged in their throats like proverbial fish bones they couldn't quite spit out. It didn't make sense to Faraj.

The prosecution was going nowhere. Three weeks into the trial and Sullivan was ready to withdraw all the charges in exchange for a guilty plea of negligent dereliction of duty, an offense that wasn't even charged in the original indictment, along with a promise of no punishment. Why was the government being so generous? The answer was obvious. It was surrendering with terms. Cornwallis at Yorktown playing "The World Turned Upside Down." It was the deal Puckett had been looking for. He could declare a victory without any more effort. The situation was as good as it got in his legal world. Faraj thought it disgusting.

When the "secret negotiations" began on Wednesday afternoon, Faraj was still clearly upset. So were Wuterich's parents. Something had triggered more than routine discomfort in their demeanors. Plans made that morning were canceled. Something was afoot. Despite Faraj's objections, the attorneys dutifully gathered in front of Jones to ask for a recess. Puckett had the steam. Mrs. Wuterich was again speaking of Puckett in glowing terms.

The negotiators told the judge they needed a break to negotiate a settlement. Jones immediately granted it. Negotiations began in the early afternoon and broke an hour later when Faraj told Sullivan that they needed to know exactly who they were negotiating with. Sullivan said he would get approval from LtGen Waldhauser. He had a secret weapon.

Sitting unobtrusively in the back of the courtroom was a Lieutenant Colonel Kirk Kumagai, the staff judge advocate to the convening authority, Waldhauser. During the trial, he identified himself to reporters simply as an observer from the Marine Corps Central Command at Elgin Air Force Base in Florida. In fact, Kumagai was far more than that. He was Waldhauser's eyes and ears and probably his brain in the matter. His presence was important because he represented a direct pipeline from Waldhauser to the proceedings.

He was so important that Faraj considered asking the judge to bar him from the courtroom. It would have caused a flap, there was no doubt about that, but before he did so, Faraj wanted to know what the former aviator was doing there.

Their conversation was more revealing than Faraj anticipated. He had an inherent mistrust of the brass following his experiences in early 2007 and again with Jones in 2010. He hadn't forgotten the troubles the defense endured from Lieutenant Colonel Bill Riggs during Tatum's Article 32 hearing. Riggs, Gen Mattis's staff judge advocate, contacted hearing officer Ware and criticized him for holding the government to "too high of a standard" when evaluating the charges against Tatum. Ware responded via email, "I viewed LtCol Riggs's comments as inappropriate and imprudent. . . . I was . . . offended and surprised by this conversation."

Riggs ended up removing himself from the case to avoid the appearance of impropriety. Faraj didn't want the hassle of dealing with that sort of problem. It deflected attention away from his client, who was on the verge on winning his freedom.

Kumagai turned out to be open and above board. He shared with Puckett and Faraj that he had had no idea that the government's case was so bad. Puckett, ever the negotiator, decided to use that nifty bit of information as leverage to push even harder for some sort of deal.

Faraj went home to go for a bike ride. The next day, there was still no word as to what the deal was. They took another break. By lunchtime Thursday Faraj told Puckett that he was not going to waste any more time waiting for the details of a deal that was neither necessary nor appropriate when they were winning the trial. They should restart the trial, and if the government wanted to make an offer, they could do it.

SOFA

While Wuterich's case was being kicked around, another element in the story of the Haditha incident was quietly percolating. It had both nothing and everything to do with Wutrerich's prosecution; it was only a coincidence they came to a head together. For three years, ever since Iraq entered into a Status of Forces Agreement (SOFA) with the United States of America, the United States had been trying to obtain an extension so it could keep troops in Iraq past January 1, 2012.

Officially titled the *Agreement between the United States of America and the Republic of Iraq on the Withdrawal of United States Forces from Iraq and the Organization of Their Activities during Their Temporary Presence in Iraq*, it had expired three days before Wuterich's court-martial got under way. Without a new SOFA, the United States would have to pull out of Iraq posthaste. Already President Obama had announced that all US troops would be leaving Iraq as soon as possible.

The oft-maligned 2012 agreement—it was not a treaty—was rejected by Iraq in 2009 as repugnant and arbitrary. The Iraqis' opinion never changed during three unrelenting years of subsequent negotiation. The SOFA the US government insisted upon securing included ironclad guarantees that US military members and civilians under the protection of the American government would receive preferential treatment if arrested and tried for crimes committed against Iraqi citizens.

When the United States offered its newest proposal for a SOFA, Coalition troops were killing almost as many innocent Iraqi civilians every week as the insurgents. The inability of the generals to rein them in was in the forefront of every negotiation. Nothing had changed by

2012 except numbers. Iraqis were still dying unavenged almost every day at the hands of Americans.

Still fresh in the minds of millions of disgruntled Iraqis when January 1, 2012, approached was the story of seven very ordinary United States Marines who had already walked away unscathed after allegedly massacring twenty-four Iraqi citizens in 2005. Unlike in the United States, the Haditha Massacre was a tawdry tale of American brutality and insensitivity in Iraq. In a revenge-driven society, that sort of thing doesn't go away. Stories about it still appeared routinely in the Iraqi press. Everyone knew the fourth suspect, the leader charged with eighteen murders, had been scheduled for court-martial numerous times without anything happening. Even Iraqi Prime Minister Nuri Kamal al-Maliki vented his spleen in the American press, calling the proposed SOFA "insulting to the sovereignty" of Iraq.

Ordinary Iraqis knew the four Marines directly involved in the massacre were subsequently charged with murder and other heinous crimes for intentionally wiping out three households of civilians. Four officers, including the battalion commander and three subordinates, were charged with covering up the alleged crimes. In Iraq there was never any doubt about how or when the Marines did what they did; the only enigma was why. What was certain was that the presumptuous and frequently trumpeted moral authority of the United States had been shredded.

By September 2011, the State Department was so concerned by its failure to obtain a SOFA it took the almost-unprecedented step of contacting the blog *Defend Our Marines* for help. The blog's focus was on the multitude of courts-martial and federal court trials under way to convict soldiers, sailors, and Marines accused of war crimes in Iraq.

The State Department was apparently stymied by the Pentagon from discovering what was happening to the Haditha defendants and other military personnel convicted or awaiting charges for alleged war crimes in Iraq.

Meanwhile, whether by design or incompetence, the Marine Corps appeared to be working equally hard to ensure the convictions of the Haditha defendants never came about. The rift between the State Department and the Pentagon grew so deep that the military refused to even share the legal status of its alleged defaulters, leaving the State Department crippled in its negotiations with its adamant Iraqi counterparts.

Iraqis universally demanded original jurisdiction in criminal cases brought against American citizens charged with injuring or killing Iraqis. The United States would have to leave Iraq or modify the agreement and expose Americans to the tender mercies of Iraqi justice.

In September 2011, State Department official Michael McClellan, spokesman and counselor for public affairs at the American embassy in Baghdad, emailed *Defend Our Marines* publisher David Allender seeking assistance in exploring *DOM*'s extensive archives for information concerning the number of Marines and soldiers accused, tried, and convicted of crimes in Iraq and Afghanistan.

"I spent much of this afternoon going through your excellent website as it is the best—and only!—website that has truly comprehensive information about trials of US service members accused of crimes in Iraq and Afghanistan," Mr. McClellan wrote. "We are most interested in the Iraq-related trials, as this is relevant to ongoing talks about a post-2011 US presence here."

The extraordinary request raised a couple of huge red flags. For instance, why did the almighty US Department of State need anything from the pedantic, frequently maligned *Defend Our Marines*? And why did the State Department need disassociated civilians to discover what happened to the young service members already convicted, sentenced, and serving time?

McClellan was seeking information, not offering it, he replied. He directed *DOM* to the Department of State in Washington, DC, for comment. In the meantime, did the blog mind sharing its archives? For reasons never answered, the State Department spokesman said it was unable to get the information anywhere else!

"Actually, what we were looking for was simply a database—how many trials, how many convictions/acquittals, sentencing, etc.," Mr.

McClellan explained. "The info on your website up to 12/2006 was actually very helpful and gave us at least some numbers to compile. This is really about having the facts at hand in case questions come up relating to SOFAs, immunities, etc. Our interest is not so much in particular trials, but the picture of trials and the results thereof. Does that make sense?"

It didn't, so *DOM* once again asked Mr. McClellan to explain.

"As for the talks, we are not making any comment at this time beyond what comes out of Washington, so just watch the news every night," Mr. McClellan replied. "Thanks again for your help—your website is a very valuable resource—believe it or not—those data simply do not exist anywhere that I have been able to find."

At the time the government was calling upon *DOM*, the State Department and the Pentagon were not communicating. Perhaps it was perceived competition, jealousy, protecting turf, or simple stupidity that brought the situation to such a dismal place. Both entities were negotiating the same SOFA with Iraq at the same time for different bosses, although all of them worked for President George W. Bush.

The bloggers reached out to all the named players for answers. A few actually responded. The Pentagon provided USMC Major Christopher Perrine, a low-level public affairs officer for the Office of the Secretary of Defense. The major immediately reminded *DOM* that he was not speaking for the Marine Corps. He was on detached duty to the Office of the Secretary of Defense as a spokesperson.

The reason OSD was handling the inquiry instead of the Department of State was because the treaty being negotiated wasn't really a treaty at all, it was merely an "agreement," Perrine explained. The Office of the Secretary of Defense apparently can negotiate agreements but not treaties. That duty rests entirely with the president and the Department of State.

"If we are going to have a continued presence in Iraq, they (service members) have to have the legal protection of a SOFA," Perrine said. The Iraqi government had been sitting on the unpopular "agreement" for two years without finding any common ground to continue pressing forward, he said.

When examined in the cold light of cruel reality, it was easy to understand why the Iraqi government would not accept a SOFA as detailed by Perrine. Coalition troops killing Iraqi citizens—and as many as one hundred thousand died—was an unintended consequence of unrestrained occupation by forces relentlessly trained to destroy the enemy, not coddle it. A kinder and gentler war received lip service but it didn't ensure the lives of the warriors expected to carry it out. Indiscriminate killing did. "Lighting 'em up" was a particularly popular pastime among American combat troops.

David Allender believed why it was happening had somehow escaped the American diplomats and military leaders addressing the slaughter with jingoist hyperbole, ridiculous rules of engagement, and ludicrous calls for combat benevolence.

While the SOFA negotiations dragged on, Wuterich remained in limbo at Camp Pendleton, a constant reminder the United States did not intend to prosecute him. They were still waiting when the 2009 SOFA expired.

The Iraqis never forgave or forgot that none of the Haditha Marines were convicted of killing fourteen women and children huddled together in dark bedrooms. The Iraqi parliament said so in September 2011 when the fledgling ruling body almost unanimously rejected any treaty with the United States that allowed for such a miscarriage of justice.

Nine months after frantic negotiations to produce a SOFA ceased, *New York Times* chief military reporter Michael R. Gordon quoted on his blog a Kurdish leader purportedly friendly to US interests to help explain the mounting storm the lack of a SOFA was already spinning in both Iraq and Syria. It was prescient and chilling.

"To many Iraqis, the United States' influence is greatly diminished. American policy is very weak," observed Fuad Hussein, the chief of staff to Massoud Barzani, the president of the semiautonomous Kurdish region in northern Iraq. "It is not clear to us how they have defined their interests in Iraq," Mr. Hussein said. "They are picking events and reacting on the basis of events. That is the policy."

MEANWHILE, BACK IN COURT

The deferred Thursday afternoon court session began on time. Jones didn't offer a reason for the break in the trial and nobody from either bench volunteered one. Mendoza, after his unexpected break from the cross examination turning him into a defense witness, returned to the stand. He seemed calmer, more relaxed, and suddenly all Marine. Mendoza had come full circle since he accused Tatum of ordering him to kill women and children. He was once again no longer sure what happened. Mendoza acknowledged that on the day the actions took place, he didn't think they had done anything wrong. He agreed with Faraj that being afraid he had done something wrong was the real reason he decided to lie. It was compelling drama.

Faraj sent Mendoza back in time, to the place where it all began, where he earned the coveted Combat Action Ribbon that separated combat Marines from pogues. Mendoza admitted that if he were to do it all over again he would do the same thing, because on that day he really was in combat. He didn't like it much, but he performed like a Marine should. Faraj had given him back his self-respect, as perverse as doing so somehow seemed. In the passion of the moment, it was easy to forget Mendoza was talking about shooting down unarmed Iraqis. How could everyone be innocent and so many people still be dead?

Mendoza tried to explain by denying that he threw a grenade at all. At the second house, Mendoza said Tatum told him to shoot two Iraqi women and several children he found on a bed in a closed room. Mendoza said he walked away but saw Tatum return and heard a loud noise, possibly gunfire or a grenade. The women and at least two of the children were later found dead. His last revelation made his story even less possible. He had never before denied throwing the grenade into the bedroom. His original account was supported by the entire fire team.

Mendoza's new version of events painted a picture of a relaxed, combat-savvy vet, which was nonsense. Why in the world would a

Marine who admittedly believed that a house contained insurgents walk into a room in that house with his rifle pointed down hanging from a sling? Faraj demanded answers. Why wouldn't he throw a grenade? He still had some. Why wouldn't his rifle be at the ready with his finger on the trigger ready to fire at a likely insurgent ready to blow his head off?

They never intended to kill civilians, Mendoza responded. Faraj consoled him. As unfortunate as the civilians' deaths were, nobody had violated the rules, he reminded the befuddled young Marine. It was easy to forget the issue was the slaughter of innocent women and children. Faraj made it about decisions. The panelists hung on every word. Faraj was making serious headway demolishing the balance of the government's waning prosecution.

By the time Mendoza stepped down, the government's case had truly unraveled. In Faraj's view, the hard-bitten jurors belonged to the defense. Faraj felt like he was controlling the momentum of the trial, but it proved to be only temporary. Friday brought another break while more negotiations were conducted. The defense had the momentum; now it was slipping away. The notion that there was something to negotiate infuriated Faraj.

Meanwhile, Faraj and Puckett were increasingly at odds as well. Faraj simply could not understand why they were negotiating. His disgust carried over into their personal relationship. The truth was about to be revealed, the jurors were clearly on their side, and they had not even presented their defense witnesses yet. Despite the obvious, Puckett pushed for the deal. In a later fit of pique, Faraj said he believed that Puckett's motivations were driven by self-preservation and promotion. Faraj had thus far dominated the trial, relegating Puckett to second chair. The attorney who once claimed he had never lost a court-martial didn't care for it. He saw himself as lead counsel, referred to himself as lead counsel, and had no patience settling for second string. He did not sit well in a backup role. The negotiations put Puckett squarely back into the spotlight. He was the deal maker. Faraj hated deals. And he hated second chair as well.

On Friday evening, January 20, fed up with the turn of events and Puckett's insistence on a deal, Faraj packed his bags and left town to avoid a total meltdown of the defense team. He felt if he didn't remove himself from the condo for the weekend, an ugly confrontation with Puckett seemed inevitable. Faraj drove to Los Angeles to stay with a friend and mentor who was also a trial lawyer and former enlisted Marine. The two former Marines discussed the trial and possible courses of action. His friend recommended that he convince Wuterich to fire Puckett. Although agreeing in principle, Faraj didn't think that was possible because of the tight-knit relationship between Wuterich, his family, and Puckett. Nonetheless, he began to consider it.

That evening, Faraj received a lengthy text message from Maj Jeffery Dinsmore asking about the rumors and what was happening. Faraj and Dinsmore—the former S-2 of 3/1 and one of Wuterich's most ardent supporters—had become friends over the years that the case developed. Faraj found himself in a dilemma. He was ethically bound to keep privileged information secret; however, Dinsmore was like a member of the defense team. He was also a subpoenaed witness. There were lines that couldn't be crossed. Faraj had decided long ago that he could win the case with Dinsmore, McConnell, and Sax. Faraj was certain they provided a narrative that could not be attacked.

"They were credible, believable, and carried themselves with the honor that every Marine Corps officer is expected to uphold. These men had no problem falling on their swords and taking responsibility for their failures when they fail. But they did not fail in this instance. The jury would know it. And because of that, they would believe them."

Faraj told Dinsmore that he had nothing to do with the deal and was resisting it, but that the decision was ultimately the client's to make. And Wuterich was in the sway of Puckett. Dinsmore said he understood, although the former recon stud was being disingenuous. Dinsmore said he had already lit into Puckett in the courthouse bathroom the preceding Thursday, and again in his minuscule office in the courthouse, mincing no words in his disgust that Puckett was "selling out" Wuterich, his battalion brothers, and the Marine Corps. Later that same night, over sushi and beer, he vented his dissatisfaction at some length. Dinsmore said he simply couldn't understand how or why Wuterich would make a deal—even though he was pleading guilty to essentially nothing—when victory was at hand.

Faraj had planned to spend the entire weekend with his friend in Los Angeles. He had no intention of seeing Puckett until Monday morning. That plan changed the next day, Saturday, when Faraj received a message saying Waldhauser had informed both sides he would not sign the deal. He told LtCol Kumagai to inform counsel to let the process run its course. Kumagai must have reported his impressions to Waldhauser. Otherwise, he had no business at Camp Pendleton.

Faraj told Puckett that he had been considering the offer and did not agree with it. Wuterich should not plea to something he did not do. "We have the upper hand," he texted Puckett. "We do NOT have the upper hand," came the reply. "We're losing and you refuse to see it."

Faraj was packed and on the road heading south to Oceanside in twenty minutes. He boiled with anger. He couldn't believe Puckett thought they were losing. That, along with the response from Waldhauser, convinced Faraj that the deal was being pushed by Puckett, even if it was initially suggested by Sullivan. Generals don't ask—they command. Faraj did not want to be associated with selling out the client. Again, he started to consider withdrawing from the case.

When he arrived at the condo, Faraj could sense the tension in the air. He was seething; he couldn't even remember if greetings were exchanged. He did remember Puckett and his wife departing within minutes of his arrival, leaving behind Mike Epstein, Maj Meredith Marshall, and Frank Wuterich. The defense was unraveling, but not because they were being defeated by the prosecution. The clash of personalities and the different views on the right strategy for disposing of the case threatened to tear the defense apart.

Marshall shared with Faraj that Puckett had been working with Wuterich to prepare him to take the stand and testify. Frank wanted to tell his story.

"Don't feel bad, Frank," Marshall reassured Wuterich in front of Faraj. "Gannon is nowhere near as good as Haytham. If you decide to take the stand, it won't be that bad."

Faraj disagreed. He sat Wuterich down and began to cross-examine him. He asked Wuterich what effect he thought saying "shoot first and ask questions later" had on the Marines in his squad. Faraj broke it down even further by discussing with Wuterich what he thought the state of mind of the Marines was after he said it and whether the statement could have caused them to believe that they could ignore the rules of engagement. Wuterich quickly realized the impressions his answer would create in the minds of the jurors. He acknowledged his performance was disastrous. Testifying would be driving down a bad road. Wuterich decided it wasn't such a good idea after all.

Afterward, Wuterich was dejected and depressed. The insincerity was overwhelming. Everyone knew Wuterich's statement to "shoot first and ask question later" was not uttered or heard by anyone. It was a fantasy. But at trial that would not matter. The statement was already in front of the jury as fact, and ultimately they would have to deal with it. If Wuterich denied saying it now, he would sound like Mendoza and Dela Cruz. If he took the stand and admitted saying it, Gannon or Sullivan would likely focus their questions on the impact that fabricated statement had on the actions in the houses. Faraj wasn't about to let that happen. Epstein caught it all on his omnipresent camera.

Faraj felt bad for Wuterich. Wuterich simply wanted to tell his story. And he had every right to. Yet because he already said on national television that he made the notorious statement—even though no one heard it—the subject was closed.

Wuterich could never take the stand. Faraj was adamant. When Puckett returned that evening, Epstein showed him the video of Wuterich being cross-examined by Faraj. After watching it, Puckett announced that Frank would not testify.

"No shit," Faraj muttered under his breath. It didn't make him feel any better.

Puckett spent most of his day trying to negotiate a deal. He talked to Kumagai again, imploring him to speak to Waldhauser, asking him to try to convince the general that a deal in Wuterich's favor was in the best interest of the Marine Corps.

Puckett had tried dealing directly with the big brass once before, in a written plea to General Joseph F. Dunford on January 13, 2011, while Dunford was the assistant commandant of the Marine Corps:

1. As a retired Marine Officer (and possible TBS classmate of yours in 1977), I feel an obligation to brief you on issues that extend far beyond the court-martial and the interests of my client. There are serious concerns I have about what the world (read: Al Jazeera) and the country will learn about what did not happen as well as what did, with the investigation and prosecution if this case must go to trial. (Ironically and coincidentally, Al Jazeera called me 10 minutes ago to ask about the scheduling of the case.) We have discovered, as a result of the passage of time and our own investigation, chilling facts about the case that will never be briefed by the prosecution team but which ought, in the best interests of the Marine Corps, to be considered at your level.

2. I want to assure you that since you are no longer the convening authority, but even if you were, there is nothing inappropriate about you speaking with me and my law partner and co-counsel, Retired Marine Major Haytham Faraj, about the wider implications of this case. We will not be bringing you a "deal" or any recommended courses of action. We're only interested in informing you about the results of our investigation and previously undiscovered facts and evidence that will be a necessary part of the trial. These, by the way, are facts that had they been discovered at the time, should have resulted in a completely different approach to the entire incident at Haditha. But then again we Marines have always been about "lessons learned."

It hadn't worked that time either. Dunford ignored him. Faraj wondered whether Puckett would fail again—even hoped he would. He saw it in the Marine Corps's interest to let the case run its course. The honor of the Corps demanded it and so did his pride. On the other hand, he was a defense attorney, and his client Frank Wuterich wanted to be free. That was the real prize. Faraj forced himself to keep his eye on the prize.

There was one last hurdle to overcome. It appeared out of the blue when Sullivan delivered a Stipulation of Fact, dated January 18, 2012, that he insisted Wuterich must sign before the deal was consummated. The stipulation placed blame for all the civilian deaths in the houses squarely on Wuterich's shoulders. In essence, he would be accepting responsibility for the civilian deaths despite the government's decision not to prosecute him anymore. Sullivan's insistence on Wuterich's acceptance of the "facts" almost derailed the plea deal:

> SSgt Wuterich agrees and admits he knew of his duty to maintain adequate tactical control of his Marines as they cleared Houses #1 and #2. That duty included an adherence to the rules of engagement at all times. SSgt Wuterich agrees and admits that through his negligent verbal order, he failed to perform his duty to maintain adequate tactical control of his Marines, resulting in the deaths of six noncombatants in House #1 and eight noncombatants in House #2.
>
> SSgt Wuterich understands and admits that his aforementioned verbal commands, "Shoot first and ask questions later," or "Don't hesitate to shoot," or words to that effect, did cause his Marines including Cpl Salinas, LCpl Tatum, and PFC Mendoza to believe that they could ignore the requirement to positively identify targets within House #1 and House #2, prior to engaging and killing individuals within those houses.
>
> I agree and admit that my verbal order to "shoot first and ask questions later" or "don't hesitate to shoot" was a negligent verbal instruction to my Marines which caused them to no longer

positively identify targets within Houses #1 and #2 prior to engaging the aforementioned noncombatants in Houses #1 and #2. SSgt Wuterich also agrees that the aforementioned negligent and instruction caused the deaths of six civilians in House #1 and eight civilians in House #2.

Faraj took one look at it and declared that he would not be part of a deal with this type of coercion. He considered it a sleazy last-minute attempt by Sullivan to gain some traction for the government's battered case. He found himself once again toying with the idea of going on the record and asking Jones to relieve him from further representation of Wuterich. It was a hard feeling to shake. He finally decided that a move like that was more about Haytham Faraj than his client. His first duty was to his client. Duty is a heavy burden sometimes—this time was one of them.

Instead of mulling over the injustice of it all, Faraj busied himself preparing for Monday morning. Faraj found Sullivan's attempt to salvage something from the flawed prosecution more than he could handle. After grousing about the inequity of it all, he left it alone. Puckett did the negotiating. He knew exactly how Faraj felt. He was the deal maker.

After a few hours of back-and-forth negotiations, an agreeable stipulation was reached. Wuterich would admit he said the imaginary words and acknowledge they "may" have led his men to kill the civilians. Nothing was certain. Faraj figured it was pretty cheap fare for fifteen lives. The last-minute negotiation wrapped things up. Puckett was happy, Wuterich was relieved, and Faraj was gloomy.

WUTERICH'S LIFE WAS now solely in the hands of Waldhauser. Puckett was still waiting to hear from Kumagai when he returned to the condo Sunday afternoon. He told Faraj the general was at an official function that Kumagai was also attending. The former Grumman EA6-B Prowler bombardier had promised Puckett he would take Waldhauser aside and speak to him about why a deal made sense.

Kumagai's powers of persuasion apparently worked. Toward the end of the day Waldhauser agreed to sign off on the proposed deal. Puckett was elated. He called SSgt Wuterich to share the good news. Faraj was ambivalent. Resigned was perhaps a better word. Who was he to tell someone who wanted to plead guilty he should not do so? He called it his lowest moment in the entire proceeding.

Faraj went to dinner that night with Epstein. They discussed the videographer's plans for the movie. "Mike had patiently waited over six years to put together a story about the incident. If he got funding he was going to make a documentary. With the end of the Haditha epic in sight, he could finally get started." As they sat discussing the movie and the end of the case, Faraj wondered if the end of the story even mattered, whether a story that failed to reveal the truth of who was responsible for the killings in the bedroom would ever be complete.

On Monday morning, Puckett shared Wuterich's decision with *North County Times* reporter Mark Walker. Walker had covered the story since the beginning. It had ripened on his home turf.

"This was his decision and his decision alone," Puckett told him, "SSgt Wuterich believed this was the right and honorable thing to do."[10]

Walker had covered the case since its inception and was understandably skeptical about the reasons for the decision. Before the court-martial even began he had predicted it would end in a deal. Like everyone else who had followed the twists and turns of the Haditha Massacre he knew it had never really been about Wuterich. In any event the cat was out of the bag. There was no turning back now.

Faraj was incensed by Puckett's indiscretion. No matter how hard he tried to keep things in perspective, he couldn't believe Puckett would reveal the decision to a reporter before it was even announced in court. He told Puckett he didn't like the timing or the way Puckett's announcement had been drafted. Faraj was also incensed by the wording of the release. He had not approved it and did not agree with it. Faraj told Puckett they had to do a better job informing the press what had really happened. He didn't want the court-martial to end on still another lie, especially one so blatant as to be almost transparent. Puckett, more conciliatory now that he thought the deal was done, surprisingly agreed. Faraj got to work outlining what he wanted to say. Puckett, his wife, and Faraj would work on it on and off for the rest of the day.

Late Monday evening, the lawyers notified LtCol Jones that a special session without members was needed for a plea hearing the next morning. Everything was over but the fat lady's song.

The truth would have to wait. Faraj tried to convince himself it didn't matter. Whatever the official truth turned out to be, it would still be a lie. Wuterich understood the evidence and had heard the witnesses. If he wanted a deal, so be it. Instead of worrying about it any longer, Faraj redirected his energy to preparing for the coming plea hearing. The requiem for the dead would have to wait. There was still no time for the truth.

That night, Faraj and Puckett collaborated on refining the final press release and the statement Wuterich would read in court. Thankfully, the rancor heating the atmosphere of their rented condo for three weeks had cooled a bit. Faraj and Puckett managed to get through the night without taking each other to task.

The press release they produced focused more on the government's decision to make a deal than on Wuterich's role at Haditha. In it, Faraj and Puckett explained how the government had used the NCIS investigation and court-martial of Wuterich to further its political agenda instead of seeking justice for the victims and the accused.

> This case began with sadness for the loss of life and ended with rage over the injustice of fabricated evidence by Naval Criminal Investigative Service interrogators who, through eight to fourteen hour interrogations of Marines, suborned perjury and encouraged lies rather than truth.
>
> SSgt Wuterich did not choose to be in Haditha. He did not choose the location of the IED or where the Small Arms Fire came

from. The Iraqi families, likewise, did not ask for the Marines to be there that day either. But the Marines did not send themselves there. They were sent by a nation that must take responsibility for the decisions it makes rather than expect that burden to be carried by the young men sent to fight its wars.

For Wuterich's statement to the court, Faraj added apologies to the families of the Iraqi victims, making sure it was contrite while still being clear that Wuterich was not taking responsibility for anything more than he was required to. It was all that was left to do. The next morning, Wuterich stood before the court and read it. More than seven years after the incident at Haditha erupted, it was finally over. Like the war that spawned it, nothing had been resolved.

January 24, 2012

Statement of SSgt Frank Wuterich to the Court

Good afternoon, Your Honor:

To begin, I would like to say a few words to the surviving Iraqi family members Safah Younis Salim, Eman Waleed Abdul Hamid, and Abd Waleed Abdul Hamid:

Words cannot express my sorrow for the loss of your loved ones. I know there is nothing I can say to ease your pain. I wish to assure you that on that day, it was never my intention harm you or your families. I know that you are the real victims of November 19, 2005.

To everyone else:

I went to Iraq to do my duty, serve my country, and do the best that I could do. When my Marines and I cleared those houses that day, I responded to what I perceived as a threat and my intention was to eliminate that threat in order to keep the rest of my Marines alive. So when I told my team to shoot first and ask questions later, the intent wasn't that they would shoot civilians, it was that they would not hesitate in the face of the enemy.

I have lived with the consequences of that day for six years. When I see those photographs, I am saddened. There are many ways that my words and decisions I made on that day have impacted my life.

I have never met a better Marine Officer than Major McConnell. If there is anyone in this world I want to emulate, it is he. So when I heard the news about my commanders being relieved because of my words or actions it absolutely devastated me. For six years, I have had to accept that my name will always be associated with a massacre, being a cold-blooded baby killer, an "out of control" monster, and a conspiring liar. There's nothing I can do about whoever believes those things. All I can do is continue to be who I've always been—me. And none of those labels have ever been, or ever will be, who I am.

I'm a divorced father of three wonderful girls who strives to be a morally better person every day. I have not been able to pursue a career serving our country, or establish a secure life for my family outside of the military. But I will always do the best I can with what I have. Regardless of the missed promotions and professional opportunities, and the lack of family security, I will always remember the loss of life that day—both for the Terrazas family, and the Iraqis in Haditha.

It's sad that the shroud of these charges and the media hype surrounding them has obscured the memory of the loss of Lance Corporal Terrazas. To his family: please know he will always be remembered by those of us who knew him best and who served proudly with him.

Many of the Marines who were there that day, along with everyone who has stood by me and supported me, may be disappointed that I pled guilty. It might suggest that I believe we behaved badly or dishonorably. The truth is, I don't believe anyone in my squad, nor any member of Kilo Co, 3/1 behaved in any way that was dishonorable or contrary to the highest ideals that we all live by as Marines. But even with the best intentions, sometimes combat actions can cause tragic results. I sit here today to take responsibility for whatever measures my words or direction contributed to the tragedy that resulted in the deaths in Haditha in 2005. In no way should my acceptance of responsibility ever be considered an indictment of the Marines or the commanders in 3/1. I have always taken responsibility for my actions and have always told the truth to the best of my recollection from the very first day I was questioned about the events of that day—both for the Terraza family, and the Iraqis in Haditha.

I also want to make clear that my commanders—then Captain McConnell and Lieutenant Colonel Chessani—always encouraged us to tell the truth. And the truth is: I never fired my weapon at any women or children that day.

Lastly, to my three girls: I know you don't understand a whole lot of what's been going on because I haven't really talked to you about any of this, but I want you know, above all else, I love you.

Regardless of the outcome, I am here to take responsibility for my actions, and to accept the consequences.

NOTES

CHAPTER 1

1. Ewers, J., "Statement of Maj Gen R.A. Huck," Bargewell Report, Enclosure (87), April 4, 2006.
2. Burnham, Gilbert, Shannon Doosy, Elizabeth Dzeng, Riyadh Lafta, and Les Roberts, "The Human Cost of the War in Iraq: A Mortality Study, 2002–2006," http://web.mit.edu/CIS/pdf/Human_Cost_of_War.pdf
3. Keen, Judy, "Bush Cheers Mongolia for Pushing Democracy," *USA TODAY,* November 20, 2005.
4. Bargewell Report, "Constraints and Limitations," Section (U), June 15, 2006, p. iv.
5. Miles, Donna, "Pace Calls Iraq Investigations Chance to Recheck Moral Compass," American Forces Press Service, June 4, 2006.
6. Gilmore, Gerry J., "Marine Commandant 'Gravely Concerned' Over Alleged Misconduct in Iraq," American Forces Press Service, June 7, 2006.
7. Bargewell, Statement of Captain J. S. Pool, Public Affairs Officer, 2d Marine Division Exchange, Enclosure (12) [hereinafter: Pool Statement Bargewell, Email traffic, January 24, 2006, between Major N. F. Murphy, MNF-W II MEF (Fwd)) PAO, Captain J. Pool, 2d Marine Division PAO], and Mr. Tim McGirk, *TIME* [hereinafter: Pool-McGirk Email exchange, Enclosure (11)].
8. Duffy, Michael, Tim McGirk, and Bobby Ghosh, "The Ghosts of Haditha," *TIME,* June 4, 2006.
9. McGirk, Tim, "Collateral Damage or Civilian Massacre in Haditha? A Time exclusive," *TIME,* March 19, 2006, http://www.time.com/time/world/article/0,8599,1174649,00.html

10. Helms, Nat, "Immunity Deal Forced on Tatum," *Defend Our Marines,* February 11, 2008; Rogers, Rick, "Immunity Given, but No Plea Deal in Place," *San Diego Union-Tribune,* February 14, 2008.

11. Associated Press, "Dismissal from Corps Sought for 2 Marines Linked to Haditha Massacre, April 19, 2012.

12. Pelley, Scott, "Wuterich's Account: The Killings in Haditha," *60 Minutes,* CBS News, August 24, 2008, http://www.cbsnews.com/video/watch/?id=2582353n

13. In re: Frank D. WUTERICH, UNITED STATES, Appellee v. Frank D. WUTERICH, Staff Sergeant US Marine Corps, Appellant, No. 08-6006. Crim. App. No. 200800183 AND CBS BROADCASTING INC., Petitioner v. NAVY-MARINE CORPS COURT OF CRIMINAL APPEALS, THE UNITED STATES OF AMERICA, and Frank D. WUTERICH, Staff Sergeant, US Marine Corps, Respondents No. 08-8020/MC/No. 08-8021/MC, November 7, 2008.

14. Marshall, S. A. Mathew W., "NCIS Interview LCpl Stephen Tatum, Report of Haditha Investigation," April 12, 2006, pp. 130–141.

15. Joint Service Committee on Military Justice, "Article 92," Manual for Court-martial (2000), US Government Printing Office, Sect. IV-24, p. 297.

16. Wuterich, Frank, "Written Admission of Guilt of Frank Wuterich," before Military Judge LtCol David Jones, January 24, 2012.

17. McLeary, Paul, "Tim McGirk on Haditha," *Columbia Journalism Review,* June 16, 2006, http://www.cjr.org/behind_the_news/tim_mcgirk_on_haditha.php?page=all

18. Bargewell, Email traffic 24Jan2006 between Major N.F. Murphy, MNF-W II MEF (Fwd)) PAO, Captain J. Pool, 2d Marine Division PAO, and Mr. Tim McGirk Time Magazine,[hereinafter: Pool-McGirk E mail Exchange, Enclosure (11).

19. Knickmeyer, Ellen, "In Haditha, Memories of a Massacre," *Washington Post Foreign Service,* May 27, 2006, http://www.washingtonpost.com/wp-dyn/content/article/2006/05/26/AR2006052602069.html

20. NCIS, "Whitt Statement," NCIS Haditha Investigation, Statement of Brian David Whitt, March 20, 2006.

21. Ware, LtCol Paul, "Investigating Officer's Report—LCpl Stephen B. Tatum to LtGen James N. Mattis," Western Pacific Judicial Circuit, August 23, 2007.

CHAPTER 2

1. Helms, Nat, "MARINE DEFENDER FIRED—Exclusive Interview with Lt Col. Colby Vokey," September 5, 2007, *Defend Our Marines,* http://warchronicle.com/TheyAreNotKillers/Blog/DefendOurMarines-MarineDefenderFired-NatHelms.htm

2.   Brahms, David M., "RE: termination of Lt. Col C Vokey," email to Nat Helms, Wednesday, September 5, 2007.

3.   Dinsmore, Jeffrey, LtCol, USMC, "Final Words from a Haditha Marine," *Defend Our Marines*, January 24, 2012, http://warchronicle.com/ DefendOurMarinesExclusive/Trial_of_SSgt_Wuterich/Final_Words_ from_a_Haditha_Marine.htm

4.   Perry, Tony, "Murder Charges Likely for Marines in Iraq Death," *Los Angeles Times*, June 6, 2006.

5.   Sax, Edward, Sgt Maj, "Sax Statement, re: US v. Wuterich," before Military Judge Lt Col David Jones, January 17, 2012, http://warchronicle.com/ DefendOurMarinesExclusive/Trial_of_SSgt_Wuterich/If_I'm_Receiving_ Fire,_I've_Got_to_Assume_the_House_is_Hostile_3281.htm

6.   Vokey/Helms, "Rumsfeld Created Haditha Group to Counter Murtha," September 15,2008, Defend Our Marines, http://warchronicle.com/ DefendOurMarinesExclusive/Rumsfeld_Haditha_15Sept08_8567. htm

CHAPTER 3

1.   Wolf, Francis, "Hearing transcript, LCpl. Justin L. Sharratt Article 32 testimony," re: US v. Wuterich, Enclosure, June 13, 2007.

2.   Roggio, Bill, "Haditha, Marine Snipers, Ansar al-Sunnah, and the Greater War," *The Long War Journal*, August 4, 2005, http://www.longwarjournal. org/archives/2005/08/haditha_marine.php#ixzz2YZ2zCTw0

3.   Mahdi, Omer, in Haditha and Rory Carroll in Baghdad, "Under US noses, brutal insurgents rule Sunni citadel: The Guardian newspaper gains rare access to Iraqi town and finds it fully in control of 'mujahideen,'" *The Guardian*, August 22, 2005.

4.   Helms, Nathaniel R., "My Men Are My Heroes: The Brad Kasal Story," Des Moines, IA: Meredith, 2007/reprint, Annapolis, MD: Naval Institute Press, 2012,   http://warchronicle.com/DefendOurMarinesExclusive/Chessani Speaks-PartTwo-23July10.htm

5.   Mahdi and Carroll, *The Guardian*.

6.   Associated Press News Dispatch, "Pro-American Mayor Mohammed Nayil al-Jurayfi of Haditha, Killed, Along with His Son, in an Ambush Wednesday," July 16, 2003, http://cryptome.org/info/haditha/haditha2.htm

7.   United States v. Wuterich et al., "Sax Trial Testimony before Military Judge LtCol David Jones, Jan. 21, 2012," Bargewell, Enclosure (60), "Interview of Sergeant Major E.T. SAX, USMC, Sergeant Major, 3d Battalion, 1st Marines," Ewers and Connell," March 31, 2006.

8. Sappenfield, Mark, "Gen. James Mattis: Petraeus's new boss boasts a salty mouth, keen mind," *The Christian Science Monitor,* July 8, 2010, http://www.csmonitor.com/USA/Military/2010/0708/Gen.-James-Mattis-Petraeus-s-new-boss-boasts-a-salty-mouth-keen-mind

9. Bargewell Report, "HET Assessment," Exhibit 081089, June 15, 2006, p. 1.

10. Dinsmore Statement, June 2, 2006, p. 4.

CHAPTER 4

1. Helms, p. 99.
2. Ibid., p.159.
3. Helms, Nat, "Firefight in Haditha: An Eyewitness Account," *Defend Our Marines,* July 17, 2007, http://warchronicle.com/TheyAreNotKillers/Blog/DefendOurMarines-FireFightInHaditha-NatHelms.htm
4. United States v. Wuterich, "Notice of Disclosure," Navy-Marine Corps Trial Judiciary, Western Judicial Circuit, December 30, 2011.
5. Helms, author's collection of digital images obtained from 3/1 Marines at Fallujah and Haditha.
6. Bargewell, Enclosure (48), "Statement; McConnell, Lucas, Cpt., 1st Marines, K Company," April 3, 2006, p. 5.
7. Bargewell, "Salinas Statement," Enclosure (35), Exhibit 000154, p.15.
8. Platt, Mark, and Nadya Manlee, "RESULTS OF INTERVIEW / EHAB, Al Askari Neighborhood, Haditha, Iraq, March 13, 2006." INVESTIGATIVE ACTION CONTROL: 13MAR06-MEBJ-0164-7HMA, NCIS, April 6, 2006.
9. Sharratt, Justin, Transcript of "Unsworn Statement," before hearing officer LtCol Paul Ware, Article 32 Hearing, June 14, 2007, http://warchronicle.com/TheyAreNotKillers/LCplSharratt/Statement.htm
10. Bargewell, Exhibits 002873–002876.
11. McDermott, Kevin Barry, "Executive Summary to United States Federal District Court, Riverside California, In the matter of United States v. Jose Nazario," May 23, 2008.
12. Helms, "My Men Are My Heroes," p. 208.

CHAPTER 5

1. Re: NMCCA 200800299, "USA. v. JEFFREY R. CHESSANI, UNITED STATES NAVY-MARINE CORPS COURT OF CRIMINAL APPEALS, WASHINGTON, D.C." March 17, 2009, http://www.jag.navy.mil/courts/documents/archive/2009/Chessani,%20J.R.%20200800299%20unpub.pdf
2. Johnson, Barry, LtCol, "McGirk," emails to author, OSA, CENTCOM, December 6/7, 2007.

3.   McGirk, *TIME,* March 17, 2006.

4.   Johnson, emails to author, OSA, CENTCOM, December 6/7, 2007.

5.   Excerpts AAR, Co B., 3rd/75th Rangers, Operation Lynx, Ft. Benning, GA, April 2007, pp. 3–5.

6.   Gresham, John D., "The Haditha Dam Seizure," *The Year in Special Operations: 2006 Edition,* Defense Media Network, Parts 1–3, http://www.defensemedianetwork.com/stories/hold-until-relieved-the-haditha-dam-seizure/ROI/AAR; 75th Rangers, "Lessons Learned Haditha Dam," USARMY, pamphlet, Ft Benning, GA, 2007.

CHAPTER 6

1.   Editorial, "The Price of Iraq," *New York Times,* May 28, 2006, http://www.nytimes.com/2006/05/28/opinion/28sun1.html

2.   Editorial, "Duty, Honor, Investigation," *Los Angeles Times,* May 31, 2006, http://articles.latimes.com/2006/may/31/opinion/ed-massacre31

3.   Bargewell, "HET Assessment," Exhibit 08108.

4.   Dinsmore, Jeffrey, "Excerpts from a Deposition," cr. LtCol Sean Sullivan, *Defend Our Marines,* March 26, 2007, http://warchronicle.com/Defend OurMarines/Documents/Depositions/CaptDinsmore26Mar07.htm

5.   Celina Dunlop, "My Lai: Legacy of a Massacre," BBC, March 15, 2008, http://news.bbc.co.uk/2/hi/asia-pacific/7298533.stm

6.   McGirk, Tim, email to author, January 22, 2012.

7.   McLeary, "Tim McGirk on Haditha."

8.   Duffy, McGirk, and Ghosh, "The Ghosts of Haditha."

9.   Navarre, Stewart, Col., "Facts About Haditha," USMC Press Release, HQ, USMC, December 21, 2006.

CHAPTER 7

1.   Re: United States v. Wuterich, "Salinas, testimony," before Military Judge LtCol Judge David Jones, January 19, 2012.

2.   Limbacher, Carl, "Haditha Child: I Knew of Bomb Plot to Kill Marines," NewsMax.com, June 3, 2006, www.freerepublic.com/focus/f-news/1642807/posts\1

3.   USMC, Scan Eagle surveillance video, Segment 1: "Aftermath of the IED—Segment 18: Capture," November 19, 2005.

4.   Helms, "Firefight in Haditha: An Eyewitness Account."

CHAPTER 8

1.   NCIS, "Statement of LCPL Justin Sharratt," Haditha Dam, Iraq, March 19, 2006, Bargewell Report, enclosures 32–40.

2. NCIS, "Sworn Statement of LCPL Justin Sharratt," February 2, 2006, Bargewell Report, enclosure 30, 000169–000177.

3. Justin Sharratt, unsworn statement, Article 32 hearing, Camp Pendleton, Calif., June 14, 2006.

CHAPTER 9

1. Watt, Col Gregory A., "Memorandum for Commander, Multi-National Corps—Iraq," 15-6 Investigation, Camp Victory, Baghdad, Iraq, APO AE 09342, March 3, 2006, p. 1.

2. Ibid., p. 2.

3. Ibid., pp. 2–3.

4. Ibid., pp. 3–4.

5. Ibid., p. 7.

6. CNN, "Marine Commanders Relieved of Duties as Unit Faces Investigation," April 8, 2005, http://www.cnn.com/2006/US/04/08/saturday/

7. Jim Miklaszewski and Mike Viqueira, "Lawmaker: Marines Killed Iraqis 'in Cold Blood,'" NBC News Network, May 17, 2006.

8. Roberts, Kristin, "General Briefed Murtha after Murder Comment, Corp Says," Reuters News Service, August 3, 2006.

9. Ricks, Thomas E., "Coverup of Iraq Incident by Marines Is Alleged," *Washington Post,* May 29, 2006, http://www.washingtonpost.com/wp-dyn/content/article/2006/05/28/AR2006052801011.html

CHAPTER 10

1. Helms, Nat, telephonic interview with LtCol Jeffrey Chessani, Camp Pendleton, CA, Defend *Our Marines,* July 21, 2010, http://warchronicle.com/DefendOurMarinesExclusive/ChessaniSpeaks-21July10.htm

2. Ibid., pp. 125–129.

3. Boot, Max, *The Savage Wars of Peace: Small Wars and the Rise of American Power,* New York: Basic Books, 2002, pp. 120–123.

4. King, Lt. Lawton, PAO, "Press Release," 1st Marine Division, USMC, Camp Pendleton, CA, April 4, 2006, http://www.foxnews.com/story/2006/04/10/three-marines-involved-in-haditha-raid-relieved-command/#ixzz2Ykog7rAr

5. Helms, "Haditha Incident Commander Speaks Out for the First Time," July 23, 2010, *Defend Our Marines,* http://warchronicle.com/DefendOurMarinesExclusive/ChessaniSpeaks-PartTwo-23July10.htm

6. Bargewell, "Statement of Sokoloski," Enclosure (13), March 31, 2006.

7. Bargewell, "Statement of Commanding Officer, Regimental Combat Team 2," Enclosure (64)(U), March 3l, 2006.

8. Miklaszewski and Viqueira.
9. Ricks, Thomas E., "Haditha Probe Finds Leadership Negligent," *Washington Post,* July 9, 2006, http://www.washingtonpost.com/wp-dyn/content/article/2006/07/08/AR2006070800904.html

CHAPTER 11

1. Bargewell Report, "Salinas Statement," Enclosure (35), Evidence # 000154, February 19, 2006.
2. Ibid.
3. Bargewell Report, Salinas Statements to NCIS, Enclosure (36), Exhibit 8, March 18, 2006, pp. 1–8.
4. McGirk, "Collateral Damage or Civilian Massacre in Haditha?" March 19, 2006.
5. Ibid.
6. Ibid.
7. Ibid.
8. Ibid.
9. Maloney, Michael S., Death Scene Examination, NCIS, March 13, 2006, pp. 1-40; Bargewell Report, "NCIS Death Scene Report," ROI Aug 3, 2006, #00553, no date.

CHAPTER 12

1. "Bargewell," Regimental Honors, 75th Ranger Regiment Association, 2010, www.soc.mil/swcs/RegimentalHonors/_pdf/sf_bargewell.pdf.
2. Schmitt, Eric, and David S. Cloud, "General Faults Marine Response to Iraq Killings, *New York Times,* July 7, 2007, http://www.nytimes.com/2006/07/08/world/middleeast/08haditha.html?
3. White, Josh, "Report on Haditha Condemns Marines," *Washington Post,* April 21, 2007, http://www.washingtonpost.com/wp-dyn/content/article/2007/04/20/AR2007042002308.html
4. Estes, Kenneth, "US Marine Corps Operations in Iraq, 2003–2006 (PDF)," History Division, United States Marine Corps, 2009, p. 33; CNN, "Marines, Iraqis Join Forces to Shut Down Fallujah Coalition Seeks to Arrest Shiite Cleric," April 6, 2004, http://www.cnn.com/2004/WORLD/meast/04/05/iraq.main/index.html
5. Estes, p. 34.
6. Petraeus, David H., Lt. Gen., "Learning Counterinsurgency: Observations from Soldiering in Iraq," The US Army Professional Writing Collection,

Military Review, January–February 2006, http://www.army.mil/professionalWriting/volumes/volume4/april_2006/4_06_2_pf.html

7. West, Bing, *No True Glory: A Frontline Account of the Battle for Fallujah*, New York: Bantam Books, 2005, pp. 68–73, 118.

8. Ibid., p. 380.

9. Bargewell Report, "Introduction," Exhibit 000004, June 15, 2006, p. iii.

10. Bargewell Report, "Limitations f.(U)," Exhibit 000005, June 15, 2006, p. v.

11. Helms, "My Men Are My Heroes," p. 110.

12. Bender, Jan M ,"On the Mean Streets of Fallujah," Video, November 7–25, 2004, http://www.youtube.com/watch?v=0N8PDBwve6g

13. Bargewell, Statement of Major W. J. Collins, Judge Advocate, Regimental Combat Team-2 [hereinafter Collins Statement], Enclosure (67), March 31, 2005, p. 83.

14. von Zielbauer, Paul, "'Negligence' Cited after Marines Killed 24 in Haditha, Iraq," *New York Times*, April 21, 2007, http://www.nytimes.com/2007/04/21/world/africa/21iht-web-0421haditha.5385943.html

15. von Zielbauer, Paul, "Propaganda Fear Cited in Account of Iraqi Killings," *New York Times*, May 6, 2007, http://www.nytimes.com/2007/05/06/world/middleeast/06haditha.html

16. Helms, Nat, "Personal Notes from Conversations with Marines," Camp Pendleton, 2007–2012.

17. Sally B. Donnelly, "Cleared of Wrongdoing in Haditha?," *TIME*, November 14, 2006, http://www.time.com/time/world/article/0,8599,1559495,00.html

18. Bargewell, "Statement of Colonel S. Davis, Commanding Officer, Regimental Combat Team 2" [hereinafter: Davis Statement], Enclosure (64)(U), March 31, 2006.

19. Ibid.

20. Bargewell Report, "Statement of Lieutenant Colonel J. Chessani et al." [hereinafter C: ERPE mail String.]; Enclosure (10), June 15, 2006.

21. Bargewell Report, "Statement of 2d Lieutenant W.T. Kallop, 3d Platoon Commander, Company K, 3d Battalion, lst Marines," Enclosure (37)(U), March l9, 2006.

22. Donald C. Winter, Secretary of the Navy, "Secretarial Letters of Censure—Huck, Sokoloski, Davis," Office of the Secretary of the Navy, Author's Notes, September 5, 2007.

23. NCIS, Dinsmore, p. 5.

24. Winter, Davis, p. 2

25. Helms, Nathaniel R. "LETTERS OF CENSURE SAY SENIOR OFFICERS BETRAYED TRUST OF THE MARINE CORPS—Defend Our Marines

Exclusive," *Defend Our Marines,* November 15, 2007, http://warchronicle.com/DefendOurMarinesExclusive/LettersOfCensure-NatHelms.htm

CHAPTER 13

1. Totten, Michael J., "5-3-5 Cards. Mentality of US Marines," MichaelTotten.com, January 2, 2008, http://www.michaeltotten.com/archives/2008/01/a-plan-to-kill.php

2. Ewers, J., and R. Connell, "Interview of Col. S. Davis," USMC, Commanding Officer, RCT-2, March 31, 2006, pp. 2–3.

3. Helms, Chessani.

4. Ewers and Connell, pp. 3–24.

5. Ewers, J., and R, Connell, Cols, USMC, "Statement of Sergeant Major E.T. Sax, 3d Battalion, lst Marines" [hereinafter: Sax Statement] Enclosure (61), March 19, 2006.

6. Petraeus, David H., Lieutenant General, US Army, "Learning Counterinsurgency: Observations from Soldiering in Iraq," *Military Review,* January–February 2006, p. 6.

7. Ricks, Thomas E., "Fiasco: The American Military Adventure in Iraq," 2006 as excerpted in *Armed Forces Journal,* August 2006, http://www.armedforcesjournal.com/2006/08/1936008

8. DOD, ANNEX E (CONSOLIDATED ROE) TO 3-187 FRAGO 02, OPORD 02-005, PDF, 2005, pp. 1–27.

CHAPTER 14

1. Al Jazeera, "Maliki: Haditha a Terrible Crime," June 1, 2006, http://www.aljazeera.com/archive/2006/06/200841010135831557.html

2. Karl, Jonathan, "Haditha Massacre Charges Imminent," ABC News, December 13, 2006.

3. Walker, Mark, "Walker General's Testimony Sought at First Haditha Hearing," *North County Times,* April 29, 2007, http://www.nctimes.com/articles/2007/04/30/news/top_stories/42907192637.txt

4. Walker, Mark, "Haditha Case Set to Unfold Starting May 8," *North County Times,* April 27, 2007.

5. UNITED STATES, Appellee v. Frank D. WUTERICH, No. 08-6006.

6. Tatum, John, and Stephanie Tatum, "An Appeal from the Parents of LCpl. Stephen B. Tatum," *Defend Our Marines* Archive, July 15, 2006, http://warchronicle.com/TheyAreNotKillers/LCplTatum/LCplTatum DefenseFund.htm

7.   Bargewell, "Statement to NCIS of Lance Corporal Humberto M. Mendoza of 24Mar 2006 [hereinafter: Mendoza NCIS Statement (24Mar06)], Enclosure (101), June 15, 2006.

CHAPTER 15

1.   Ware, Paul, LtCol, USMC, "Investigating Officer's Report—Wuterich (PDF)," October 2, 2007, pp. 1–37.

CHAPTER 16

1.   In re: Frank D. Wuterich, Staff Sergeant (E-6) United States Marine Corps, Petitioner, "PETITION FOR EXTRAORDINARY RELIEF IN THE NATURE OF A WRIT OF MANDAMUS AND BRIEF IN SUPPORT" v. David M. Jones, Lieutenant Colonel, United States Marine Corps (in his official capacity as Military Judge), and The United States, Respondent, Case No. 200800183, August 25, 2011.

2.   White, Josh, "Report on Haditha Condemns Marines," *Washington Post,* April 21, 2007, http://www.washingtonpost.com/wp-dyn/content/article/2007/04/20/AR2007042002308.html

3.   In re: Wuterich v. United States, "Notice of Disclosure (PDF)," Navy–Marine Corps Trial Judiciary, Western Judicial Circuit, by Gannon, N. L., Major, December 30, 2011.

4.   White, Josh, "Third Marine Is Cleared of Charges, Given Immunity," *Washington Post,* March 29, 2008 http://www.washingtonpost.com/wpdyn/content/article/2008/03/28/AR2008032801923.html

5.   Bowman, Tom, Steve Inskeep, and Renee Mantagne, (Hosts), "Five Marines Expected to Face Charges in Killings," *Morning Edition,* NPR News, November 21, 2006, http://www.npr.org/templates/story/story.php?storyId=6517848

6.   Helms, Nathaniel R., "Maybe War Should Be On Trial: Testimony of Hector Salinas," *Defend Our Marines,* Jan 12, 2012, http://warchronicle.com/DefendOurMarinesExclusive/SSgt_Wuterich_CM_Day_Six/Maybe_War_Should_Be_on_Trial_287.htm

7.   Watson, Julie, "US Marine Testifies Would Have Leveled Iraqi Home," Associated Press, January 13, 2012. http://arabnews.com/world/article562864.ece

8.   Helms, Nathaniel R., "No Case Evident Yet," *Defend Our Marines,* January 21, 2012, http://warchronicle.com/DefendOurMarinesExclusive/Trial_of_SSgt_Wuterich/Week_Two_Report_%20No_Case_Evident_Yet.htm

9.   NCIS, Results of Interview with Safah Younis Salim, Wuterich IO Report to Lt Gen J. Mattis (PDF), June 8, 2006, Item 13a, Enclosure I, p. 4.

10.   Walker, Mark, "EXCLUSIVE: Wuterich Attorney Speaks about Plea Deal," *North County Times,* January 23, 2012, http://www.utsandiego.com/news/2012/Jan/23/exclusive-wuterich-attorney-speaks-about-plea-deal/